Discourse as
Structure and Process

Discourse as Structure and Process

Discourse Studies:
A Multidisciplinary Introduction
Volume 1

edited by

Teun A. van Dijk

SAGE Publications
London • Thousand Oaks • New Delhi

Contributors

Charles Antaki is Reader in Language and Social Psychology in the Department of Social Sciences, University of Loughborough, Loughborough, England. His research interests are in conversation, positioning, and identity. Among his publications is *Explaining and Arguing: the Social Organisation of Accounts* (1994).

Robert de Beaugrande is Professor of English at the University of Vienna. His major concern is the development of a dialectical interaction between theory and practice in issues relating to discourse, society, and education. A corresponding and comprehensive plan for research and application is presented in his latest book, *New Foundations for a Science of Text and Discourse* (1996).

Susan Condor is Lecturer in social psychology and culture and communication in the Department of Psychology, Lancaster University. Her research interests include the discursive construction of national identity, stereotypes and categories in talk, and the commonsense understanding of time and history.

Susanna Cumming is Associate Professor of Linguistics at the University of California, Santa Barbara. Previously she taught at the University of Colorado, Boulder, where she was a member of the Linguistics Department and the Institute of Cognitive Science. She is interested in discourse and grammar and related issues, including syntactic change, the lexicon in discourse, and computer text generation. Her primary language area is Malay/Indonesian; she has written a book on constituent order change (*Functional Change: the Case of Malay Constituent Order*, 1991) and is currently working on various issues concerning grammar in Indonesian conversation.

Suzanne Eggins lectures in semiotic approaches to text/discourse in the School of English at the University of New South Wales. She studied systemic linguistics under Michael Halliday at Sydney University and completed a PhD in systemic analyses of casual conversation. Her research interests include: conversation analysis, cohesion in text, theory and analysis of popular culture texts (especially romantic fiction), and the linguistics of factual writing. Publications include: *An Introduction to Systemic Functional Linguistics* (1994) and *Analysing Casual Conversation* (co-authored with Diana Slade, 1997).

Linda B. Forrest is a PhD student in the Department of Linguistics at the University of Oregon. Her research interests include language and cognition, and the neurobiology of language.

Morton Ann Gernsbacher is the Sir Frederic C. Bartlett Professor of Psychology at the University of Wisconsin–Madison. Her research explores the general cognitive processes and mechanisms underlying language comprehension. She has held a Fulbright Research Scholar Fellowship that allowed her to be a visiting scientist at the Max Planck Institute for Psycholinguistics, and a Research Career Development Award from the National Institutes of Health. She is a Fellow of the American Psychological Association and the American Psychological Society, and is president of the Society for Text and Discourse. She is author of *Language Comprehension as Structure Building* (1990), editor of the *Handbook of Psycholinguistics* (1994), and co-editor of *Coherence in Spontaneous Text* (forthcoming).

Ann M. Gill is Professor and Chair of the Department of Speech Communication at Colorado State University. She has written *Rhetoric and Human Communication*, (1994), a textbook introducing students to the operation of rhetoric in their everyday lives and to the linguistic nature of human experience. Her published work also includes rhetorical analyses of courtroom and judicial discourse and essays on freedom of speech.

Susan R. Goldman is Professor of Psychology and Co-director of the Learning Technology Center, Peabody College of Vanderbilt University. Her research explores text comprehension, reading, complex learning, question answering, and the use of interactive video-based materials in instructional settings. She has been conference program chair for the Society for Text and Discourse and the American Educational research Association. She has published chapters on computational modeling of text comprehension in edited books by Weaver, Mannes and Fletcher (1995) and by Britton and Graesser (1995).

Arthur C. Graesser is Professor of Psychology and Co-director of the Institute for Intelligent Systems at The University of Memphis. His research explores text comprehension, reading, inference generation, knowledge representation, question asking and answering, conversation, tutoring, and human–computer interaction. He is past president of the International Association for the Empirical Studies of Literature, a founder of the Society for Text and Discourse, a Fellow of the American Psychological Association, and associate editor of *Discourse Processes*. He is author of *Prose Comprehension beyond the Word* (1981), co-author (with L.F. Clark) of *Structures and Procedures of Implicit Knowledge* (1985), co-editor (with G.H. Bower) of *Inferences and Text Comprehension* (1990), and co-editor (with B.K. Britton) of *Models of Understanding Text* (1995).

Rob Grootendorst is Associate Professor of Discourse and Argumentation Studies in the Department of Speech Communication at the University of Amsterdam, the Netherlands. His research is in the area of descriptive and normative pragmatics and has concentrated on argumentation. He is co-author of the international journal *Argumentation*, and co-founder of the International Society for the Study of Argumentation (ISSA). His main books in English, co-authored by Frans van Eemeren, are *Speech Acts in Argumentative Discussions* (1984), *Argumentation, Communication and Fallacies* (1992), *Reconstructing Argumentative Discourse* (with Sally Jackson and Scott Jacobs, 1993) and *Fundamentals of Argumentation Theory* (with Francisca Snoeck Henkemans et al., 1996). Several of his books have been translated into Chinese, Dutch, French, German and Russian. Grootendorst received, with Frans van Eemeren, the Medal of David the Invincible of the Armenian Academy of Science 1986, the Daniel Rohrer Award 1989, and the Best Research Awards 1992 and (with Sally Jackson and Scott Jacobs) 1993 from the American Forensic Association.

Sally Jackson is a member of the Communication Faculty at the University of Arizona in Tucson, Arizona. Her main research interest is argumentation. With chapter co-authors van Eemeren, Grootendorst, and Jacobs, she wrote *Reconstructing Argumentative Discourse*, which in 1994 received the Outstanding Research Award from the American Forensic Association. 'Structure of conversational argument: pragmatic bases for the enthymeme', co-authored by Jacobs, received the Golden Anniversary Monograph Award from the Speech Communication Association in 1981, and 'Conversational argument: a discourse analytic approach', also co-authored by Jacobs, received the Daniel Rohrer Award from the American Forensic Association in 1983.

Scott Jacobs is a member of the Communication Faculty at the University of Arizona. His most significant publications in argumentation are *Reconstructing Argumentative Discourse*, co-authored with van Eemeren, Grootendorst, and Jackson and recipient of the Outstanding Research Award from the American Forensic Association; 'Structure of conversational argument: pragmatic bases for the enthymeme', co-authored with Jackson and recipient of the Golden Anniversary Monograph Award from the Speech Communication Association; and 'Conversational argument: a discourse analytic approach', co-authored with Jackson and recipient of the Daniel Rohrer Award from the American Forensic Association. He has also received from the Speech Communication Association the Outstanding Dissertation Award, the Karl Wallace Award, and the Charles Woolbert Award.

Myung Hee Kim is a lecturer at Ewha Women's University and Kangwon National University in South Korea. Her interests lie in discourse pragmatics, interactions between language and cognition, and language typology.

Regina Leite-García is Professor in the Faculty of Education, at the Federal University Fluminense, (UFF) in Rio de Janeiro. She has published widely on the politics of pedagogy. Among her recent publications is *Cartas Londrinas ed outros lugares sobre o lugar da educação* (Relume Dumara, 1995).

Gunther Kress is Profesor of Education/English at the Institute of Education, University of London. He has written on issues of representation and ideology. His most recent book, *Before Writing: Rethinking Paths to Literacy*

(Routledge, 1996), brings a social semiotic perspective to the question of literacy.

J.R. Martin is currently Associate Professor of Linguistics at the University of Sydney. His research interests include systemic theory, functional grammar, discourse analysis, register, genre and ideology, focusing on English and Tagalog – with special reference to the transdisciplinary fields of educational linguistics and social semiotics. Recent publications include Harcourt Brace Jovanovich's *Language: a Resource for Meaning* programme (co-authored with Frances Christie, Brian and Pam Gray, Mary Macken and Joan Rothery, 1990, 1992), *English Text: System and Structure* (1992), *Writing Science: Literacy and Discursive Power* (with M.A.K. Halliday, 1993), *Deploying Functional Grammar* (with C. Matthiessen and C. Painter, 1996) and *Genres and Institutions: Social Processes in the Workplace and School* (co-edited with F. Christie, 1997).

Elinor Ochs is Professor of Applied Linguistics at UCLA. Her research focuses on language socialization across the life span, across societies, and across situations. Ochs has analysed narrative as a socializing medium among families, physicists, and sufferers of mental disorders. She is the author of *Acquisition of Conversational Competence* (with B. Schieffelin, 1983), *Culture and Language Development: Language Acquisition and Language Socialization in a Samoan Village* (1988), and *Constructing Panic: the Discourse of Agoraphobia* (with L. Capps, 1995).

Tsuyoshi Ono is a faculty member at the University of Arizona where he teaches Japanese language and linguistics. He has a PhD in linguistics from the University of California, Santa Barbara; his dissertation was on the discourse and grammar of Barbareño Chumash (a Californian language). He has worked extensively on grammar and interaction in Japanese and English, and he is currently building a corpus of Japanese conversation. His research interests also include language change and research methodology, and he is working on a model of syntax which is adequate to account for conversational data.

Ming Ming Pu is Assistant Professor of Linguistics at Northern State University. Her research interests include discourse and psycholinguistics.

Barbara Sandig is Professor of German Linguistics at Saarland University in Saarbrücken, Germany. Her research interests focus on (German) stylistics (mainly of non-literary texts), text types, speech acts and evaluation in language. She has authored *Stilistik der deutschen Sprache* (1986). She has also edited a number of books on stylistics and a book about *Tendenzen der Phraseologieforschung* (1994), and has published numerous articles.

Margret Selting is Professor of Communication Theory and Linguistics at Potsdam University, Germany. Her research interests include conversational analysis, stylistics, interactional phonology and syntax. She has authored *Verständigungsprobleme* (1987) and *Prosodie im Gespräch* (1995). She co-edited a book on interpretive sociolinguistics and stylistics with Volker

Hinnenkamp (*Stil und Stilisierung*, 1989). Another book, *Prosody in Conversation* (1996), has been co-edited with Elizabeth Couper-Kuhlen. She has also published numerous articles, among others in the *Journal of Pragmatics*.

Russell S. Tomlin is Professor of Linguistics and a member of the Institute of Cognitive and Decision Sciences at the University of Oregon. His research interests include discourse, psycholinguistics, and functional theory.

Teun A. van Dijk is Professor of Discourse Studies at the University of Amsterdam. After earlier work in literary studies, text grammar and the psychology of text comprehension, his research in the 1980s focused on the study of news in the press and the reproduction of racism through various types of discourse. In each of these domains, he published several books. His present research in 'critical' discourse studies focuses on the relations between power, discourse and ideology. He is founder editor of the international journals *Text* and *Discourse and Society*, and editor of the four-volume *Handbook of Discourse Analysis* (1985). He has lectured widely in Europe and the Americas, and has been visiting professor at several universities in Latin America.

Frans H. van Eemeren is Professor of Discourse and Argumentation Studies and Chairman of the Department of Speech Communication at the University of Amsterdam, the Netherlands. He is also director of the research project Argumentation and Discourse Analysis of the Institute for Functional Research of Language and Language Use (IFOTT). His research is in the area of descriptive and normative pragmatics and has concentrated on argumentation. He is co-editor of the international journal *Argumentation*, and co-founder of the International Society for the Study of Argumentation (ISSA). His main books in English, co-authored by Rob Grootendorst, are *Speech Acts in Argumentative Discussions* (1984), *Argumentation, Communication, and Fallacies* (1992), *Reconstructing Argumentative Discourse* (with Sally Jackson and Scott Jacobs, 1993), and *Fundamentals of Argumentation Theory* (with Francisca Snoeck Henkemans et al., 1996). Several of his books have been translated into Chinese, Dutch, French, German and Russian. Van Eemeren received, with Rob Grootendorst, the Medal of David the Invincible of the Armenian Academy of Science 1986, the Daniel Rohrer Award 1989 and the Best Research Awards 1992 and (with Sally Jackson and Scott Jacobs) 1993 from the American Forensic Association.

Theo van Leeuwen is Professor of Communication Theory in the School of Media, London College of Printing. His most recent books are *The Media Interview: Confession, Contest, Conversation* (with Philip Bell) and *Reading Images: the Grammar of Visual Design* (with Gunther Kress).

Karen Whedbee is Assistant Professor in the Department of Communication and Journalism at the University of Maine, Orono. She is working on a book about John Stuart Mill's theory of rhetoric and argumentation. She specializes in the history of rhetoric and political communication.

Preface

This book offers a first introduction to discourse studies, a new cross-discipline that comprises the theory and analysis of text and talk in virtually all disciplines of the humanities and social sciences. For the main areas of discourse studies, the respective chapters feature literature reviews, explanations of theoretical frameworks and many concrete discourse analyses.

Besides providing a current state of the art, the chapters in this book have especially been written for newcomers to the field: students who take a special course in discourse analysis or choose this topic as part of their own discipline, as well as scholars from other disciplines who (finally) want to know what this study of discourse is all about. Esoteric jargon has been avoided in favor of a style of presentation that is accessible to all students and scholars in the humanities and social sciences.

There are several other introductions to the study of discourse. Most of them are now dated, or suffer from other limitations, such as very partial (and sometimes partisan) coverage of only a few domains of this new discipline. The chapters in the two volumes of the present book offer insight into a broad range of topics and areas, ranging from linguistic, stylistic and rhetorical approaches, to psychological and especially also social directions of research. Some deal with written texts, others with informal as well as institutional dialogue in a multitude of social contexts. Some focus on abstract structures of discourse, others on the orderly organization of ongoing talk by language users as well as on the broader social, political and cultural implications of discourse. The book highlights most important dimensions and levels of discourse description, and the authors do so from different theoretical perspectives. And in addition to more theoretical and descriptive approaches, critical and applied perspectives are represented here. In sum: this is the most complete introduction to discourse studies to date.

However, the study of discourse is a huge field, and it is being practiced by many scholars in many countries. Thus, despite their comprehensive set-up, even two volumes are unable to cover everything. For instance, there was no space for a chapter on the sound structures of discourse. Of the many discourse genres discussed as examples throughout the various chapters, only two important ones, namely argumentation and storytelling, could be dealt with in separate chapters.

The same is true for the various social domains and issues of discourse analysis: space limitations only allowed us a separate chapter on political discourse analysis, so that no special treatment could be given to, for example, medical, legal and educational discourse, among many other discourse domains. But again, the variety of the examples in the various chapters amply makes up for this limitation. Of the pressing social issues dealt with in separate chapters, we have focused on those of gender and ethnicity, although discourse is obviously involved in the reproduction of many other forms of domination and inequality, such as those of class, age, nationality, religion, language, sexual orientation, and so on.

The authors who contribute to this book are among the most prominent in the discipline, worldwide. Women and men from several countries were invited to join this project, so as to guarantee theoretical, analytical and cultural diversity – a criterion that is often ignored or impossible in one-author monographs. For the same reason, several chapters are co-authored by well-known senior as well as bright junior scholars in the field.

Despite this variety, however, many theoretical approaches, in many countries and many languages, are not represented by separate chapters here. Thus, as is so often the case, the requirement of English as a dominant academic language prohibited contributions from prominent discourse scholars who only write in, for example, Japanese, Chinese, Russian, French, Spanish, German and Italian, among other languages. Linguistic limitations and lack of cross-cultural data also prevented most authors from analysing more examples from more languages and more cultures, an aim that only an ideal book with multilingual authors can ever realize.

The book has been divided into two separate volumes that may be read independently of each other. The first focuses on the analysis of verbal structures and cognitive processes, the second on discourse as interaction in society. This division roughly corresponds to the traditional separation between the study of discourse in the humanities and psychology on the one hand, and in the social sciences on the other. As several chapters show, this division has become increasingly arbitrary, and there are several chapters that precisely aim to integrate these different approaches. Despite the inevitable specialization of each mature discipline, I hope that increasing integration will overcome the current divisions in the field.

I would like to see this book as an ongoing project, in which future editions in several languages follow the developments in the field, and in which new versions of chapters realize as much as possible the scholarly and social ideals of theoretical, analytical and cultural diversity. Readers from all over the world have a special responsibility in such an endeavor, and are invited to send me their critical comments as well as suggestions for improvement. I hope that teachers will provide feedback about their experiences with the use of this book in class. It is only in this way that the book may become a joint project of the growing global community of students and scholars of discourse.

Teun A. van Dijk

1

The Study of Discourse

Teun A. van Dijk

What is Discourse?

This two-volume introduction provides an elaborate answer to the simple question novices tend to ask when they note the ubiquitous presence of the term 'discourse' in the humanities, the social sciences and even in the mass media: 'What exactly is discourse, anyway?'

It would be nice if we could squeeze all we know about discourse into a handy definition. Unfortunately, as is also the case for such related concepts as 'language', 'communication', 'interaction', 'society' and 'culture', the notion of discourse is essentially fuzzy. As is so often the case for concepts that stand for complex phenomena, it is in fact the whole discipline, in this case the new cross-discipline of *discourse studies* (also called 'discourse analysis'), that provides the definition of such fundamental concepts.

However, we need to begin somewhere, and we usually do this with a brief and general characterization of the phenomena being studied in a discipline. This will be the task of this chapter. Further details and references about various domains of discourse studies will then be given in the chapters that follow. After this summary of the major characteristics of discourse, I briefly sketch the development of the discipline of discourse studies and then formulate some general principles shared by many contemporary approaches to discourse. In a way, thus, this chapter gives an introduction to the introductions in the rest of the book.

From Common Sense to Theory

Before we begin with the more theoretical description of discourse one expects to find in the discipline of discourse studies, a few words are in order about the common-sense notion of 'discourse' as we know it from everyday language use and the dictionary. Here, the term 'discourse' usually refers to a form of language use, public speeches or more generally to spoken language or ways of speaking, for instance when we refer to 'the discourse of former President Ronald Reagan'.

Another, increasingly popular but still informal, use of the term may be found in the media and some of the social sciences, for instance, when they refer to 'the discourse of neo-liberalism'. In this case, 'discourse' refers not merely to the language use of neo-liberal thinkers or politicians, but also to the ideas or philosophies propagated by them. Indeed, studies of neo-liberalist discourse may not pay attention to language use at all.

Discourse analysts try to go beyond such common-sense definitions. They agree that discourse is a form of *language use*. But since this is still quite vague and not always adequate, they introduce a more theoretical concept of 'discourse' which is more specific and at the same time broader in its application. They want to include some other essential components in the concept, namely *who* uses language, *how, why* and *when*.

One characterization of discourse that embodies some of these *functional* aspects is that of a *communicative event*. That is, people use language in order to communicate ideas or beliefs (or to express emotion), and they do so as part of more complex social events, for instance in such specific situations as an encounter with friends, a phone call, a lesson in the classroom, a job interview, during a visit to the doctor, or when writing or reading a news report.

These examples also suggest that whatever else may happen in these sometimes complex communicative events, the participants are *doing* something, that is, something else beyond just using language or communicating ideas or beliefs: they interact. To emphasize this interactional aspect of discourse, it is sometimes also described as a form of *verbal interaction*.

Even after this first approximation to the concept of discourse, we already have encountered its three main dimensions: (a) *language use*, (b) the *communication of beliefs* (cognition), and (c) *interaction* in social situations. Given these three dimensions, it is not surprising to find that several disciplines are involved in the study of discourse, such as linguistics (for the specific study of language and language use), psychology (for the study of beliefs and how they are communicated), and the social sciences (for the analysis of interactions in social situations).

It is typically the task of discourse studies to provide *integrated* descriptions of these three main dimensions of discourse: how does language use influence beliefs and interaction, or vice versa, how do aspects of interaction influence how people speak, or how do beliefs control language use and interaction? Moreover, besides giving systematic descriptions, we may expect discourse studies to formulate *theories* that *explain* such relationships between language use, beliefs and interaction.

Text and Talk

Although we now have a first characterization of what discourse analysts understand by 'discourse', there are some complications that need to be resolved. First of all, language use is of course not limited to spoken language, but also involves *written* (or printed) language, communication and interaction, as is the case when we read our daily newspaper, our textbooks, our mail (on paper or e-mail), or the myriad of different text types that have to do with our academic or other work. Although many discourse analysts specifically focus on spoken language or *talk*, it is therefore useful to include also written *texts* in the concept of discourse. There are many similarities between the ways people speak and write when using language to communicate their ideas, and the same is true for listening or reading to spoken and written discourse.

However, such an extension of the concept is not without complications. Thus, talk as we know it from everyday conversations, parliamentary debates or job interviews, is typically a form of interaction, involving language users as speakers and recipients. This is less obvious for such types of text as letters, news reports, textbooks, laws or scholarly contributions like this one. These seem to be *objects*, or products of verbal acts, rather than forms of interaction.

And yet, just like talk, texts also have 'users', namely authors and readers. So we may also speak of 'written communication' or even of 'written interaction' although the participants here do not usually interact face-to-face, and the readers seem to be more passively involved in the interaction: except for an exchange of letters or in a media debate they seldom react to writers by writing back. This does not mean of course that when reading and understanding they are less active than listeners. Thus, despite a number of notable differences, there are enough similarities between spoken and written language use, communication and interaction to warrant inclusion of both these *modes* of discourse in one general notion of 'discourse'.

It is true though that discourse analysts also sometimes use their own notions somewhat casually. Although they may characterize discourse as a communicative event or as a form of verbal interaction, they often focus on the verbal dimensions, that is, on what is actually being said or written by language users as part of such an event or action. Thus, in the same way as 'text' is mostly used to refer to the product of writing, 'talk' is often studied as the product of speaking or as ongoing interaction, without paying much attention to the language users involved or the other aspects of the whole communicative event. Theoretically, it is however emphasized that discourse studies should deal both with the properties of text and talk and with what is usually called the *context*, that is, the other characteristics of the social situation or the communicative event that may systematically influence text or talk. In sum, discourse studies are about *talk and text in context*.

The Ambiguity of 'Discourse'

There is another complication. So far, I have used the term 'discourse' in a rather *abstract* way, as was also the case for 'language' and 'communication'. Thus, when we characterize discourse as a communicative event we refer to discourse in *general*. In a similar but slightly different way we may also generally refer to specific types or social domains of language use and discourse, for example with such terms as 'medical discourse' or 'political discourse'.

On the other hand, we use the word 'discourse' more *concretely*, as a count noun, and refer to a single, *particular* conversation or news report, as in 'this discourse' or 'a discourse on the front page . . .'. In that case, we may even use the plural 'discourses' when referring to several instances of text or talk.

Usually this ambiguity is not much of a problem: from the context or the surrounding text (the 'co-text) we may generally infer whether the general or the particular meaning is used. However, we should be aware of the theoretical difference between the abstract use of 'discourse' when referring to a *type* of social phenomenon in general, and the specific use when we are dealing with a concrete example or *token* of text or talk.

Unfortunately, the ambiguity does not stop here. Above we have already encountered another use of 'discourse' (as in 'the discourse of liberalism') which is not limited to language use or communicative interaction, but which may rather or also refer to ideas or ideologies. Although we find this usage also in discourse studies, it is obvious that it makes the term even more fuzzy than it already is, and many discourse analysts will therefore avoid it. Sometimes this very general system of discourse and ideas is called an *order of discourse*, a notion we may find in more philosophically inspired discourse studies.

Delimiting discourses

There is a third complication. In most situations we are able to identify and delimit a particular discourse: as is the case for an interaction or a communicative event, we know where it begins and where it stops or whether we have one or more discourses. But there are situations where this is less obvious. Whereas a (one) conversation usually can be identified and delimited as such, what about a long parliamentary debate about an issue, a debate that may go on (with interruptions or 'adjournments') for days? Is this one discourse, or a compound discourse consisting of various installments (on different days), or a sequence of discourses (the speeches of MPs), or what? The same would be true for a debate on an issue on the editorial page of a newspaper, or the serial installments of a movie on television, or the various 'articles' in an encyclopedia, or in this very book for that matter.

In other words, as soon as we begin to look somewhat closer at the everyday reality of discourse, we encounter complications which we are unable to solve with common-sense notions of discourse. In that case we may need theoretical notions that define the beginning or the end of text and talk, their unity or coherence, intertextual relations between different discourses, intentions of speakers or writers, settings, time, place, and other aspects of the communicative context. Thus, given the examples just mentioned, we might have to distinguish between 'simple' and 'compound' discourses, or between discourses and 'discourse complexes'.

Theoretical Description

At this point, then, the limitations of a more intuitive and informal characterization of discourse as it was given above show that we need a more explicit and theoretical approach to account for the many properties of text and talk.

Instead of simply saying, for instance, that discourse is a form of 'language use', we need to spell out what this means, for instance by describing what such language use consists of, what its *components* are, how these components are *ordered*, or how they may be combined into larger constructs. Similar questions may be asked about the process of communication or about the actions being accomplished when people engage in discourse.

At this point the descriptions of discourse focus on various *structures*. Thus, a grammar may describe sentences as series of words that occur in a specific *order*. Some of these sequences make grammatical or meaningful sentences, while others do not. Similarly, if we want to provide a *structural description* of discourse, we might start by considering it as a sequence of sentences, that is, as sentences that follow each other in a specific order. Some of these sequences will constitute meaningful, coherent and acceptable discourses, but others will not. In other words, a structural description should spell out the various relations and conditions that define the 'discursivity' of sequences of sentences.

From this point on, common sense and some school knowledge about language and grammar will soon no longer be sufficient to answer the more specific and technical questions about these and other structures of discourse. We need to know more about the properties of the sentences or other components and constructs of discourse, as well as about their mutual relations, about the rules that govern the way they may or should be combined or the other conditions or constraints that may be involved. This is true not only for a description of discourse as language use, but also for its other main dimensions, namely the study of discourse as the communication of beliefs, or as a form of social interaction, as well as for the ways language use, communication or interaction are related to the social context.

Obviously, such an enterprise is not a simple matter. Therefore, as is the case for specialization in other disciplines, discourse analysts may focus on one aspect, level or dimension of text or talk, or even on one general class of discourse, like media discourse. Such a division of labor may follow the theoretical distinctions being made between different properties of discourse, as I already did for the very general distinction between the *language use, communication (cognition) and interaction* dimensions of discourse.

Each of these dimensions may itself show different characteristics. For instance, when we focus on discourse as a form of language use, that is, on the verbal aspect of utterances, linguistics usually makes a metaphorical distinction between different *levels* of such utterances, as if they were buildings or other constructions. Similarly, I begin with what is rather metaphorically called the 'superficial' or 'observable' level of *expression*, and then work 'down' to the 'deeper' or 'underlying' levels of *form, meaning* and *action*. Once we know a bit more about discourse as language use, we move to a characterization of its communicative and interactional dimensions. This order of analysis is rather arbitrary: we might just as well have started with these latter dimensions, especially since these are often used to explain why language use has the properties it does.

Discourse as Verbal Structure

Sound, Sight and Body

As was the case, historically, in modern linguistics, discourse analysis may also begin with the analysis of a separate level of observable manifestations or *expressions*, namely auditory *sounds* and visual *marks* (letters, figures, colors, etc.) on paper, boards or computer screens (or of course electronic traces on computer disk). This is how language is used when we speak or write, hear or read discourses. We may then focus, as does *phonology*, on the *abstract structures* of these sounds of spoken discourse, and examine how pronunciation, emphasis, intonation, volume and other properties that result from speech contribute to the typical sound structures of discourse. Thus, sounds may relate sentences (for instance through contrastive emphasis), signal verbal acts such as questions, mark the beginning or the end of a discourse segment, or characterize change of speakers.

This book unfortunately had no place for a separate chapter on the phonological study of the sound structure of discourse, but it would be a perfectly legitimate part of an introduction to discourse studies. It does, however, have a chapter on the written, printed, or graphical aspects of discourse (see Chapter 10, Volume 1, by Gunther Kress, Regina Leite-García and Theo van Leeuwen). Also because of the bias of traditional linguistics for spoken language, the *visual* aspect of discourse was (and still is) often ignored in discourse studies. However, within the sister discipline of semiotics (the study of signs), it is made clear that especially in these times of multi-media communication, such an analysis of the visual dimensions of discourse is indispensable. Studies of advertising, textbooks or television programs obviously need such cross-media or *multi-modal* analysis.

In spoken discourse, sounds do not come alone either. Several types of *non-verbal activity*, such as gestures, face-work, bodily position, proximity, applause and laughs, will usually and relevantly accompany talk, and therefore need analysis in their own right as part of the whole communicative event. Again, this is a domain of discourse analysis that has remained relatively unexplored. Yet, together with the sounds of discourse, non-verbal activity plays an important role in the interpretation of the meanings and functions of discourse in face-to-face interaction (or of course in understanding discourse in movies). Being angry shows not only in the selection of special words, or in the volume, pitch or intonation of sounds, but also in displaying an angry face or angry gestures. This example clearly shows that communicative events consist of more than just words.

This discussion about the auditory, visual and bodily aspects of discourse presupposes a well-known distinction made by language users themselves as well as by discourse analysts, namely between two different *modes* of discourse: *talk* and *text*. Talk or spoken discourse comprises everyday conversations and other types of dialogue, such as parliamentary debates, board meetings or doctor–patient interaction. Text or written discourse, like the one you are now reading, defines the large set of discourse types comprising, for example, news reports in the newspapers, scholarly articles, novels, textbooks and advertising. In a more technical sense, the term 'text' has sometimes been used in discourse analysis to refer to, for example, the abstract ('underlying') structures of discourse, or to transcripts of talk. Here, however, we only use the term more or less in its everyday meaning of 'written discourse'.

The lists of different discourse types just formulated also show something else. We may use properties of discourse, such as whether they are spoken or written, as criteria for a *typology* of discourse: they define sets or classes of discourse types. Combinations of such criteria may be used to define 'natural' discourse types, or *genres*, that is, types that are also known and used as such by language users, such as conversations, ads, poems and news reports in the paper.

Order and Form

This decomposition of discourse into its various levels or dimensions may be continued also for the other aspects that characterize talk or text. Still following the lead of linguistic grammar, for instance, we may expect that discourse analysis also pays attention to the abstract *forms* of sentences in discourse, such as the *order* of words, phrases or clauses or other properties of sentences that are studied in *syntax*.

Unlike traditional linguists, however, discourse analysts go *beyond the sentence boundary* in this case, and focus on the ways the forms of sentences are influenced by surrounding sentences in text and talk. This means that in a discourse approach to grammar, the well-formedness or grammaticalness of sentences is *relative*. For instance, an isolated sentence consisting of only a verb would usually be not only ungrammatical but also partly incomprehensible. But as part of a discursive sequence of sentences, such *incompleteness* may be quite normal, because the 'missing' grammatical (and other) information can be supplied by a previous sentence.

The *order* of words or phrases in a sentence is not arbitrary. It may have various *functions* in relation to other sentences in discourse. For instance, in English and many other languages the first noun phrase (NP) of a sentence generally tends to express information that is already known ('given') to the recipient (for example, because it was inferred from previous sentences or from the context) whereas the latter parts of the sentence tend to express information that is 'new'. Word order may also have other functions, such as signalling contrast, or emphasis, or a choice among several alternatives. Similarly, the 'normal' word order of a sentence may change as a consequence of the structure or the information of previous sentences.

One of the phenomena most studied in discourse syntax is how sentence forms signal the distribution of *information* throughout a discourse. We may tell a story about a woman and may begin to refer to her by using a name such as 'Jane Doe', or a full indefinite NP such as 'a lawyer', identifying the person. Then later we may refer to the same person with a definite NP such as 'the woman' or 'the lawyer', or only with pronouns such as 'she' or 'her'.

In sum, the formal structure of sentences in discourse is not independent of the rest of the discourse (or the context). Interestingly, however, it is not merely the form of previous sentences that plays a role, but also what information is conveyed by these sentences, what or who they refer to, what the recipients are assumed to know already, or what they focus their attention on. These are all notions that rather belong to a semantic or cognitive approach to discourse (see below). This shows that the syntactic study of discourse (such as about the discursive functions of word order, definite NPs or pronouns) needs to be integrated with a study of other levels and dimensions of discourse. This is also the reason why Chapter 4, Volume 1, by Susanna Cumming and Tsuyoshi Ono, who discuss these aspects of discourse in more detail, is called not 'Discourse Syntax' but more broadly 'Discourse and Grammar'.

Meaning

Crucial in many discourse descriptions is the level of *meaning*, as it is typically analysed in *semantics*. 'Meaning' is, however, a very fuzzy concept, which itself has many meanings. At this point, however, we mean the abstract, conceptual meanings of words, sentences, sequences of sentences and whole discourses. Linguists often call these abstract meanings of discourse *semantic representations*.

Psychologists and cognitive linguists take a more empirical approach to meaning and emphasize that it is not so much that discourse itself 'has' meaning, but rather that meaning is something *assigned* to a discourse by language users. This process of meaning assignment we all know under such terms as 'understanding', 'comprehension' or 'interpretation'. In this case, meaning is rather associated with the *mind* of language users. Also the notion of *information* will be used in such a more psychological approach to meaning, although it should be emphasized that information is a more general notion: people have much information (including knowledge) that is not necessarily expressed in discourse meaning.

In the same way, some social scientists may claim that such meanings are shared and social, and should therefore be associated not so much with the mind, but rather with·interaction, or social groups or societal structures. We shall come back to these cognitive and social approaches to meaning and other aspects of discourse below.

Note that in everyday language (and in the social sciences) also the term *content* is often used to refer to the meaning or information of a discourse. Discourse analysts usually avoid this rather vague term, which is still used in such methods of text analysis called 'content analysis' (a method which in fact has less to do with meaning than with the more observable aspects – mostly words – of discourse).

Each level of discourse description has its own, typical concepts. Thus, in semantics we have a special term for the meaning of a whole clause or sentence, namely a *proposition*. Thus, whereas discourse syntax focuses on the formal structure of sentences, discourse semantics rather studies the structure of propositions, and especially the relations between propositions in a discourse. As is the case for all other levels of discourse analysis, here we find the *discursive relativity* principle: propositions are influenced by previous propositions in text or talk. Indeed, one need not be a discourse linguist to know that the meaning of a sentence depends on what has been said (meant) before.

One semantic notion, already briefly mentioned above, is fairly crucial in such an analysis, namely that of *coherence*: how do the meanings of sentences – that is, propositions – in a discourse 'hang together'? We may study such coherence relations for sentences that immediately follow each other (the *micro level* of analysis), but also for the meaning of discourse as a whole (the *macro level* of analysis). In both cases we in fact are explaining what makes discourses *meaningful*, and how a discourse is different from an arbitrary (incoherent) set of sentences.

At the *micro level*, meaning relations between propositions of a discourse obey a number of coherence conditions. These relations may have a *functional* nature. For instance one proposition may function as a specification, generalization, illustration or contrast with respect to a previous proposition. In a simple sequence like 'John is late. He is always late', the second sentence expresses a proposition that is a generalization of the proposition expressed in the first sentence.

A typical example of another functional relation is specification, which we find each day in our newspaper in the news reports. These usually begin with sentences that express very general propositions (in their headline and lead) followed by sentences that express propositions that provide increasingly specific details. Similarly, the chapters in this book often use the functional relation of example or illustration: after mentioning a general property of a discourse, they may give one or more examples (as I did in the previous paragraph).

In the same way, a semantic analysis of discourse may spell out how meaning or information is emphasized or being placed in or out of *focus*. Also, depending on their discursive 'environment', meanings may function as the *topic* of a sentence, that is, what/who the sentence 'is about'. Thus, in the example of the previous paragraph, the concept 'John' (expressed by the words *John* and *he*) is the topic of the two sentences. In all these cases, these various functions of meaning depend on the meaning or information of the previous part of the discourse or the context (or rather on the knowledge the language user invested in them or inferred from them).

The semantics of discourse is not restricted to such functional or other *meaning* relations between propositions. It also needs another notion, that of *reference* – the ways discourse and its meanings are related to the real or imaginary events that people talk *about*, namely its so-called *referents*. One seemingly simple rule for the local coherence of a discourse is that its propositions must refer to (be about) events or situations that are related (according to the speaker at least). Thus, discourse may be coherent if its sentences refer to facts that are causally related, as in the constructed example 'Jean was late. Her plane was delayed. She had to wait for hours.'

As suggested, such coherence is relative to the speakers and their knowledge. This brings in a cognitive aspect which we shall deal with below. Often such a coherence condition also means that the propositions of a discourse will be about the same people or objects, which are sometimes called *discourse referents*. We have seen in the section on syntax that such discourse referents may be referred to by different expressions, depending on whether the recipient is supposed to know or to think about the referents. Full descriptions may be needed in order to identify a new (or recall a previously mentioned) discourse referent, but after that a simple pronoun (and sometimes not even that) may suffice to know what or whom we are now talking about. (Chapter 3, Volume 1, by Russell S. Tomlin, Linda Forrest, Ming Ming Pu, and Myung Hee Kim gives details of these and many other aspects of discourse meaning).

With the description of the *macro level* of discourse meaning we leave traditional linguistics and grammar behind us, and encounter such typical discourse notions as *topics* or *themes*. Discourse topics (which are not the same as sentence topics) are so to speak the global meanings of discourse, of which they define the overall (macro) coherence. If we formulate the topic(s) of a text or talk, we answer such mundane questions as 'What was she speaking/writing about?', questions that in this case ask for the *upshot* or *gist* of a discourse, that is its *most important information*. Topics are crucial for text and talk. Without them we don't know what we are talking or reading about. They define the overall 'unity' of discourse, and are typically expressed in such discourse segments as headlines, summaries or conclusions. They also happen to be the information that we usually remember best of a discourse. In sum, global meanings or topics are essential in processes of communication.

For instance, the news report that opens today's newspaper may have as its main topic 'that an agreement has been signed for peace in Bosnia'. Such a topic embodies at an abstract and higher level of meaning the more detailed information conveyed by the rest of the news report, and thus also defines the global coherence of such a text. In a sense, the topic 'summarizes' the more detailed meanings of a discourse. In the same way, scholarly articles, everyday conversations or parliamentary debates may also have one or more of such topics.

Style

Most linguistic grammars are limited to the levels of expression (sound and form) and meaning of sentences. We have gone beyond the limitations of such grammars and also paid attention to meaning and referential relations between sentences, and even to (global) meanings of whole discourses. However, discourse has many more properties and these are not usually accounted for in grammar or even in linguistics.

One other aspect of discourse, for instance, is its *style*, a notoriously difficult notion to define. One way of defining style is in terms of *variation*. For instance, in order to describe the civil war in Bosnia, we may refer to the various groups of participants in terms of 'fighters', 'rebels', 'insurgents', 'terrorists', etc. The *choice* of a specific word in this case may depend on the type of discourse (for example news report, editorial or political propaganda), or on the group membership, position or opinion of the speaker or writer. That is, in order to refer to the same people, we may use different lexical items. If such variation is a *function of the context* (speaker, perspective, audience, group, etc.) we usually call it a property of the style of the discourse.

We may also use variable pronunciation, writing, visual elements, gestures, word order, or sentence order, to describe the same events, and also this functional variation may be part of the style. In sum, style is usually a context-bound variation of the *expression* level of discourse. The meanings in that case remain the same: if not, we would speak not of a stylistically variant discourse, but of a different discourse altogether. But even then we might find stylistic variation: we may speak about the same topic or events (referents) and do so with different local meanings (details), as would be the case for accounts of the 'same' events in a serious 'quality' broadsheet and a tabloid newspaper. Obviously, two different news reports, next to each other in the same paper, and about different topics or events, would not constitute stylistic variants of each other. In other words, this concept of style usually assumes that at least something (meaning, topic, events) remains the same, so that we are able to compare *how* the discourses 'say the same thing'.

A stylistic analysis may also define a collection of *typical* discursive characteristics of a genre (story vs report), a speaker (calm vs emotional), a group (women vs men), a social situation (formal vs informal), a literary period (classic vs romantic), or even a whole culture (Anglo vs Latino), and so on. Usually, we then will focus not only on contextual variations of words or sentence forms, but also on many other properties of discourse to be discussed below, such as typical ways of storytelling or politeness strategies. There are many other aspects of style not mentioned here, and these will be dealt with in Chapter 5, Volume 1, by Barbara Sandig and Margret Selting (for cultural variations of style, see also Chapter 9, Volume 2, by Cliff Goddard and Anna Wierzbicka; other chapters also regularly refer to style).

Rhetoric

Closely related to a stylistic analysis is another dimension of discourse which we may call *rhetorical*, although rhetoric originally had a much broader meaning, namely the art or study of persuasive public discourse (see Chapter 6, Volume 1, by Ann M. Gill and Karen Whedbee). In this broader sense, which goes back to Antiquity, rhetoric may be considered as the forerunner of what we would now call discourse studies. One central element of this classical rhetoric focused on the special means that make discourse more memorable and hence more *persuasive*, namely the *figurae* or figures of speech. Whereas all discourse necessarily has style, not all discourse has such figures, which we may also call 'rhetorical structures': alliteration, rhyme, irony, metaphor, hyperbole, etc.

Thus, more generally, rhetorical analysis will typically focus on such persuasive 'devices', that is, special structures at all discourse levels that attract attention, for example because of unexpected repetition, inverse order, incomplete structures or changes of meaning. Although traditionally studied especially for structures within sentences, it goes without saying that also whole sequences or discourses may be more or less hyperbolical, ironic or metaphorical. And although these rhetorical structures are typically related to the persuasiveness of discourse, it need hardly be emphasized that such a persuasive *function* of text or talk is not limited to its rhetoric, but may also depend on style or meaning or coherence.

Schemata

There is one other level of discourse which is not often dealt with separately and in a homogeneous way, namely that of its overall formal structures, also called *schematic structures* or *superstructures*. Still, this separate level is not difficult to define. If for instance we admit that discourses have an overall meaning or topic, what still seems to be lacking is an abstract overall *form* in which these global meanings will fit. That is, in the same way as the form of sentence is described in terms of word order (syntax), we may decompose the form of whole texts and talk into a number of fixed, *conventional components* or *categories* and formulate rules for their characteristic order. Indeed, also without theoretical knowledge about schematic structures, we are usually able to identify the 'beginning' and the 'end' of a discourse, or the headline of a news report, or the opening greetings of a conversation, or the conclusions of an argument. It should be stressed again that these are *formal* notions: whatever the meaning (content) of a news report, it will always have a headline category, which has as its function to begin and summarize the report. And whatever we say at the end of a conversation or a meeting or write at the end of an article, it will usually *function* as some kind of closure category.

In sum, in an abstract sense we may analyse a discourse in terms of a number of typical formal *categories* and their specific *order* and *function*, much like we do when we analyse a sentence in terms of subject, object, etc. Thus, many types of discourse will begin with a summary and end with a conclusion category. Arguments may consist of various premises and a conclusion, and stories may be abstractly composed of categories among which a complication and a resolution appear to be crucial. That is, together with their style, various genres may be described in terms of these typical schematic categories. Whereas news reports and other stories, as well as many scholarly discourses, typically begin with summaries and end with some kind of conclusion, poems, advertisements and other types of discourse do not.

Note that, as elsewhere so far, we are here dealing with *abstract* structures. How language users actually go about constructing their concrete texts and conversations, and thus how they 'accomplish' coherence, topics, summaries, headlines or closures, requires another type of analysis. Moreover, a story may typically exhibit narrative structures, but obviously has many more properties than such a schematic organization, for example accounts and explanations of actions, character and situation descriptions, temporal organization and a variable style and perspective, all depending on context and narrative genre. These and other aspects of narrative and argumentative texts are dealt with, respectively, in Chapter 7, Volume 1, by Elinor Ochs, and Chapter 8, Volume 1, by Frans H. van Eemeren, Rob Grootendorst, Sally Jackson and Scott Jacobs.

Discourse as Action and Interaction in Society

With each next step in the definition and analysis of discourse, we encounter structures that are further removed from the traditional scope of linguistics. Indeed, we now enter a domain that comes closer to that of the social sciences, namely that of *action* and *interaction*. That is, discourses do not only consist of (structures of) sound or graphics, and of abstract sentence forms (syntax) or complex structures of local or global meaning and schematic forms. They also may be described in terms of the social actions accomplished by *language users* when they communicate with each other in *social situations* and within *society* and *culture* at large. It is also for this reason that the chapters on discourse as action and interaction are grouped together in a separate volume of this book.

Speech Acts

The first approach to the study of language use as action is still fairly abstract, and was initiated in the philosophy of language. It emphasizes the fact that when people use language they are doing several things at the same time. Thus, what was described above as abstract structures of sounds, may also be described more actively as a *locutionary act*, that is, producing an utterance in some language. At the same time, 'meaning' may be characterized more actively as a verb and not as a noun, that is, as a *semantic* (or *propositional*) *act*. New in this approach, however, was the focus on the *social* dimension of what we do when we produce a meaningful utterance in some context, that is, the accomplishment of a *speech act* or *illocutionary act*, such as an assertion, a question, a promise, a threat or a congratulation.

Whereas the abstract forms of sentences obey syntactic rules that govern their well-formedness, and semantics has its own conditions of meaningfulness, these speech acts must also satisfy a number of typical conditions, which are called *appropriateness conditions*. These conditions, however, pertain not only to the expression (words, syntax, etc.) or meaning of the utterance, but also to their situational *context*, such as the intentions, knowledge or opinions of the speaker. For instance, one condition for the appropriateness of the speech act of a promise is that the speaker intends to do something and believes that this future act will please the hearer. The theoretical account of such speech acts and their conditions is usually located in a field commonly called *pragmatics*, which more generally focuses on the study of language use as action in the sociocultural context. Since this is also one major goal of discourse studies, we may consider pragmatics as a subdiscipline of discourse studies (see Chapter 2, Volume 2, by Shoshana Blum-Kulka, for details).

Whereas the initial studies of speech acts, following the usual sentential bias of traditional linguistics and philosophy of language, focused on isolated speech acts, a discourse approach will of course be interested again in the *sequences* of speech acts which are realized by text or talk. Also at this level, thus, we may specify conditions of *pragmatic coherence* for such sequences, for example when some speech act may express the appropriateness condition, such as an acceptable reason, for a previous or following speech act (as in 'Could you please shut the door? It is so cold in here', where the assertion accomplished by the utterance of the second sentence provides an explanation for the reasonableness of the preceding request).

Also in analogy with the semantic account of discourse meaning, we may further assume that sequences of speech acts may be 'summarized', at a more abstract level, as one global speech act, or *macro speech act*. Indeed, a whole news report may function as a complex assertion, an editorial as one macro accusation, and a ransom note overall as a macro threat, even when their constituent speech acts are of a different nature (a ransom note may consist only of assertions). That is, the macro speech act here may be defined as the overall illocutionary function of the discourse as a whole, defining at the same time its overall pragmatic coherence.

Conversation as Interaction

Interestingly, once we engage in the analysis of discourse as action and interaction, we find that text and talk are part of a complex hierarchy of different acts. Thus, besides the speech acts introduced above, people engage in various types of *interaction*, such as taking turns in conversation, attacking others and defending themselves, opening and closing dialogues, negotiation, agreeing and disagreeing with each other, responding to previous turns or preparing next turns, presenting themselves in positive ways, face keeping, being polite, persuading each other, teaching, and so on. Many of these acts may be accomplished at the same time. This means that besides the sequential analysis of such actions, we also need to do a 'vertical' analysis of all the acts we may accomplish 'by' accomplishing others, like buying a house *by* signing a contract.

The vast domain of *conversation analysis*, and in broader terms all studies of discourse as interaction, deal with various types of these social acts as they are accomplished in their social and cultural contexts. Thus, 'simply' taking turns at talk follows complex rules and strategies for selecting next speakers at specific positions of talk. Similarly, people make complex moves in 'doing' politeness, for instance in order to avoid hurting the 'face' of their interlocutors. Conversations are not simply stopped, but participants go through complex collaborative 'work' to close talk appropriately, and the same is true for initiating, closing or changing topics. Very detailed studies, at the boundary of sociolinguistics, discourse analysis, ethnography and sociology, have been made of a myriad of these and other properties of 'talk' as 'situated' social interaction, whether in informal conversations between friends in a bar, or in more formal talk in institutions. Chapter 3, Volume 2, by Anita Pomerantz and B.J. Fehr, and Chapter 4, Volume 2, by Paul Drew and Marja-Leena Sorjonen, provide further details about this influential approach to discourse.

Abstract Structures versus Actual Language Use

The analysis of discourse as interaction does not merely focus on another 'level' of verbal utterances, besides expressions, forms or meanings. Indeed, it may take into account *all* previous levels discussed above, but always as part of what language users actively do or *accomplish* as participants of talk. In other words, the conduct of discourse is an activity that may involve the contextually relevant, strategic production of sound, making gestures, fabricating semantic representations or performing speech acts as well as engaging in interactional forms of turn-taking, impression formation, negotiation, persuasion, or the reproduction of racist prejudices. Yet, in a sense we may say that the earlier levels of verbal activity are oriented towards the accomplishment of the relevant *social* actions. Language users speak in order to be understood and to communicate ideas, and they do that, both as individual persons and as social group members, in order to inform, persuade or impress others or in order to accomplish other social acts in social situations, institutions or social structures.

Moreover, whereas many of the linguistically inspired earlier studies of discourse often have a more abstract nature, and provide structural descriptions and formulate general rules, such as of coherence or narrative structures, the interactional approach is rather congenial with the sociolinguistic emphasis on the study of *actual language use.*

Thus, instead of abstract, ideal structures, there has been a general tendency in discourse analysis, also outside the study of conversation, to avoid the study of abstract or ideal structures, and to focus on how people actually speak and write in social situations. This may mean that sentence forms are incomplete or not quite meaningful, that speech acts are in fact inappropriate, or that negotiation, topic change or closing a conversation seem to fail. We may find false starts, repetitions, contradictions, irrelevancies, redundancies and other breaches of the normative rules for appropriate discourse. In sum, actual language use, especially in mundane, spontaneous everyday communication, may appear very 'messy'.

And yet, instead of simply treating such manifestations of messiness as 'errors' or 'deviations' from general rules, we need to study them in their own right. Indeed, what may appear as a violation of some rule or regularity, may turn out to have a very specific interactional or *contextual function.* That is, besides the 'normative' aspects of language and discourse, as we know them from the rules of grammar, the rules of well-formed news report formation, or the abstract conditions of speech acts, this more realistic and 'empirical' approach takes text and talk as how they actually *are.*

Nevertheless, most scholars will seek for *order,* even in what at first sight may appear as irregularity and messiness. Thus, even in ongoing spontaneous speaking and writing, language users follow rules and effective strategies when making a sentence, a topic or a headline, concluding a meeting, congratulating or disagreeing. These rules and strategies are not personal, but socially shared, implicitly known and used in a speech community. Even apparent mistakes, flaws, problems, inconsistencies, deviations, and other breaches of the rules may be managed in a meaningful and orderly way. This allows not only the participants themselves but also the discourse analysts to *make sense* of what is going on.

Cognition

Making sense, understanding, interpretation, meaning and many other notions used above belong not only to the realm of discourse structures and social interaction, but also to that of the *mind*. For instance, both an abstract and a more realistic account of word order, sentence meaning, coherence, narrative schemata, speech acts or conversational interaction always presuppose that language users have *knowledge*. They know the rules that govern such structures, they know the strategies and the contexts in which they apply. To understand a sentence, to establish coherence between sentences or to interpret the topic of a text presupposes that language users share a vast repertoire of sociocultural *beliefs*. The choice of lexical items, the variation of style or the use of rhetorical devices similarly presupposes that language users express *opinions* or *ideologies*, and thus contribute to the construction of new ones or the modification of existing ones with their recipients.

Thus, although it is sometimes useful to abstract from the mental nature of grammars, rules, norms, knowledge or opinions in an account of discourse and communication, it is obvious that a fully fledged theory of discourse would be seriously incomplete without a mental (cognitive or emotional) component. It is especially cognitive psychology that has focused on these mental dimensions of language use, for instance in terms of the various mental *processes* and *representations*, usually located in the *memory* of language users. These play a role in the production as well as in the comprehension of text and talk.

At one level of analysis, such processes and representations are unique, in the sense of characterizing individual language users in specific communicative contexts. Such uniqueness explains the *personal variation* of all discourse: discourses are generally different from each other, even when produced in similar social situations, if only because different language users make different uses of the same sociocultural repertoire of knowledge.

On the other hand, and more interestingly, the knowledge language users have about grammar and discourse rules is of course *socially shared*, so that mutual understanding is possible. With other members of their group, community or culture, social actors share norms, values and rules of communication, as well as *social representations* such as knowledge and opinions. In other words, in addition to individual cognition, discourse especially involves *sociocultural cognition*.

As is the case in the interactional approach to discourse, a cognitive approach is not limited to mental representations of abstract rules and other forms of knowledge. Also here, analysts are interested in how language users *actually* go about producing and understanding discourse. Psychologists are interested not so much in ideal language users as in real ones. Besides rules, therefore, they focus on *strategic processes* that are consciously or unconsciously applied by language users in the production or understanding of sentences, topics or stories.

Similarly, as is the case for an interactional approach, a cognitive discourse analysis emphasizes that such mental processes are *constructive*. The mental representations derived from reading a text are not simply copies of the text or its meaning, but the result of strategic processes of construction or sense-making which may use elements of the text, elements of what language users know about the context, and elements of beliefs they already had before they started to communicate.

And again as in interaction, such processes are *context-sensitive*: for instance, they may depend on the aims, interests, goals, expectations or other mental representations of the language users. Unlike the rules of grammar, these processes are not necessarily systematic but may contain mistakes, operate with incomplete information and function at various levels at the same time, *as long as they are fast and efficient* in order to reach the goals of communication and interaction, such as mutual understanding and the appropriate accomplishment of the desired actions in a specific situation.

In other words, some phonological or graphical information may be combined with some syntactic, semantic or contextual information in order to quickly infer, within the time span of say one or two seconds, which speech act or other act is being accomplished by a speaker. Of course, this also requires that mistakes may later be corrected, as we also know from repairs in conversation.

In sum, actual understanding is always an ongoing (on-line), tentative process, which allows for continuous reinterpretation. Thus, partial mental analysis of a fragment of a text may interact with the activation and contextual adaptation of general knowledge and opinions from memory. Bottom-up processes of word and sentence understanding may be combined with abstract, top-down 'guesses' about the expected structures of a sentence, story or conversation. Various modules may be put to work to do specialized jobs, such as processing words, clause structure, semantic coherence or speech acts or closing a conversation.

During understanding language users thus gradually build not only a representation of the text and the context, but also representations – in so called mental *models* – of the events or actions the discourse is *about*. What we usually remember of text or talk, thus, is not so much their exact words, or even their meanings or actions, but rather such a model, that is a schematic representation of our (subjective) beliefs about some event or situation. If we tell others about what we have read in the paper this morning, we are thus not so much reproducing news reports as communicating our (sometimes biased) models constructed on the basis of such reports.

And conversely, when we want to say something, a model will serve as the starting point for the production of discourse. Some beliefs will be selected as relevant for communication in the present context and will serve as input to the construction of the (local and global) meaning of the discourse.

The same is true for interaction: language users activate or build, and continuously update, a model of the current context, and of the actions they engage in, actively or passively. Making sense of text or talk, then, involves the construction of such models based on semantic meanings of the discourse, as well as on its interactional meanings or functions, together with the specific application of more general, socially shared knowledge and opinions. These are merely some of the aspects of a cognitive account of discourse: for details, see Chapter 11, Volume 1, by Arthur C. Graesser, Morton A. Gernsbacher and Susan R. Goldman.

Although the main tenets of this cognitive analysis of discourse processing are widely accepted in psychology, some interactional approaches prefer to focus on the observable and social, and hence on the discursive constructions of mental representations and processes. The mind is here seen as interactionally and socially relevant only when actually displayed in text and talk. Rather than to speculate about what such invisible minds may look like or do, it is here proposed to systematically examine the discursive nature of the mind (for details, see Chapter 12, Volume 1, by Susan Condor and Charles Antaki).

Discourse and Society

Most of the studies of discourse take place in one or more of the main areas described above: form, meaning, interaction and cognition. However, we have also seen that the *context* plays a fundamental role in the description and explanation of text or talk. Although there is no explicit theory of context, and the notion is used by different scholars with a wide variety of meanings, we may briefly define it as the structure of all properties of the social situation that are relevant for the production or the reception of discourse. Context features not only influence discourse, but also vice versa: discourse may typically also define or change such context characteristics.

In the same way as we distinguished between local and global structures in discourse, we may also speak of *local* and *global* structures of contexts. Among the local contextual constraints of discourse, we find for instance a setting (time, location, circumstances), participants and their various communicative and social roles (speaker, chairperson, friend, etc.), intentions, goals or purposes, and so on. The global context becomes relevant as soon as we identify ongoing discourse or other actions as constitutive of organizational or institutional actions and procedures (legislation, a trial, teaching, news reporting, etc.), and when participants are involved in the interaction *as members* of social categories, groups or institutions (women vs men, blacks vs whites, young vs old, supervisors vs subordinates; or the various participants in education, parliament, the court or the police) (for detail, see Chapter 4, Volume 2, by Paul Drew and Marja-Leena Sorjonen, and Chapter 7, Volume 2, by Dennis K. Mumby and Robin P. Clair).

In sum, as soon as we take such a contextual approach to discourse more seriously, we involve many aspects of society and culture in our analysis. For instance, the selection of specific pronouns as forms of more or less polite address (as is the case for *tu* and *vous* in French) presupposes that language users (and discourse analysts) know about social relations. Lexical variation (for example, between 'terrorist' and 'freedom fighter') implies that speakers have different opinions and ideologies. Speech acts such as commands presuppose differences of power and authority. At all levels of discourse, we thus find the 'traces' of a context in which the social properties of the participants play a fundamental role, such as their gender, class, ethnicity, age, origin, position or other forms of group membership.

This does not mean that such social contexts are always 'given' or 'static' and that language users and their discourses passively 'obey' the constraints of their group, society or culture. On the contrary, discourse and its users have a 'dialectic' relation with their context: besides being subject to the social constraints of the context, they also contribute to, construe or change that context. Flexible negotiations may be engaged in as a function of the demands of the present context and the more general constraints of culture and society. Group power may be obeyed in discourse, but also challenged. Social norms and rules may be creatively changed or broken and such violations may give rise to new social arrangements.

Gender

Many men – sometimes blatantly, sometimes more subtly – engage in the sexist ways of speaking (with or about women) which prevail in their group. When actively doing so, they at the same time contribute to the reproduction of the system of gender inequality. Of course, they may also (partly) change such social constraints and challenge the status quo, for example by refraining from exercising control over virtually all aspects of text, talk or context, such as genre, topic, style, turn-taking or storytelling, at the expense of female participants in communicative events (for details of the role of gender in discourse and communication, see Chapter 5, Volume 2, by Candace West, Michelle M. Lazar and Cheris Kramarae).

Ethnicity

Similar remarks of course hold for the relations of text and talk on the one hand, and 'race' and ethnicity on the other, and more generally for intra- and intercultural discourse and communication. Thus, a history of slavery and segregation, continuing racism, as well as cultural factors have created the conditions for special discourse patterns in the African American community in the United States. More generally, ethnic or 'racial' groups may develop their specific ways of speaking, which may give rise to mutual influence and adaptation, as well as to problems of intercultural communication and understanding. Intercultural and interethnic relations may also take the form of dominance: people may engage in the reproduction of ethnocentrism and racism through prejudiced talk about ethnic or 'racial' minorities and (other) immigrants from the South (for details, see Chapter 6, Volume 2, by Teun A. van Dijk, Stella Ting-Toomey, Geneva Smitherman and Denise Troutman).

Culture

What is here summarized for the study of the role of discourse in society, also applies to the even broader account of the role of discourse in *culture*. For virtually all forms of discourse discussed above we have witnessed variations among social actors and especially among groups. The same is true for cultural characteristics and variation. Telling a story, accomplishing a command, being polite and changing topics are not subject (only) to general or universal rules: people across the globe may do these things in different ways.

These cultural differences may be related to other aspects of culture, such as norms and values, social relations or institutions. We have seen that as soon as members of such ethnic groups or cultures communicate with (or about) those of other groups or cultures, discourse differences may either be cooperatively and tolerantly accepted, or give rise to misunderstanding and conflict, and even to dominance, exclusion and oppression of the less powerful. Hence, the study of intra- and intercultural communication is an important domain of a multidisciplinary discourse analysis (for details, see several chapters of this book, more specifically Chapter 9, Volume 2, by Cliff Goddard and Anna Wierzbicka).

Social Discourse Analysis

It is this broader account of discourse in society and culture which may be seen as the culmination of discourse studies. In such a vastly complex framework we are able to go beyond the mere study of discursive sentence combinations, coherence, speech acts, conversational turns or topic change. Whereas some of the properties of these structures and strategies are relatively autonomous and context-free, many of them interact with many of the properties of the local and societal contexts briefly summarized above.

Indeed, if we want to *explain* what discourse is all about, it would be insufficient to merely analyse its internal structures, the actions being accomplished, or the cognitive operations involved in language use. We need to account for the fact that discourse as social action is being engaged in within a framework of understanding, communication and interaction which is in turn part of broader sociocultural structures and processes. Thus, storytelling may be constitutive of corporate culture, argumentation and rhetoric in parliament may be an inherent part of legislation, and educational discourse may define the social process of schooling. We have seen that specific properties of talk about immigrants may contribute to the reproduction of racism. Gender inequality may be expressed and confirmed by male text and talk but also challenged by feminist discourse. Political power abuse usually takes place through various properties of discourse, and may involve propaganda, manipulation or legitimation as types and functions of discursive communication, but so might political resistance (for details, see Chapter 8, Volume 2, by Paul Chilton and Christina Schäffner). In sum, what appears to be mere local talk and text in many ways enacts as well as constitutes complex processes and structures at the more global, societal level.

Obviously, such forms of *social discourse analysis* are not exactly simple. They require integrated analysis at all levels and dimensions discussed thus far. Although even here we may focus on only a few properties of discourse, such as on the use (and abuse) of a pronoun or speech act, or on how topics are controlled, the relationships between discourse and societal structures are often indirect and highly complicated. Thus, use of pronouns, for instance, may need to be linked with sentence structures, meaning, interaction, mental models, identity and socially shared beliefs before it can be linked with power differences between (members of) groups or institutional structure and routine.

In sum, if discourse analysis is a multidisciplinary enterprise, this is most certainly the case for such a social discourse analysis. This is equally true for all forms of *applied discourse analysis* which deals with the practical applications of discourse studies in, for example, education, the media, politics, law or other fields where various forms and uses of text and talk play such a fundamental role (see Chapter 11, Volume 2, by Britt-Louise Gunnarsson).

Critical Discourse Analysis

Finally, even when engaging in social discourse analysis, the analysts may do so in a distanced and disinterested way, trying to be 'objective', as the dominant norms of scholarship require. However, they may also become more actively involved in the topics and phenomena they study, as one would most probably do (whether intentionally or not) as soon as one studies power abuse, dominance and inequality as it is expressed or reproduced by discourse. The critical scholars make their social and political position explicit; they take sides, and actively participate in order to uncover, demystify or otherwise challenge dominance with their discourse analyses.

Instead of merely focusing on their discipline and its theories and paradigms, such discourse analysts focus on relevant social *problems*. That is, their work is more issue-oriented than theory-oriented. Analysis, description and theory formation play a role especially in as far as they allow better understanding and critique of *social inequality*, based on gender, ethnicity, class, origin, religion, language, sexual orientation and other criteria that define differences between people. Their ultimate goal is not only scientific, but also social and political, namely *change*. In that case, social discourse analysis takes the form of a *critical* discourse analysis.

An increasing number of discourse analysts have shown interest in such a critical approach to text and talk. Beyond observation, systematic description and explanation, they decide to make one crucial further step, and see the discourse analytical enterprise also as a political and moral task of responsible scholars. They emphasize that it is not always possible, or desirable, to neatly distinguish between doing 'value-free' and technical discourse analysis on the one hand, and engaging in social, cultural or political critique on the other. They will claim that one can no less study racist discourse without a moral position about racism than a medical researcher can study cancer or AIDS without taking a position about the devastating nature of such diseases, or a sociologist can study the uprising of exploited peasants without being aware of the nature of their oppression and the legitimacy of their resistance.

In sum, discourse is an inherent part of society and partakes in all society's injustices, as well as in the struggle against them. Critical scholars of discourse do not merely observe such linkages between discourse and societal structures, but aim to be *agents of change*, and do so in solidarity with those who need such change most (for details, see Chapter 10, Volume 2, by Norman Fairclough and Ruth Wodak).

Types of Discourse Studies

After this elementary introduction to the various structures, levels and dimensions of discourse, and the corresponding approaches in discourse studies, we may step back for a moment and consider the resulting framework in more general terms. As we shall see below, when we examine some of the basic principles of doing discourse studies, we may distinguish some general *types*, *styles* or *modes* of analysis.

One prevalent one is that between studies of *text* and *talk*. Text analysis tends to deal more often with (abstract) structures of written discourse as a fixed object, whereas the study of talk rather focuses on more dynamic aspects of spontaneous interaction. The first will be more inspired by linguistics, and the latter rather by the social sciences. And yet, despite the vast differences of these approaches, they are both after *order*, *rules*, *regularities* in the detailed analysis of *structures* and *strategies* of text and talk. Both are more descriptive, less explanatory and tend to ignore broader (for example cognitive or societal) contexts.

In the same way we might distinguish between more *abstract*, formal studies, for instance in grammar and artificial intelligence, and more *concrete* studies of actual texts and talk in specific, socio-historical contexts, that is, of the ways actual language users and social actors go about (often quite imperfectly) speaking, making sense and doing things with words.

Another well-known distinction is that between *theoretical and descriptive* approaches on the one hand, and *applied and critical* ones on the other, the latter rather focusing on social issues, relevance and the use of discourse analysis in society.

We may even distinguish between 'styles' of research, cross-cutting the various distinctions made above, and establish a distinction between more *empirical* research working with concrete discourse data, corpora and their analyses or experiments on the one hand, and more *philosophical*, speculative or impressionistic ways to write about discourse on the other hand.

Another obvious criterion for different approaches is based on discourse types of genres. Indeed, many discourse analysts exclusively focus on conversation, whereas others prefer to study news, advertising, narrative, argumentation, or political discourse, among the myriad of other genres or domains of the world of text and talk. Each of these approaches may have developed its own concepts, methods and procedures.

Other distinctions or categorizations may be made. All of them may be practical and, like beginners or outsiders, experienced discourse analysts also often make them in their everyday lives. They often associate themselves more with one direction or orientation than another; some scholars feel more inclined to meticulous analyses of real talk, whereas others prefer to focus on abstract theory building.

But then again, many others may at least in principle reject such a division of the field into directions, approaches or schools. They may precisely advocate that constant renewal in the field comes from new combinations of approaches, across subdisciplines, methods, theories or types of phenomena studied. They may refuse the artificial distinction between theory, description and application, and may study the same phenomena both in text and in talk, and do so in abstract terms as well as in the more empirical terms of actual language use and interaction. Given their broad orientation, critical scholars for instance may want to consider *all* levels and dimensions, and all methods and approaches, as long as they contribute to our insight into the role of discourse in society and the reproduction of inequality. It is this variety that is one of the appealing characteristics of contemporary discourse analysis.

At the same time, as we shall see below, *integration* of approaches may run parallel to variety and subdisciplinary specialization. Across the various directions of research above, this chapter has identified three main approaches: (a) those which focus on *discourse* 'itself', that is on structures of text or talk; (b) those which study discourse and communication as *cognition*; and (c) those which focus on *social structure and culture*. This triangle of discourse–cognition–society is indeed the site of multidisciplinary discourse analysis.

However, we have seen above that each point of the triangle is related to the two others. We are unable to explain text structure and interaction without a cognitive account, and cognition without the realization that knowledge and other beliefs are acquired and used in discourse and in social contexts; whereas cognition, society and culture, as well as their reproduction, need language, discourse and communication. Thus, wherever we start in the triangle, we will soon discover that systematic description, analysis and explanation need to follow the interdisciplinary sides that connect with the other points of the triangle. Any form of exclusion or reduction will soon run into problems when it is unable to account for part of the phenomena it set out to study 'in their own right'. In sum, adequate discourse analysis, even when temporally studying only some aspect of the discourse triangle, will soon need to become multi-disciplinary and integrated.

The Emergence of Discourse Studies

Under different names, this modern study of discourse, as briefly described above, emerged in the 1960s more or less at the same time in several disciplines in the humanities and the social sciences. Of course, text and talk have been analysed before that, for instance in literary scholarship, history and mass communication research, and at least since ancient rhetoric provided a detailed account of the properties of public speaking.

Ethnography

However, it was only in the mid 1960s that the idea of a new and more systematic and explicit cross-discipline for the study of discourse began to take shape. Anthropology set the stage with the first ethnographic accounts of 'communicative events' or 'ways of speaking' in their cultural contexts. It emphasized that speakers of a language not only know their grammars, but as cultural members also have a broader communicative competence. They also share cultural knowledge of rules about how to talk together appropriately, for instance how to warn someone, how to tell a story, or how to engage in disputes or political debates.

Structuralism and Semiotics

Inspired by the so-called Formalists and other Russian scholars of the 1920s and 1930s, structuralism offered a broader framework for the study of narrative, myths, literature, film and other semiotic practices, first in France, later also elsewhere. These approaches had much influence on the structuralist analyses of other than literary texts or stories, for instance in media studies. Typically lacking in these studies were accounts of cognitive processes as well as of social interaction and societal structures.

Discourse Grammar

Some linguists, mainly outside the generativist mainstream, began to realize that the study of language amounted to more than writing formal grammars of isolated sentences. They began to think in terms of text or discourse grammars and other linguistic approaches to discourse, and especially focused on semantic and functional relations between sentences, for instance on how texts are coherent and how information or focus is distributed in texts. As is the case for the structuralist (literary, semiotic) approaches to discourse, this linguistic approach ignored actual language use and hence also the social dimensions of discourse. On the other hand, these discourse grammars did establish connections with ideas on discourse processing in psycholinguistics and cognitive psychology.

Sociolinguistics and Pragmatics

At the same time, sociolinguistics and pragmatics emerged as new directions of research in the language sciences. Some of this work also focused on the discursive nature of language use, speech acts and verbal interaction. As is the case for the studies in the 'ethnography of communication', mentioned above, these approaches were not satisfied with a formal account of discourse structures, but emphasized the necessity to study actual language use in their socially and culturally variable contexts.

Ethnomethodology

Also at the end of the 1960s, an approach in phenomenological microsociology called 'ethnomethodology' began to focus on the rich field of everyday interaction and especially on conversation. It examined in detail such apparently mundane phenomena as how people change turns at talk, and what kind of social interaction is accomplished by such talk, as explained above. This development would later have a tremendous influence in several other disciplines: conversation analysis became one of the core domains of the new cross-discipline of discourse studies. In this approach few links were established with formal linguistic and cognitive studies of text or talk, while at the same time there was some distance from more classical (macro) sociological ways of accounting for social structure.

Cognitive Psychology

A few years later, in the early 1970s, and inspired by questions of learning and knowledge acquisition, cognitive and educational psychology started its successful and influential research on the mental processes of text comprehension. Especially within the broader framework of what later would be called 'cognitive science', this development took place in close cooperation with the computer simulation of text understanding and the study of the role of knowledge in the field of artificial intelligence. As suggested above, some of this work also integrated insights from text-linguistic approaches.

Social Psychology and Discursive Psychology

Surprisingly lagging behind, despite its attention to many discourse-relevant phenomena (such as socialization, persuasion and attribution), social psychology followed suit only in the later 1980s. However, given the obvious relevance of discourse in social interaction and the construction of social representations, some social psychologists, mainly in Great Britain, developed their own 'discursive psychology'. Departing from the dominant cognitive paradigm, and inspired by ethnomethodological principles, they especially emphasized the interactional accomplishment of psychological phenomena such as understanding, explanation, opinions and ideologies.

Communication Studies

Slowly, and throughout the 1970s and 1980s, the various branches of communication studies witnessed a growing awareness of the usefulness of detailed discourse analysis of, for example, mass media messages as well as of interpersonal, intercultural or business communication. Indeed, we may expect that the many overlaps between the concerns of discourse and communication studies will in the future lead to further integration or even a merger of these different approaches to communication and language use.

Other disciplines

Similar remarks may be made about the emergence of discourse analysis in the other disciplines of the humanities and social sciences. Thus, interestingly, the study of interaction in the courtroom drew attention not so much in *legal studies* as in the sociology or social psychology of talk and interaction. On the other hand, historians hardly needed to be reminded of the eminently textual nature of most of their sources, and of the narrative aspects of *historiography*, as was the case for *theology*, studying the Bible or other sacred texts. In fact, in this long list of the various discourse disciplines only *political science* seems to be systematically absent. And yet, it needs little argument that text and talk are central and constitutive parts of the political process. Instead of detailed discourse analyses of political text and talk, however, there is a rich tradition here of the study of political communication and rhetoric, a tradition going back at least to the rhetoric of Aristotle and other classical rhetoricians.

Diversity and Integration

As is the case in other new scholarly domains, such as biochemistry or cognitive science, interdisciplinary endeavors often bring most interesting forms of theoretical renewal. Similarly, the enthusiastic discoveries of the fascinating world of discourse and its sociocultural contexts took place especially at the boundaries of the established disciplines, where theoretical and methodological cross-fertilization is most intense.

However, given the different philosophies, approaches and methods in their various 'mother-disciplines', the various developments of discourse analysis hardly produced a unified enterprise. True, text grammarians and cognitive psychologists understood each other and worked together. The same soon happened between microsociology, sociolinguistics and ethnography. However, vast domains of the study of discourse remained rather disparate and isolated, as was initially the case for stylistics, rhetoric and argumentation studies.

Obvious links, such as between mind and interaction, were not established, thus keeping most of the psychological and social approaches to discourse apart until today. Ideas on the coherence of written texts were not taken up in the study of the coherence of conversations, and vice versa, strategies of interaction in situated talk were often ignored in the study of texts. Fundamental notions, such as 'meaning', were dealt with in totally different ways in formal discourse semantics, cognitive psychology and the sociology and ethnography of interaction.

Other regrettable forms of fragmentation took place along the inevitable linguistic boundaries, especially between the English- and French-speaking worlds of discourse and discourse analysis. Some famous French structuralist and post-structuralist scholars were (sooner or later) available in English, and even became fashionable internationally, especially in the more literary and philosophical directions of discourse studies. Italian, Spanish and Latin American studies of discourse were initially mainly oriented towards these French approaches. The more analytical and empirical directions of most work in English had little impact in this Latin sphere. Conversely, those writing in English were seldom reading studies in French, or those in German or Russian for that matter. Largely unwittingly, such scholars, mainly in the USA and the UK, thereby expressed and reproduced the cultural hegemony of English and of English-language scholarship in the world, as is unfortunately also the case for this book.

However, despite this diversity in the vast 'trans-discipline' of discourse studies, the last decade has also witnessed many attempts at integration. For the study of the 'mental side' of discourse, cognitive science provided a unified framework for the integration and mutual inspiration of linguistic, cognitive, neurological, logical and formal philosophical approaches. On the sociocultural side, the common focus on situated social interaction and talk required synthesis and favored mutual interest among scholars working in pragmatics, sociolinguistics, sociology and ethnography.

Some scholars never accepted the deep division between cognition on the one hand, and interaction, society and culture on the other, and favored the study of cognitive anthropology or social cognition as a basis for the study of discourse as involving both sociocultural and cognitive dimensions.

In sum, discourse studies on the one hand partly reproduced the well-known disciplinary limitations of specialization or arbitrary divisions of labor and interest (as between cognitive and social psychologists or between sociologists and ethnographers). But on the other hand, it defined a *domain* of study which by itself promoted cross-disciplinary influence and integration. Despite the usual specialization, therefore, we may expect further integration of various directions of discourse studies in the future. This will especially be the case when young researchers are no longer educated only in one of the mother-disciplines mentioned above, but will be able to focus on discourse studies as an autonomous discipline. For them, writing grammars, analysing cognition, or studying interaction and societal structures will not be totally different things, but simply different aspects of one, complex scholarly enterprise, namely to describe and explain discourse.

Principles of Discourse Analysis

Having explained the different properties of discourse and the corresponding domains of discourse analysis, we finally need to summarize some of the basic principles of 'doing' discourse analysis. Despite a vast variety of approaches and methods, each discipline, even a cross-discipline such as discourse studies, usually has a number of norms that most scholars somehow will follow in order to do 'good' scholarship in that domain. Some of these principles have developed as a critical reaction against earlier dominant paradigms in the respective mother-disciplines of discourse studies. This implies that these norms are historical, and subject to change. Although each of these normative principles would require lengthy explanation, I merely summarize them here, and refer to the chapters in this book for more detailed discussion and illustration. At some points, however, I briefly state my own (critical) view of currently prevailing principles.

1 Naturally Occurring Text and Talk Perhaps most pervasive in the study of discourse is the virtually exclusive focus on actually or naturally occurring talk and text. Unlike much work in formal linguistics and philosophy, invented or constructed examples (as we used above) are avoided in favor of examples and corpora of 'real data', for instance tape or video recordings of conversations, or actual texts used in the mass media or education. Data are in principle not edited or otherwise 'sanitized', but studied 'as is', that is, close to their actual appearance or use in their original contexts.

2 Contexts Discourse should preferably be studied as a constitutive part of its local and global, social and cultural contexts. Text and talk in many ways signal their contextual relevance, and therefore context structures need to be observed and analysed in detail, also as possible consequences of discourse: settings, participants and their communicative and social roles, goals, relevant social knowledge, norms and values, institutional or organizational structures, and so on. Despite the general recognition of the importance of contextual analysis, this principle is unfortunately more preached than actually practiced.

3 Discourse as Talk Whereas much earlier discourse study, such as in literature or the media, focused on written texts, most contemporary discourse studies are oriented towards the analysis of ongoing verbal interaction in informal conversations as well as other, more formal or institutional dialogues. Indeed, talk is often considered as the basic or primordial form of discourse. On the other hand, although the earlier neglect of mundane, everyday conversation warranted such an orientation in discourse studies, it should not lead to a corresponding neglect of the vast domain of written (and sometimes no less mundane or everyday) texts in society.

4   Discourse as Social Practice of Members   Both spoken and written discourse are forms of social practice in sociocultural contexts. Language users are engaged in discourse not merely as individual persons, but also as members of various groups, institutions or cultures. Through their discourse, thus, language users may enact, confirm or challenge more comprehensive social and political structures and institutions.

5   Members' Categories   It has become widespread practice, especially in conversation analysis, not to 'impose' preconceived notions and categories of analysts, but (also) to respect the ways social members themselves interpret, orient to and categorize the properties of the social world and their conduct in it, including that of discourse itself. Obviously, such a principle should not be interpreted to mean that analysts do not go beyond common-sense categories of language users, or should not develop theories that systematically and explicitly account for discourse as social practice.

6   Sequentiality   The accomplishment of discourse is largely linear and sequential, in the production and understanding both of talk and of text. This first implies that at all levels, structural units (sentences, propositions, acts) should be described or interpreted relative to preceding ones, as is most obvious in various forms of coherence. This discursive relativity may also involve *functionality*: later elements may have special functions with respect to previous ones. It also implies that language users operate, both mentally and interactionally, in an 'on-line' or 'ongoing' fashion, that is tentatively, possibly erroneously, but with the opportunity to reinterpret or repair previous activities and understandings.

7   Constructivity   Besides being sequential, discourses are constructive in the sense that their constitutive units may be *functionally* used, understood or analysed as elements of larger ones, thus also creating *hierarchical* structures. This applies to forms as well as to meaning and interaction.

8   Levels and Dimensions   Discourse analysts tend to theoretically decompose discourse at various layers, dimensions or levels and at the same time to mutually *relate* such levels. These levels represent different types of phenomena involved in discourse, such as sounds, forms, meanings, or action. Language users on the other hand strategically manage several levels or dimensions of discourse at the same time.

9   Meaning and Function Both language users and analysts are after meaning: in their understanding and analysis, they will ask things like 'What does this (she) mean here?', or 'How does this make sense in the present context?' As is the case for other principles, this principle also has functional and explanatory implications: '*Why* is this being said/meant here?'

10   Rules Language, communication as well as discourse are assumed to be rule-governed. Text and talk are analysed as manifestations or enactments of these socially shared grammatical, textual, communicative or interactional rules. At the same time, however, the study of actual discourse will focus on how rules may be violated, ignored or changed, and what the discursive or contextual functions are of such real or apparent violations.

11   Strategies Besides rules, language users also know and apply expedient mental as well as interactional strategies in the effective understanding and accomplishment of discourse and the realization of their communicative or social goals. This relevance of strategies may be compared to the game of chess: chess players need to know the rules in order to play chess in the first place, but will use tactics, gambits, and special moves within an overall strategy to defend themselves or to win.

12   Social Cognition Less generally recognized but no less relevant is the fundamental role of cognition, that is, of mental processes and representations in the production and understanding of text and talk. Few of the aspects of discourse discussed above (meaning, coherence, action, etc.) can be properly understood and explained without having recourse to the minds of language users. Besides personal memories and experiences of events (models), the shared sociocultural representations (knowledge, attitudes, ideologies, norms, values) of language users as group members also play a fundamental role in discourse, as well as its description and explanation. Indeed, in many ways, cognition is the interface between discourse and society.

Conclusion

Contemporary discourse analysis has come a long way since the early linguistic studies of pronouns and semantic coherence, the first observations of turn-taking in talk, the initial ethnographic studies of 'ways of speaking' in various cultures, or the early experiments with text comprehension. It has become not only a vast and multidisciplinary enterprise involving at least half a dozen disciplines, but also fairly sophisticated in several of its areas. So much so that unavoidable specialization has taken place and mutual comprehension is not always guaranteed. In that respect discourse analysis has come of age, and is now much like the other disciplines in the humanities and the social sciences, although its cross-disciplinary nature guarantees continuous renewal and inspiration at the borders of existing domains of knowledge. That is, despite vast differences of approach and method, we now find systematic analyses of text and talk from formal linguistics and artificial intelligence, to cognitive, social and educational psychology, to literary scholarship, semiotics and virtually all the social sciences.

In this first introduction I have characterized discourse as essentially involving three main dimensions, namely language use, cognition, and interaction in their sociocultural contexts. Instead of vaguely summarizing, paraphrasing or quoting discourse, as is still often the case in social scientific approaches, discourse analytical studies distinguish various levels, units or constructs within each of these dimensions, and formulate the rules and strategies of their normative or actual uses. They functionally relate such units or levels among each other, and thereby also explain *why* they are being used. In the dame way, they functionally connect discourse structures with social and cultural context structures, and both again to the structures and strategies of cognition. Discourse analysis thus moves from macro to micro levels of talk, text, context or society, and vice versa. It may examine ongoing discourse top down, beginning with general abstract patterns, or bottom up, beginning with the nitty-gritty of actually used sounds, words, gestures, meanings or strategies. And perhaps most importantly, discourse analysis provides the theoretical and methodological tools for a well-founded critical approach to the study of social problems, power and inequality.

Following a number of characteristic principles, discourse analysis is thus taking its own place within the humanities and the social sciences. It has shown that it is able to provide insights in many social and mental phenomena that other disciplines might ignore or neglect. In that sense, discourse analysis is *not* a method one can simply apply while doing psychological, sociological, anthropological or political scientific research. As is the case for other important new cross-disciplines, such as the cognitive and neural sciences, or interdisciplines such as molecular biology or biochemistry, discourse studies claims to be an autonomous domain of study, with its own characteristic objects and phenomena, theories, methods and principles. For linguists and psychologists, discourse studies emphasizes that language use and thought typically and functionally manifest themselves in discursive social interaction. For social scientists, discourse analysis stresses that social and political institutions, organizations, group relations, structures, processes, routines, and many other relevant phenomena, also need to be studied at the level of their actual manifestations, expressions or enactment in discourse as language use, communication and interaction.

There are few disciplines that offer such a broad, multidisciplinary, multicultural and socially relevant approach to human language, cognition, communication and interaction. Few disciplines allow students to focus on small but significant details of text and talk, as well as on the fascinating processes and representations of the social mind, and at the same time on the fundamental social and political issues and problems of our time. Few disciplines offer so many opportunities to combine formal precision with broad explanatory frameworks on how people use language, think and interact, and thus enact and reproduce their groups, societies and cultures.

Recommended Reading

For references and recommended reading about the various levels and dimensions of discourse analysis, see the respective chapters of this book. For the history of discourse studies, especially also in the field of linguistics, see also Chapter 2, Volume 1, by Robert de Beaugrande and references given there. The other chapters usually also give a historical overview of the respective domains and directions of discourse analysis.

For new developments in the various domains of discourse studies, see the journal *Text*, and for discussion of the social, political and critical dimensions of discourse analysis, see the journal *Discourse and Society*. Pragmatic approaches to discourse appear in the *Journal of Pragmatics*. Psychological (but also other) studies on discourse may be found in the journal *Discourse Processes*.

Earlier well-known overviews of and introductions to discourse analysis and its major domains include the following books:

Atkinson and Heritage (1984): one of the classic selections of articles on conversational interaction. See Chapters 3 and 4, Volume 2, for other references.

Beaugrande and Dressler (1981): a classic and still useful history of and introduction to the grammar and other linguistic aspects of discourse.

Brown and Yule (1983): a well-known introduction to the analysis of discourse, focusing especially on such semantic aspects as topic, focus, information, coherence and reference.

Coulthard (1994): besides the many collections and overviews of spoken discourse analysis, this volume especially deals with aspects of written texts, such as expository discourse, newspaper editorials, narrative and scholarly discourse.

Drew and Heritage (1992): besides the overviews and selections of studies on informal conversations, this volume extends conversational analysis to the study of talk in institutional settings, for example media interviews, doctor–patient interaction, job interviews, and courtroom interaction.

Fairclough (1995): one of the recent books that focuses on the various aspects of a more critical approach to discourse, such as ideology, power and hegemony.

Renkema (1993): translated from the Dutch, this book provides a first introduction to both written and spoken discourse analysis. It also discusses the psychology of text comprehension.

Schiffrin (1993): this book is especially useful as an introduction to the study of discourse as interaction, such as pragmatics, conversation analysis and the ethnography of speaking.

Tannen (1994): one of the recent books of an author who has written extensively about conversation and the differences between male and female styles of talk. For discussion of this approach and further references, see Chapter 5, Volume 2, by Candace West, Michelle M. Lazar and Cheris Kramarae.

van Dijk (1985): this is a detailed overview of the whole field of discourse analysis, focusing on the various disciplines (vol. 1), levels (vol. 2), conversational interaction (vol. 3) as well as societal functions of discourse (vol. 4).

van Dijk and Kintsch (1983): a general and still influential discussion of the various cognitive strategies of discourse comprehension, and of the role of knowledge and models in processing.

References

Atkinson, J.M. and Heritage, J. (eds) (1984) *Structures of Social Action: Studies in Conversation Analysis.* Cambridge: Cambridge University Press.

Beaugrande, de R. and Dressler, W.U. (1981) *Introduction to Text Linguistics.* London: Longman.

Brown, G. and Yule, G. (1983) *Discourse Analysis.* London: Cambridge University Press.

Coulthard, R.M. (ed.) (1994) *Advances in Written Text Analysis.* London: Routledge.

Drew, P. and Heritage, J. (eds) (1992) *Talk at Work: Interaction in Institutional Settings.* Cambridge: Cambridge University Press.

Fairclough, N.L. (1995) *Critical Discourse Analysis: Papers in the Critical Study of Language.* London: Longman.

Renkema, J. (1993) *Discourse Studies: an Introductory Textbook.* Amsterdam: Benjamins.

Schiffrin, D. (1993) *Approaches to Discourse.* Oxford: Blackwell.

Tannen, D. (1994) *Gender and Discourse.* New York: Oxford University Press.

van Dijk, T.A. (ed.) (1985) *Handbook of Discourse Analysis* (4 vols) London: Academic Press.

van Dijk, T.A. and Kintsch, W. (1983) *Strategies of Discourse Comprehension.* New York: Academic Press.

2

The Story of Discourse Analysis

Robert de Beaugrande

In the mid 1990s, providing a user-friendly introductory survey of the research trends which have contributed to discourse analysis is a tough problem. My solution is to 'tell a story' highlighting the main ideas that have helped or hindered discourse analysis, crediting projects or researchers only for illustration. Many citations and references are found elsewhere.[1]

'Science' as Map-Making

In the popular 'story of science', scientists *observe* things in the *real world* and then *describe* or *explain* them *accurately*, steadily piling up more *facts* and marching on towards the *final truth*. A more accurate, though less dramatic, story would tell of scientists *drawing a series of maps* for a rugged and periodically shifting *terrain* that is not *located* in the 'real world' of ordinary experience yet is *connected* to it in ways the scientists determine. This terrain requires *specialized methods* for observing, describing, or explaining. Each map fits the vision of its makers and the intentions of its users, putting some features or places into sharp perspective and ignoring others, just as ordinary maps look different if they show roads, climates, altitudes, or mineral deposits. No scientific map is ever final or complete, just as no ordinary map ever becomes identical with the terrain.

Again like an ordinary map, a scientific map gets *tested* by seeing how well it helps people find things. The *natural sciences* make maps of a *sparse terrain* – one that can be disconnected from the rich and messy world of ordinary reality. Looking at the world around us and the society we live in, we do not see the forces and particles of physics, or the compounds and polymers of chemistry, or even the cells and neurons of biology. But these sciences give us reliable maps revealing these things in the *underlying order* of reality, and give special instruments for observing, such as microscopes and particle accelerators. Some instruments can even *intervene* in those orders, for example by splitting atoms, synthesizing compounds, or removing unhealthy cells.

The *human sciences*, in contrast, face a *rich terrain* closely connected to human activities. Here, observing ordinary experience is much easier than deciding what 'underlying order' to look for and what instruments to use for observing, let alone for intervening, for example to render humans more co-operative (see final section).

The human sciences have drawn two kinds of maps. *Outside maps* try to record what people are *actually observed to do*, such as how people within a culture and a society behave in the roles of chiefs, priests, warriors, hunters, farmers, and so on. *Inside maps* try to infer from observations and intro-spections what people *think and believe* and how they *organize their knowledge of the world and of their society*. Drawing *both* kinds of maps together might be worthwhile, using the one kind to better understand the other and trying to show the whole big picture of human life. But until recently, most scientists and philosophers have recommended drawing *only one kind or the other* to suit the changing fashions of science. The recent struggle to regain the big picture was a major motive for discourse analysis, as we shall see.

Disconnecting the 'Science of Language' from Discourse

This general 'story of science' sets the scene for our more specific 'story of language science'. Surely, science should investigate the capacities of human beings for using the *natural languages* developed by a culture or society for communication in everyday life. But language is *immensely rich* – vastly connected to many things in many ways. How can science tackle it or keep it from spilling into the terrain of other human sciences, like history, anthropology, sociology, and psychology?

The 'language science' of the twentieth century, known as *modern linguistics*, resolved to *disconnect language* and study it *by itself*.[2] But in the world of human beings, you won't find a language by itself – the Dutch language strolling by the canals, or the English language having a nice cup of tea, or the German language racing madly along the autobahn. You only find *discourse*, that is, *real communicative events*. So ever since, linguists have been trying to reconstruct language disconnected from discourse, believing that it *should* be done to create a proper 'science' and not seriously questioning whether it *actually could* be done.

Let's watch what happened in the 'story of language science' during the first half of the twentieth century. Language got *divided up* into various *'domains' to be studied separately*, starting with the ones that are *easier to disconnect from discourse*. Linguistics made a fine start by describing the *simplest language sounds* in the domain of *phonology*. It offered a grand vision of 'underlying order': beneath all the *practical sound-units* that speakers of a language actually produce or recognize lies an *ideal system of theoretical sound-units* called *phonemes* we can precisely describe. In *physical* terms, for pronouncing the sound of 'd' in an English word like 'daunting', the front teeth stop the flow of air and the vocal chords vibrate; just try it. If the vocal chords didn't vibrate, you'd get 't' in 'taunting'. So we can classify the sound of 'd' as the 'voiced dental stop' in the system of

'English phonemes'. The system nicely connects back to the real world and yields a convincing 'map' of the anatomy of the mouth, nose, and vocal tract with the locations and events for producing 'phonemes'. In *mental* terms, each 'phoneme' must allow us to *tell the difference* between words that are also *different in meaning*, say 'daunting' versus 'taunting'. So we get both an *outside map* of how sounds are pronounced, and an *inside map* of what sounds speakers tell apart in words. Moreover, our 'phonemes' match the *letters* in the *alphabet*, which was tidied up and enlarged to make the *international phonetic alphabet* for recording the 'phonemes' of any language.

The next domain of language to study was the *simplest meaningful forms*, called *morphemes*, described by *morphology* – strategically, the two names rhymed with 'phonemes' and 'phonology'. These *theoretical units* correspond to *word-parts* as *practical units*. You find 'morphemes' by writing down language samples and 'segmenting' them into the smallest pieces that still seem to mean something. For example, the utterance 'the labels seemed blurred and unreadable' would have 6 words but 11 morphemes:

(1)   the + label + s + seem + ed + blur + ed + and + un + read + able

Written this way, little 'maps' show language data as a left-to-right series of smallest meaningful units in the same order they are spoken or written. Again, the connection to reality seems clear through the visual image of the segments. But wait: a visual image is far less 'real' and permanent than the human vocal tract; and written segments can mislead. If we had 'ineffable' or 'impossible', not 'unreadable', in sample (1), where are the morphemes? English has no verbs 'to eff' or 'to poss'; a native speaker may not know that the stems were borrowed from Latin via French. Do we count them anyway?

Other problems soon arise. How do we make the whole big map of *all* the 'morphemes' in a language, like the phonologists' map of all the phonemes? Listing all word-parts plus all indivisible words is an enormous job. And *identifying* the 'morphemes' by segmenting transcribed utterances doesn't tell us just how to *classify the pieces*. In (1), we already see *different types of meanings*. Some units like '-ed' have *sparse* meanings (such as 'past tense'), while others like 'read' have *rich* meanings (such as 'inspect and understand writing'). The *sparse* ones come in *little sets*, such as the set of *present and past endings on verbs*, whereas the *rich* ones come in *big sets*, such as the set of *verbs* like 'blur' and 'read'. Not surprisingly, the sparse little sets were picked to be the main 'morphemes', while the rich big sets were called *lexemes*, the *theoretical units* corresponding to *words* as *practical units*, and handed over to the domain of *lexicology*.

We readily recognize the pattern in the science of language called 'modern linguistics'. The resounding success in describing sounds established the idea that you can indeed disconnect language from real discourse and discover an underlying order. After that, language science had some standard 'rules':

1   Study *one domain of language at a time.*
2   Describe each domain as a *system of theoretical units* corresponding to the *practical units* in the data.
3   Describe each unit by the *features* that clearly identify it from the rest (for example, being a 'voiced dental stop' or being 'past tense').
4   Investigate by carefully *transcribing* the native speaker's utterances, *segmenting* them into units, and *classifying* the units.

These 'rules' worked well in 'phonology' and got transferred into 'morphology', where they worked under more special conditions. In 'lexicology', they started to break down because the number of units is so vast and many have no features to clearly identify them. So lexicology was often left along the margins of linguistics or assigned to 'lexicographers', who explore how to make dictionaries.

The next domain had an old name waiting for it: *syntax*, a name for 'tying things together'. The units to be tied would presumably be 'morphemes' and 'lexemes'. But what does the 'tying'? We can only *inspect the pieces*; we have to *infer the ties*. And the usual tactics of segmenting data and then classifying the pieces involve *untying the pieces*, which doesn't help much.

To be consistent, the *theoretical units* would be *syntagmemes*,[3] corresponding to *phrases* and *clauses* as *practical units*. But *how many units* would the whole system have, and how should we *find and classify* them? Compare sample alternative wordings (1a)–(1d): do we give each sentence its own separate description or do we try to show how they are all related?

(1a)   the labels were blurred and unreadable
(1b)   the labels were blurred and unread
(1c)   the labels were too blurred to be readable
(1d)   the blurred labels weren't readable

Linguists decided to show the relations among similar sentences. The 'outside maps' of the units as we find them 'in' language data were traded for 'inside maps' of *underlying patterns and rules* that explain how units get tied together to produce the data we find.

This shift raised another important issue for our story: not *which data you study* but *where you go searching for your data*. The project of studying 'language by itself' doesn't say where because language isn't found by itself. The search methods that most firmly established linguistics as a science were developed by *fieldwork linguistics*. You draw *outside maps* by going out to 'work' in the 'field' of cultural and social activities and *carefully recording what native speakers of previously undescribed languages are actually observed to say*. Your work is difficult and obliges you to live for extended periods in remote areas. In exchange, you have the privilege of working at the cutting edge of your science and describing a language that was unknown to other scientists.

Also, you have the huge practical advantage of meeting *authentic data* of *natural language* in *actual contexts of situation*, instead of *language by itself*. Gradually, you join the social practices of interaction and conversation, which supply *continual tests*: if your conclusions are wrong, you'll get corrected, misunderstood, teased, or ignored. So you have constant opportunities to check your results before you present them as a 'map'. And you can justly claim to have made the map the hard way, without relying on personal intuitions the way you could do for your own native language.

The other search method has no special name, so I invented the term *homework linguistics*. You draw *inside maps* of language by staying at home or in your office and using *introspection* and *intuition* to determine what native speakers *know about their language*. Being a native speaker yourself, you might decide that *fieldwork and authentic data aren't necessary for doing linguistics*. You can do your homework with your own *invented data* and state the 'rules' you were presumably following.

At this point in our story the main definition of a 'language' also got shifted: it became not a *set of systems of theoretical units corresponding to the practical units you find in the data*, but rather a *system of underlying patterns and rules that arrange and transform the data*. Looking back at samples (1a)–(1d) this system would *explain* a complicated pattern by *transforming* it into simpler patterns, such as by changing (1a) into (1e).

(1a)   the labels were blurred and unreadable
(1e)   something blurred the labels + someone couldn't read the labels

The system did not have to explain *why* the more complicated pattern might be *actually uttered*. So linguistics could continue officially studying 'language by itself', represented by handfuls of invented sentences and still disconnected from ordinary discourse.

But here our story begins to look bleak. After three decades of research on syntax, no such system of underlying patterns and rules has yet been produced for any natural language. All we have is a pile of fragments such a system might contain, but no idea how they fit together and how we can supply the rest. The problem is simple and, I am convinced, unsolvable: the arrangement of words in phrases and sentences is *decided only partly by syntax*, and *partly by speakers' knowledge of the world and of their society*. To explain the arrangement, we must *reconnect* language with that knowledge and *shelve the project of describing language by itself*. And we must quit *working with invented data* and start *working with authentic data*. These prospects are precisely what discourse analysis intends to achieve.

Reconnecting the 'Science of Language' to Discourse: Large-Corpus Linguistics

My story so far naturally has been too simple. Many distinguished linguists never proposed to disconnect language from discourse, such as American tagmemics, the Prague School, and British systemic functional linguistics, whose projects are reviewed later in this chapter. And fieldwork linguists, as I said, maintained the connection in practice regardless of their official theories.

Nonetheless, the majority view in linguistics has usually been that discourse is too rich and diversified, too intimately tied to the ordinary world of human activities, such as casual conversations among friends or family, to be a proper object for science. In the vision of one leading discourse analyst, Joseph Grimes (1975: 2), 'linguists' might feel 'like the Dutch boy with his finger in the dike', fearfully imagining 'the whole wild sea out there . . . business letters, conversations, restaurant menus, novels, laws . . . movie scripts, editorials, without end'. So we can appreciate why 'discourse analysis' has, until recently, rarely been a title for academic courses, or for chapters in introductory textbooks, or for sections in conferences on linguistics.

Today, the scientific trend carrying the label of *discourse analysis* is increasingly conceived to be a programmatic counter-current to the self-conscious 'disconnection programme' sketched in the previous section. We emphatically define language as a *system integrated with speakers' knowledge of the world and society*. This system should be described in *linguistic, cognitive, and social terms, along with the conditions under which speakers use it*. Our precepts might seem to make the job of describing language messier and less disciplined than the old programme. In fact, I shall claim just the opposite.

For the old programme, language was a *uniform and stable system defined in its own terms*: it had *one ideal underlying order* beneath the mass of particular data. If this idea were correct, then linguistics should plainly reveal three kinds of success:

1 The *coverage* of a language should keep getting wider.
2 The various descriptions should *converge*.
3 Linguists or linguistic schools should reach a firm *consensus* about how to proceed.

But we actually see a mixed picture: very high success in phonology and fairly high in morphology, middling in lexicology, and low in syntax. In my story, the mix has to happen because these domains are not equally easy to disconnect from real discourse, especially after you've booted out fieldwork with authentic data in favour of homework with invented data. To make real headway on coverage, convergence and consensus, we must regard language as a diverse and dynamic system designed to provide the means for human communication. The system does not have or need *one underlying theoretical order* because it is *constantly creating multiple modes of practical order wherever discourse takes place*. When you try to disconnect the system from discourse, those modes of order dissolve, and you start imagining all sorts of complicated rules for 'assigning structures', 'disambiguating meanings', and so on – for solving the very problems you've created by disconnecting. But if you insist on connections between language discourse, these problems don't arise.

To see my point, let's examine one recent linguistic approach, which has by far the most real data ever assembled. *Large-corpus linguistics*, as pioneered by John McHardy Sinclair and his team, exploits the advanced technology of powerful computers with spacious memories to gain 'access to a quality of evidence that has not been available before' (Sinclair 1991: 4). Intriguingly, the Sinclair team, whose 'functional linguistics' I cited at the start of this section, were among the earliest linguists to call their research 'discourse analysis' (for example, Sinclair and Coulthard 1975; see later). Today, Sinclair compares his computer to the instruments and technologies that enabled swift advances in other sciences, such as the microscopes and particle accelerators I mentioned at the beginning of the chapter. Of course, the computer differs by displaying evidence that was easy to observe before, but too plentiful and diverse to manage. The computer enables us to see patterns that don't emerge either from modest sets of samples or from introspection and intuition – a very different 'underlying order' than sets of 'theoretical units' and 'syntactic rules'. Instead of just making general statements about 'the English language', we can use the data base to explore how general or specific our statements ought to be.

My data here were taken from the 'Bank of English' corpus at the University of Birmingham, storing around 200 million words of authentic spoken and written English discourse from books, newspapers, radio broadcasts, telephone conversations, mailings, radio broadcasts, and so on. The primary data display consists of the *key words* we pick to search for, plus their *collocations*, that is, the 'company they usually keep'.[4] For the English verb 'warrant' as key word, some of the corpus data I found are shown here:[5]

< their *circumstances* simply do not warrant **charitable assistance**. <t> For >
< bark disease. *Degenerating trees* warrant **specialist attention**. Felling or >
< Costa Rica's *economic conditions* warrant the **cut in aid**, which the country >
< insists there is enough *evidence* to warrant an **investigation** # One suggestion >
< the *national objectives* at stake warrant the **deaths of U.S. troops** # Oil, >
< these *old homes* are chilly enough to warrant guests **wearing thermal long johns** >
< *revelations of an affair* did not warrant my **leaving the Government**. <t> I >

Before looking at the data, I had no clear idea of the meaning and uses of the verb 'warrant', and I hardly use it myself. Now, I can define the meaning as: 'provide an occasion where a reaction would be appropriate or expected'. I can also tell which people are likely to utter such data: ones who might be expected to react, or somebody reporting what they said. The contexts imply public exposure, where the discourse would raise large issues like 'economic conditions' or 'national objectives'. So the typical speaker represents some institution or authority, and the data also tell what kind: government, judiciary, military, sports, business, science, and medicine. To use the word is to engage in a *subtle gesture of power* – maybe why I don't use it.

The data also showed me something else my intuition couldn't supply: the occasions doing the 'warranting' are usually *bad* ones, so that the reaction would control the ill effects or punish the persons responsible. The most common collocation was whether 'evidence warrants an investigation' or a 'trial', recalling the legal discourse with the noun 'warrant' in collocations like 'search warrant' or 'warrant for arrest'. So if we read 'there wasn't a single incident to warrant any action from me' we can assume it was a bad 'incident' calling for retaliatory 'action'. Often, the situation is even more specific: when something bad happens or gets discovered, excuses are made why the expected reaction *won't* happen, as when the 'revelations of an affair did not warrant my leaving the Government', or when somebody else's 'circumstances simply do not warrant charitable assistance' from me. Such uses are *gestures for showing power while denying responsibility*.

Authentic discourse samples also show that infrequent data may be no harder to manage than frequent data. We easily tell what is meant when 'degenerating trees warrant specialist attention' or when 'old homes are chilly enough to warrant thermal long johns'. Even odd or vague data appear simple, e.g.:

(2)   < shampoos are effective enough to warrant only one shampoo per wash. >

(3)   < the White House says these air leaks do not warrant military interception >

Example (2) was probably intended to praise a commodity, the shampoos (substances) that 'warrant only one shampoo' (one act of use). In military discourse like (3), an 'air leak' can have the unusual meaning of aeroplanes or missiles rather than air passing through.

As you see, describing authentic language data does *not* get messier and less disciplined when we retain the connections to human knowledge of world and society. On the contrary, the data only get that way when we try to disconnect them by segmenting them into theoretical units or writing 'underlying rules' or 'features'.

Large corpuses offer valuable support for the project of discourse analysis to return to authentic data. This support is all the more vital now that the label has caught on, and many studies claim to be 'discourse analysis' while still writing abstract 'rules' for invented data, rather like a textbook called 'modern astronomy' but still teaching astrology.

Large-corpus linguistics also promises unprecedented advances in *coverage* as big teams of linguists with sophisticated software collaborate in the description of corpus data. Descriptions would tend to *converge*, thanks to maintaining rich connections. And we should reach a *consensus* because we are using our shared linguistic, cognitive, and social skills, which are also shared by the people who produced the data in the first place.

Now, Joe Grimes was right about that 'whole wild sea' that a science of discourse must confront, as quoted near the start of this section. But having so much data has the advantage of forcing us to consider and explain the *human relevance* that justifies us doing one project in discourse analysis rather than some other. Even my brief demonstration with 'warrant' raised the issues of power and responsibility you soon encounter when you quit segmenting or analysing 'sentence structures' and start asking who says what and why.

Language and Discourse, Science and Power

The popular 'story of science' (invoked at the very beginning), observing things in the 'real world' and describing or explaining them accurately, handily conceals the prospect that *science has power* – power to say what the 'truths' shall be, who gets to state them and decide what they mean, and who gets to learn them and where. Even better concealed is the prospect that *science also has responsibility* – to consider and influence how its results will be used to make life better or worse, safer or riskier, more humane or inhumane. This responsibility is greatest when the object of investigation happens to be discourse, the main human channel for organizing life and deciding who knows or does what: whether knowledge and power will be shared or hoarded, whether people accept or deny responsibility for what they do or say, and so forth.

Now, if a science of discourse analysis neglects its responsibility, we are not just being cynical or lazy; we are also bypassing the most humanly relevant issues within our own domain. If participating in discourse carries social responsibility, participating in a science of discourse carries far more, as we get a steadily clearer and larger picture of how some people are much better than others at using discourse to reach their goals.

To prevent misunderstandings, we must stress the contrast between our programme and the *campaign of traditional grammar*. Since ancient times, *language guardians* have been rallying to 'preserve good language' and 'rescue it from destruction by vulgar speech'. They have invoked such lofty ideals as 'logic' and 'purity', but their real motive has been to *legitimize the language variety of powerful people as the only 'correct' or 'proper usage'*. In this way, other people could be *disempowered* by excluding them from public discourse or else forcing them to participate with feelings of anxiety or humiliation. So most of the 'incorrect' or 'improper' usages were picked out from the normal language of the social groups who were to be disempowered.

We must understand that the issues of usage over which the campaign was usually fought were *unrelated to successful communication*, and why. They were technical or finicky points worked out or just made up by the 'language guardians', typically schoolmasters or clerics who were naturally self-conscious about their speech and keen to supplement their meagre incomes by giving lessons or writing books and treatises about 'correct usage'. Having no scientific methods of gathering and sorting data, the guardians just followed their own intuitions and wishful thinking.

Over the years, long disorganized lists have been compiled and passed along, in handbooks or schoolbooks, of all the things you should or should not say. In school, pupils are regaled with bales of confusing and impractical advice purporting to 'improve' their language. Most of the pupils who prosper come from social backgrounds whose language varieties already resemble the 'proper' variety. A few others succeed in switching to the 'proper variety' through great diligence, but risk sounding a bit awkward in 'proper society' and very awkward among friends and family. The rest just leave school convinced they still don't speak or write 'good English', now regarded as a mysterious game whose rules change from teacher to teacher and never get clearly explained. Indeed, it's a game everybody is told to play if they want a good life, but the rules are made so confusing and complicated that people need special lessons at exclusive places fittingly called, until recently, 'grammar schools'.

In this game, prissy and irrelevant rules have a good market value to mystify ordinary people. If you proclaim it 'wrong' to 'put a preposition at the end of a sentence', people struggle to say fussy thing things like (4) and hesitate to say things like (5) and (6), where the alternatives are plain awful.

(4)   to whom did you give it? (not: whom did you give it to?)
(5)   what did she look like? (awful: like what did she look?)
(6)   he's worth listening to (awful: to him is worth listening)

Such 'rules' are in effect *unworkable solutions for imaginary problems*, and reveal an insensitivity for English grammar: an expression such as 'look like', 'listen to', or 'pay for' is not verb plus preposition but rather a phrasal verb that can no more be taken apart than can 'resemble' or 'hear'.

I am not suggesting some grand conspiracy among teachers of English; many have sincerely aspired to improve the English language and to help ordinary people. Instead, educational practices have evolved and survived to suit the *fundamental contradiction in the ideology of Western societies between inclusive theory and exclusive practice* (Beaugrande, 1996). In theory, all citizens have the same basic human rights to free speech, public education, scientific training, and so on; in practice, the great majority are systematically excluded. We can find this contradiction in all our democratic institutions, above all in our public schools, which in theory offer everyone equal chances to succeed by merit and in practice programme many young people for a lifetime of failure and poverty (Lemke, 1990). Applied to language, the same contradiction favours approaches that in theory teach everyone to speak 'properly' and in practice select pupils from privileged backgrounds – quite apart from what the teachers might intend.

The first organized resistance against the campaign of language guardians was mounted when 'modern linguistics' declared its resolve to *describe actual usage*: what people do say and not what language guardians think they should say. 'The non-standard speaker' was sensibly counselled to 'take pride in simplicity of speech and view it as an advantage' (Bloomfield, 1933: 499). But this resolve was stunted by the project, sketched earlier, of orienting the description toward some *ideal underlying order* of 'units' and 'rules', which was too near the old ideals of 'logic' and 'purity' invoked by grammarians. Providing accurate registers of the 'phonemes' and 'morphemes' of many languages and language varieties does not yet account for the effective discourse strategies genuinely essential to successful communication. Nor does it supply practical alternatives for language teachers who would gladly relinquish the old campaign against 'incorrect grammar'. So the prospects for concerted interaction between English teachers and linguists have not moved very far beyond the programmatic stage of hopeful talk about a 'revolution in teaching' (Postman and Weingartner, 1966).

I raise these issues because we can expect the programme of discourse analysis for supporting effective communication to be both accidentally misunderstood and deliberately misrepresented in contexts of institutional power, where language is currently a major pretext for denying human rights (Phillipson and Skuttnabb-Kangas, 1994). Language guardians will resent us for demystifying their campaign not to 'improve language' but to protect privilege and legitimize social and ethnic discrimination. Homework linguists with fancy 'theories of syntax' will call us 'unscientific' and absurdly lump us together with the language guardians. Both of our opponents' parties are high in power and low in responsibility, and bent on maintaining the status quo.

Yet another danger looms, as Teun van Dijk has foreseen. If we do discover and describe the strategies for effective communication, our results can be co-opted by the same manipulators, indoctrinators, and exploiters who have long been using discourse to seize and secure their power – politicians, demagogues, bureaucrats, profiteers, and advertisers. We cannot prevent them, but we can help ordinary people use discourse to resist their schemes and scams, provided we can make our results widely available in plain language and in readable (or listenable) sources. Either we take our own advice and communicate effectively – or we don't deserve to be believed any more than our opponents, the snobbish guardians and glib homeworkers.

The Programme of Discourse Analysis: Looking Back

So far, I have told you why discourse analysis was resisted for so long and why I think its time has come. I have also suggested why large-scale projects for helping people to participate in discourse more effectively run counter to powerful interests in society and science. Next, we can look at the resources and outlooks for a programme of discourse analysis along the lines I have been pursuing.

It's essential to consider which *disciplines* might be *contributors*. One obvious candidate we have already met: the linguists who developed methods for *fieldwork on previously undescribed languages*. Instead of 'language by itself', you analyse discourse encountered in human inter-action, a principle emphasized by American *tagmemics* (for example, Pike, 1967). Also, you benefit from being 'defamiliarized' from your own culture and meeting 'strange' ways of saying and doing things. Evelyn Pike told a story about one culture whose language she was studying, where locations are expressed by the points of the compass rather than the sides of the body. At the approach of a poisonous snake, somebody yelled 'jump to the east!'

Fieldwork also reveals differing notions about what a language needs to express. For example, Mumiye, a Niger-Congo language, has special forms to indicate when an action is 'progressive' (is continuing) or 'durative' (goes on for a longer time), such as '-yi' in (7) and (8) and 'naa' in (9) (data reported by Danjuma Gambo, in Longacre et al., 1990: 151f). The piece-by-piece translations indicate what the morphemes contribute, while the idiomatic translations suggest what an English speaker might say:

(7) kpanti nwang kn   sha-yi
     chief   sat   food eating-DURATIVE
     'the chief sat eating and eating'
(8) sombo da-yi   di ya bii ka   jaa gbaa
     squirrel go-DURATIVE go take FOCUS child hoe
     'the squirrel was going to go take a small hoe'
(9) kura   gbãa   yuu naa
     tortoise returning road PROGRESSIVE
     'the tortoise was returning on the road'

English has no special form for 'durative'; and its 'progressive' form with '-ing' need not indicate that something went on for a long time. Often, it indicates an action going on when something else happened (such as 'the tortoise was returning when he met the squirrel'). For some actions, we can use repetition ('eating and eating') but for others this would sound odd (for example, 'returning and returning' might suggest several different returns rather than one long one). Yet we can rely on our world-knowledge, for example that tortoise take a long time to travel – just as the world-knowledge of Mumiye speakers grasps a small hoe as a 'child hoe' although nobody saw hoes bear children.

Studying discourse data from unfamiliar languages makes you more sensitive to data from familiar ones. People's sensitivities to a language like English have long been dulled and distorted by unreliable schoolroom 'grammars' (see previous section). Moreover, English has been dominated by *written culture*, encouraging the belief that the order of language only emerges when written down in neat sentences – a belief shared by many homework linguists. So we have not properly appreciated the different and highly elaborate order of everyday spoken language, as uncovered by 'conversational analysis' (see below).

In contrast, the more remote languages of Africa, Asia, Oceania, and South America have been centred on *oral cultures*. They have been spared campaigns against 'incorrect' usage, and the bookish equation of orderly language with written language; some never devised writing systems at all. High values were placed on speaking skills in communal activities such as story-telling, which vitally supported cultural traditions against the ravages and dislocations of slavery and colonialism. Whole systems of spoken *discourse signals* were developed to organize the story-line with its individual events and their participants, as discovered by Longacre and his group (1990) in some 40 languages of East and West Africa. In Gimira, an Omotic language of Ethiopia (data reported by Mary Breeze, in Longacre et al., 1990: 27f), a 'switch reference marker' (shown as S/R) is used at the high point of a story when the main characters alternate major actions. We see the marker in the nasal sound '-n/m' affixed to verb-forms in the story (10) about a man named Gartn who was up a tree collecting honey when he was spotted by a hungry leopard (FUT = future; LOC = location; SUB = subject; STAT = static verb-forms indicating the setting):[6]

(10) panc'i   yi tok'an   yisti iňc gapmk'an   wognsi
      leopard-SUB his foot-LOC being tree branch-LOC having-sat
      hammsagyis   maki bak'u. Taci peški hamišidni iču   Gartn
      go-FUT-STAT-he saying waited thinking   not-to-go refused Gartn
      nasi   esa   myac'a kabnsi   yi apm   hazn m'msi
      man-SUB honey bees   having-wrapped his face-LOC throwing-S/R
      myac'am   dusti   woc'i   koškan wot'i šičamm
      having-eaten by-bees being-stung running valley descending
      yiam   gurt'i   yisti dodn   wornti   hank'u.
      leaving-S/R by-it trembling being ground-LOC descending went

> 'The leopard being at the foot of the tree, he had been sitting on the tree branch and waiting, saying and thinking it would go. It refused to go. Gartn wrapped the honey and the bees and threw them in its face. The bees stung it and it ran away down into the valley. After it had gone, trembling he descended to the ground and left.'

Both the piece-by-piece translation and the more idiomatic one show rapid switches of the agent (the one who does the action) between 'leopard' and 'Gartn', who are named only once each. We can use world-knowledge to infer from context who is meant, though I have cleared up the English translation by switching between the pronouns 'he' and 'it'. The switch reference marker only appears for the two decisive actions of Gartn's 'throwing' ('haz-n') and the leopard's finally 'leaving and descending' ('šičam-m') from the valley, and not for less decisive actions like 'sitting' and 'thinking'. We see here how forms and patterns relate to the *total discourse* and are not merely 'morphemes' or 'sentence structures' to segment and classify.

We can still find a few discourse signals in traditional English stories. In an 1878 rendering of the familiar folktale 'Tom Tit Tot'[7] (a demonic cousin of Rumpelstiltskin), 'well' systematically appears at important turning points in the story, often with a shift of time:

(11)   Well, once there were a woman and she baked five pies [through a misunderstanding, the king proposes marriage to her daughter if she will spin for him] Well, so they was married [king orders her to spin or die] Well, she were that frightened [she bargains with a demon to do the spinning; she must guess his name or be 'his'] Well, the next day her husband took her into the room and there were the flax [demon appears and spins] Well, when her husband he come in: there was the five skeins [a cycle of spinning and name-guessing begins] Well, every day the flax and the vittles was brought [king unwittingly reveals name] Well, when the gal heerd this, she fared as if she could have jumped outer her skin for joy [she tells the demon his name] Well, when that heerd her, that shrieked awful and away that flew into the dark

We hardly notice such uses of 'well' because the word has many other functions, for example as a conversational signal indicating you are about to give a spontaneous opinion.[8] Also, these functions do not figure in traditional grammar books; and 'well' is not deemed 'proper' for written English.

Data like those from Mumiye and Gimira indicate why fieldwork naturally leads into discourse analysis. But only around the mid 1970s did such work adopt the *term* 'discourse analysis' (led by Grimes, 1975; 1978; Longacre, 1976). By then, linguistics was turning away from the project to disconnect language from discourse and favouring alternative projects.

The most important alternative was *functional linguistics*, which has had several branches. A Czechoslovakian branch, sometimes called the *Prague School* and founded by Vilém Mathesius and his pupils, exploited their knowledge of Slavic languages like Czech and Slovak, where the order of words in a sentence is more flexible than in English and depends crucially on degrees of 'knownness' and 'focus'. In comparison to the more ordinary version (12), the English order (12a) emphatically focuses on the 'problems' by fronting the expression ahead of the sentence subject. In contrast, the Czech version in (12b) (REFL PRON = reflexive pronoun) is not emphatic, showing that 'what is regarded as unusual in one language need not appear so in another' (Firbas, 1992: 125f).

(12)   a computer could take in its stride most of these problems
(12a)   most of these problems a computer could take in its stride
(12b)   většinou   problémů by   si   počítač
        with most problems it-would REFL PRON computer
        hravě   poradil
        with-great-ease it-cope

The *functional sentence perspective*, as this approach has been called (bibliography in Firbas and Golková, 1976), revealed previously unnoticed ways for text and context to influence the arrangement of English sentences. In Katherine Mansfield's short story 'At the Bay' (analysed by Firbas, 1992: 26ff, 74ff), the setting is made the opening *theme* for Linda Burnell's appearance on the scene. As in many discourse beginnings, the *communicative dynamism* – how 'informative' the content is – starts out high for the opening sentence (13.1) presenting first the 'setting' and then the main person in the story as the subject of the sentence and her 'dreaming' action as the main verb. Putting the setting in a long phrase ahead of the subject suggests that the story will highlight the setting.

(13.1)   In a steamer chair under a manuka tree that grew in the middle of the front grass patch, Linda Burnell dreamed the morning away. (13.2) She did nothing. (13.3) She looked up at the dark, close, dry leaves . . .

Though we cannot anticipate a 'steamer chair' or an exotic 'manuka tree', it is normal for a chair to be placed 'under a tree' and for a tree to 'grow' in a 'grass patch'; in such a pastoral setting, 'dreaming' is a typical action too. In contrast, the dynamism of (13.2) is uniformly low: the pronoun subject 'she' is already identified, and the activity of 'doing nothing' is expected from a 'dreaming' person. The dynamism of (13.3) is a bit higher, with the same pronoun subject 'she'; and someone in a reclining chair under a tree easily looks up and sees 'leaves', though we might not anticipate them being 'dark' or 'close'.

Starting the story-line for the whole discourse in this way indicates that the main character is Linda Burnell and that we'll learn what she 'dreams' about. Also, prominently placing the setting at the start suggests that the dream will be associated with the tree; a lengthy reverie about 'flowers' indeed ensues, and about Linda 'feeling like a leaf'. As a British writer, Mansfield probably hoped the 'manuka' species of tree would make the story more informative than a typical British tree. In the Gimira story (10), in contrast, the 'tree' setting remains unspecified, the 'thematic' focus of attention being the plight of a man who, if 'dreaming' about anything, is dreaming about being safe at home away from leopards.

The British branch of functionalism, led by linguists like J.R. Firth, Michael Halliday, and John Sinclair, also rejected the disconnection of 'language by itself' and studied what speakers actually say. Sinclair's group pioneered 'discourse analysis' through fieldwork on *classroom discourse*. Instead of 'linguistic units' and 'rules', the main terms highlighted *discourse moves* like *initiation, nomination*, and *follow-up* by the teacher, and *bid* and *response* by a learner, as in (14):[9]

(14)   Initiation   T   Give me a sentence using an animal's name as food, please.
         Response   L1   We shall have a beef for supper tonight.

Follow-up	T	Good. That's almost right, but 'beef' is uncountable so it's 'we shall have beef', not 'we shall have a beef'.
Initiation		Try again, someone else.
Bid	L2	Sir.
Nomination	T	Yes Freddie.
Response	L2	We shall have a plate of sheep for supper tonight.
Follow-up	T	No, we don't eat 'sheep', we eat 'mutton', or 'lamb'.
Initiation		Say it correctly.
Response	L2	We shall have a plate of mutton for supper tonight.
Follow-up	T	Good. We shall have mutton for supper. Don't use 'a plate' when there's more than one of you.

Such discourse plainly occurs only in classrooms, pursuing the old campaign for 'correct' usage (see earlier). The pupils are not to tell what they like to eat and why, or how to cook it. The task is far more artificial: saying 'an animal's name as food', which easily traps pupils with the tricky English usage of French loan-words for the foods (e.g. 'mutton', 'beef', 'veal') instead of the animals' usual names. Communication is subordinated to fine points of usage that the teacher illustrates without giving useful explanations.

Several British functionalists were guided by knowing oriental languages like Chinese, rather than Slavic ones; and they too brought new insights into English. They developed a view of language being a *network of options* that are assigned their functions when language is used in discourse. Instead of 'correctness', the key criterion is *markedness*, for example to emphasize 'these problems' in (12a). This 'network' view carries the British brand name of *systemic functional linguistics* and assumes that the organization of a language is expressly designed to support its use.

One classic demonstration, also a model for *stylistics*, was given by Halliday (1973) for William Golding's *The Inheritors*. To evoke a 'Neanderthal tribe's point of view', Golding uses clause patterns whose 'subjects are not people' but 'parts of the body or inanimate objects'; the effect is 'an atmosphere of ineffectual activity' and 'helplessness', and a 'reluctance to envisage the "whole man" . . . participating in a process' (1973: 123, 125). When the Neanderthal Lok watches a person from a more advanced tribe shooting an arrow at him, the event is expressed as a series of natural processes performed by a 'stick' and a 'twig':

(15)   The bushes twitched again . . . The man turned sideways in the bushes and looked at Lok along his shoulder. A stick rose upright and there was a lump of bone in the middle . . . The stick began to grow shorter at both ends. Then it shot out to full length again. The dead tree by Lok's ear acquired a voice. 'Clop!' His ear twitched and he turned to the tree. By his face there had grown a twig. (Golding, 1955: 106f)

These choices deliberately omit the connection between 'stick' and 'twig' in a single weapon of bow and arrow, plus the causes and effects involved, such as bending and releasing the bow, seen head-on as a stick 'growing shorter at both ends' and then 'shooting out to full length' and propelling the 'lump of bone' and its shaft to 'the tree by his face'. Lok's notion of a 'dead tree' suddenly 'growing a twig' symbolizes the Neanderthals' archaic and mystified world-view, dooming them to a destruction they can neither understand nor resist, at the hands of a more evolved people.

Another contributor to discourse analysis would be the discipline of *sociolinguistics*, which reconnects language with society by studying the language varieties corresponding to differences in social, regional, and economic status. These varieties differ not just in sound patterns, but also in discourse patterns, depending especially on whether the participants come from a more 'written' or more 'oral' culture. When shown a series of pictures and asked to tell the story, middle-class children from written cultures specified nouns for things like 'boys' and 'window' in (16), whereas the working-class children from oral cultures, assuming anybody can see what's meant, used pronouns like 'they' and 'he' and pointing expressions like 'there', as in (16a):[10]

(16)   three boys are playing football and one boy kicks the ball and it goes through the window

(16a)   they're playing football and he kicks it and it goes through there

In Basil Bernstein's (1964) unwisely named *deficit hypothesis*, working-class people with a more 'restricted code' are also more limited in their mental capacities than middle-class people with a more 'elaborated code'. This hypothesis triggered a storm of controversy because both common sense and science wrongly assume that 'intelligence' is a fixed and innate capacity, which would lead to the offensive hypothesis that the working class is genetically inferior; Bernstein was claiming instead that social conditions create disparities in mental capacities, including ones for using language. The idea that intelligence is a social construct is repugnant to many Western scientists and educators, because it demystifies our fundamental contradiction between inclusive theory and exclusive practice (see previous section), and the alibi of education that failure is caused by the biological and psychological limitations of individuals. Moreover, Bernstein's work suggested that the 'remedial programmes' tacked onto ordinary schooling to bring pupils' language varieties into line with the 'standard' would be ineffective – as we now know. Improvement demands transforming the social conditions under which intelligence and discourse competence are constructed, away from producing and legitimizing inequalities and toward supporting equality in practice as well as in theory (see next section).

The most detailed picture of real talk in society has been supplied by the *analysis of conversation* in *ethnomethodology*. Its home discipline was *sociology*, which developed its own methods to study language rather than borrowing them from linguistics. Harold Garfinkel (1974) reported coining the term *ethnomethodology* after such terms as 'ethnoscience' or 'ethnomedicine' for people's common-sense knowledge of what 'science' or 'medicine' do. His method proposed studying real conversational data and uncovering the participants' common-sense 'methodology' for ordinary social interactions.

This method focused far more on *real speakers* than linguistics, and upon *oral culture*, this time in familiar languages like English. Conversation is usually managed by its participants quite tightly and fluently, with few conspicuous breaks or disturbances. The significance of utterances is clearly a function of the ongoing interaction as a whole rather than just the meanings or words or phrases. Witness this bit of taped conversation collected by Emmanuel Schegloff (1987: 208f) (small capitals show emphasis; brackets show overlap; colons indicate lengthened sounds):

(17.1) B: WELL, honey? I'll probl'y SEE yuh one a' these days
(17.2) A: OH::: God YEAH
(17.3) B: ⌈ Uhh huh!
(17.4) A: ⌊ We–
(17.5) A: But I c– I jis' ⌈ couldn' git down ⌈ there
(17.6) B: ⌊ Oh–   ⌊ Oh I know I'M not askin
            ⌈ yuh tuh ⌈ come down
(17.7) A: ⌊ Jesus   ⌊ I mean I just didn't have five minutes yesterday

Two middle-aged sisters who haven't visited each other for some time are conversing on the telephone. Sister B probably intends to signal a closing with the usual reference to a future seeing (17.1), as in English 'see ya', French 'au revoir', German 'auf Wiedersehen', etc. But sister A understands a complaint about not having visited, and makes excuses for why she 'jis' couldn' git down there' (17.5). Sister B displays that she appreciates A's problems and signals that she was not pressing her claims to a visit (17.6), overlapping with A's excuse of 'not having five minutes yesterday' (17.7).

Ethnomethodologists like Schegloff emphasize that the conversational analysis can document its own interpretations with those made by the actual participants, in this case, A's misunderstanding and B's venture to amend it. The theory thus stays far closer to the practice than in 'homework linguistics'. Though 'often unnoticed or underappreciated in casual observation or even effortful recollection of how talk goes', the 'detailed practices and features of the conduct of talk – hesitations, anticipations, apparent disfluencies, or inconsequential choices . . . are strikingly accessible to empirical inquiry' (Schegloff, 1992). This lesson should be noted by linguists and philosophers.

The empirical lesson came more easily to the discipline called *text linguistics* (early survey in Dressler, 1972). Predictably, some early 'text linguists' tried constructing a disconnected theoretical unit of 'language by itself' called (what else?) the *texteme* and represented by complicated and impenetrable formulas. But a text disconnected from context resembles a miscellaneous array like a pattern on wallpaper.

Most text linguists gradually reconnected texts to discourse participants' knowledge of world and society. We developed the concept of *textuality*: not just a set of 'theoretical units' or 'rules', but a *human achievement in making connections wherever communicative events occur* (cf. Beaugrande and Dressler, 1981). The connections among linguistic forms like words or word-endings make up *cohesion*, and those among the 'meanings' or 'concepts' make up *coherence*; *intentionality* covers what speakers intend, and *acceptability* what hearers engage to do; *informativity* concerns how new or unexpected the content is; *situationality* concerns ongoing circumstances of the interaction; and *intertextuality* covers relations with other texts, particularly ones from the same or a similar 'text type'.

We can demonstrate these seven principles with a short 'classified' advert from *Psychology Today* (August 1983, p. 82) under the heading 'Parapsychology':

(18)   HARNESS WITCHCRAFT'S POWERS! Gavin and Yvonne Frost, world's foremost witches, now accepting students. Box 1502P, Newbern, NC 28560.

Here, general intertextuality specified the text type 'classified advert'. Intention and acceptance are typical: the writers publicize an offer for the readers to take up. The 'text type' shapes the modest cohesion, showing just one ordinary sentence, a command with the imperative ('harness!'), and one incomplete phrase resembling a sentence (like 'are now accepting students'). No command is given to 'contact us', 'write us', or 'dispatch us your raven or your flying broom with a parchment of inquiry' – just the address. These choices are strategic, especially the opening commands implying that the action can be successfully performed – precisely what readers need to be convinced of here.

Coherence centres on the topic of 'witchcraft', which common sense holds to be the activities of 'witches' and to grant extraordinary 'powers'. This central topic is combined somewhat picturesquely with the 'student' topic of enrolling in courses and (not mentioned here!) paying fees. The concept 'foremost' helps connect the two topics, since stories of 'witches' often tell of superlatives, and students should be attracted to the 'foremost' authorities in a field. In return, a submerged contradiction impends between claiming to be able to 'harness' such 'foremost powers' versus being obliged to seek fee-paying 'students' instead of just using the 'powers' to conjure up spirits who reveal buried treasure.

The informativity (or 'communicative dynamism' in the 'functional sentence perspective') starts out high, not merely by claiming that witchcraft has real 'powers' in today's world but also by inviting ordinary readers to 'harness' them. Also quite high is the extravagant, untestable claim to being the 'world's foremost', although such inflated claims are so commonly made in US advertising that American readers may not be surprised. Perhaps the offer to 'accept students' has some surprise value too (shouldn't witches have 'apprentices'?), though less so in a classified column offering paid services.

The situationality seems the most significant principle of textuality here. The Frosts[11] evidently expect some readers to believe the advert and to become 'students'. This prospect must be viewed in the social context of rising superstition, especially in areas like the American Southeast (in this case North Carolina), as a desperate response to a 'modernism' too complicated and interconnected for many people to comprehend or control (Beaugrande, 1996). The feeling of powerlessness creates a vacuum some people try to fill by 'harnessing powers' of any imaginable kind.

This social point can be supported by specific intertextuality by noticing how other ads in the same magazine offer to solve your problems:

(19)   Master the power of suggestion for $49.95.
(20)   HOW TO REPROGRAM YOUR SUBCONSCIOUS FAST! New Secret Technique (Microshifting).
(21)   DISCOVER HOW MIND POWER BREAKTHROUGH WORKS! Latest Subliminal and Hypnosis/Sleep-Learning tapes.
(22)   NEW SUBLIMINAL TIME COMPRESSION 'audio' technique crystallizes perception, resolves problems, energizes creativity. Free scientific report.
(23)   ERASE DEBTS with little-known law – CREATE wealth!

Despite some diversity, the shared discourses' strategies are obvious. To explain why these marvellous plans or devices are not famous already, they are called 'new', 'secret', 'little-known', etc. Calling them also 'fast' and easy panders to the readers' presumed inability and impatience to solve their own problems. How much you must pay is rarely mentioned, as in (19) (for Americans, $49.95 is much less than $50), versus 'free' information, as in (22). Powerless people are probably short on cash, and might think you'll be safe from bill-collectors once you have magic powers for turning them into hoptoads. These quasi-'scientific' 'parapsychological' aids may contrast starkly with 'witchcraft', but nothing prevents a desperate person from combining 'subliminal' and 'hypnotic' tactics with magical incantations in order to leave nothing untried. In the words of a well-known social psychologist, 'the United States sometimes seems to be a huge carnival of disorder and self-help, with shamans and prophets seeking new converts and rallying followers, all promising comfort, solace, and a better life' (Erchak, 1992: 117).

Reconnecting language to knowledge of the world has also been the main issue in the discipline of *artificial intelligence*. Computer programs that can interact more 'intelligently' with humans must understand discourse in 'natural language', not just the artificial programming languages invented for computers. This work shows how much rich world-knowledge is involved just in participating in simple conversations or accepting a brief story and answering questions about it, such as for a prosaic news item like (24):[12]

(24)   A New Jersey man was killed Friday evening when a car swerved off Route 69 and struck a tree. David Hall, 27, was pronounced dead at Milford Hospital. The driver, Frank Miller, was treated and released. No charges were filed, according to investigating officer Robert Onofrio.

The program can apply a *schema* or *script* for 'vehicle accidents', specifying relevant data about what caused the accident, who was killed or injured, and whether charges were filed. This prior knowledge supports the swift comprehension of the news item along with appropriate inferences, for example that the 'driver' lost control rather than deliberately heading for the tree with the intent to knock it down and cart it home for firewood.

But how much world-knowledge and how many inferences are likely to be humanly relevant? In principle, North American readers should know that the 'tree' was a large northern outdoor tree rather than a dwarf bonsai on a window sill or a Christmas tree in a shopping mall; that Hall was taken to 'hospital' by an ambulance and not by Miller's car or by canoe, rickshaw, or skateboard; that Miller was 'treated' by dressing his injuries and not by giving him a fancy dinner; that he was 'released' by being allowed to leave the hospital rather than being unlocked from the chains into which the irate police had clapped him; that Onofrio is an 'officer' in the highway patrol and not on a ship or in a bank; and so on. Yet it seems unreasonable to demand that all this be *stored* in human memory. Such things would more likely be *constructed* only if the context required it.

This conclusion has in fact been reached in the discipline of *discourse processing*. This field crystallized in the late 1970s and early 1980s to support research in 'the many disciplines that deal with discourse – sociolinguistics, psycholinguistics, linguistics proper, sociology of language, ethnoscience, educational psychology (e.g. classroom interaction), clinical psychology (e.g. the clinical interview), computational linguistics, and so forth' (Freedle, 1977: xvi). As Freedle's wide vision suggests, the field is a *transdiscipline* strategically situated to address issues or problems from multiple angles.

The central issue had not received adequate attention elsewhere: how do people actually process a discourse during real communication? For centuries, various disciplines have discussed 'using language' and 'interpreting texts' without really explaining how language can operate so quickly and easily. Philosophers and grammarians had assumed some ideal logical system, perhaps instilled by God or innately transmitted among humans; linguists had assumed some underlying orderly system of units and rules. But nobody felt responsible for drawing detailed inside maps of the system at work.

Discourse processing finally took the issue seriously, and what they found was a big surprise. Instead of holding a complete system ready with great batches of rules, *processing designs its own series of systems on line.* The key evidence came from robust experimental findings on *priming* in human text reception during reading (Kintsch, 1988). An item such as a word is *primed* when it's active in memory, as if standing at attention and waiting to be called. Primed items are consistently recognized and responded to more rapidly than others, for example by pressing a key to signal that a word either is or is not an English word (a 'lexical decision task'). Surprisingly, the experiments indicated that when a word is recognized, *all* its meanings are initially 'activated', not just the relevant one for the context. Yet very soon the irrelevant ones are 'deactivated', while the relevant ones raise their activation and spread it out. Suppose you are a speaker of American English reading a text on a moving computer display containing this passage:

(25)   The townspeople were amazed to find that all the buildings had collapsed except the mint.

The text suddenly halts at 'mint', and the display gives you a target item to decide if it's a real word. For a brief interval of roughly half a second, your response would show priming for both the relevant 'money' and the irrelevant 'candy', but not for the inferable 'earthquake' (what made the 'buildings collapse'). Thereafter, the irrelevant item would lose its activation while the relevant and the inferable items would gain. Evidently, the context 'self-organizes' during this tiny interval without running complicated rules.

Several important conclusions follow that may profoundly change our views of language and discourse. One of them I have anticipated: language works so well by connecting with world-knowledge, for example about buildings collapsing. Another one seems more disturbing: what people use in communicating is not *the* language but *one small version* of it that *self-organizes expressly to support the discourse.* Drawing maps of how that is done goes far beyond our accepted theories, which would make it resemble a tremendous miracle. But in real life, it's not miraculous, it's ordinary, in fact easy. How can that be?

Reconnecting language to knowledge of society has been a main issue in the disciplines of *social psychology* (for example, Billig, 1986; Potter and Wetherell, 1987), *social cognition* (Fiske and Taylor, 1984), and *rhetorical psychology* (Billig, 1991).[13] An *ideology* is popularly held to consist of fixed ideas, for example that communism is the root of all evil, including violence at rugby matches (you didn't know? stay tuned!). In discourse, however, an ideology can easily produce inconsistencies, typically linked to the basic contradiction between favouring human rights (inclusive theory) and restricting who should have them (exclusive practice). We can thus observe the same concept being used in discourse for opposite images of different social groups, such as the concept of 'violence' among New Zealanders talking about rioting at a rugby match against the South African Springboks in April 1981. For the police, interviewees explained the violence as an understandable 'human' response to 'provocation' (26),

(27). But for the protestors, the violence was either a pleasurable goal for 'trouble-makers' who had no 'moral' positions on the 'issue' of apartheid (28) or else the action of 'well-meaning' people 'stirred up' by 'extremists' (29) and 'communists' (30):[14]

(26)   policemen are only ordinary people/they must have had a lot of provocation and I don't blame them if at the last they were a bit rough

(27)   I think the police acted very well/they're only human if they lashed out and cracked a skull occasionally, it was/hah/only a very human action

(28)   I feel very strongly that it gave trouble-makers who weren't interested in the basic moral of it an opportunity to get in and cause trouble to beat up people/to smash property

(29)   it was mainly extreme groups which took over/um and stirred people up

(30)   what really angered me that a certain small group of New Zealanders . . . who are communists I believe/led a lot of well-meaning New Zealanders who abhor apartheid and organized them you know/to jump up and down and infringe the rights of other New Zealanders

These discursive constructs make it possible to ignore or excuse the 'infringement of rights' both by 'skull-cracking' police and by the South African government. The violence on one side was a 'human' reaction to wilful and malicious 'trouble-makers' who did not favour human rights but 'infringed' them. The adaptive value of such accounts is obvious in a country that has long infringed the rights of the Maoris, a black minority who are not even immigrants but the original inhabitants of New Zealand.

Ideology can also harness language for inverting things into their opposites. In modern times, the scariest example is how preparations for war get transformed into means to 'keep the peace' because, as with the bugbear of 'communism', huge sums of money can be made in the defence industry that makes such 'generous contributions' to political parties. How this transformation affects language and discourse was described by George Orwell in 1946 with an uncanny prescience of the future (say, Americans in Vietnam in the 1970s or South Africa's mercenaries in Anglo and Mozambique in the 1980s):

> In our time, political speech and writing are largely the defence of the indefensible. Things like the continuance of British rule in India, the Russian purges and deportations, the dropping of atom bombs on Japan can indeed be defended but only by arguments that are too brutal for most people to face . . . political language has to consist largely of euphemism, question-begging, and sheer cloudy vagueness. Defenceless villages are bombarded from the air, the inhabitants driven out into the countryside, the cattle machine-gunned, the huts set on fire with incendiary bullets: this is called *pacification*.

Yet such glaring abuses should not distract us from the subtler 'politicizing' of public discourse at large and increasingly also the discourse of the home, the school, and the workplace, where delicate hierarchies of power are played off to block or undermine solidarity (cf. Apple, 1985; Wilden, 1987). As the material crisis worsens the competition for diminishing world resources, *cultural differences* are made into grounds for *confrontation*. The *de facto multiculturalism* of most 'modern' societies is fiercely attacked by a militant right-wing *monoculturalism* that mystifies claims to cultural supremacy for middle- and upper-class native white males behind an allegiance to the values of 'law and order', 'patriotism', 'family', and 'Christian morals' (cf. Fish, 1994). Few people would object to such values or, if they do, right-wing discourse has a gallery of buzzwords ready to hurl at them: 'soft on crime', 'unpatriotic', 'Satanic', and (of course) 'communist'.

Predictably, the chief targets of right-wing monocultural discourse are ethnic minorities and immigrants (cf. van Dijk, 1987; 1991; Essed, 1991), where old feelings of racism and colonialism can handily be reawakened (if they ever were asleep). A leading discourse strategy is to *transform the victims into victimizers*[15] by hatching 'conspiracy theories' and making the minorities and their defenders into scapegoats for the economic and political problems actually caused by the greed, waste, and corruption of the ruling white males. Consider:[16]

(31)   Our traditions of fairness and tolerance are being exploited by every terrorist, crook, screwball, and scrounger who wants a free ride at our expense. (*Daily Mail*, 28 November 1990)

(32)   Nobody is less able to face the truth than the hysterical 'anti-racist brigade'. Their intolerance is such that they try to silence or sack anyone who doesn't toe their party line. (*The Sun*, 23 October 1990)

(33)   Liberal academics [have] abandoned scholarly objectivity to create academic disciplines that were in actuality political movements . . . ethnic studies, women's studies etc. have one intent only, that is: undermining the American education system through the transformation of scholarship and teaching into blatant politics. (*Florida Review*, 12 October 1990)

Such discourse betrays a characteristic *motivation gap*: making victims into victimizers requires accusing them of seizing the initiative to do things for which they could have no reasonable motivation, such as 'academics' striving to 'undermine the education system' that gives them a livelihood. The discourse either doesn't mention the real initiative coming from the right wing or else portrays it only as 'fighting back'. Historical parallels to the anti-Semitic discourse of the Hitler era are all too patent.

Discourse analysis must not just describe and demystify the discourse of cultural confrontation and victimization. If we make angry counter-attacks on racists, we get drawn into their own mode of confrontational discourse. Developing alternative strategies for cultural integration and co-operation is much harder, and certainly will not be achieved without concerted projects and explicit models, to which I now turn.

The Programme of Discourse Analysis: Looking Ahead

Our highest and hardest goal will be to achieve the *wholeness of a trans-disciplinary perspective* where we can *make connections* among the vast panorama of issues crowding onto our agenda, and can draw both 'inside maps' and 'outside maps' in co-ordination with each other. Such an expansive programme poses daunting tasks indeed, but is urgently justified by the geopolitical situation today. The close of the twentieth century is pervaded by a sense of impending *crisis*, even among the dwindling portions of the world's population whose fortunes are still secured. Some of the causes are widely known, especially the *material crisis* of resources brought on by the wasteful exploitation of the environment for immediate profit and by the voracious consumption of surplus commodities by small elites. Far less attention has been devoted to the twin *knowledge crisis* and *communication crisis*. The 'modern' world as a whole possesses an exploding body of specialized knowledge that is locked up in discourse accessible to only a few people concentrated in centres of wealth and power, and not to many persons who need it for controlling their own lives and careers. They desperately struggle on to cope with life in a 'modernized' world where everything seems connected but almost nobody understands how. So people *fail to make connections*, especially their responsibilities to family, neighbourhood, society, and future generations, and subsist on selfishness, confrontation, and exploitation. Alienation and anxiety abound, punctuated by senseless violence.

The failure to connect is clearly reflected in *regressive strategies* that are *short term* in rushing toward immediate goals, *confrontational* in asserting your goals by denying other people's, and *destructive* of resources. *Progressive strategies* are *long term* in weighing your goals against future conditions, *co-operative* in integrating your goals with other people's, and *constructive* of new resources. Clearly, progressive strategies *can be* supported through discourse but are *unlikely to be* unless we can provide explicit models showing how.

So discourse analysis increasingly raises the prospect of not merely *describing discursive practices* but *transforming them into more progressive practices*. Our framework would be the *ideology of ecologism*, wherein theory and practice are reconciled through human co-operation in consciously sustaining a life-style in harmony with our social and ecological environment, and in programmatic opposition to the dominant *ideology of consumerism*. It is unfortunately no exaggeration to say that the survival of the planet over the next century or so hinges on developing more progressive strategies of discourse for sharing and accessing crucial knowledge and for communicating about our problems and conflicts.

For such a challenge, we can pursue *concurrent transdisciplinary programmes*. Our *cultural programme* would assess how discourse can help consolidate cultural groups and encourage mutual respect, and can demonstrate how *multiculturalism* is the highest opportunity for realizing the whole spectrum of human potential. Our *social programme* would address the relations between discourse and the processes of *socialization* in such arenas as the home, the school, and the workplace. Our *cognitive programme* would address the access and use of knowledge through discourse in an age of rising specialization. Finally, our *linguistic programme* would address the strategies for using language resources in progressive modes.

Could our .own 'story' ever come to some *happy end*? If we take the question literally, no. Our vast programme can have 'no end', much as utopia is always in front of us (Freire, 1980): ours is a 'never-ending story'. But we can be more than 'happy' if we manage to provide a relevant and useful description of the processes and practices of discourse in the service of ecologically sound coexistence.

Notes

1 Sources include Koch (1972), Dressler and Schmidt (1973), Beaugrande (1980; 1985; 1984; 1996), Cicourel (1980), Beaugrande and Dressler (1981), Kalverkämper (1981), Brown and Yule (1983), Benson and Greaves (1985), Coulthard (1985), van Dijk (1985), Macdonnell (1986), Heinemann and Viehweger (1991), Coulthard (1992), Mann and Thompson (1992).

2 For a detailed discourse analysis of linguistic works, see Beaugrande (1991).

3 From Pike (1967), but less popular than other '-emes'.

4 Firth (1968: 106ff, 113, 182).

5 See Beaugrande (1995) for a fuller analysis with more samples.

6 I have made the idiomatic translation a bit more readable.

7 On this story, see Beaugrande (1980).

8 See Schriffrin (1987) on 'discourse markers' in English.

9 Sinclair and Brazil (1982: 45) offer this as 'an example of the kind of follow-up that is familiar to teachers' without saying if it is from a native or a foreign language classroom.

10 From Hawkins (1969): not actual data but clusters of tendencies that he found.

11 Could this be a pseudonym associated with the poems 'Two Witches' by Robert Frost?

12 Data adapted from Cullingford (1978: 4ff, 130–72). A problem with AI research is the invented quality of English texts made easier for the computer. I have rewritten Cullingford's text into a version more typical for radio or newspaper.

13 On problems in these intermediary fields with balancing the social against the cognitive or psychological when representing beliefs or attitudes, see van Dijk (1987: especially Chapter 5).

14 Data from Potter and Wetherell (1987: 122ff).

15 My translation of Ruth Wodak's term *Opfer-Täter-Umkehr*.

16 I am indebted to Teun van Dijk for (31) and (32); compare van Dijk (1991) and Essed (1991).

References

Apple, M. (1985) *Education and Power*. Boston: ARK.

Beaugrande, R. de (1980) *Text, Discourse, and Process*. Norwood, NJ: Ablex.

Beaugrande, R. de (1984) *Text Production*. Norwood, NJ: Ablex.

Beaugrande, R. de (1985) 'Text linguistics in discourse studies', in T. van Dijk (ed.), *Handbook of Discourse Analysis*. London: Academic. pp. 41–70.

Beaugrande, R. de (1991) *Linguistic Theory: the Discourse of Fundamental Works*. London: Longman.

Beaugrande, R. de (1995) 'The "pragmatics" of doing language science: the "warrant" for large-corpus linguistics', *Journal of Pragmatics*, 25.

Beaugrande, R. de (1996) *New Foundations for a Science of Text and Discourse*. Norwood, NJ: Ablex.

Beaugrande, R. de and Dressler, W. (1981) *Introduction to Text Linguistics*. London: Longman.

Benson, J.D. and Greaves, W.S. (eds) (1985) *Systemic Perspectives on Discourse*. Norwood, NJ: Ablex.

Bernstein, B. (1964) 'Elaborated and restricted codes', *American Anthropologist*, 66 (2): 55–69.

Billig, M. (1986) *Social Psychology and Intergroup Relations*. London: Academic.

Billig, M. (1991) *Ideology and Opinions: Studies in Rhetorical Psychology*. London: Sage.

Bloomfield, L. (1993) *Language*. Chicago: Holt.

Brown, G. and Yule, G. (1983) *Discourse Analysis*. Cambridge: Cambridge University Press.

Cicourel, A. (1980) 'Three models of discourse analysis: the role of social structure', *Discourse Processes*, 3: 101–32.

Coulthard, M. (1985) *An Introduction to Discourse Analysis*. London: Longman.

Cullingford, R. (1978) 'Script application'. Dissertation, Yale University.

Dressler, W. (1972) *Einführung in die Textlinguistik*. Tübingen: Niemeyer.

Dressler, W. and Schmidt, S.J. (eds) (1973) *Textlinguistik: Kommentierte Bibliographie*. Munich: Fink.

Erchak, G. (1992) *The Anthropology of Self and Behaviour*. New Brunswick, NJ: Rutgers University Press.

Essed, P. (1991) *Understanding Everyday Racism*. London: Sage.

Firbas, J. (1992) *Functional Sentence Perspective in Written and Spoken Communication*. Cambridge: Cambridge University Press.

Firbas, J. and Golková, E. (1976) *An Analytic Bibliography of Czechoslovakian Studies in Functional Sentence Perspective*. Brno: Pyrkyn University.

Firth, J. (1968) *Selected Papers of J.R. Firth 1952–1959* (ed. F.R. Palmer). London: Longman.

Fish, S.E. (1994) *There is No Such Thing as Free Speech*. Oxford: Oxford University Press.

Fiske, S.T. and Taylor, S.E. (1984) *Social Cognition*. Reading, MA: Addison-Wesley.

Freedle, R. (ed.) (1977) *Discourse Production and Comprehension*. Norwood, NJ: Ablex.

Freire, P. (1980) *Conscientização: Teoria e prática da libertação*. São Paulo: Moraes.

Garfinkel, H. (1974) 'The origins of the term "ethnomethodology"', in E.M. Turner (ed.), *Ethnomethodology*. Harmondsworth: Penguin.

Golding, W. (1955) *The Inheritors*. London: Faber and Faber.

Grimes, J. (1975) *The Thread of Discourse*. The Hague: Mouton.

Grimes, J. (ed.) (1978) *Papers on Discourse*. Arlington: Summer Institute of Linguistics.

Halliday, M.A.K. (1973) *Explorations in the Function of Language*. London: Arnold.

Hawkins, P. (1969) 'Social class, the nominal group, and reference', *Language and Speech*, 12: 125–35.

Heinemann, W. and Viehweger, D. (1991) *Texlinguistik: Eine Einführung*. Tübingen: Niemeyer.

Kalverkämper, H. (1981) *Orientierung zur Textlinguistik*. Tübingen: Niemeyer.

Kintsch, W. (1988) 'The role of knowledge in discourse comprehension: a "construction-integration model"', *Psychological Review*, 95 (2): 163–82.

Koch, W.A. (ed.) (1972) *Strukturelle Textanalyse – Analyse du récit – Discourse Analysis*. Hildesheim: Olms.

Lemke, J. (1990) *Talking Science*. Norwood, NJ: Ablex.

Longacre, R.E. (1976) *An Anatomy of Speech Notions*. Lisse: de Ridder.

Longacre, R.E. et al. (1990) *Storyline Concerns and Word Order Typology in East and West Africa*. Los Angeles: UCLA Department of Linguistics.

Macdonnell, D. (1986) *Theories of Discourse*. Oxford: Blackwell.

Mann, W.C. and Thompson, S.A. (eds) (1992) *Discourse Description*. Amsterdam: Benjamins.

Orwell, G. (1946) 'Politics and the English language', in *Inside the Whale and Other Essays*. Harmondsworth: Penguin, 1979. pp. 143–58.

Phillipson, R. and Skuttnabb-Kangas, T. (eds) (1994) *Linguistic Human Rights*. Berlin: de Gruyter.

Pike, K.L. (1967) *Language in Relation to a Unified Theory of the Structure of Human Behavior*. The Hague: Mouton.

Postman, N. and Weingartner, C. (1966) *Linguistics: a Revolution in Teaching*. New York: Delacorte.

Potter, J. and Wetherell, M. (1987) *Discourse and Social Psychology*. London: Sage.

Schegloff, E. (1987) 'Some sources of misunderstanding in talk-in-interaction', *Linguistics*, 25: 201–18.

Schegloff, E. (1992) 'To Searle on conversation: a note in return', in H. Parrett and J. Verschueren (eds), *On Searle on Conversation*. Amsterdam: Benjamins. pp. 113–28.

Schriffrin, D. (1987) *Discourse Markers*. Cambridge: Cambridge University Press.

Sinclair, J. McH. (1991) *Corpus, Concordance, Collocation*. Oxford: Oxford University Press.

Sinclair, J. McH. and Brazil, D. (1982) *Teacher Talk*. Oxford: Oxford University Press.

Sinclair, J. McH and Coulthard, M. (1975) *Toward an Analysis of Discourse*. Oxford: Oxford University Press.

van Dijk, T. (ed.) (1985) *Handbook of Discourse Analysis*. London: Academic.

van Dijk, T. (1987) *Communicating Racism: Ethnic Prejudices in Thought and Talk*. Newbury Park, CA: Sage.

van Dijk, T. (1991) *Racism and the Press*. London: Routledge.

Wilden, A. (1987) *The Rules Are No Game*. London: Routledge and Kegan Paul.

3

Discourse Semantics

Russell S. Tomlin, Linda Forrest, Ming Ming Pu and Myung Hee Kim

The Problem of Meaning

It is remarkable how well, how routinely, we communicate with one another. Whether we relate the common and trivial events of our day-to-day lives or argue passionately for our ideologies; whether we read a simple newspaper account of a world event or an academic paper on the intricacies of human language; whether we compose a simple thank-you note or a legal brief, our problems remain the same: how can we ensure that our comprehender gets the message we intend, and how do we derive the message intended from what we hear or read? Our problems as linguists also remain the same: for the comprehender, whether listening or reading, we must describe and account for how meaning is derived from any of these multiple sources; and, for the producer, whether speaker or writer, we must account for how meaning is conveyed. This problem of meaning, this problem of *discourse semantics*, is a complex one, involving interplay among a wide array of linguistic and non-linguistic processes.

Let us consider a very simple example, the text fragment in (1).

(1) Text fragment
1 . . . puck knocked away by Dale McCourt,
Ø picked up again by Steve Shutt/
Now Shutt coming out, into the Detroit zone/
He played it out in front/
5 There's Lemaire with a shot.
and it was blocked by Reed Larson/

The fragment is a short segment transcribed from the concurrent and on-line description of an ice hockey game. The professional announcer rapidly produces his description as the events unfold before him. One can see that the announcer alternates between active and passive voice (lines 4 vs lines 1, 2, and 6), between nominal and pronominal form, and between existential or presentative clause type (line 5) and simple clauses (line 3). What is it about the message the announcer must convey that leads to the selection of these alternative structures? Our initial and intuitive guesses, some grounded perhaps in our traditional schooling, is that the difference between the active and passive is related to which referent is given more emphasis or is somehow, at least at the moment, more important; that the selection of the proper names versus the pronoun is related to keeping clear which referent one targets at a given moment, and that the selection of the existential is tied to whether or not the referent has been recently 'on stage,' as it were, as the action unfolded.

This chapter provides an introduction to the concepts and processes underlying our intuitions about how matters of emphasis and importance and prior knowledge contribute to the meaning one derives from text and discourse during comprehension, and how they contribute to and shape decisions about the use of language structures in the service of larger meanings.

The remainder of this section provides a framework for this effort.

Metaphors of Discourse Interaction

The way one thinks of discourse has a strong effect on the kind of theory or model of discourse semantics one creates. The most naive metaphor can be called the *conduit metaphor* of discourse. In this view, the speaker packages his intended meaning into a textual artifact. This artifact, in essence, *contains* the meaning intended by the speaker. It is conducted to the listener in either spoken or written form. The text is then unpacked and its meaning extracted from the text artifact by the listener.

Within the conduit metaphor one is invited to think of language and texts as *containing* meaning. It invites one to think of meanings as inherent to the text itself or to the clauses and words which make it up. Failure by the speaker to be clear derives from a failure to match well intended meaning with the details of text as produced. Failure by the listener to comprehend arises from the failure to extract proper semantic detail or nuance from the text itself. Language, in a sense, is viewed as a precision instrument, which is used to craft a precise meaning, fully embodied in the text. The text becomes both the target of analysis and the source, sometimes the only source, for explanatory information regarding its structure and meaning.

An alternative metaphor, the one we will embrace here, can be called the *blueprint metaphor* of discourse. In this view, the speaker holds a conceptual representation of events or ideas which he intends should be replicated in the mind of the listener. The listener is neither helpless nor passive in the endeavor but actively engages in constructing her own conceptual representation of the matters at hand. The speaker behaves as a sort of architect and his linguistic output, the text, can be viewed less as a fully fleshed out semantic construct than as a blueprint to aid the listener during the construction of a conceptual representation. Just as a true blueprint contains no actual building materials but depicts by convention how existing materials should be employed in constructing a given edifice, so the text itself contains little or no meaning *per se* but serves by convention to guide the listener in constructing a conceptual edifice.

One can demonstrate the utility of the blueprint metaphor over the conduit metaphor with a brief demonstration or 'thought' experiment. Consider a simple task – like putting on your favorite sweater. Try to write a passage which instructs a naive reader – a very naive reader – on how to put on a sweater. No matter how much detail is provided in the text itself, the text will never alone, never without the employment of other sources of information, be adequate to get the sweater on. The conceptual model of sweater-wearing the speaker has in mind is more complex than can be captured in the text, and the text can only be helpful to the reader as it exploits and builds on conceptual models of sweaters and donning and whatever else can be brought to bear on the task.

Building or interpreting text blueprints requires dealing with two fundamental problems. The first is integrating the semantic information provided in each utterance into a coherent whole.[1] The speaker must select pertinent concepts and events from his experience and organize this in a way helpful to the listener. The listener must integrate utterances heard into a coherent representation which permits her to access or construct concepts and events virtually identical to those held by the speaker. We can call this the problem of *knowledge integration*.

The second fundamental problem is managing the flow of information between speaker and listener in dynamic, real time interaction. The speaker will help the listener succeed in knowledge integration in part by directing the listener's efforts to process the information provided through the text. For example, the speaker will help the listener by exploiting information held in common as a prelude to or anchor for information the speaker believes will be novel or unexpected for the listener. The coherence of the knowledge held by the listener will be affected by how cohesive the information is that the speaker offers. We call this the problem of *information management*.

Knowledge integration requires effective information management, but effective information management is not enough to account for knowledge integration.

What Is Linguistic and What Is Not

The social and cognitive processes of discourse creation and comprehension involve a complex array of both linguistic and non-linguistic processes. It will prove immensely useful to keep in mind that both sorts of processes are implicated in our understanding of discourse and text and that the dividing line between linguistics and psychology cannot be neatly drawn. These processes include at least three different types:

1 *Morpho-syntactic codings*: grammatical codes employed automatically and generally non-consciously by speaker and listener to shape the flow and decoding of information during production and comprehension.

2 *Implicatures*: signals employed under routine conditions by the speaker and which result in common and rapidly drawn inferences by the listener.

3 *Planning and inference*: high level processes of planning on the part of the speaker and inference on the part of the listener which set general directions for less global processing by speaker and listener.

These issues will be dealt with more fully in the next main section where we discuss the problem of knowledge integration in discourse.

Four Central Threads of Information Management

The ease with which the listener can integrate knowledge into a coherent vision of the concepts and events the speaker has in mind is determined largely by how well the speaker controls the flow of information to the listener. Information flow (Chafe, 1979; 1980a; 1987; 1994) depends on the effective control of four distinct kinds of information:

1 *Rhetorical management*: participants must be clear about the goals and intentions of the discourse interaction as these constrain greatly the propositional content of production and the construal of what is heard.

2 *Referential management*: participants must keep track of the referents and propositions they have in common.

3 *Thematic management*: participants must keep track of the central elements around which the discourse is developed.

4 *Focus management*: the participants must keep track of which referents they are dealing with at any given moment and must take steps to ensure they are on the same one(s).

Each of these four threads will be pursued in separate sections in this chapter.

The Granularity of Discourse Interaction: Three Key Levels

Discourse is neither flat nor linear in its organization; it is hierarchical, with clauses forming higher order structures, paragraphs, which in turn combine to form larger episodes or sections of discourse. For our purposes, it is important to distinguish three key levels:

1 *Global coherence*: the participants develop a sense of what the overall narrative or procedure or conversation deals with.

2 *Episodic coherence*: the participants are sensitive to smaller scale units which contribute to global coherence but which display an internal gist of their own.

3 *Local coherence*: the participants make sense of the contribution of individual sentences or utterances.

These three levels of granularity will be important to keep in mind as we pursue each of the four threads of information management.

Historical Perspective

The pragmatic notions discussed below emerged from research traditions seeking answers to questions of discourse and syntax (see Cumming and Ono, Chapter 4 in this volume), in particular to questions of typological differences between languages. For example, the precursor to Prague School work on *functional sentence perspective* was a volume by Weil (1887), originally published in 1844, which appealed to pragmatic and cognitive rationales to explain differences between the less constrained word orders of Latin and Ancient Greek and the more constrained word orders of modern European languages.

In the same vein, Prague School research was directed, as it is directed today, at explaining differences between languages like Czech and English. All of the pragmatic notions discussed below arose historically from attempts to explain otherwise opaque structural contrasts. Why, after all, should a language 'need' simple voice alternants like English passive, let alone complex systems typical of Philippine Austronesian languages like Tagalog or Cebuano, when the essential semantic content of passive and active is identical?

The central concepts employed in developing theories of discourse semantics have a long history. This chapter will respect that history, linking current conceptualizations with their historical antecedents.

Methodological Issues and Dilemmas

While it is not particularly fashionable to be concerned with methodology, it is nevertheless important to examine a number of issues tied to the methods employed in the analysis of discourse semantics. Of particular interest will be the contributions made to discourse studies by introspection, by text counting procedures, and by experimental methods. Methodological issues are taken up later in the chapter.

Cognitive and Discourse Semantics

There has always been an interest in the relationship between discourse and text structure and their processing and storage in the mind. As early as the nineteenth century, scholars such as von der Gabelenz appealed to primitive ideas of attention in discussing 'psychological subject' (related to notions of topic and theme). Similarly, early psychologists like Stout also explained linguistic behavior by appeal to the activity of the mind (cf. Lambrecht, 1994 or Gundel, 1974). More recently, many linguists, within both discourse studies and more general linguistics, have begun to appeal to cognitive notions in their theoretical efforts, in particular to ideas of activation (memory) and attention. The penultimate section examines the promise this line of research holds for the future of discourse semantics.

Knowledge Integration in Discourse

To appreciate the richness and complexity of discourse semantics in discourse production and comprehension, let us consider two examples. First, from the point of view of the speaker, consider the drawing in Figure 3.1. Describe the scene as you examine it for the first time, perhaps even recording your description, for a listener who cannot see the drawing.

There are a number of important matters one must deal with in developing a theory of discourse semantics. First, the speaker must have in mind some sort of *conceptual representation*[2] of the subject matter under discussion. It is this representation which is the fundamental 'meaning' the speaker works with in constructing a discourse. Most of the time as linguists we think of the conceptual representation as a set of propositions, sometimes referred to as a text representation or text base (Kintsch, 1974; van Dijk and Kintsch, 1983), but a conceptual representation need not be simply or only propositional. In the case of the Figure 3.1 the speaker will form some sort of *visual* representation for the picture, which he will access when speaking. For other kinds of experience, there may well be other kinds of representation. For example, a conceptual representation for, say, tasting coffee may well be different from one for listening to music, which in turn may be distinct from that for shifting gears in a car. And, we must remember that we can create conceptual representations as well as access them from memory or perceptual experience.

In addition, one should keep in mind that conceptual representations are *dynamic*. While the picture in Figure 3.1 is itself static, our viewing of it is not: our eyes move from one element to another, pausing here and there, skipping here and there, forming smaller scale images and impressions. In the same vein, most conceptual representations are dynamic: we do not view pictures so much as we do scenes and other sorts of unfolding events. Even our abstract efforts are dynamic, as we leap from idea to idea or slog through a difficult argument. Conceptual representations are thus foundational for understanding discourse production.

The conceptual representation alone, though, is not the meaning of the discourse. Somehow the speaker must select information from the overall conceptual representation and build a text from that selected information. The speaker will select information he believes the listener needs, and that information will be presented to help the listener make good sense of what is heard. How the speaker *manages* information plays a critical role in discourse production and comprehension. Discourse management involves (at least) four independent threads.

One, the speaker never *merely* outputs a conceptual representation via language. The speaker always has some *purpose* or *goal*, perhaps even several, in mind. Such goals constrain how conceptual representations are searched, and they constrain the selection of information to convey. The picture in Figure 3.1 will yield different descriptions depending on whether the speaker is asked to 'describe what seems to be happening' or 'evaluate

Figure 3.1   *Scene example (artwork by Jennifer Jones, 1995)*

the quality of the drawing'. In each case the speaker will access a visual representation of the picture, but the information selected and ultimately incorporated into a verbal description will be different. We can think of these different goals or purposes in speaking as distinct *rhetorical goals* for discourse production and the associated selection processes as defining an area we will call *rhetorical management*.

Two, constrained by rhetorical goals, the speaker accesses the conceptual representation, dynamically selecting referents and propositions for the listener. As he does so, the speaker makes real time decisions about which referents and propositions are more central or important to the developing discourse. Such *starting points* ultimately assist the listener in building her own conceptual representation. We can think of important referents or starting points as specifying the *thematic organization* of discourse and the associated pragmatic notions and processes as defining an area we will call *thematic management*.

Three, in parallel with thematic management, the speaker will also monitor dynamically which referents and propositions seem to be available to the listener already and which require introduction or reintroduction. Referents and propositions fall coarsely into two classes: those that the speaker believes the listener can readily access, the information in common; and those that the speaker believes the listener will need explicit assistance to access, the targeted information. We can think of the interlocking pattern of referents and propositions held in common or not as defining the *referential organization* of discourse, and the associated pragmatic notions and cognitive processes as defining an area we will call *referential management*.

Finally, the speaker will monitor dynamically which referents and propositions he wishes to ensure are brought to the attention of the listener. From time to time, the speaker may not be certain that the listener has the right referent in mind at the right time, or he may wish to somehow *highlight* or *emphasize* a particular referent or proposition. We can think of efforts to highlight or emphasize or steer the listener's attention to particular referents and propositions as defining the *focus organization* of discourse, and the associated pragmatic notions and cognitive processes as defining an area we will call *focus management*.

These four arenas of discourse management define the central problems of information management in discourse. While there is an extensive literature dealing with each of these areas, there is at present no single, comprehensive model of how they fit together to account for knowledge integration (but cf. Vallduví, 1992 or Lambrecht, 1994). Still, one useful model for understanding what the speaker does is Levelt's (1989) blueprint for the speaker. In Levelt's model there are three principal components. There is a *conceptualizer*, which is responsible for the creation of a pre-verbal message, the central proposition to be encoded, annotated in some way for pertinent pragmatic statuses like *topic*, *focus*, or *given*. The pre-verbal message is then processed by an *utterance formulator*, which (in concert with the lexicon) assigns first a grammatical representation to the message and then a phonological representation. The phonological representation is then processed by an *articulator*, which is responsible for the generation of overt speech.

A model of discourse semantics will deal with the creation of Levelt's pre-verbal messages with its pragmatically annotated propositions. Figure 3.2 (based loosely on Levelt, 1989) presents a simple model of production, setting out the contribution of the four arenas of discourse management to the overall discourse creation task.

Briefly, the conceptualizer operates on a conceptual representation to produce something like a pre-verbal message or annotated proposition. The conceptual representation may come from several sources – current perception, long term memory, or some creative production. The

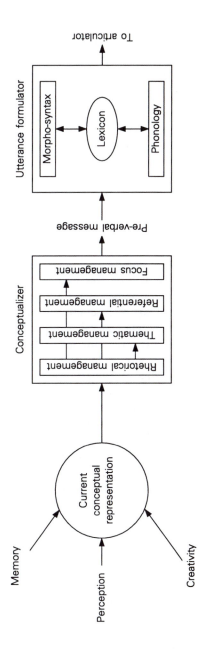

Figure 3.2 *A blueprint for the speaker*

conceptualizer employs rhetorical management to select a particular event or other conceptualization for communication consistent with the speaker's global and local plans for the discourse. This selected event is, in turn, and in parallel, annotated for thematic, referential, and focus statuses (all discussed below). The output of this process is a pre-verbal message, a proposition annotated for fundamental pragmatic statuses and ready for processing by the utterance formulator.

Turning to comprehension, one can see that the listener's problem parallels the speaker's, but it is not simply its reversal. The listener will form a conceptual representation as discourse is encountered. She will use information extracted from the text in concert with information already at hand to construct a conceptual representation. Consider the discourse sample in (2) and imagine the scene created in your mind as you read it.

(2)   A boy with a pail on his head is trying to catch a frog who is falling off a tree stump and the boy has accidentally caught his dog with the net.

The listener encounters utterances one at a time in real time. She will attempt to create a conceptual representation of the events the speaker blueprints via the text, and she will do this by employing all of the information at her disposal. Most researchers see the listener as creating some sort of *text representation*. This text representation is something like the gist of the text, a cohesive and complete general picture of the events or other subject matter discussed. The text representation is generally taken to be a set of propositions linked to one another to form a coherent whole. Perhaps the best known such model is that of Kintsch and van Dijk (1978). A text representation for them is a set of propositions, linked together through common referents and other features of events like time or place, and connected to a higher order discourse theme or *macroproposition*. Other models (Gernsbacher, 1990; Kintsch, 1988; Reinhart, 1981; Vallduví, 1992) follow this general pattern. None of these models grapples with the larger problem of how the text representation – the understanding of the message – is tied to developing the final conceptual representation which the text blueprints, for instance the (possible) mental image resulting from comprehending (2).

In dealing with the text blueprint as it arrives in dynamic time, the listener employs at least three distinct kinds of knowledge to decode the text and integrate its information into a text representation. The listener exploits the *morpho-syntactic details* of her grammar as they code the flow of information in the text and discourse. She entertains *implicatures* derived from the pragmatic interpretation of the sentences in the text against the wider discourse context. And, she employs general processes of *inference* to help make wider connections between the current text and her larger store of knowledge.

Morpho-syntactic coding can be exemplified by something like the particle *wa* in Japanese (Hinds et al., 1987). While the details are not agreed to by all researchers, speakers of Japanese appear to use *wa* to direct the listener's attention to the key referent in the utterance, its *topic* as some argue. Listeners who encounter *wa* automatically treat the noun phrase so marked as the key referent of the clause, integrating following information against this central referent. These decisions are largely automatic and non-consciously managed by speaker and listener.

Implicatures can be exemplified by something like the English conjunction *and*. In narrative discourse, when two clauses are conjoined by *and*, it is common for a listener to conclude that the event reported by the second clause occurred after the event reported by the first. However, the temporal order of events is *not* part of the meaning of *and*, since there are many uses of *and* which do not involve temporal order at all. The understanding of order derives from implicature, an understanding of event order arising from the interplay of the basic meaning of *and* with the larger context in which the conjunction is used (Levinson, 1983).

Planning and inference can be exemplified by simple inference across clauses. Suppose Mary has a new acquaintance, Sita, and has learned enough about her to know that Sita was raised in one of two national capitals, London or New Delhi. Upon hearing Sita utter (3a), Mary draws the inference that Sita is from London, permitting Mary to utter (3b):

(3a) I used to enjoy playing in the snow in our garden when I was a child and seeing all the trees covered in snow.
(3b) Did you ever see the Trafalgar Square Christmas Tree all covered in snow?

The inference Mary draws that Sita was raised in London derives not from any facts about language, but through Mary's employment of world knowledge while interpreting Sita's observation in (3a). Such inferences are important for knowledge integration, but the processes are strictly speaking non-linguistic.

It is important to see that all of these processes are involved in knowledge integration. But it is also important to see that these contributions are distinct. It is easy for the linguist to include facts about implicature and inference in descriptions of the function of linguistic forms in discourse. It is easy for the psychologist or psycholinguist to conclude that his or her observations about language use are facts about the linguistic system when they might be due to non-linguistic processes of planning or inference. Two excellent resources to help guard against such confusions can be found in Levinson (1983) or Leech (1983).

There are two useful models of knowledge integration in comprehension: Gernsbacher's (1990) structure building model and Kintsch's (1988) construction-integration model. In Gernsbacher's *structure building model*, the listener's goal is to build a coherent mental representation or 'structure' of the information in the discourse. In order to achieve this goal, the listener uses many general cognitive processes and mechanisms. Some processes and mechanisms are involved in 'laying a foundation' for the mental structure.

Once the foundation has been laid, the listener develops her mental structure by *mapping* incoming information onto the previous structure. However, the new information can only be mapped onto a current structure if it coheres with earlier information. If the new information is less coherent, listeners must *shift* to begin building a new structure.

In Gernsbacher's framework, these mental representations are built from memory cells which are activated by incoming information. If that information is coherent with previous information, it is more likely to activate similar memory cells. But if it is less coherent, it is not as likely to activate similar memory cells. Instead, it will activate different memory cells, and these newly activated cells become the foundation for a new structure or substructure. When memory cells are activated, they transmit processing signals which either enhance or suppress the activation of other cells. A group of memory cells is enhanced as long as the information they represent is needed in building the mental structure. When that information is no longer needed, they will be suppressed.

Kintsch's (1988) *construction-integration model* also deals well with knowledge integration. This model attempts to describe explicitly how knowledge is retrieved from memory and utilized in understanding utterances. Consider the sentence, *Mary baked a cake for Sally and burned her fingers*. In order to understand the utterance, the listener needs to know more than merely the words and phrases that were uttered by the speaker. She also needs to have a good deal of general knowledge about how the world works, in this case, that baking entails that the object will be very hot for a period of time. She must also know how language works, for example, that the verb *bake* requires an agent and that this role is filled by Mary in this sentence. Further, the listener needs to know specific information about the situation in which the words were uttered. It is not clear from the words alone whether Mary baked the cake as a gift for Sally, or whether Sally was obligated to make a cake and Mary did it in her place.

Kintsch's model of knowledge use in discourse comprehension has two stages. In the first stage, the words in the utterance are used as the raw material from which a mental representation of the meaning of the utterance is constructed. This mental representation is a network of linked propositions called a text base. In the second stage, the network is edited and integrated with other knowledge stored in memory. Each proposition in the utterance activates its closest neighbors in a general knowledge network. This process of spreading activation results in a text base which contains not only the propositions that were uttered by the speaker, but propositions retrieved from knowledge stores which are related to the propositions in the utterance. Thus, after the second stage of processing, the text base contains clusters of related propositions that combine the information in the utterance with the world knowledge and language knowledge stored in memory.

As we have seen, knowledge integration involves the meshing of non-linguistic or real world knowledge and knowledge about one's language with the actual utterances in the discourse. The speaker must employ non-linguistic knowledge to observe and understand events in the world and their relevance to the listener. Then he must use this knowledge and knowledge about his language to choose particular linguistic structures which will be informative to the listener. The listener, for her part, must interpret these linguistic structures using her own linguistic and non-linguistic knowledge. This task is made easier if the speaker manages well his task of providing the listener with appropriate information. In the next four sections, we will explore how speakers manage the task of controlling information for their listeners.

The Rhetorical Management of Discourse

While a detailed discussion of rhetorical management falls outside the scope of the present chapter (but see Gill and Whedbee, Chapter 6 in this volume, for a rich discussion), most of the key concepts discussed below depend on their rhetorical setting for a full understanding. The process of speaking involves both information and action. The informational component includes the details of propositional content as well as pragmatic matters – emphasis, importance, presupposition – which guide how the semantic content should be interpreted. The action component includes the details of discourse planning – both global and local – which help direct pragmatic matters for the speaker and help constrain interpretation by the listener.

It is well known that the use of linguistic structures in discourse is related to linguistic actions taken by the speaker. At the sentence level, the linguistic action of, say, *issuing a command* can be carried out through a number of linguistic structures: an imperative (*Give me your money*; *Let me have your money*), an interrogative (*Could I have your money*), or a declarative (*I want your money*). These examples demonstrate that the form of an utterance is separable from the action, in this case the *speech act*, which the utterance carries out.

The key insight of speech act theory (Levinson, 1983; Searle, 1969; 1979) is that language is used to *do* things (Austin, 1962). Speech act analysis of discourse focuses on local matters affecting clause or sentence type. But language as action is reflected in higher level aspects of discourse organization as well. For example, Swales (1981) examined some 48 introductions to scientific and technical articles. He identified four crucial component actions within each introduction. These actions, which Swales called *moves*, capture critical kinds of information selected by the speaker from his conceptual representation of the subject matter. As shown in Figure 3.3, a typical introduction to a scientific article is composed of four moves: (1) establishing the field, (2) summarizing previous research, (3) preparing for present research, and (4) introducing present research.

There are numerous threads of research, many apparently unknown to each other, which pursue work in this area. Probably the best known is

Subject	HLA antigens in patients with scabies

Move 1 Establish the field	The cell-membrane molecules which are determined by the closely linked genes in the HLA chromosomal complex may be divided into two different classes (Thorsby, 1979): (a) The HLA-ABC molecules, which are determined by allelic genes at the A, B, and C loci, are present on probably all nucleated cells and are highly polymorphic. (b) The HLA-D/DR molecules which have a more restricted tissue distribution are present mainly on B lymphocytes and monocytes/macrophages. Typing for these antigens has become a tool of steadily increasing interest.
Move 2 Summarize previous research	Patients with certain diseases have an increasing frequency of particular HLA antigens compared to healthy individuals (Dausset and Svejgaard, 1997). This is also true for some dermatological diseases. The strongest appears to be the association between D/DR and dermatitis herpetiformis (Solheim et al., 1977), but discoid lupus erythematosus (Stenszky, Nagy, and Szerze, 1975), psoriasis (Williams et al., 1976), vitiligo (Retornaz et al., 1976) and lichen planus (Lowe, Cudworth, and Woodrow, 1976; Halevy et al., 1979) have been found to be associated with certain HLA antigens.
Move 3 Prepare for present research	The reason for these associations are unknown, but probably involve HLA gene control of T cell immune responses (Thorsby, 1978). Immunological mechanisms are also involved in patients with scabies (Mellanby, 1944; Falk, 1980; Falk and Bolle, 1980a, b).
Move 4 Introduce present research	In view of these observations we looked for an association between scabies and any of the HLA-ABC antigens.

Figure 3.3   *Analysis of article introductions (Swales, 1981)*

the British tradition of discourse analysis associated with Coulthard and Sinclair (Coulthard, 1977; Coulthard and Montgomery, 1981; Sinclair and Coulthard, 1975). Their classic work (Sinclair and Coulthard, 1975) examined the structure of classroom discourse in British schools. Mehan (1979) has developed similar lines of research within education.

Researchers in artificial intelligence have examined the goal oriented structure of discourse and its relation to the structure of the knowledge that the discourse is about. Grosz (1974) examines the language used in assembling a water pump, investigating connections between knowledge representations and referential form. Such task-based discourse work has been conducted by Cohen and Perrault (1979), Baggett (1982), McKeown (1985), Sidner (1983), and others.

Linguists have also examined the organization of discourse in this fashion. Early work by Propp (1958) investigated the prototypical organization of Russian fairy tales. Grimes (1975) developed an inventory of rhetorical predicates to capture the intentional structure of discourse. More recently, Levy (1979) examined the structure of informal interviews of students completing course schedules. Hinds (1979) looked at procedural discourse in Japanese. Mann and Thompson (1986) offer a rich system for describing the fine-grained details of rhetorical management in natural discourse.

All of these efforts propose an inventory of hierarchically organized actions of one kind or another. High level structures can be decomposed into constrained sets of lower order units; lower order units combine in constrained ways to form higher levels of discourse organization. So, Swales's introduction is decomposed into four moves; the four distinct move types combine to form a well formed introduction.

Understanding rhetorical management is important for discourse semantics for a number of reasons. One, the integration of information into or from the text is never merely a matter of processing individual utterances. The utterances are integrated with respect to higher order considerations, and these considerations are what is managed by the rhetorical component. Two, as this volume details elsewhere, there is an important role to be played by the syntax, what we have called morpho-syntactic coding, in signaling one or another information status as the discourse unfolds. The determination of which information is thematic or focused and so on is very much tied to the higher order rhetorical goals for which the discourse was initiated.

The Referential Management of Discourse

One of the characteristics of connected and coherent discourse is that entities, once introduced at a given point in text, are often referred to again at a later point. The problem of how reference is managed in discourse production and comprehension has been the focus of considerable research on discourse processing because it is fundamental in understanding the relationships among cognitive processes, knowledge integration, and information management.

The key insight within referential management is that certain concepts seem to be held in common or shared by both speaker and listener, while others are not. Information held in common forms part of the conceptual scaffolding on which speaker and listener depend for effective communication. The key questions are: (1) what does it mean to say that speaker and listener 'share' information, and (2) how is referential management related to higher level aspects of rhetorical and discourse structure?

Virtually every theory of discourse structure draws a distinction between *given information* and *new information* (also referred to as *old* vs *new*, *known* vs *unknown*, or *shared* vs *new*). Each clause or utterance is theorized to contain elements the speaker believes he holds in common with the listener and elements the speaker believes he does not. So, in the discourse fragment in (4), the bold-faced NPs are generally taken to be given information and the italicized NPs new information.[3]

(4)   Text fragment from popular novel *Sarum* by E. Rutherford (1988: 17)
      1   The next day **he** discovered *the lake.*
          It was *a small, low hill about five miles inland*
          that first attracted **his attention.**
          It looked like [*a place from*
      5   *which he could spy out the land and*
          where they could camp at least for the night].
          When **he** reached **the place**, however,
          he was surprised and delighted to find
          that hidden below **it** and in his path
      10 lay *a shallow lake about half a mile across.*
          At **its eastern end**, *a small outlet* carried **its water** away towards **the sea.**
          Tracing round **the lake**
          he found that
          it was fed from **the north** and **the west** by *two small rivers.*
      15 On **its northern side** was *a flat, empty marsh.*
          The water, sheltered by **the hill**, was very still;
          there was *a sweet smell of fern, mud and water reed.*
          Over **the surface of the lake**, *a heron* rose
          and *seagulls* cried.
      20 Protected from **the wind** it was warm.
          It did not take **him** long to make *a small raft*
          and cross **the little stretch of water.**

Overall, this paragraph describes a new location encountered by the main character in the novel. Several of the clauses exhibit straightforward cases of given information as well as straightforward cases of new information.

The bold-faced NPs in 1, 2, 7, 8, 12, 13, 21 represent given information because they have been mentioned before in the text. The italicized NPs in 1, 2, 10, 11, 15, 18, 19, 21 represent new information, for they have just been introduced. Other cases are a bit less clear. The NPs in 3, 11, 14, 15, 20 are marked bold, and their putative status as given must be related to knowledge shared by writer and reader about lakes and their environs. But then lakes also include native birds, like herons and gulls, so one wonders why the NPs in 18 and 19 cannot count also as given.

Such observations have led a number of researchers to propose more or less complex systems of given and new information.

Conceptual Foundations for Given and New Information

There are two basic ideas about given and new information: (1) given information represents a referent shared in some way by speaker and listener; or (2) given information is a cognitively activated referent.

Given Information as Shared Information   Traditionally, referential management is taken to require that a given semantic argument also hold a
pragmatic status like *old* or *given* or *known* information. Within the Prague
School, Mathesius (1939) suggests that one portion of the utterance
represents information that is assumed to be possessed by the listener from
the preceding context or may be inferred by her from the context. Such
information is *known* (*old*, *given*) information. It is contrasted with the
portion of the utterance which the speaker presents as *new* (*unknown*)
information and which is the content of the utterance. Mathesius examined
how this status of information is signaled via strategies such as word order,
intonation, and other constructions. These ideas were developed by other
Prague School scholars, such as Daneš and Firbas.

Halliday (1967a; 1967b) is concerned with relating each unit of information in a given sentence to the preceding discourse. He draws a distinction between *given* information and new information. New information
represents information the speaker treats as not known to the listener.
Given information represents information the speaker treats as known to
the listener. Halliday links the status of new information to focal sentence
intonation. Unlike Prague School researchers, Halliday draws a further
distinction between *known* and *unknown* information. For Halliday, information is known if the speaker assumes the listener can identify the referent
and is unknown if the speaker assumes the listener cannot identify the
referent. DuBois (1980) also considers the importance of identifiability in
referential management.

Prince (1981) finds these intuitively appealing notions to be too
simplistic. She proposes a multi-way distinction in types of information
(types of statuses of referents). One, a referent is *new* when it is introduced
into the discourse for the first time. New referents may be *brand-new*, that
is newly created by the speaker, or simply *unused*, that is entities the listener
is assumed to know about but which have not been mentioned previously
in the discourse. Two, a referent is considered *evoked* if it is already part of
the discourse. An evoked referent may be *textually evoked* if the listener
had evoked it earlier on instructions from the speaker (as by the speaker's
mention of the referent), or it may be *situationally evoked* if the listener
knows to evoke it all by herself, such as 'you' referring to the listener.
Three, a referent is *inferable* if the speaker assumes the listener could have
inferred it, using knowledge and reasoning. A referent may be inferable
either from the text or from the situation.

Given Information as Degree of Memorial Activation   Chafe (1976; 1987;
1994) discusses information status in terms of what is activated (or not
activated) in consciousness. He argues that the linguistic phenomena such
as *given* and *new* information are manifestations of our basic cognitive
activities. Our minds contain a very large amount of knowledge or information but only a very small amount of this information can be focused
on, or be 'active', at any given moment. He proposes that a particular

concept may be in any one of the three different activation states at a particular time of discourse processing: *active* (corresponding to the 'given'), *semi-active* (accessible), or *inactive* (corresponding to the 'new').

> An active concept is one that is currently lit up, a concept in a person's focus of consciousness. A semi-active concept is one that is in a person's peripheral consciousness, a concept of which a person has a background awareness, but which is not being directly focused on. An inactive concept is one that is currently in a person's long-term memory, neither focally nor peripherally active. (Chafe, 1987: 25)

A speaker normally makes changes in the activation states of certain concepts which are partially reflected in their referential choice. If the speaker assumes, prior to uttering an intonation unit, that a concept is already active in the listener's mind, he will verbalize that concept in an attenuated manner, most probably pronominalizing it. If he assumes that a concept is not presently activated in the listener's consciousness, he will verbalize that concept in a less attenuated manner, most probably nominalizing it.

Clark and Haviland (1974) relate these notions to memorial processes in their discussion of the 'given–new strategy'. That is, each sentence produced by a speaker contains some information that is old or given, and some that is new. The old information serves as an indication of where, in the listener's memory, she will find information related to that conveyed by the present sentence, and thus 'an instruction specifying where the new information is to be integrated into the previous knowledge' (1974: 105). Consequently, pronouns and definite noun phrases (NPs) are more likely to refer to old or given entities and indefinite NPs to new information.

Givón (1983) also considers referential management in cognitive terms. He observes that the speaker estimates to what extent a given referent is mentally accessible to his listener. If accessibility is gauged to be high, the speaker will use an attenuated referential form to index the referent (ellipsis or pronominalization). If accessibility is judged to be lower, the speaker will use a longer form, perhaps a simple nominal NP or one with some modification. If accessibility is estimated to be very low, the speaker may introduce a referent into the conceptual representation through (at least in English) an indefinite NP or some other appropriate device.

Referential Management and Knowledge Integration

One important problem in reference management has been understanding how speaker and listener keep track of referents during discourse production and comprehension. Keeping track of referents involves three related problems: (1) introducing referents to the discourse, (2) sustaining reference once a referent has been introduced, and (3) reintroducing referents after a long hiatus. Virtually every approach at present employs some notion of managing a mental model or conceptual representation for this purpose. Speakers will use particular linguistic forms (see Cumming and Ono, Chapter 4 in this volume) to introduce referents to the discourse, typically indefinite NPs or focal sentence intonation or later word order. Such introductions can be thought of as moving a referent from off stage onto the stage, or from some long term memory store into the current conceptual representation.

Speakers use other linguistic forms, most typically anaphoric forms, pronominalization or definite NPs, to signal referents which are already available to the listener. Such referents can be thought of as activated or emplaced within the conceptual representation. Speakers may also reintroduce a referent after a long hiatus or some other interruption.

Keeping track of referents over time involves important interplay between the activation status of a referent and the granularity of discourse. Of numerous linguistic and psycholinguistic approaches to reference management in discourse, the episode model (van Dijk and Kintsch, 1983; Fox, 1987; Marslen-Wilson et al., 1982) has been the most influential. It considers the use of *anaphora* to be a function of a particular discourse structure – the paragraph or *episode*. The basic assumption underlying the model is that while texts may be produced in a linear fashion, they are nevertheless hierarchically organized and processed as episodes – semantic units dominated by higher level macropropositions (van Dijk and Kintsch, 1983). This episode organization has dramatic consequences for reference tracking in texts.

The notion of episode as a semantic unit dominated by a macroproposition has been found to have psychological relevance in several studies. Black and Bower (1979), for example, demonstrated in a psychological study of story processing the existence of episodes as chunks in narrative memory. Similarly, Guindon and Kintsch (1984) in their experiment studying the macrostructure of texts found that macrostructure formation appears to be a virtually automatic process. That is, people appear to form macrostructures during reading and derive relevant macropropositions of a passage as soon as possible. Their findings provided evidence for the episode and the *macrostructure* theories of Kintsch and van Dijk (1978) and Schank and Abelson (1977).

Gernsbacher (1990) supports the episodic organization of stories, reporting that comprehenders capture the episode structure of narratives in their mental representation by building separate substructures to represent each episode. Readers build new mental substructures for new episodes, where information on the previous episode is less accessible to them. It is therefore harder for readers to draw coherence inferences across two episodes than within the same episode.

The cognitive basis of discourse organization helps us further understand the relationship between discourse structure and anaphora. An episode, as a semantic unit subsumed under a macroproposition, is the textual manifestation of a memory chunk which represents sustained attentional effort and endures until an episode boundary is reached. Attention shifts when the processing of the episode is completed. In other words, 'the macroproposition remains in Short Term Memory for the rest of the interpretation of the same episode. As soon as propositions are interpreted that no longer fit that macroproposition, a new macroproposition is set up' (van Dijk, 1982: 191). At an episode boundary, where a change of macro-proposition occurs (that is, new agents, places, times, objects or possible worlds are expected to be introduced), the encoding load is much heavier, the reference under concern is less accessible, and hence a more explicit anaphoric form (such as an NP) is required to code the referent. Within an episode, when the macroproposition is maintained, the referent under consideration is more accessible and hence a less explicit anaphoric form (such as a pronominal) is sufficient to code the reference.

Indeed many studies on anaphora have reported the alternation between nominal and pronominals to be a function of the paragraph or episodic structure. Hinds (1977), for example, discusses how paragraph structure controls the choice of NPs and pronouns. He finds that noun phrases are used to convey 'semantically prominent' information in peak sentences of a paragraph while pronouns are used to indicate 'semantically subordinate' information in non-peak sentences. Fox (1987) demonstrated that structural factors of discourse establish the basic patterns of anaphora: NPs are generally used at the beginning of a 'development structure' to demarcate new narrative units, whereas pronominals are used within that structure. Marslen-Wilson et al. (1982) also argue that a speaker's use of referential devices is governed by discourse structure and the context of speaking. The general pattern of anaphora is that NPs and proper names are used to establish initial reference at an episode when a particular referent is in a state of low focus, whereas pronouns are used to maintain reference within an action sequence when a particular referent is in a state of high focus.

While the episode model presupposes the importance of cognitive con-straints and hierarchical organization of discourse, it faces difficulties to the extent that structural units such as paragraph, episode, event and theme are not well defined theoretically. Many structural units are hard to identify in spoken and written texts, and are prone to misinterpretation.

Tomlin (1987a) attempts to solve the problem of prior studies by introducing the attention model, where he ties the use of anaphora directly to the cognitive activities of attention and memory. He argues that an episode represents sustained attentional effort and endures until attention is diverted (that is, an episode boundary is reached). In his study, each episode was represented by a slide picture; the shutter release cycle of the slide projector, which imposed a sufficiently strong perceptual disruption for the subject, served as the episode boundary. He demonstrated experi-mentally that NPs are used at the boundary of episodes when attention shifts, while pronominals are used within episodes when attention is sus-tained (see Tomlin and Pu, 1991).

Another important model of referential management is the distance model proposed by Givón (1983), which argues for a correlation between anaphora and referential distance in discourse, such as number of clauses between a given anaphor and its antecedent. The distance model may be a manifestation of a psychological factor, such as short term memory decay. The 'iconicity principle' underlying the model is that the longer the distance, the harder it is for the listener to identify the referent, and so a more explicit referential form (such as a full noun phrase) is required. The shorter the distance, the easier it is for the listener to identify the referent, and hence a less explicit referential form (a lexical pronoun or a zero anaphor – ellipsis) is required.

The Thematic Management of Discourse

The key insight within thematic management is that certain concepts and propositions seem more central or important to the development of the discourse than others. Such central concepts and propositions provide the framework or scaffolding around which the details of the discourse are emplaced. Such central concepts and propositions seem to be what is better remembered when a discourse is interpreted. The key questions are: (1) What makes a concept or proposition more central? (2) How is that centrality tied to the developing discourse? (3) What does the speaker do to convey centrality to the listener? and (4) How does the listener know when to construe a concept or proposition as central?

Thematic management in discourse concerns four interrelated problem areas. First, at least historically first, is the problem of clause level *theme* or *topic*. In general, it appears that each clause in a discourse contains one key element – the *theme* – which is somehow the *central* referent at that moment, a *point of departure* for the clause, the referent *about which* the remainder of the clause predicates something. Second, there is the problem of higher level paragraph or *discourse theme*. In this area, one is concerned with either the centrality or the significance of a referent globally or with the aggregate propositional goal of a discourse or some major component unit. Third, there is the problem of *foregrounding* in discourse. Propositions in a discourse can be sorted into at least two coarse sets. Some propositions relate key concepts or events in discourse; others in one way or another elaborate or provide supporting information. The former are called *fore-grounded* propositions; the latter *background*. Finally, there is growing interest in the cognitive underpinnings of thematic management, in particular the relationship of theme to cognitive processes of memory, attention, and consciousness.

Theme or Topic: Conceptual Starting Point

There are several quite excellent reviews of ideas and issues of clause level theme or topic (Goodenough, 1983; Gundel, 1988b; Jones, 1977). Each clause or utterance is theorized to contain one element which is more important or central to the discourse; or, more technically, which serves as the *starting point* of the utterance; or which serves as the element *about which* the predication is asserted.

To understand the idea of theme or topic requires that one deal with a number of interrelated matters. One, there is the theoretical definition of theme or topic, which is generally articulated in terms of *starting point* or *aboutness*. Two, there is its manifestation through syntactic form, most generally discussed in terms of constituent order (initial or preposed), or syntactic subject, or other morpho-syntactic cues (such as *wa* in Japanese: Hinds et al., 1987). Three, there is the interplay between these two areas, the extent to which the definitions of theme or topic include information about its syntactic manifestation.

In the paragraph fragment in (5), the bold-faced NPs are ostensibly clause level themes. In each case, the referent seems introspectively to satisfy requirements of importance, centrality, starting point, and aboutness.

(5) Text fragment from popular novel *Sarum* by E. Rutherford (1988: 206)
  1 Late in the winter, while **the snow** was still on the ground,
     a new figure of great significance arrived on the island.
     He was tall, middle aged, with a thin, kindly face and receding
        hair.
     He had two peculiarities that Porteus observed:
  5 **he** stooped when he spoke to people,
     as though Ø concentrating intently on what they said;
     but when Ø not involved in conversation
     his eyes often seemed to grow distant
     as though **he** were dreaming of some far off place.
  10 **He** was Julius Classicianus, the new procurator and replacement
        for the disgraced Decianus Catus.
     His responsibility included all the island's finances.
     Under the Roman system of divided authority, **he** reported direct
        to the emperor.

From a global point of view, this paragraph introduces a new character to the novel, one Julius Classicianus, and provides his initial description.[4] This paragraph illustrates well the basic ideas and issues surrounding clause level theme or topic. First, several of the clauses exhibit prototypical cases of clause level theme (3, 4, 5, 10, 12). In each of these cases, the referent of the bold-faced NP is the central or most important character in this paragraph. It is also the referent about whom the predication is asserted. And, it is also the referent from which the description proceeds. Though it cannot be a defining characteristic of theme, it is also not an accident that the relevant NP in each case is the subject of the clause. It is on such cases that the central theoretical ideas of theme and topic have been constructed.

Second, several of the clauses illustrate cases which remain problematic in discussions of theme and topic. One, it is not clear how to treat the subject of clause 2, *a new figure of great significance*. Some argue that this NP is *not* a theme because the information is referentially new, unlike the NPs in the prototypical cases. Others argue that this NP *is* thematic precisely because its referential status is in principle independent of its thematic status, and in this clause it is this NP which is the starting point of the utterance and about which a predication is asserted.

Two, it is not clear how to treat the subjects of clauses 8 and 11. Neither denotes the principal character of the paragraph, so it is difficult to sustain a view that the referent is somehow important. Yet for each clause itself, the bold-faced NP seems to be the starting point of the utterance and the NP about which the utterance is predicated.

Three, there are a number of subordinate clauses, some embedded, which have either explicit or elliptic subjects. It remains unclear exactly how the thematic status of key NPs in these clauses is to be treated.

With these observations in mind, we can turn to explore more carefully major ideas about clause level theme and topic.

Conceptual Foundations for Theme and Topic

Despite individual variation in the formulation of definitions and the specific terms defined, there are essentially three basic ideas of what constitutes a clause level theme or topic: (1) the theme is what the sentence is *about*, (2) the theme is the *starting point* of the sentence, and (3) the theme is the *center of attention* for the sentence.

Theme as Aboutness Classical scholarship on language and logic distinguished those portions of a sentence about which something is predicated and that which is predicated of it. In classical terms the difference between *subject* and *predicate* was exactly this sort of difference. Modern and contemporary research developed this idea, leading to many formulations of clause level theme or topic in terms of aboutness. A particular referent counts as theme when it is this referent that the remainder of the sentence is about. One classic 'test' for aboutness comes from Gundel (1974; 1988b): in a given context, a particular NP will count as a topic (for Gundel) if it can be included in a preposed adverbial with *As for*. Thus, the bold-faced NP in example (5), clause 8, counts as a topic because this referent felicitously fits into the following sentence:

(6)   As for **his eyes**, they seemed to grow distant . . .

Theme or topic as *aboutness* dominates current research in this area. It begins with classical research from the Prague School, proceeds through Halliday (1967b; 1973; 1976) and Halliday and Fawcett (1987), and features prominently in much current research (Gundel, 1974; 1988b; Hajicovà, 1984; Lambrecht, 1994; Reinhart, 1981; Vallduví, 1992).

Theme as Starting Point Another way of conceptualizing theme is as the starting point of the utterance as a message. In this view, the speaker plans his message to proceed from a point of view held in common with the listener out to a message novel to the listener. The starting point helps to frame the utterance, tying the predication to something already known and shared by the discourse participants. It is a common feature of this approach to require that theme be given or known information. This approach differs from *aboutness* largely in terms of its greater emphasis on the dynamic nature of discourse, on its processing over time or its flow in time (Chafe, 1994).

This approach is reflected in the early work of Weil (1887) and very early formulations of Prague School thinking (Mathesius, 1929). More recent work employing this view includes Chafe (1994) and MacWhinney (1977).

Theme as Center of Attention   There is yet a third view of theme which ties the clause level theme or topic to some notion of attention. Early work in this area observes that certain concepts come to mind first in the production of utterances, and it is this coming into consciousness that defines the theme. Thus, van der Gabelenz (discussed in Gundel, 1974: 24) distinguishes *psychological subject*, 'the idea which appears first in the consciousness of the speaker . . . what makes him think and what he wants the hearer to think of', from *psychological predicate*, 'that which is joined to the psychological subject'. There is also important work in psycholinguistics which takes this view (Prentice, 1967; Sridhar, 1988; Tannenbaum and Williams, 1968). More recently, some linguists have examined how cognitive theories of attention are tied to the classical notions of theme or topic (Tomlin, 1983; 1995; 1997).

Historical Foundations of Theme and Topic

Historically, theoretical ideas of theme and topic, at least as they affect contemporary scholarship, have emerged from Prague School research. Similar ideas are taken up by Halliday, Dik, and an array of researchers in North America.

Prague School Formulations of Theme and Topic   For contemporary work in discourse the most important source of ideas for theme and topic has been the Prague School (Daneš, 1974; Firbas, 1964b; 1974). Its precursor, Henri Weil, merits mention at the outset, for Weil published an early (1844) treatise on comparative word order studies in which he attributed the flexible word orders of Latin and ancient Greek to a pragmatic notion he called 'the march of ideas' (Weil, 1887). In Super's (1887) translation, Weil observes that it is important for the speaker to place the listener at the same point of view as the speaker, that this can be done by providing a word of introduction preceding the remark intended about it. The interlocutors can then lean on something present and known in order to reach out to something less present and unknown. Weil treats the central notion of his 'march of ideas' as a point of departure, an initial notion on which the two intelligences meet.

The Prague School founder, Vilem Mathesius, was much influenced by Weil, and Mathesius's treatment of theme remains seminal for the field.

For Mathesius (1929; 1939; 1975) the theme was the *starting point of the utterance*. It was information already known to both speaker and listener which served also as the point of departure for the sentence as a whole. In later formulations the theme (or foundation) was also something that is being spoken about in the sentence. Thus, in example (5), lines 3, 4, 5, 10, the information conveyed by the bold-faced NP is in each case the theme because it is known to both interlocutors and because it serves as the conceptual starting point against which other information is construed, what is called the *rheme* (or sometimes *core* for Mathesius in particular).

This basic view of theme is sustained in one or another formulation among Prague School researchers. So, for example, Travnicek (discussed in Firbas, 1964b) defines the theme as the sentence element that links up directly with the object of thought, proceeds from it, and opens the sentence thereby. Travnicek rejects the notion that theme must be known or given information. Beneš (also discussed in Firbas 1964b) distinguishes the *basis* of the sentence from the *theme*. The basis is the opening element of the sentence which links up the utterance with the context and the situation, selecting from various possible connections one that becomes their starting point, from which the further utterance unfolds. The theme, following Firbas, is the element with the lowest degree of communicative dynamism.

One important variation in this arena is found in work by Jan Firbas (1964a; 1964b; 1974; 1987a; 1987b; 1992). While other Prague School efforts pursued a bipartite treatment of the sentence into theme and rheme or topic and comment, Firbas considered the information in the utterance to contribute to its development continuously. He articulated a scalar idea of sentence information he called *communicative dynamism* (CD). Information in the utterance was seen to fall somewhere on a continuous scale of novelty, beginning with elements with the lowest CD and moving through the utterance to those of highest CD. Thematic elements are those with the lowest degree of CD.

Halliday and Systemic Grammar   A second tradition of research on theme is found in Halliday's (1985) systemic grammar. Halliday (1967b; 1976) treats theme not as the starting point of the utterance but as the clausal element *about which* the remainder of the clause is predicated. Thus, in example (5) the elements identified as theme are the elements for which the remainder of the sentence provides elaborative predication. The difference in use between active and passive clauses in English (see Cumming and Ono, Chapter 4 in this volume, for more detail) is very much tied to whether it is the semantic agent or patient about which the remainder of the sentence is predicated.

Dik and Functional Grammar   While most discussions of theme and topic select one of these terms as their clause level thematic notion, Dik's (1978) theory of functional grammar employs both. A given sentence is composed, in part, of a theme as well as a possible topic. For Dik, a theme is an extra-clausal element preposed to the clause itself, and designates the universe of discourse with respect to which subsequent predication is construed as relevant or connected. Dik's theme is well illustrated by preposed adverbials headed by *As for* in English:

(7) *As for Professor Smith*, she's always helpful to students.

The preposed adverbial is the theme in that it specifies the universe of discourse (*Professor Smith*) against which the predication is construed as relevant (always *helpful to students*).

Topic represents a different notion within functional grammar. A topic presents the entity *about which* the predicate predicates something in the given setting. Thus, the answer to the question in (8), being about John, begins with John as its topic.

(8) To whom did John give the book?
     JOHN gave the book to *Mary*.
     TOPIC   FOCUS

It is possible to observe individual sentences with both theme and topic:

(9) *As for sushi, my favorite* is made with fresh tuna.
     THEME   TOPIC

The preposed theme specifies the universe of discourse within which the predication is to be construed; the topic represents the particular entity the predication is about.

North American Traditions There is no established North American school for discourse studies analogous to the Prague School or systemic grammar or Dik's functional grammar. There are, however, a number of important lines of research dealing with theme (and topic). Gundel (1974; 1988a; 1988b) offered an early treatment of topic in which topic is defined in terms of aboutness. Chafe (1976; 1980a; 1994) approaches the problem through a notion of *starting point*, which he treats as the conceptual beginning of information flow in discourse. Lambrecht (1994) defines topic in terms of aboutness. Vallduví (1992) develops a notion of topic similar to Reinhart's, incorporating ideas of aboutness with initial position. Tomlin (1983; 1995; 1997) argues for a cognitive account of theme, tying classical notions of theme to attention and its dynamic employment during discourse production.

There are numerous other efforts of interest to students of discourse. These include Goodenough (1983), Hawkinson and Hyman (1974), Jones (1977), Keenan (1976) and Keenan and Schieffelin (1976), among others.

Multiple Uses of the Terms 'topic' and 'theme'

The expression 'topic' is used widely to capture ideas similar to clause level theme. A careful look at the literature reveals at least three distinct uses.

'Topic' as Thematic Element   In some writing a clause level *topic* is identical to clause level theme, the two terms being used virtually synonymously. This can be found in many places (Dahl, 1969; 1974; Hajicovà, 1984; Sgall, 1987).

'Topic' as a Composite Grammatical Unit   In other work, the term *topic* is used to capture an extra-clausal adjunct generally preposed in the clause. In models of discourse which adopt this strategy a topic represents a composite between a pragmatic notion akin to theme and a structural reflex of that notion, typically but not always initial position. Thus, a topic can be distinguished from a theme or from a subject (which in such cases is treated as having a thematic component). Li and Thompson (1976) drew a distinction at one point between subject prominent and topic prominent languages, the latter characterized by topics which are defined as preposed and discourse central. More recently, Lambrecht (1981; 1987a; 1987b) describes a topic slot for French, this slot being located sentence initially but outside the core clause. In a similar vein, Dik and his colleagues also define a clause external unit, though they use the term 'theme' to describe this unit.

There has even been some effort to capture the notion of topic within the configurational structures of government and binding theory and its predecessors (Chomsky, 1965; Aissen, 1992).

'Topic' as Referent   Perhaps the greatest departure from original Prague School senses of theme and topic is found in the literature of *topic continuity* (Givón, 1983; 1989). For Givón the notion of topic is tied to the accessibility of a referent in a conceptual representation. The more accessible a referent is, the higher its degree of topicality. Since topicality is defined by a scale, all referential elements in the utterance in principle can be assigned a topicality value of one kind or another. Thus, every referent to one degree or another is a topic.[5]

Discourse Level Theme (Global Theme)

To understand the problem of higher level or discourse level theme, we must distinguish between the centrality or significance of a referent globally and the aggregate propositional goal of a discourse or some major component of a discourse.

Generally, in a stretch of connected discourse, one referent emerges as central, or the one that the propositions in the discourse are about. This global significance of one referent affects choices made at the clause level; that is, the clause level theme is in some way a local reflection of some higher level unit of discourse – something like a paragraph or episode. Given two competing referents at the clause level, it seems natural that the local theme would be related to the same but more general or higher order theme. That is, if a given paragraph or episode is about Mary (and not really about John), then clauses in that paragraph dealing with both Mary and John should tend to treat Mary as clause level theme because Mary contributes to better cohesion with the higher level episode or paragraph theme.

In much the same way as clause level matters are tied to higher level paragraphs or episodes, so, too, are these mid-level units connected to yet higher level structures. While the embedding of lower level units into higher ones is ultimately recursive, in most discourse studies one seldom looks beyond the three levels of organization and development: clause level or local; paragraph or episode; and overall text or discourse or global.

The term 'global theme' is also related to the notion of what the overall discourse is about. In this case, the global theme has the form of a proposition rather than a noun phrase (Jones, 1977; Keenan and Schieffelin, 1976; van Dijk, 1985). Although not as strong as the claims on local sentence level themes, there has been a recognition of the importance of global theme. As an illustration, consider the following passage (from van Dijk, 1985: 298):

(10)   This morning I had a toothache. I went to the dentist. The dentist has a big car. The car was bought in New York. New York has had serious financial troubles.

Although each sentence is connected with the previous one by having a common referent, the passage as a whole lacks coherence, owing to the lack of a global theme. Rochester and Martin (1977) report that connected but incoherent discourse is characteristic of thought-disordered and schizophrenic patients.

Related to global theme is the notion of macrostructure formulated by van Dijk (1977; 1980; 1985). Macrostructure is the global semantic structure of a discourse and may be expressed by its title or headline or by summarizing sentences. Macrostructure propositions are derived by macrorules, that is, by eliminating those propositions which are not relevant for the interpretation of other propositions (deletion), by converting a series of specific propositions into a more general proposition (generalization) and by constructing a proposition from a number of propositions in the text (construction), and from activated world knowledge.

Work in the field of psycholinguistics has demonstrated that a well defined global theme facilitates text comprehension; it functions as an advance organizer (Frase, 1975), scaffolding (Anderson et al., 1978), or anchor point (Pichert and Anderson, 1977) by evoking a mental model (representation) in the comprehender. Such a representation might be called *schema* (Rumelhart, 1980), *frame* (Minsky, 1975), *script* (Schank and Abelson, 1977), or *scenario* (Sanford and Garrod, 1980). The fact that comprehenders construct discourse models as well as linguistic representations has been corroborated in a number of studies. In one of the most frequently cited experiments, Bransford and Johnson (1972) asked their subjects to listen to and later recall the following passage:

(11)   The procedure is actually quite simple. First you arrange things into
       different groups depending on their makeup. Of course, one pile may
       be sufficient depending on how much there is to do. If you have to
       go somewhere else due to lack of facilities that is the next step,
       otherwise you are pretty well set. It is important not to overdo any
       particular endeavor. That is, it is better to do few things at once
       than too many. In the short run this may not seem important, but
       complication from doing too many can easily arise. A mistake can
       be expensive as well. The manipulation of the appropriate
       mechanisms should be self-explanatory, and we need not dwell on
       it here. At first, the whole procedure will seem complicated. Soon,
       however, it will become just another facet of life. It is difficult to
       foresee any end to the necessity for this task in the immediate future,
       but then one never can tell.

Their results indicated that the subjects who were provided with the title
'washing clothes' before reading the passage recalled it significantly better
than those who were provided with no title, or those who were provided
with a title after reading it.

    Lastly, how do sentence level theme and discourse level theme interact
with each other? There has been widespread speculation that the
assignment of lower level themes is a function of the higher level themes.
Although this may be true, Kim's (1994) experimental study which separ-
ated global theme from local theme showed that their influences on subject
assignment in English are both significant and suggested that they, in fact,
have separate functions in discourse production.

Foreground and Background: Propositional Centrality

Like other central discourse notions, the idea of *foreground* versus *background* information in discourse arises from attempts to explain structural
alternations in language for which no obvious semantic explanations are
apparent. Consider, for example, the paragraph in (12):

(12)   Sample paragraph
       It was a calm, peaceful day *as the little fish took its daily swim
       throughout its home territory. Gracefully sliding up to the surface of the
       water,* **the little fish is startled by one of its feared enemies – the crab.
       They stare at each other surprisedly,** *though the little fish soon realized
       its danger. Before the little fish could escape unharmed,* **the crab began
       to attack frantically,** *its long claws snapping at any part of the fish.
       Without thinking twice about it,* **the fish dashed away from the crab.**[6]

The italicized clauses are all dependent adverbial clauses; the bold-faced
clauses are all straightforward independent clauses. The critical question is
this: what determines whether a given proposition in this fragment shows
up as a dependent clause or as an independent clause? The classical

answer, reflected in any of dozens of composition texts, appears simple enough: the more important ideas are found in the independent clauses, the less important and supporting ideas are found in the dependent clauses. And it is this classical idea that is captured and developed in the various treatments of the discourse notion of *foreground* versus *background information*.

The earliest work on foregrounding (Longacre, 1968; 1976a; Grimes, 1975; cf. also Labov and Waletzky, 1967) distinguished *backbone* information from *background* information and employed this distinction to account for syntactic alternations in a number of languages. Longacre (1976a), for example, examined the use of the *waw*-predicate construction in biblical Hebrew. On the surface, there seems to be no semantic difference between clauses with the *waw*-predicate and those without. However, in looking at their distribution in text data, in particular the Flood narrative in the Old Testament, Longacre observed that the subset of clauses with the *waw*-predicate construction formed a coherent abstract of the overall narrative while the remaining clauses did not. Thus, it appeared that the *waw*-predicate construction was used to signal the importance of the clauses forming the backbone of the narrative.

Later work by Hopper (1979) developed the original ideas of Longacre and Grimes. For Hopper, information could be characterized as either foreground or background. Foreground information in narrative discourse includes 'the parts of the narrative belonging to the skeletal structure of the discourse' (1979: 213). Background information is 'the language of supportive material which does not itself relate the main events' (1979: 213). Hopper examined the distribution of foreground and background information in a number of languages, claiming that foreground clauses correlate with both independent clauses and perfective aspect (Hopper, 1979; Hopper and Thompson, 1980). Further, Hopper linked foreground information with the event line of narrative discourse (Hopper, 1979; Labov and Waletzky, 1967). The clauses which relate events falling on the main event line are foreground clauses, while those which do not fall on the main event line are the background ones.

Most work on the foregound–background distinction has been directed at narrative discourse. However, narrative is not the only kind of discourse one's treatment of foregrounding ultimately must deal with. Expository discourse in particular requires a treatment of foregrounding which is not dependent on the notion of event line for its theoretical definition (Jones and Jones, 1979). Tomlin (1984; 1985; 1986) offers a treatment of foregrounding which alleviates the dependence on event line for both theoretical and empirical purposes. In this treatment, foregrounding is viewed as a thematic matter. The centrality of any given proposition in discourse arises from the intersection of the theme of the discourse at that point – the subject matter being developed – and the rhetorical goal of the discourse, whether that goal is to narrate, or describe, or evaluate, and so on.

Focus Management

The central observation within focus management is that certain concepts and propositions seem to be more novel or unexpected from the listener's viewpoint. In fact, the novel concepts and propositions appear to be the target of the speaker's utterance, that is, what the speaker wishes the listener to specifically add to her mental representation. The key questions are: (1) What makes a concept or proposition more novel? (2) How is the novel concept tied to the developing discourse? (3) What does the speaker do to convey the novelty to the listener? and (4) How does the listener know when to construe a concept or proposition as novel?

One problem is that of the newness of particular pieces of information in the utterance. Generally, each clause contains one element which contains new information. This central new idea is the *focus*. Traditionally, it has been linked with the Prague School notion of *rheme* (as opposed to *theme*) and *newsworthiness* (Mithun, 1987). A second aspect of focus is that the information may not be expected by the listener because it clashes with information that she already has. So, the focus may be the speaker's attempt to get the listener to replace some incorrect information with the correct information. Finally, focus is related to the cognitive notion of prominence or salience. Focus is the information that 'stands outs' from other information. If discourse were not like this, in Longacre's words, 'the result [would be] like being presented with a piece of black paper and being told, "This is a picture of black camels crossing black sands at midnight"' (1976b: 10). This unequal prominence of some elements over others is necessary for human cognition. We perceive something when it 'leaps out' from the surrounding area.

Focus as Prominence

The term 'focus' is used by linguists to refer to the resources available to speakers for packaging information in order to make some information stand out for the listener. While thematic management is concerned with how the speaker lets the listener know what information is more central to the discourse, focus management is concerned with how the speaker lets the listener know what in particular she should notice about that central element.

All languages provide speakers with a variety of devices for making some information seem more prominent or significant than other information. In English (as in many other languages), some words can be said with extra stress. For example, consider these sentences:

(13)   I'M not mad at you.
(14)   I'm not mad at YOU.

In each case, the actual words are the same, but by putting extra stress on different words, slightly different meanings can be conveyed. Sentence (13) implies that while I'm not mad at anyone, someone else is, in fact, mad at you. On the other hand, (14) implies that I *am* mad at someone, but my anger is not directed towards you. By making one word stand out more than the others, the listener is invited to infer why that particular piece of information is important and contrast it with other possible situations. In these situations, the focused information is said to have a contrastive function.

Intonation is not the only device speakers can use to make certain information stand out to listeners. Languages may also use special constituent orders, morphological markers, or grammatical constructions to make some information more prominent. For example, English has a special structure called a cleft-sentence, which fulfills this function. Cleft-sentences have the form 'It was X that Y', where X is an NP and Y is a statement about the referent of the NP. This structure focuses whatever element is in the X slot. Whatever is in the Y slot is assumed to be true, that is, it is presupposed. Consider the following sentences:

(15)   It was Mary that went to the party.
(16)   It was the party that Mary went to.

In (15), 'Mary' is the focused information. The speaker presupposes that there was a party and that someone went to it. He or she uses the cleft-sentence to tell the listener to associate the notion 'someone' with the person 'Mary'. This is very different from the structuring of information (16). Here the speaker presupposes that Mary went somewhere. He or she uses this cleft-sentence to tell the listener that the notion of 'somewhere' should be associated with 'the party'.

Another common device for focusing information is to put it in a special position by altering the usual word order of the sentence. Usually, focused elements appear first or last in a sentence where they are more likely to be noticed, rather than being put in the middle. In English, the speaker can move constituents that normally occur at the end of the clause to the beginning in order to make them more prominent. For example, in the sentence

(17)   Coffee I like, but tea I don't.

'coffee' and 'tea' have been moved to the beginning of their respective clauses. In that position, they are more salient to the listener and the contrast between them is heightened. This strategy of moving NPs to the first or last position in order to focus them is found over and over again in the world's languages. It probably reflects speakers' intuitive capitalization on universal properties of human cognitive processing in order to meet their discourse goals.

Formulations of Focus

These differences of importance between the elements of a sentence were first characterized by Weil (1887 (1844)). He proposed that the 'focus' of one sentence is related to the topic (or theme) of the next. His work was followed by the Prague School scholars who were interested in the communicative dynamism of the elements of sentences (Firbas, 1974; Vachek, 1966). Recall that the communicative dynamism of an element is the degree to which it moves the sentence forward. The focus or 'rheme' is the part of the sentence with the highest degree of communicative dynamism, that is the predicate or the comment portion of the sentence or 'what is being said about' the theme. In the Prague School framework, sentences might not have a topic, but every sentence had a focus. If there were no focus, there would not be any information relevant for communication. Thus,

(18)   A girl broke a VASE.

has a focus but not a topic/theme, since none of the information has been previously talked about.

Halliday (1967a) elaborated the Prague School work, investigating what he called *information structure*. Like the Prague School scholars, he used ideas of the newness or givenness of information. For Halliday, focus was the new information marked by pitch prominence, while theme was the element expressed in the first position of a sentence. From Halliday's point of view, WH-words ('what', etc.) were themes; this was contrary to the Prague School, which argued that they were focus, but never theme. Also, notice that Halliday's approach does not work for cleft-sentences. In these constructions, the first element is not 'what's being talked about'. Another problem with this approach is that the surface structure of natural languages has both ambiguity and synonymy. That is, a single structure can have more than one meaning (ambiguity), and several structures can have the same meaning (synonymy). Consequently, an element of structure, such as first position, cannot be used directly to define notions of meaning.

Following Halliday's work and later work by Chomsky (1970), the importance of topic and focus in determining the meaning of sentences (that is, their semantic representation) was recognized and accepted by most linguists. It is often assumed that, in many European languages, focus is primarily in the last position. In this position, it need not be marked with stress. When a focused element occurs earlier in the sentence, it receives intonational stress and the NPs which follow it are theme. Other languages use variations of these strategies. For example, in Yagua (Payne, 1992), focused information occurs in the first position in the sentence and is also sometimes repeated in the last position, just in case the listener missed it.

An important contribution to the study of focus was Chafe's (1976) work on the statuses of referents, that is the ideas that nouns within a sentence represent. One status is the 'speaker's assessment of how the addressee is able to process what he is saying against the background of a particular context' (1976: 27). Here, focus has to do with how the message is packaged, that is, how the speaker presents the message to the listener, rather than the content of the message *per se*. The speaker packages messages in different ways, depending on his assessment of the listener's mental state, that is what she is presently thinking about. Also, the speaker makes judgments about what is important and needs to be emphasized, what has been said in previous discourse, and what the listener already knows.

Chafe investigates focus of contrast (or contrastiveness) as one packaging phenomenon. In English, this is conveyed by high pitch and stress on one element of the sentence. For example, consider the sentence:

(19)   RONALD made the hamburgers.

This conveys information that: the speaker knows that, out of a group of possible candidates the listener might be thinking of, Ronald rather than one of the others did it. According to Chafe, in using this construction, (1) the speaker assumes that both the speaker and the listener know that someone made hamburgers (Chafe calls this background knowledge); (2) the speaker assumes that the listener entertains or perhaps actually believes that someone other than Ronald did it; and (3) the speaker asserts that Ronald is the correct someone. Thus, by focusing one element of the sentence, the speaker may directly contradict a previous assertion of the listener. Chafe calls the asserted alternative the 'focus of contrast'. He suggests, as a rule of thumb, that a phrase beginning with the words 'rather than . . .' can felicitously follow the assertion. Chafe argues that focuses of contrast assert the correctness of a particular referent, but the referent itself is *not* new information; the speaker assumes it is already in the mind of the listener. Chafe also permits a single sentence to have more than one focus of contrast. For example, in

(20)   RONALD made the HAMBURGERS.

the assertion is that the particular referents have a particular pairing or relationship or role in the event under discussion.

A very useful and detailed discussion of the different types of focus phenomena found in language was presented by Dik (Dik et al., 1981; Dik, 1989). Dik regards focus as a pragmatic function and studies it within the framework of functional grammar. He tries to determine what different categories of focus there must be if we are to account for all the focus phenomena of different languages. Like others, Dik (1978; 1989) contrasts topic and focus:

1 *Topic*: the topic presents the entity 'about' which the predication predicates something in the given setting.
2 *Focus*: the focus represents what is relatively the most important or salient information in the given setting.

According to Dik, 'A constituent with Focus function presents information bearing upon the difference in pragmatic information between Speaker and Addressee, as estimated by the Speaker' (1978: 149). For example, consider these sentences:

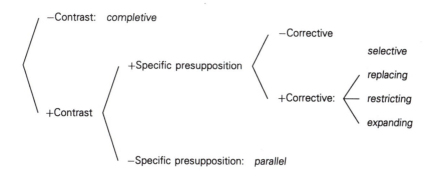

Figure 3.4 *Dik's overall model of focus*

(21) A: What did John buy?
     B: John bought an umbrella.

Speaker A indicates a difference between himself and the listener about the identity of a particular item and B's answer eliminates the difference. The NP 'an umbrella' is the important or salient information which eliminates the difference and thus is the focus.

Examples using WH-questions, such as the one above, are critical to Dik's approach to focus. In fact, Dik takes WH-questions as diagnostic of what the focus of a sentence is. Thus, the answer to the question 'Who ate what in the restaurant?' must have two referents which are assigned focus. Consequently, focus is different from functions like agent and subject. A function such as subject cannot be assigned to more than one constituent per predication, while focus may be assigned to more than one constituent in a predication. Dik also makes clear that focused information is not necessarily new information, although it may well be. The focus function is defined as presenting information about the *difference* in pragmatic information between speaker and addressee, and this information need not be new. The speaker may focus information to stress its importance and to reactivate that information in the listener's memory.

Dik subcategorizes the focus function based on the uses to which it can be put. These subtypes of focus function are organized as in Figure 3.4. Each of the six subtypes of focus has a special function. Let's examine these different functions using examples drawn from Dik et al. (1981). Consider the following exchange:

(22) A: What did John buy?
     B: John bought COFFEE.

In B's statement, the focused element, 'coffee', is a *non-contrastive completive focus* because it simply emphasizes information that is meant to fill some gap in the listener's information. Alternatively, all *contrastive focus* types put some piece of information in opposition to other information, either implicitly or explicitly. One way to do this is with *selective focus*, which selects one item from among a set of several possible values. For example, in a slightly different exchange,

(23)   A: Did John buy coffee or rice?
       B: John bought COFFEE.

B's use of 'coffee' is a selective focus, because it selects one item from a group. This differs from *replacing focus*, which attempts to remove some incorrect information from the listener's mental representation and replace it with the correct information. So, in the exchange

(24)   A: John bought rice.
       B: No, John bought COFFEE.

B is attempting to remove the incorrect information, 'rice', and replace it with the correct information, namely 'coffee'. A speaker may also try to correct the listener's information by using *restricting focus* to narrow the value of the information even further than he or she believes the listener has. For example, consider the exchange:

(25)   A: John bought rice and coffee.
       B: No, John only bought COFFEE.

In this case speaker B notes that A's information includes correct and incorrect information. By focusing 'coffee', B attempts to restrict the information to the correct items. Speakers may also use *expanding focus* to add more information when the listener's information seems to be incomplete, although essentially correct. This can be seen in the following:

(26)   A: John bought rice.
       B: Yes, but he also bought COFFEE.

Here B's remark adds information to A's essentially correct statement. Finally, the speaker may use *parallel focus* to contrast two pieces of information within one linguistic expression. This case is illustrated by the sentence

(27)   JOHN bought COFFEE, but PETER bought RICE.

Here, all four NPs have the focus function, but what the speaker is specifically contrasting are the pairs of relationships.

More recently, Lambrecht (1994) has investigated the issue of focus. Like Chafe and Halliday, Lambrecht has been concerned with how information is structured. He seeks to understand how speakers manipulate the focus of an utterance to meet what they assume are the needs of the listener. For Lambrecht, the focus is that portion of the proposition which is asserted, that is what the listener is expected to know or take for granted as a result of hearing the sentence uttered. Asserted information is contrasted with presupposed information, that is what the speaker assumes the listener *already* knows or is ready to take for granted. Lambrecht has identified three distinct types of focus: predicate focus, argument focus, and sentence focus. Each type occurs in distinctly different types of communicative situations. Consider the exchange

(28)   Q: What happened to your car?
       A: My car broke down.

According to Lambrecht, the answer in this exchange is an example of a *predicate focus*. Here, the speaker's car is presupposed since it is already known to the listener; the focus, or information not known to the listener (who asked the question in the first place), is the predicate 'broke down'. Consider this same answer in reply to a different question:

(29)   Q: I heard your motorcycle broke down?
       A: My car broke down.

In this case, the speaker uttering the answer presupposes that the listener knows that something belonging to the speaker broke down; the speaker asserts that that thing is the speaker's car, and thus the argument 'car' is the focus of the proposition. Thus, Lambrecht terms this an example of *argument focus*. Finally, consider this same answer in response to another question:

(30)   Q: What happened?
       A: My car broke down.

Lambrecht calls this an example of *sentence focus*. In this case, there is no presupposed information at all; the entire sentence is the focus.

Prince (1978) has tried to understand the functions of two different English focus constructions by studying their use in natural discourse. These constructions, known as clefts (or it-clefts) and pseudo-clefts (or WH-clefts), are shown in the following examples:

(31)   (a)   John lost his keys.   neutral construction
       (b)   What John lost was his keys.   pseudo-cleft
       (c)   It was his keys that John lost. cleft

Although all three sentences convey the same basic information, they differ in the way they package the pieces of information. Specifically, they differ in terms of what information is *focus* and what is presupposition. Logically, both (b) and (c) presuppose that 'John lost something' while (a) does not (see Prince, 1978: 884 for a more thorough discussion). The information that is not presupposed in (b) and (c) is the identity of the 'something', namely, 'the keys', which is the focus. Since both (b) and (c) have the same presuppositions and the same focus, many linguists have considered them essentially synonymous (Bolinger, 1972; Chafe, 1976). Prince's investigation of the phenomena as they occur in natural discourse showed that this is not the case.

In order to explain the difference between clefts and pseudo-clefts, Prince drew a distinction between 'given' information and 'known' information.

1 *Given information*: information which the cooperative speaker may assume is appropriately in the hearer's consciousness.
2 *Known information*: information which the speaker represents as being factual and as already known to certain persons (often not including the hearer) (1978: 903).

Thus, Prince adds the idea that the speaker is acting cooperatively to Chafe's definition of 'given' as 'material which the speaker assumes is already in the addressee's consciousness' (1974: 112). It is important from Prince's viewpoint that the speaker does not necessarily believe that the information is, in fact, activated in the listener's mental representation, only that it would be appropriate if it were. Thus, a professor may felicitously begin a lecture or course with the sentence (## = discourse initial utterance)

(32) (a) ##What we're going to look at today (this term) is . . .

but not with the sentence

(33) (b) *##What one of my colleagues said this morning was . . . (1978: 889).

The professor may assume that, at the beginning of a course, students appropriately have activated the information that some content will be taught, but the information that the professor had a recent conversation with a colleague is not appropriately activated in that situation. Thus, the information in the WH-clause of a pseudo-cleft is information the speaker may cooperatively assume is in the listener's consciousness. In contrast, the information in the that-clause of cleft sentences is *not* assumed to be in the listener's mind, though, of course, it may be. In discourse, clefts seem to have a number of functions, such as focusing new or contrastive information or presenting the information as known without making any claim that the listener is thinking about it.

As we have seen, speakers try to make some information more prominent or salient to their listeners. Depending on which language they are using, they have a number of devices at their disposal in order to achieve this goal of focusing information.

Methodological Issues and Dilemmas

No discussion of information management and knowledge integration in discourse can be considered complete without an examination of methodological issues in text and discourse analysis. There are three principal methodological strategies employed in the analysis of text and discourse: (1) introspection-based analysis, (2) text counting methods, and (3) experimental and quasi-experimental methods.

Introspection in Analysis of Text and Discourse

The most conventional method of linguistic analysis – the introspective examination of discourse data – remains a central and important strategy in discourse studies. Introspection-based methods, typical of early efforts within the Prague School and early developments out of the generative tradition in linguistics, emphasize creation of precise theoretical definitions of key pragmatic notions coupled with introspection in their use. The most common strategy is to offer a pragmatic notion as the explanatory basis for some unexplained structural alternation, define in clear prose that theoretical notion, and then map discourse onto that definition. Argumentation consists largely of documenting numerous examples congruent with one's definition and hypotheses.

Some introspective analysis deals with hypothetical discourse data created by the analyst. Such analyses can be problematic because the intuitions on which they are based are often not as reliable, as consistent from speaker to speaker, as are the judgments of acceptability on which analogous claims in sentence syntax are made. Much stronger are introspective analyses conducted on authentic discourse data. Such efforts, typical of Prince and her associates (Birner, 1994; Prince, 1978; 1985; Ward, 1988), involve the collection of massive amounts of genuine discourse data, both written and spoken, which are subjected to painstaking analysis.

Despite its limitations, this strategy remains an extremely useful one for postulating important theoretical ideas and demonstrating their feasibility for addressing difficult problems.

Text Counting Strategies

Introspection has been either augmented or replaced by text counting methods of one kind or another. There was an active tradition in Europe in the 1950s and 1960s of quantitative textual analysis, though this tradition has been largely ignored among North American linguists. More recently, Givón and his students have developed an array of text counting methods intended to increase the reliability of text analysis and through this their cross-linguistic utility.

Within this tradition, critical theoretical notions are operationalized through a set of heuristic counting procedures. For example, one can get a quantifiable handle on the thematic centrality of a referent by observing how reference to a particular endures over the course of a text or text episode. Referents of greater thematic centrality should display greater *topic persistence* (Givón, 1983), where topic persistence is operationalized in terms of the frequency with which a reference recurs over the ten clauses immediately following a given reference of interest.

Text counting methods offer the advantage of increased reliability in discourse analysis. If the methods are transparent, the results should turn out the same no matter who conducts the analysis, a clear advantage over introspective efforts. There are two limitations, though, for text counting.

First, text counts only work well when the theoretical notions they serve as heuristics for are clearly defined and clearly linked to those heurisitics. Second, the data collected under text counting methods require careful statistical analysis, which at present is difficult to complete (Tomlin, 1987b).

Experimental and Quasi-Experimental Strategies

There is increasing interest in finding ways of conducting discourse research within traditions of experimental studies. One direction is the employment of films or pictures to collect comparative discourse samples from speakers of various languages. In this tradition, the linguist obtains a drawing or a film and asks speakers to describe it. Since each speaker in the effort performs more or less the same task, the data collected should be reasonably comparable. Perhaps the best known effort of this sort is Chafe's 'Pear Film' (Chafe, 1980b), though others have followed this direction (Givón, 1991; Tomlin, 1985). These efforts are properly described as quasi-experimental: the collection of data is more controlled but there is no manipulation of variables required of true experimental work.

There is increasing interest in experimental studies of discourse within linguistics. There is, of course, a huge literature of experimental studies in discourse comprehension, but the employment of experimental methods by linguists is considerably rarer (Forrest, 1992; Kim, 1993; Sridhar, 1988; Tomlin, 1995; Tomlin and Pu, 1991). Experimental studies are important because the control employed in their development permits extremely strong conclusions to be drawn. Under the proper conditions, the observations made regarding language use will be due exclusively to the variables independently manipulated in the experiment. While significant results may offer extremely strong conclusions, experimental studies are often seen as problematic when the experimental task lacks the ecological validity seen in naturally occurring discourse data.

There is little point at this moment in time in advocating any of these strategies as the correct one to employ. Rather, it seems more valuable to emphasize the need to provide convincing evidence from an array of studies as the best overall strategy in studies of discourse semantics. Introspection provides deep and relatively inexpensive insights into how language may work. Text counting studies reveal systematic patterns of language use which reflect important features of the underlying system revealed in the rich data of human performance. Experimental studies demonstrate in a more narrow or constrained context the details of how pragmatic notions interact with or impact on linguistic form.

Cognitive Approaches to Discourse Semantics

The long term future of studies in discourse semantics lies in the development of cognitive models of discourse comprehension and production. There are two directions of note at this time: (1) cognitive treatments of fundamental discourse notions, and (2) large scale models of discourse processing.

Cognitive Treatments of Fundamental Discourse Notions

It has been extremely difficult to develop definitions which are both theoretically satisfying and empirically manageable for basic notions in information management – theme, given/new, foregrounding, focus, etc. This has led a number of investigators to pursue a strategy in which discourse notions are operationalized in cognitive terms or in which traditional ideas are outright replaced by cognitive alternatives.

Within referential management, there has been considerable interest in recasting traditional notions of given and new in cognitive terms, in particular in terms of memory, or memorial activation. Chafe offers such a treatment, though he does not connect his theory directly with the cognitive literature. Building on Chafe's effort, others have incorporated ideas from the study of memory (see Cowan, 1988 for review) into a model of referential management based on experimental manipulation of episodic structure and memorial activation (Tomlin and Pu, 1991).

Within thematic management, there has been, as discussed above, considerable interest in demonstrating a connection between theme or topic and attention. A large scale review of ideas in attention is outside the scope of this chapter, but there are several quite excellent summary articles available (Cowan, 1988; Posner and Raichle, 1994; Tomlin and Villa, 1994). Recent work by Tomlin and his students argues that the idea of theme itself can be reduced to cognitive terms, in particular to attention detection at the moment of utterance formulation detection (Forrest, 1992; Tomlin, 1995; Tomlin and Villa, 1994). In this view, the cognitive processes of attention are not merely the cognitive reflexes of linguistic theme or topic; rather the notion of theme or topic is treated as an artifact emerging from the employment of attention within a conceptual representation during discourse production.

Within focus management, there is interest in developing a cognitive account of focus. There are a number of important treatments of focus which appeal to cognition, notably Lambrecht (1994) and Vallduví (1992). Some others have been looking at focus as another arena involving attention (Erteschik-Shir, 1986; Levelt, 1989). Under this treatment, focus is seen not as a status for NPs or arguments, but as the outcome of directing the listener's attention to a referent during discourse production and comprehension. One such treatment of interest is Erteschik-Shir's notion of dominance, in which a constituent is dominant if the speaker intends to direct the attention of the listener to a particular referent. Tomlin (1995) and Hayashi (1995) take a similar tack in seeking to explain the function of *wa* in Japanese.

All of these efforts show more in common than just the desire to overcome the problems of developing adequate theoretical definitions within information management. These approaches are moving away from a conceptualization of text structure holding pragmatic statuses (for example, that NP is a topic; that argument is a focus) toward a conceptualization of discourse and grammars that is dynamic. In this view, morpho-syntactic cues reveal the memorial and attentional characteristics of the speaker's conceptual representation and direct those of the listener to conform to the speaker's conceptual representation. Attention and memory flow through conceptual representations in real time; there is every reason to believe, as Chafe (1974) observed early on, that information flows through discourse over time.

Models of Knowledge Integration

Just as investigators are moving increasingly toward cognitive treatments of information management, so too are researchers dealing with knowledge integration. Knowledge integration requires large scale models of how individual propositions are incorporated into textual representations and then integrated to generate final conceptual representations in the listener.

The two models of particular importance in this area have already been discussed: Gernsbacher's structure building model and Kintsch's construction-integration model. Both of these models seek to account for how the listener takes propositions encountered one at a time and builds a text representation by integrating the immediate proposition with knowledge already in hand. But a more comprehensive model of knowledge integration in discourse is needed. One, a more comprehensive model must deal more effectively with the role of morpho-syntax in aiding knowledge integration. Neither Gernsbacher nor Kintsch deal fully with how the form of an utterance (as opposed to its content) contributes to knowledge integration. Two, it must deal with how text representations, the set of connected propositions tied closely to the actual text blueprint, are to be related to deeper conceptual representations, in production as well as comprehension. Three, it must also deal explicitly with the dynamic nature of language use and conceptualization. The temporal features of language use probably do not sit outside of discourse semantics but constrain the kinds of systems that ultimately operate as humans create discourse together.

Conclusions

Summary: Key Issues in Discourse Semantics

In this chapter we have discussed the central issues and concepts of discourse semantics. This area involves two main problems. The first is the problem of knowledge integration: how the individual propositions in a text and discourse are integrated to reflect well the speaker's conceptual representation and to optimize the creation of an appropriate conceptual representation in the listener. The second is the problem of information management: how information is organized and distributed as the speaker and listener interact during the blueprint creation process. In this area we looked at four distinct arenas of information management: rhetorical management, referential management, thematic management, and focus management. Each contributes in a distinct way to increase the efficacy of knowledge integration as the discourse unfolds.

This effort has two serious limitations. First, we have not looked at formal models of discourse semantics. This is an area better left to those more knowledgeable, although interested readers might wish to examine important works such as Kamp and Reyle (1993). Second, it is not possible to provide as detailed a look at the work of individual scholars as one might wish to do. We have settled on trying to extract for our readers the most central insights in each arena. Hopefully, this effort will lead some to a more careful examination of the original sources and related work.

The Future of Studies in Discourse Semantics

The future of studies in discourse semantics is no more predictable than other futures, but there are certainly some directions one can discern. The most important direction is the development of cognitive models of language use. One can expect to see an increased integration of ideas from cognitive psychology, ideas from attention and memory, into linguistic treatments of knowledge integration and information management. This integration will not be easy to accomplish because it will require of us the development of cross-disciplinary and multidisciplinary skills and knowledge that traditional academic disciplines do not readily cultivate. The static descriptive systems linguists know best, a legacy of our structuralist heritage, make it difficult for us to appreciate the dynamic nature of language processing, tempting us to relegate such matters to the periphery when we do not really know they belong there.

In a similar vein, one should expect to see also important developments arising from neuroscience. Even though word and sentence level studies still predominate in this area, the connection between language and brain as scenes and discourses are viewed and heard should prove a fruitful domain. In addition, the neurosciences offer new methods and technologies, in particular ERP and fMRI techniques, which may assist us in providing convincing empirical evidence for our textual and behavioral work.

Finally, we should expect to see increasing collaboration between the field and the laboratory. It is the desire to construct plausible theories of discourse semantics and language use that prompts the interest in empirical and experimental work. Anything we can do to increase our empirical rigor and theoretical sophistication will be welcome. But we must just as much remember that theories which make no connection to actual languages and their description fail to make their full contribution to the study of language. Thus, the future of discourse semantics requires that we deal with each of the thousands of languages, described and undescribed, distributed across the globe. There is really plenty to do.

Notes

1 Discourse semantics is not concerned with the semantic interpretation or processing of each component in the utterance or sentence. For example, it is not concerned with how semantic roles are managed (agent vs patient vs instrument) or with how lexical knowledge is accessed (what 'dog' means in 'The dog chewed my shoe').

2 The term *conceptual representation* is virtually identical in meaning to another expression *mental model* (Johnson-Laird, 1983) used to capture cognitive representations of events and other mental representations.

3 The NPs in this example are not exhaustively analysed. We have focused on a number of pertinent cases to illustrate ideas in referential management.

4 Note that this is a description of the rhetorical goal of this paragraph.

5 This use of 'topic' does not imply a confusion in Givón's writings about a notion of theme. This is separately discussed in several places (Givón, 1983).

6 This text fragment is taken from a set of edited written protocols generated by a group of undergraduate students who narrated a brief animated film they had recently viewed (Tomlin, 1985).

References

Aissen, J. (1992) 'Topic and focus in Mayan', *Language*, 68: 43–80.

Anderson, R.C., Spiro, R.J. and Anderson, M.C. (1978) 'Schemata as scaffolding for the representation of information in connected discourse', *American Educational Research Journal*, 15: 433–40.

Austin, J.L. (1962) *How To Do Things with Words*. Oxford: Clarendon Press.

Baggett, P. (1982) 'Information content equivalent movie and text stories', *Discourse Processes*, 5: 73–99.

Birner, B.J. (1994) 'Information status and word order: an analysis of English inversion', *Language*, 70: 223–59.

Black, J.B. and Bower, G.H. (1979) 'Episodes as chunks in narrative memory', *Journal of Verbal Learning and Verbal Behavior*, 18: 309–18.

Bolinger, D. (1972) 'A look at equations and cleft sentences', in E.S. Firchow, K. Grimstad, N. Hasselmo and W.A. O'Neil (eds), *Studies for Einar Haugen Presented by Friends and Colleagues*. The Hague: Mouton. pp. 96–114.

Bransford, J.D. and Johnson, M.K. (1972) 'Contextual prerequisites for understanding: some investigations of comprehension and recall', *Journal of Verbal Learning and Verbal Behavior*, 11: 717–26.

Chafe, W. (1974) 'Language and consciousness', *Language*, 50: 111–33.

Chafe, W. (1976) 'Givenness, contrastiveness, definiteness, subjects, topics, and points of view', in C.N. Li (ed.), *Subject and Topic*. New York: Academic Press. pp. 25–56.

Chafe, W. (1979) 'The flow of thought and the flow of language', in T. Givón (ed.), *Discourse and Syntax*. New York: Academic Press. pp. 159–81.

Chafe, W. (1980a) 'The deployment of consciousness in the production of narrative', in W. Chafe (ed.), *The Pear Stories: Cognitive, Cultural, and Linguistic Aspects of Narrative Production*. Norwood, NJ: Ablex. pp. 9–50.

Chafe, W. (ed.) (1980b) *The Pear Stories: Cognitive, Cultural, and Linguistic Aspects of Narrative Production*. Norwood, NJ: Ablex.

Chafe, W. (1987) 'Cognitive constraints on information flow', in R. Tomlin (ed.), *Coherence and Grounding in Discourse*. Amsterdam: John Benjamins. pp. 21–51.

Chafe, W. (1994) *Discourse, Consciousness, and Time*. Chicago: University of Chicago Press.

Chomsky, N. (1965) *Aspects of the Theory of Syntax*. Cambridge, MA: MIT Press.

Chomsky, N. (1970) 'Deep structure, surface structure, and semantic interpretation', in R.J.a.S. Kawamoto (ed.), *Studies in General and Oriental Linguistics*. Tokyo: TEC Corp.

Clark, H.H. and Haviland, S.E. (1974) 'Psychological processes as linguistic explanation', in D. Cohen (ed.), *Explaining Linguistic Phenomena*. Washington, DC: Hemisphere. pp. 91–124.

Cohen, P.R. and Perrault, C.R. (1979) 'Elements of a plan-based theory of speech acts', *Cognitive Science: a Multidisciplinary Journal of Artificial Intelligence, Psychology, and Language*, 3: 177–212.

Coulthard, M. (1977) *An Introduction to Discourse Analysis*, London: Longman.

Coulthard, M. and Montgomery, M. (ed.) (1981) *Studies in Discourse Analysis*. London: Routledge and Kegan Paul.

Cowan, N. (1988) 'Evolving conceptions of memory storage, selective attention, and their mutual constraints within the human information-processing system', *Psychological Bulletin*, 104 (2): 163–91.

Dahl, Ö. (1969) *Topic and Comment: a Study in Russian and Transformational Grammar*. Stockholm: Almqvist and Wiksell.

Dahl, Ö. (1974) 'Topic–comment structure in a generative grammar with a semantic base', in F. Danes (ed.), *Papers on Functional Sentence Perspective*. The Hague: Mouton. pp. 75–80.

Daneš, F. (1974) 'Functional sentence perspective and the organization of the text', in F. Daneš (ed.), *Papers on Functional Sentence Perspective*. The Hague: Mouton. pp. 106–28.

Dik, S. (1978) *Functional Grammar*. Amsterdam: North-Holland.

Dik, S. (1989) *The Theory of Functional Grammar*. Dordrecht: Foris.

Dik, S., Hoffmann, M.E., Jong, J.R.d., Djiang, S.I., Stroomer, H. and Vries, L.d. (1981) 'On the typology of focus phenomena', in T. Hoekstra, H.v.d. Hulst, and M. Moortgat (eds), *Perspectives on Functional Grammar*. Dordrecht: Foris. pp. 41–74.

DuBois, J.W. (1980) 'Beyond definiteness: the trace of identity in discourse', in W. Chafe (ed.), *The Pear Stories: Cognitive, Cultural and Linguistic Aspects of Narrative Production*. Norwood, NJ: Ablex. pp. 203–73.

Erteschik-Shir, N. (1986) 'Wh-questions and focus', *Linguistics and Philosophy*, 9: 117–49.

Firbas, J. (1964a) 'From comparative word-order studies (thoughts on V. Mathesius' conception of the word-order system in English compared with that in Czech)', *Brno Studies in English*, 4: 111–28.

Firbas, J. (1964b) 'On defining the theme in functional sentence analysis', *Travaux Linguistiques de Prague*, 1: 267–80.

Firbas, J. (1974) 'Some aspects of the Czechoslovak approach to problems of functional sentence perspective', in F. Daneš (ed.), *Papers on Functional Sentence Perspective*. The Hague: Mouton. pp. 11–37.

Firbas, J. (1987a) 'On the delimitation of theme in functional sentence perspective', in R. Dirven and V. Fried (eds), *Functionalism in Linguistics*. Amsterdam: John Benjamins. pp. 137–56.

Firbas, J. (1987b) 'On two starting points of communication', in R. Steele and T. Threadgold (eds), *Language Topics*. Amsterdam: John Benjamins. pp. 23–46.

Firbas, J. (1992) *Functional Sentence Perspective in Written and Spoken Communication*. Cambridge: Cambridge University Press.

Forrest, L.B. (1992) 'How grammar codes cognition: syntactic subject and focus of attention'. Unpublished MA thesis, University of Oregon.

Fox, B.A. (1987) *Discourse Structure and Anaphora in Written and Conversational English*. Cambridge: Cambridge University Press.

Frase, L.T. (1975) 'Prose processing', in G.H. Bower (ed.), *The Psychology of Learning and Motivation: Advances in Research and Theory*. New York: Academic Press. pp. 1–47.

Gernsbacher, M.A. (1990) *Language Comprehension as Structure Building*. Hillsdale, NJ: Lawrence Erlbaum.

Givón, T. (ed.) (1983) *Topic Continuity in Discourse: a Quantitative Cross-Language Study.* Amsterdam: John Benjamins.

Givón, T. (1989) *Mind, Code and Context: Essays in Pragmatics.* Hillsdale, NJ: Lawrence Erlbaum.

Givón, T. (1991) 'Serial verbs and the mental reality of "events": grammatical vs cognitive packaging', in E. Traugott and B. Heine (eds), *Approaches to Grammaticalization,* vol. 1. Amsterdam: John Benjamins. pp. 81–127.

Goodenough, C. (1983) 'A psycholinguistic investigation of theme and information focus'. Unpublished PhD dissertation, University of Toronto.

Grimes, J. (1975) *The Thread of Discourse.* The Hague: Mouton.

Grosz, B. (1974) 'The structure of task oriented dialogue' (in German), in *IEEE Symposium on Speech Recognition: Contributed Papers.* Pittsburgh, PA: Carnegie Mellon University Computer Science Department. pp. 250–3.

Guindon, R. and Kintsch, W. (1984) 'Priming macropropositions: evidence for the primacy of macropropositions in the memory for text', *Journal of Verbal Learning and Verbal Behavior,* 23 (4): 508–18.

Gundel, J. (1974) 'The role of topic and comment in linguistic theory'. PhD dissertation, University of Texas, Austin.

Gundel, J. (1988a) 'Universals of topic–comment structure', in M. Hammond, E. Moravcsik and J. Wirth (eds), *Studies in Syntactic Typology.* Amsterdam: John Benjamins. pp. 209–39.

Gundel, J.K. (1988b) *The Role of Topic and Comment in Linguistic Theory.* New York: Garland.

Hajicovà, E. (1984) 'Topic and focus', in P. Sgall (ed.), *Contributions to Functional Syntax, Semantics, and Language Comprehension.* Amsterdam: John Benjamins. pp. 189–202.

Halliday, M.A.K. (1967a) 'Notes on transitivity and theme in English, Part 1', *Journal of Linguistics,* 3: 37–81.

Halliday, M.A.K. (1967b) 'Notes on transitivity and theme in English, Part 2', *Journal of Linguistics,* 3: 199–244.

Halliday, M.A.K. (1973) *Explorations in the Functions of Language.* London: Edward Arnold.

Halliday, M.A.K. (1976) 'Theme and information in the English clause', in G. Kress (ed.), *Halliday: System and Function in Language.* London: Oxford University Press. pp. 174–88.

Halliday, M.A.K. (1985) *An Introduction to Functional Grammar.* London: Edward Arnold.

Halliday, M.A.K. and Fawcett, R.P. (eds) (1987) *New Developments in Systemic Grammar: Theory and Description.* London: Frances Pinter.

Hawkinson, A.K. and Hyman, L.M. (1974) 'Hierarchies of natural topic in Shona', *Studies in African Linguistics,* 5: 147–70.

Hayashi, A. (1995) 'American learners' use of Japanese *wa*'. MA thesis, University of Oregon.

Hinds, J. (1977) 'Paragraph structure and pronominalization', *Papers in Linguistics,* 10: 77–99.

Hinds, J. (1979) 'Organizational patterns in discourse', in T. Givón (ed.), *Discourse and Syntax.* New York: Academic Press. pp. 135–57.

Hinds, J., Maynard, S.K. and Iwasaki, S. (eds) (1987) *Perspectives on Topicalization: the Case of Japanese 'wa'.* Amsterdam: John Benjamins.

Hopper, P. (1979) 'Aspect and foregrounding in discourse', in T. Givón (ed.), *Discourse and Syntax.* New York: Academic Press. pp. 213–41.

Hopper, P. and Thompson, S. (1980) 'Transitivity in grammar and discourse', *Language,* 56: 251–99.

Johnson-Laird, P.N. (1983) *Mental Models.* Cambridge, MA: Harvard University Press.

Jones, L.B. and Jones, L.K. (1979) 'Multiple levels of information in discourse', in L. Jones and L. Jones (eds), *Discourse Studies in Mesoamerican Languages: Discussion.* Arlington, TX: Summer Institute of Linguistics. pp. 3–28.

Jones, L.K. (1977) *Theme in Expository English.* Lake Bluff, IL: Jupiter Press.

Kamp, H. and Reyle, U. (1993) *From Discourse to Logic.* Dordrecht: Reidel.

Keenan, E.L. (1976) 'Toward a universal definition of subject', in C.N. Li (ed.), *Subject and Topic.* New York: Academic Press. pp. 305–33.

Keenan, E.O. and Schieffelin, B. (1976) 'Topic as a discourse notion', in C.N. Li (ed.), *Subject and Topic*. New York: Academic Press. pp. 337–84.

Kim, H.W. (1994) 'An experimental study of two functions of the Korean topic marker: thematic and contrastive'. Unpublished MA thesis, University of Oregon.

Kim, M.-H. (1993) 'The interaction of global and local theme in English narrative'. Doctoral dissertation, University of Oregon.

Kintsch, W. (1974) *The Representation of Meaning in Memory*. Hillsdale, NJ: Lawrence Erlbaum.

Kintsch, W. (1988) 'The role of knowledge in discourse comprehension: a construction-integration model', *Psychological Review*, 95 (2): 163–82.

Kintsch, W. and van Dijk, T. (1978) 'Toward a model of text comprehension and production', *Psychological Review*, 85: 363–94.

Labov, W. and Waletzky, J. (1967) 'Narrative analysis: oral versions of personal experience', in J. Helm (ed.), *Essays on the Verbal Arts*. Seattle: University of Washington Press.

Lambrecht, K. (1981) *Topic, Antitopic, and Verb Agreement in Non-Standard French*. Philadelphia: John Benjamins.

Lambrecht, K. (1987a) 'Aboutness as a cognitive category: the thetic-categorical distinction revisited', in J. Aske, N. Beery, L. Michaelis and H. Filip (eds), *Proceedings of the Thirteenth Annual Meeting of the Berkeley Linguistics Society*. pp. 366–82.

Lambrecht, K. (1987b) 'On the status of SVO sentences in French discourse', in R. Tomlin (ed.), *Cohererence and Grounding in Discourse*. Amsterdam: John Benjamins. pp. 217–61.

Lambrecht, K. (1994) *Information Structure and Sentence Form*. Cambridge: Cambridge University Press.

Leech, G.N. (1983) *Principles of Pragmatics*. London: Longman.

Levelt, W.J.M. (1989) *Speaking*. Cambridge, MA: MIT Press.

Levinson, S.C. (1983) *Pragmatics*. Cambridge: Cambridge University Press.

Levy, D.M. (1979) 'Communication goals and strategies: between discourse and syntax', in T. Givón (ed.), *Syntax and Semantics: Discourse and Syntax*. New York: Academic Press. pp. 183–210.

Li, C.N. and Thompson, S.A. (1976) 'Subject and topic: a new typology of language', in C.N. Li (ed.), *Subject and Topic*. New York: Academic Press. pp. 457–89.

Longacre, R.E. (1968) 'Discourse, paragraph, and sentence structure in selected Philippine languages'. Santa Ana, CA: Summer Institute of Linguistics.

Longacre, R.E. (1976a) 'The discourse structure of the Flood narrative', in G. Macrae (ed.), *Society of Biblical Literature: 1976 Seminar Papers*. Missoula, MT: Scholars Press. pp. 235–62.

Longacre, R.E. (1976b) *An Anatomy of Speech Notions*. Lisse: Peter de Ridder Press.

MacWhinney, B. (1977) 'Starting points', *Language*, 53: 152–68.

Mann, W.C. and Thompson, S.A. (1986) 'Relational propositions in discourse', *Discourse Processes*, 9: 57–90.

Marslen-Wilson, W., Levy, E. and Tyler, L. (1982) 'Producing interpretable discourse: the establishment and maintenance of refence', in R.J. Jarvella and W. Klein (eds), *Speech, Place, and Action*. Chichester: Wiley. pp. 339–78.

Mathesius, V. (1929) 'Zür Satzsperspektive im modernen Englisch', *Archiv für das Studium der neuren Sprachen und Literaturen*, 155: 202–10.

Mathesius, V. (1939) 'O tak zvaném aktuálnim clelneni vetném (On the so-called actual bipartition of the sentence)', *Slovo a Slovcesnost*, 5: 171–4.

Mathesius, V. (1975) 'On the information-bearing structure of the sentence', in S. Kuno (ed.), *Harvard Studies in Syntax and Semantics*. Cambridge, MA: Harvard University Press. pp. 467–80.

Mayer, M. (1967) *A Boy, a Dog, and a Frog*. New York: Dial Press.

McKeown, K.R. (1985) *Text Generation: Using Discourse Strategies and Focus Constraints to Generate Natural Language Text*. Cambridge: Cambridge University Press.

Mehan, H. (1979) *Learning Lessons*. Cambridge, MA: Harvard University Press.

Minsky, M. (1975) 'A framework for representing knowledge', in P.H. Winston (ed.), *The Psychology of Computer Vision*. New York: McGraw-Hill.

Mithun, M. (1987) 'Is basic word order universal?', in R.S. Tomlin (ed.), *Coherence and Grounding in Discourse*. Amsterdam: John Benjamins. pp. 281–328.

Payne, D.L. (ed.) (1992) *Pragmatics of Word Order Flexibility*. Amsterdam: John Benjamins.

Pichert, J.W. and Anderson, R.C. (1977) 'Taking different perspectives on a story', *Journal of Educational Psychology*, 69: 309–15.

Posner, M.I. and Raichle, M.E. (1994) *Images of Mind*. New York: Scientific American Library.

Prentice, J.L. (1967) 'Effects of cuing actor vs. cuing object on word order in sentence production', *Psychonomic Science*, 8: 163–4.

Prince, E. (1978) 'A comparison of WH-clefts and it-clefts in discourse', *Language*, 54: 883–907.

Prince, E.F. (1981) 'Towards a taxonomy of given-new information', in P. Cole (ed.), *Radical Pragmatics*. New York: Academic Press. pp. 223–56.

Prince, E.F. (1985) 'Topicalization and left-dislocation: a functional analysis', *Annals of the New York Academy of Sciences*, 433: 213–25.

Propp, V. (1958) *Morphology of the Folktale*. Bloomington, IN: Indiana University Research Center in Anthropology, Folklore, and Linguistics.

Reinhart, T. (1981) 'Pragmatics and linguistics: an analysis of sentence topics', *Philosophica*, 27 (1): 53–94.

Rochester, S.R. and Martin, J.R. (1977) 'The art of referring: the speaker's use of noun phrases to instruct the listener', in R.O. Freedle (ed.), *Discourse Production and Comprehension: Advances in Discourse Processes*. Norwood, NJ: Ablex.

Rumelhart, D. (1980) 'Schemata: the building blocks of cognition', in B. Spiro, B.C. Bruce and W.F. Brewer (eds), *Theoretical Issues in Reading Comprehension*. Hillsdale, NJ: Erlbaum.

Rutherford, E. (1988) *Sarum*. New York: Ivy Books.

Sanford, A.J. and Garrod, S. (1980) 'Memory and attention in text comprehension: the problem of reference', in R. Nickerson (ed.), *Attention and Performance VIII*. Hillsdale, NJ: Lawrence Erlbaum.

Schank, R.C. and Abelson, R.P. (1977) *Scripts, Plans, Goals, and Understanding*. Hillsdale, NJ: Lawrence Erlbaum.

Searle, J.R. (1969) *Speech Acts*. Cambridge: Cambridge University Press.

Searle, J.R. (1979) *Expression and Meaning: Studies in the Theory of Speech Acts*. Cambridge: Cambridge University Press.

Sgall, P. (1987) 'Prague functionalism and topic vs. focus', in R. Dirven and V. Fried (eds), *Functionalism in Linguistics*. Amsterdam: John Benjamins.

Sidner, C.L. (1983) 'Focusing in the comprehension of definite anaphora', in M. Brady and R.C. Berwick (eds), *Computational Models in Discourse*. Cambridge, MA: MIT Press. pp. 267–330.

Sinclair, J.M. and Coulthard, R.M. (1975) *Towards an Analysis of Discourse*. Oxford: Oxford University Press.

Sridhar, S.N. (1988) *Cognition and Sentence Production: a Cross-Linguistic Study*. New York: Springer-Verlag.

Swales, J. (1981) *Aspects of Article Introductions*. Aston ESP Research Report no. 1. The Language Studies Unit, University of Aston in Birmingham.

Tannenbaum, P.H. and Williams, F. (1968) 'Generation of active and passive sentences as a function of subject and object focus', *Journal of Verbal Learning and Verbal Behavior*, 7: 246–50.

Tomlin, R.S. (1983) 'On the interaction of syntactic subject, thematic information, and agent in English', *Journal of Pragmatics*, 7: 411–32.

Tomlin, R.S. (1984) 'The treatment of foreground–background information in the on-line descriptive discourse of second language learners', *Studies in Second Language Acquisition*, 6: 115–42.

Tomlin, R.S. (1985) 'Foreground–background information and the syntax of subordination', *Text*, 5: 85–122.

Tomlin, R.S. (1986) 'The identification of foreground–background information in on-line descriptive discourse', *Papers in Linguistics*, 19: 465–94.

Tomlin, R.S. (1987a) 'Linguistic reflections of cognitive events', in R. Tomlin (ed.), *Coherence and Grounding in Discourse*. Amsterdam: John Benjamins. pp. 455–80.

Tomlin, R.S. (1987b) 'The problem of coding in functional grammars', paper presented at the UC Davis Conference on the Interaction of Form and Function in Language, Davis, California, April 1987.

Tomlin, R.S. (1995) 'Focal attention, voice, and word order: an experimental, cross-linguistic study', in P. Downing and M. Noonan (eds), *Word Order in Discourse*. Amsterdam: John Benjamins. pp. 517–54.

Tomlin, R.S. (1997) 'Mapping conceptual representations into linguistic representations: the role of attention in grammar', in J. Nuyts and E. Pederson (eds), *With Language in Mind*. Cambridge: Cambridge University Press. pp. 162–89.

Tomlin, R.S. and Pu, M.M. (1991) 'The management of reference in Mandarin discourse', *Cognitive Linguistics*, 2 (1): 65–95.

Tomlin, R.S. and Villa, V. (1994) 'Attention in cognitive science and SLA', *Studies in Second Language Acquisition*, 16 (2).

Vachek, J. (ed.) (1966) *The Linguistic School of Prague: an Introduction to its Theory and Practice*. Bloomington, IN: Indiana University Press.

Vallduví, E. (1992) *The Informational Component*. New York: Garland.

van Dijk, T.A. (1977) 'Sentence topic and discourse topic', in B.A. Stolz (ed.), *Papers in Slavic Philology 1: In Honor of James Ferrell*. Ann Arbor, MI: Department of Slavic Languages and Literature, University of Michigan.

van Dijk, T.A. (1980) *Macrostructures*. Hillsdale, NJ: Lawrence Erlbaum.

van Dijk, T.A. (1982) 'Episodes as units of discourse', in D. Tannen (ed.), *Analyzing Discourse: Text and Talk*. Washington, DC: Georgetown University Press.

van Dijk, T.A. (ed.) (1985) *Handbook of Discourse Analysis*. London: Academic Press.

van Dijk, T.A. and Kintsch, W. (1983) *Strategies of Discourse Comprehension*. New York: Academic Press.

Ward, G. (1988) *The Semantics and Pragmatics of Preposing*. New York: Garland.

Weil, H. (1887) *The Order of Words in the Ancient Languages Compared with that of the Modern Languages* (1844) (trans. C. Super), 3rd edn. Boston: Ginn.

4

Discourse and Grammar

Susanna Cumming and Tsuyoshi Ono

This chapter deals with the relation of discourse to grammar, setting forth
what we will call a 'discourse-functional approach' to grammatical
phenomena. Discourse-functional grammarians view discourse – that is,
spoken, signed or written language used by people to communicate in
natural settings – as the primary locus for the grammars of the world's
languages, not only as the place where grammar is manifested in use, but
also as the source from which grammar is formed or 'emerges' (Hopper,
1988). In this view, grammar originates in recurrent patterns in discourse,
and these patterns continually shape it. This approach to grammar is
distinct from what might be called the 'autonomist' approach, which views
grammar as having an existence entirely independent of its communicative
uses.

Discourse-functional approaches to grammar have two goals. The first
goal is a descriptive one: given the richness of the grammatical resources
languages typically have for expressing the 'same' content, how do speakers
choose among them? That is, what are the functions of the grammatical
and lexical alternations of a language? We can ask, for instance, how
speakers choose between a full noun phrase and a pronoun, or between two
alternative orders for subject and verb. The second goal is explanatory: why
do languages have the resources they have? That is, why are particular
grammatical resources, such as pronouns, available in many or all
languages, and why are certain functions typically realized by certain kinds
of forms? This second concern has consequences for language universals
and typology: for instance, the universal tendency for subjects to precede
objects can be explained in terms of the fact that subjects typically have
referents which are related to the discourse topic, and that topical
information tends cross-linguistically to occur early in the clause.

Discourse linguists interested in grammar have tended to focus on three
general kinds of explanations. Cognitive explanations appeal to the
cognitive resources and processes used by interactants in producing and
understanding language. Social or interactional explanations appeal to the
dynamics of the interactional situations in which language (especially
spoken language) is produced and consumed, and with the social and/or
cultural norms, resources, and goals of interactants. Finally, diachronic
explanations focus on the relationship between discourse-functional

pressures on grammars and grammatical change; this type of explanation is often called 'grammaticalization', a topic which is beyond the scope of the present chapter.

These three sources of explanation are not, of course, mutually exclusive; they are interrelated in many complex ways. Discourse linguists believe that the great variety of formal repertoires among the world's languages comes about through the interaction of different functional pressures, which sometimes compete – forcing speech communities to 'choose' between two or more well-motivated outcomes – and sometimes converge, leading to very general or even universal patterns of language structure (see Du Bois, 1985).

Historical Overview

The school of linguistics characterized above emerged in its present form in the mid 1970s, when 'functional' linguists in the US began to distinguish themselves from 'formal' (autonomist) linguists. This new school of linguistics owed much to older European social and communicative approaches, especially the Firthian approach as extended by Halliday (see, for example, Halliday, 1967–8 and other works summarized in Halliday, 1985), and the Prague School tradition developed under the name 'functional sentence perspective' by Firbas (1966), Daneš (1974), Mathesius (1975) and others. These approaches viewed the social setting of language, its communicative function, and especially the management of information in discourse, as central to understanding grammar.

A group of American linguists were also working on discourse at this time. Dwight Bolinger contributed a long series of studies (for example, Bolinger, 1952; 1986; 1989) which demonstrated the importance of understanding language in use; moreover, he was a pioneer in understanding the special characteristics of spoken language, especially intonation. Pike (1954), Longacre (1972) and Grimes (1975) represented an approach to linguistics which always saw discourse as central to understanding language.

Another thread that was centrally important to the nascent discourse functionalism of the mid 1970s was the typological school of linguistics inspired by the seminal work of Greenberg (1966) and others, which focused attention for the first time on universal properties of human languages. Greenberg and his followers included observations about statistical tendencies in the languages of the world, as well as correlations between characteristics of different syntactic subsystems – such as word order in the noun phrase and the clause. These new observations demanded explanations, which discourse-functional approaches were in a good position to provide.

The mid 1970s also saw the inception of several other streams in related disciplines which have continued to influence and be influenced by the discourse-functional approach to grammar in the years since. Since one aspect of the discourse-functionalist approach centrally involves cognitive factors, results in psycholinguistics and, more recently, cognitive science have continued to be brought to bear on problems of grammar in discourse. Yet another important pair of influences on the discourse-functional approach comes from the fields of anthropology on the one hand and sociology on the other. Since the contributions from other disciplines are covered extensively elsewhere in this volume, we will not consider them further here.

Methodology and Data

As suggested above, a discourse-functional linguist believes that the use of language to communicate in natural settings is fundamental to the organization of languages. The primacy of grammar in discourse both as an object of description and as a source of explanations has had important methodological consequences for discourse grammarians.

Most importantly, unlike 'autonomist' grammarians, discourse grammarians have over the last three decades increasingly restricted their attention to naturally occurring data, as opposed to invented examples. Increasingly, too, discourse-functional linguists have attempted to include in their database as much as possible of the context within which the discourse occurs – not just the linguistic context, but also the ethnographic and extralinguistic context, including both its social and its physical aspects. This is because context can often provide clues to locally relevant functional pressures not detectable from the linguistic signal alone. Awareness of the importance of context in grammatical choice has led to increasing interest in the nature of 'context' as an object of study in itself. Many discourse linguists have come to the realization that we have to understand discourse and its context as mutually creating and constraining, rather than seeing this simply as a unidirectional process.

Another concomitant of the discourse-functional perspective has to do with the issue of text frequency. Many discourse grammarians feel that text frequency is vital to understanding the discourse motivations for particular grammatical constructions. This is because they have come to realize that those functional pressures that have the most opportunity to affect communicators are those most likely to affect language form: in the words of Du Bois (1985), 'grammars code best what speakers do most.' This observation has had two significant consequences for the methodology of discourse approaches to grammar. First, many discourse grammarians have adopted a quantitative methodology, and have been very concerned with statistical correlations between particular grammatical forms and aspects of the linguistic and non-linguistic context. Second, many discourse grammarians have recently begun to focus increasingly on the form of language which occupies most of the time and attention of most language users everywhere in the world: everyday 'talk in interaction'. While other discourse genres and styles, produced under different kinds of functional constraints and pressures, are still considered relevant, interactive talk is seen as having a privileged position as a source of explanation for language structure and change. For this reason, the examples given in this chapter in so far as possible are taken from interactional data.

These factors are responsible for the distinctive methodological characteristics associated with studies in the discourse-functional mold: an insistence on carefully recorded natural data and an interest in quantitative and distributional information about grammatical patterns.

Conceptual Tools

There are a number of explanatory themes, or 'conceptual tools', which have been especially important in discourse-functional work and which tend to recur. In the following sections we will outline the themes that have emerged as most central. For each theme, we will give examples of grammatical phenomena that have been usefully addressed in terms of that theme.

By far the largest share of research in studies of discourse and grammar is related to the theme of 'information flow', which has to do with the way information is distributed within and across clauses. Increasingly, however, researchers have realized that information flow doesn't give the whole story. Quantitative approaches to information flow often treat the text as 'flat', an unstructured series of clauses; but in fact texts are structured, and this fact also has consequences for grammatical resources.

While both information flow and text-structure considerations can be seen as primarily relating to the discourse context of an utterance, other kinds of contextual factors are relevant too. In this chapter we discuss the speaker's attitude towards a referent or a proposition, and factors having to do with the interaction, that is which relate not just to the speaker or the hearer, but to the communication between them. We also discuss the impact that results from discourse approaches to grammar have had on our understanding of the basic categories of grammatical analysis.

Finally, we provide our view of the future of discourse-functional approaches to linguistics and list some outstanding research questions.

Information Flow

'Information flow' is perhaps the best-known and most widely exploited of the conceptual tools employed by discourse-functional grammarians. More or less the same range of phenomena appears in the literature under a variety of names; the terminology we adopt here is that of Chafe (1994), but other widely used terms include 'communicative dynamism', 'givenness', 'topicality', 'thematicity', and 'focus'. The idea underlying information flow

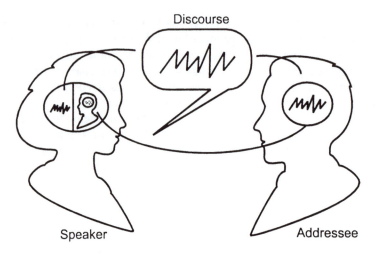

Figure 4.1   *A simplified model of information in discourse*

is that a primary function of language is to convey information from the speaker to the addressee. Information differs in how accessible it is, or how easy to process, from either the speaker's or the addressee's point of view. From the speaker's point of view, we can think in terms of information which is in or out of attention or the 'focus of consciousness' (to use Chafe's term). From the addressee's point of view, we can think in terms of information which is more or less expected or predictable given the setting and the previous discourse (Prince, 1981; Givón, 1983). We expect information which is relatively accessible or predictable to be coded with less linguistic work; conversely, information which is relatively inaccessible or surprising should be coded with special, heavy or 'marked' linguistic mechanisms. Moreover, predictability may have· several different sources, which may be distinguished by linguistic coding devices (as the discussion below of the difference between pronouns and definite articles shows).

Information flow is generally taken to be a cognitive matter, to be understood in terms of the dynamic mental states of the speaker and addressee during discourse production and consumption. Since it is speakers who make linguistic decisions, discourse grammarians are primarily interested in the speaker's mental states. On the other hand, since speakers take addressees' needs (as assessed through discourse history, observation, and general expectations) into account when producing discourse, the mental state of the addressee – or, more accurately, the speaker's model of the mental state of the addressee – must also be taken into account. These relationships are shown in Figure 4.1.

What is misleading about this figure is that it suggests that the 'same' information is present in the mind of the speaker, in the linguistic signal, and in the mind of the addressee, and moreover that the speaker's rep-resentation of the addressee is exact. This is of course unlikely to be the case. However, it does correspond to the folk model interactants have about communication. For this reason it is a relevant view, and a convenient one to adopt as a first approximation.

Since access to the mental representations constructed by speakers and hearers in natural settings is difficult to obtain, discourse-functional linguists often operationalize aspects of these representations in terms of characteristics of the discourse itself. For instance, 'less accessible/predictable' may be operationalized as 'not recently mentioned' or 'distant in the text'. Alternatively, using experimental means, researchers may manipulate speakers' representations. For instance, they may provide material to verbalize by showing subjects a film and asking them to describe what happened, as in Chafe (1980) and Tomlin (1987).

Information flow factors have been cited in relation to a very wide range of grammatical phenomena. Perhaps the most fundamental are matters relating to the quantity of information in a unit (especially with regard to noun phrase form) and its arrangement (as realized in the order of elements and their roles in argument structure). The following sections discuss information flow in relation to noun phrase form, constituent order, and argument structure; for additional topics, see the recommended reading at the end of the chapter.

Noun Phrase Form

One of the most fruitful areas of investigation by discourse-functional linguists is the choice – traditionally characterized as 'optional' – among different referential forms such as full noun phrases, pronouns, and 'zero anaphora' (simple omission), and also the use of articles (such as, English *the* and *a*) and other determiners. The major finding has been that the degree of explicitness of a referential form correlates with how accessible the speaker judges the referent to be in the hearer's mind (Chafe, 1976; 1987; 1994). Full noun phrases are associated with referents which the speaker judges are not active in the hearer's consciousness, while pronouns are associated with active concepts. Articles, on the other hand, are associated with an information status factor that Chafe (1976) characterized as 'identifiability': the speaker's assumption that a hearer can identify a referent, based either on prior mention in discourse or on knowledge obtained from other sources. Definite marking (*the*) is associated with identifiable referents, while indefinite marking (*a*) is associated with non-identifiable ones.

Consider the following example, from a conversation about work in a paper recycling mill (*mayate* is a Mexican Spanish term for an African-American).[1]

(1) 1 G: . . Can you imagine man?
     2   . . . They hired summer help,
     3   . . They're paying seven fifty,
     4   to stock boost,
     5   three machines man.

6   . . . Two dudes.
7   . . A mayate,
8   . . and a white dude.
9   D: Nobody in finishing?
10   . . . Just two guys they hired?
11   G: . . . Uh,
12   . . . and one more,
13   . . on the tables.
14   . . . Uh,
15   . . . Zamorra's uh . . brother-in-law.
16   D: . . Is that right?
17   G: . . . Yeah.
18   D: . . . Wow.
19   G: . . . So they got three new guys.
20   . . . But they're summer help.
21   . . But the mayate,
22   . . . apparently,
23   . . it seems like he's,
24   . . . worked in a –
25   D: . . . paper company before.
26   G: Yeah.
27   He knows about paper.

In this example, speaker G is attempting to establish a referent for speaker D. The first mention of the referent, *a mayate* (line 7), is accomplished with a noun phrase marked with *a*. The next reference, which doesn't occur until several lines further down (line 21), is accomplished with a noun phrase marked with *the*. By this time, the referent is identifiable (by virtue of prior reference), but it has not been mentioned recently enough to be considered active in the hearer's consciousness. The third and fourth references, occurring directly afterwards (lines 23 and 27), are accomplished with personal pronouns (*he*); this reflects the fact that the referent was mentioned in the immediately previous context, and thus the speaker can assume that the referent is active in the mind of the hearer.

This illustrates the following general pattern: when a referent is not active in the hearer's consciousness at the time of mention, it is likely to be expressed with an indefinite noun phrase. When it is identifiable but not fully active (for instance, it has been introduced but not mentioned recently), a definite noun phrase will be used. Finally, when it is fully active (for instance, because it has just been mentioned), a pronoun will be used.

Another factor relevant to the choice of the full noun phrase *the mayate* in line 21 is the fact that the immediately preceding line contains a reference to a set of which the *mayate* is a member (the 'three new guys'). Thus, there are three human referents available in the context. It is generally the case that environments which contain more than one semantically compatible referent give rise to the use of full noun phrases rather than pronouns (Clancy, 1980; Givón, 1983; Fox, 1987b); Givón calls this situation 'potential interference'.

As suggested above, there are other sources of identifiability besides prior mention in the text. In line 13 of example (1), the noun phrase *the tables* is definite because G and D have worked in the same environment, and therefore G can assume that D is able to identify the tables he means.

Noun phrase form relates not only to the past history of a referent, but also to the speaker's intent to trace the identity of the referent in *subsequent* discourse. Du Bois (1980) and Wright and Givón (1987) have shown that English *this* is used for non-identifiable referents when the same referent continues to be mentioned in the following discourse. Consider 'this group of elephants' in line 6 of the following example:

(2)   1   A: and they went to the river,
      2   for a picnic,
      3   and,
      4   . . this and that,
      5   . . and on the way back,
      6   . . . they saw this group of elephants.

[Digression about who was at the picnic]

      7   A: [And] they started walking.
      8   . . toward these elephants.
      9   . . and these gals were taking pictures.
      10   And all of a sudden,
      11   one of them turned around.
      12   . . . and started to come toward him.

The noun phrase in line 6 introduces the elephants for the first time in this narrative. The use of *this* rather than *a* reflects the fact that the narrator intends to say more about the elephants (in fact, the ensuing story has to do with how one of the elephants tramples one of the women at the picnic).

Though it is generally accepted that information flow factors are the primary factors involved in selecting noun phrase form, various other factors have also been shown to be relevant; some of these will be discussed below.

Constituent Order

Constituent order – the order of elements in the clause, especially the relative positions of the verb, subject and object – is another area where information status has long been recognized as playing a crucial role. The Prague School linguists observed that, especially in languages with relatively flexible constituent order, given information tends to come earlier in the clause than new information. In Indonesian, for instance, the subject of the existential/locative verb *ada* 'be (at)' precedes the verb when it is given information, but follows it when it is new information. This is illustrated in examples (3) and (4) respectively.[2]

(3)   katakan   saja   yang   map   hitam   itu,
          say   just   REL   folder   black   that

          . . . Map   hitamnya,
          . . . folder black:the

          S   V
      →   **dia**   ada   di   lemari   sini.
          they   be   at   cupboard   here

          'Say for instance the black folders . . . the black folders, they're in the cupboard here.'

(4)   . . . Tapi,
          . . . But

          ada   s- --
          be —

          V   S
      →   ada   **dua**   **hal**   **yang**   **mau**   **saya**   **kasih**   **tahu**,
          be   two   thing   REL   want   I   give   know

          sama   anda-anda   ya?
          to   you:PL   yes

          'But, there's o- there are two things I want to tell you, OK?'

While English is a relatively fixed word-order language, it also has a tendency to arrange given and new information in this way, as reflected in the glosses of the above examples: *they are in the cupboard* vs *there are two things I want to tell you*. In the latter sentence, the 'fixedness' of English word order is respected by the presence of the 'dummy subject' *there*, but the understood subject of the sentence is *two things I want to tell you*, which comes clause-finally.

While the pattern illustrated here (old information first, new information last) is widespread, there is a competing pattern in many languages which favors initial position for certain kinds of unexpected information, especially information which is contrastive or 'resumptive' (that is, it has been mentioned before but not for some time). This pattern is commonly found, for instance, in Classical Malay, a language which is a precursor of Modern Indonesian but which exhibits significantly different constituent order patterns. Classical Malay has the same pattern for 'brand-new' arguments as Modern Indonesian does: they are introduced clause-finally. However, unlike Modern Indonesian, predictable arguments also tend to follow the verb, as illustrated in the following passage (both the King of China and the princess have been mentioned in the immediately preceding context).[3]

(5)

		V	S		
Maka	terlalulah	suka	**hati**	**raja**	**Cina**
then	very:EVT	happy	heart	king	China

		V	O					
oleh	beroleh	**puteri**	**anak raja**	dari	**Bukit Siguntang itu.**			
because	obtain	princess	child king	from	Bukit Siguntang that			

		V	A	Obl		
Maka	disambut	**baginda**	dengan	sempurnanya	kebesaran
then	PAS:welcome	he:HON	with	complete	greatness
dan	kemuliaan,				
and	honor				

		V	A
lalu	diperisteri	**baginda**;
then	PAS:marry	he:HON

	V	V	S	Obl			
beranak	bercuculah	**baginda**	dengan	tuan	puteri	itu.	
have:child	have:grandchild	he:HON	with	lady	princess	that	

'Then the king of China was very happy because of receiving the
daughter of the king from Bukit Siguntang. He received her with the
highest respect and honor, and married her; he had children and
grandchildren by that princess.'

However, arguments which are given but unexpected for some reason (usually
because there has been a shift in actor, topic, or setting) tend to precede
the verb, and are often marked by the 'topic' particle *pun*. The following
example illustrates a 'contrastive' context: in line 3, the Sang Sapurba is the
experiencer, whereas in line 4, the experiencer is the Chinese prince.

(6) 1

	V	S			
Kalakian,	ada	**seorang**	**anak**	**ceteria**	**Cina,**
then	be	one:CL	child	prince	China

2

	V	S
terlalu	baik	**rupanya**;
very	good	appearance:his

3

	V	A	
maka	dikasihi	**oleh**	**Sang** **Sapurba**;
then	PAS:love	by	Sang Sapurba

4 S

→

		V	Obl			
ia	**pun**	sangat	kasih	akan	duli	Sang Sapurba.
he	TOP	very	love	to	dust	Sang Sapurba

'There was a Chinese prince, very handsome; Sang Sapurba
loved him, and he (in turn) greatly loved Sang Sapurba.'

This function for clause-initial position has been called 'newsworthiness', and is discussed with relation to polysynthetic languages in Mithun (1987).[4]

Preferred Argument Structure

Another area where information flow factors have been shown to be crucially relevant to linguistic coding is the area of 'argument structure', a term which refers to the syntactic and semantic roles of the noun phrases in a clause. It has been noted for some time, for instance, that subjects tend strongly to have a given referent (Li, 1976). This is usually held to derive from the fact that subjects – especially of transitive verbs – tend to be agents, agents tend to be human, and humans tend to be discourse topics; thus they are likely to be given. Du Bois (1985; 1987) has extended this analysis, showing that new information also has preferences: new referents are much more likely to be introduced as objects of transitive verbs or as subjects of intransitive verbs in many different languages. Example (4) above showed the use of an intransitive verb to introduce a referent (existential and locative verbs are particularly suited for this function); the following examples, excerpted from examples (1) and (2) respectively, show how transitive verbs are used to introduce new information in object position. (Note that the subjects of both verbs are pronouns, in accordance with the tendency for transitive subjects to be given.)

(7)   . . . So they got three new guys.
(8)   . . . they saw this group of elephants.

Thus, objects of transitive verbs tend to contain new information and subjects of transitive verbs tend to contain given information, while intransitive subjects are sometimes given (like transitive subjects) and sometimes new (like transitive objects). Du Bois argues that this observation explains the fact that most languages of the world exhibit one of two major case-marking patterns: one in which subjects of intransitives have the same case marking as subjects of transitives (the so-called 'nominative-accusative' pattern, found in Indo-European languages and elsewhere), and another in which subjects of intransitives have the same case marking as objects of transitives (the so-called 'ergative' pattern, found in many Native American, Australian, and Pacific languages and elsewhere).

Discourse Structure

Another group of general principles often invoked in explaining the distribution of grammatical patterns in discourse is related to discourse structure. According to this view, grammar creates and reflects the higher-level organization of text in several ways. Certain grammatical phenomena, such as preverbal adverbial clauses (Thompson, 1987) and full noun phrases (Fox, 1987b), may signal text-structure unit boundaries; while other phenomena, such as pronouns (Fox, 1987b) and clause-chaining morphology (Longacre, 1985), may be associated with unit-internal locations. Alternatively, certain kinds of grammatical patterns may be associated with particular kinds of text-structure units: for example, simple past verbs with narrative clauses and intensifiers with evaluative clauses (Labov, 1972). Finally, types of inter-unit relation may be signaled by grammatical and lexical choice (especially certain kinds of subordination and subordinating linkers).

A text-structure account of a particular grammatical phenomenon requires, of course, a theory of discourse structure as a basis. Discourse grammarians have appropriated such theories from a wide variety of different sources, including anthropology, sociology, and artificial intelligence. A characteristic of these approaches is that they tend to associate markedly different kinds of structures to different discourse genres. Because of this, the inventory of units, labels and relations can be very different for, for example, folkloric narrative, personal narrative, written narrative, conversation, and written expository discourse. Since the topic of discourse structure is dealt with elsewhere in this book, a detailed account of these approaches would be out of place here; we will simply provide several examples illustrating some of the ways discourse structure considerations have been brought to bear on grammatical alternations.

Initial Adverbial Clauses

Adverbial clauses are clauses which are subordinate to a main clause and which may be placed either before or after the clause they modify. In English, they are usually introduced with 'subordinating conjunctions' such as *before, because,* or *although.* Since they can occur in more than one position, it becomes relevant to examine the factors which determine where they actually occur. Considerable research has been devoted to the discourse-functional factors which determine the position of the adverbial clause relative to the main clause. A comparison of these studies, which include Chafe (1984) and Thompson (1987) on narrative, Matthiessen and Thompson (1988) on expository discourse, and Ford (1993) on conversation, reveals that the most general function associated with initial position for adverbial clauses is that of creating and reflecting discourse structure by signaling shifts in time, place or orientation. For instance, consider the following Classical Malay example:

(9)   Maka Sang Sapurba pun   berangkatlah ke   Bentan.
       then Sang Sapurba TOP   depart   to   Bentan

→ **Setelah datang ke Bentan,** lalu masuk ke dalam negeri.
   after   come   to Bentan then enter to   inside country

'So Sang Sapurba left for Bentan. After arriving in Bentan, he went into the country.'

The text prior to this passage describes Sang Sapurba's preparations for his trip to Bentan, and the subsequent text describes his activities after he arrives there. The initial adverbial clause thus serves to signal a text structure boundary – here, a switch in the time frame and location of the action.

Noun Phrase Form

It has been suggested that after some types of discourse boundaries, such as episode boundaries, world shift (such as from the story itself to the actual situation where story telling occurs), and nested topic (where a digression is followed by a return to the original topic), the referent becomes less accessible, so it has to be expressed in a more explicit form (Chafe, 1976; 1987; Fox, 1987a; 1987b; Tomlin, 1987). In example (1) above, for instance, G uses the full noun phrase the *mayate* in line 21 after a digression (initiated by D) concerning how many people were hired and what their roles were. Earlier, we discussed this example simply in terms of the distance between the two references; however, a more careful account might note that the full noun phrase occurs directly after a text-structure boundary, a common pattern. There are cases where a full noun phrase can be used after a text-structural break even when the same referent has been mentioned in the immediately preceding clause. Fox (1987a) presents many examples such as the following:[5]

(10)   That did it for the Ewok. He jumped up, grabbed a four-foot-long spear, and held it defensively in her [i.e. Leia's] direction. Warily he circled, poking the pointed javelin at **her**, clearly more fearful than aggressive.

       'Hey, cut that out,' **Leia** brushed the weapon away with annoyance.

The use in the second paragraph of the full noun phrase *Leia* – rather than a pronoun, which is what a distance account might predict – reflects the presence of a text-structure boundary – in the terms of Rumelhart (1975), the boundary between an 'initiating event' and a 'reaction'.

Speaker Attitude

The range of phenomena associated in the literature with 'speaker attitude', also called 'stance', 'perspective', 'empathy', 'subjectivity', 'interpersonal metafunction' and so on, has been held to influence a wide range of aspects of linguistic form. Unlike information flow factors, attitude factors reflect neither the content of an utterance nor its informational aspects, but rather how the person views or assesses the state of affairs being described – or how they wish to be seen by their interlocutor as viewing it. Here, we will discuss the influence of speaker attitude on noun phrase form and argument structure.

Noun Phrase Form

There have been studies which suggest that referential choice is determined by these attitudinal factors. Several studies show that in some languages the explicitness of referential forms correlates with the degree of empathy (Clancy, 1980; Duranti, 1984): the more empathy the speaker feels towards the referent, the less explicit the form used (for example, zero anaphora and pronoun).

The converse is also true: sometimes a fuller form is used to indicate lack of empathy. Mayes and Ono (1991) also suggest that a particular set of explicit forms (anaphoric demonstrative plus noun) in Japanese is used to indicate a certain social distance between the speaker and the referent, regardless of the degree of the accessibility of the referent in the hearer's mind. Consider the following example:[6]

(11) H: iwayuru furui   taipu   no   eigyoo-   moo
        so-called old   type   of   sales:person EMPH
        'Because (he) is an old world sales-'

     T: ne.
        PRT
        'Yeah.'

     H: tenkeitekina eigyooman   da   kara   ano   hito.
        typical   sales:person be   because that person
        'typical sales person, that person.'

     T: honto   yan   nacchau   **ano** **hito**.
        really disgusted become   that   person
        '(I'm) really tired of that person.'

The use of the more explicit *ano hito* in the last clause can be explained by the speakers' stance toward the referent. In the context of the conversation, the participants were complaining about a co-worker. The use of *ano hito* clearly indicates a certain social/emotional distance and thus a lack of empathy between the speaker and the referent. The unusual constituent order of the final clause in this example is probably also stance-related: Ono and Suzuki (1992) report some instances where predicates indicating strong emotion are expressed before their arguments in Japanese, which is otherwise known for rigid predicate-final order.

Argument Structure

Several researchers have suggested that there is a direct relationship between the stance taken by a speaker and the mapping of event participants onto case roles in discourse. In such accounts, agents or subjects are generally held to have a special syntactic status, either because the speaker takes their 'point of view' (as suggested in, for example, Chafe, 1994), or because they are held socially 'responsible' for the event (the account preferred in, for example, Duranti and Ochs, 1990; Duranti, 1994). Consider the following example from a traditional Samoan village council meeting (Duranti, 1994: 132). Tafili reveals a rumor that has forced her brother Savea to file a suit against Inu. First, Tafili says:[7]

(12)   e (le)aga 'o 'upu gei ou ke kaukala iai,
          because these words I am going to talk about,

→   "ua   fa'akau   Savea   e   **Igu**   i   kupe.' . . .
          PST   buy   Savea   ERG   Inu   with   monies
          'Savea has been bought by Inu with money.' . . .

ia 'ua kakau ai lāga kulāfogo 'upu gā,
          so it has been necessary to try in court those words,

In the quote reporting the rumor, Inu is marked by *e* (an 'ergative' marker, which makes it explicit that Inu is the agent of a transitive clause). Duranti suggests that this case marker is associated with attributed responsibility – relevant here, because this is an accusation of wrongdoing. However, later in the same meeting, Savea says:

(13) → e   leai   ā   se   kupe   a   **Igu**   o   maimau
          TA   NEG   EMPH   ART   money   of   Inu   PRED   wasted
          there is no money of Inu's wasted

e   kokogi ai   sa'u   fāsefulu   kālā . . .
          TA   pay   PRO   my   forty   dollars
          to pay my forty dollars . . (or 'to pay forty dollars for me')

Here, the same event is described, but this time Inu is marked by the genitive marker *a*. Apparently, in this scene, Savea is reframing the event in a way which minimizes Inu's responsibility.

We have seen in this section that many of the factors usually associated with information flow considerations – including pronoun use, constituent order, and case marking – may also be associated with factors relating to the speaker's attitude. In the next section, we explore additional social factors in relation to grammatical choice.

Interactional Factors

Pressures from the demands of conversational interaction have been associated with a wide range of grammatical alternations. Various aspects of syntax can be understood as motivated by goals that arise for interactants out of the turn-taking system of conversation (described by Pomerantz and Fehr in Chapter 3, Volume 2 of this work). Here, we will focus on the effects of interactional pressures on two areas of syntactic choice, both of which relate to motivations for presenting information in a particular sequence.

Left-dislocation

'Left-dislocation' is the construction found in sentences such as *Sandy, she likes garlic*. According to traditional accounts, this construction involves 'fronting' a noun phrase and replacing it with a 'pronoun copy'; it is viewed as a simple, monoclausal construction. However, both Keenan and Schieffelin (1976) and Geluykens (1992) have shown that this construction is likely to be interactionally complex, involving contributions from more than one interactant, and that it is designed to fulfill interactional goals. For example, Geluykens (1992: 36) presents such examples as the following:

(14) → A: well **Sir Garnet Wolseley**
        B: yes ((sure oh oh))
        A: he was the one who did all the army reforms in the eighteen eighties

Here, speaker A introduces a referent in the discourse with a noun phrase, and only after the introduction has been confirmed by speaker B does A come back and say something about the referent. Thus, the left-dislocation construction is distributed across three turns by two speakers, and involves negotiation between them as to the identifiability of the referent. So the examination of left-dislocation in discourse shows that its use involves heavy interactional work, and this further suggests that the existence and characteristics of the construction itself may be interactionally motivated.

Final Adverbial Clauses

We suggested earlier that the function most commonly associated with initial position for adverbial clauses has to do with text-structuring considerations. Ford (1993) has addressed the function of adverbial clauses in other positions in conversation. She suggests that when an adverbial clause is produced in final position following a falling intonation contour, it is motivated by interactional factors. For example, Ford (1993: 115) finds examples such as the following in her conversational data:[8]

(15)   1 A: Did you get ye=r your first pay check from it?
         3   . . at least?
         4 R: No= I won't get that for a couple weeks yet.
         5 A: Oh,
         7   . . W'l
 → 8 R: 'Cause it takes a long time.
         9 A: at least it's in the bank,
       10 R: . . . Yeah it will be.

In this example A asks R a question in lines 1–3. R's answer in line 4 is somewhat unexpected, as shown by A's utterance *oh* in line 5. Ford suggests that the adverbial clause in line 8 is used in response to A's signal

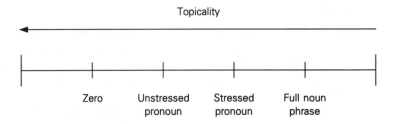

Figure 4.2   *A scalar category*

of interactional trouble, that is as a clarification for the unexpected answer. Thus we see that interaction motivates the use of final adverbial clauses in English.

The Nature of Analytical Categories

One of the most fundamental ways in which discourse-functional linguistics has divided itself from autonomist linguistics is in its treatment of the basic categories of analysis. Discourse-functional linguists have explicitly rejected the idea that the categories of grammar are Aristotelian, that is, that they are structured such that a given item either is or is not a member of a category, and tests should be discoverable to determine which is the case (see, for example, Givón, 1989 for arguments against this view). Rather, they have proposed a number of other models of category structure, using a variety of terms including hierarchies, scales, continua, and prototypes. These proposals all have in common the view that category membership can be a matter of degree.

The simplest type of non-Aristotelian category views category member-ship as scalar, where different degrees of category membership can be plotted along a single dimension. For instance, Givón (1983) proposes that the category 'topic' is scalar. He suggests that topicality itself is continuous (a referent at a particular point in discourse may be more or less topical), but that a given language will divide up the continuum according to its inventory of linguistic forms. For instance, a language which contrasts 'zero anaphora', a set of unstressed pronouns, a set of stressed pronouns, and full noun phrases will divide up the topicality continuum as in Figure 4.2. As shown in this figure, phonologically 'lighter' material falls closer to the left end of the scale, while phonologically 'heavier' material falls closer to the right end.

Some types of linguistic categories don't fit the 'scale' model well, because they can be viewed as varying along more than one dimension. An alternative model is the prototype structure suggested by Rosch (1978), in which a 'central' member of a category has a collection of related charac-teristics, but non-central members can diverge in various ways according to how many and which of these characteristics are lacking. In the next two sections, we will present two analyses of this type.

Transitivity

One example of a category distinction which is traditionally viewed as Aristotelian is the distinction between transitive and intransitive verbs. This distinction is addressed in an influential paper by Hopper and Thompson (1980). This paper proposes that the distinction between 'transitive' and 'intransitive' verbs – in traditional grammars, simply a matter of whether the verb has an object – needs to be broken down into distinct factors, in order to explain various cross-linguistic correlations between the argument structure of a verb and various grammatical characteristics. The factors cited by Hopper and Thompson include matters relating to the agent (such as volitionality), the verb (such as telicity, having an endpoint), and the patient (such as affectedness) as well as the overall argument structure of the clause. These factors (which, taken together, are characterized as 'discourse transitivity') are shown to correlate with each other in a sample of languages. In Tongan, for instance, there is a 'transitive' marker -'*i*, which is used when the object is totally affected by the action of the verb, *and* as a marker of perfective aspect:

(16) (a) Na'e   taipe   'e   he   tangata 'a   e   topi.
        PAST   type   ERG DEF man   ABS DEF letter
        'The man is typing the letter.'

    (b) Na'e   tanu-'i   'e   he   tangata 'a   e   ika.
        PAST   bury-TRANS ERG DEF man   ABS DEF fish
        'The man buried the fish.'

This example illustrates the convergence of various aspects of transitivity which are in principle independent. This convergence is illustrated in Figure 4.3. That these three factors might be coded by separate linguistic devices (as they are in many languages) is represented in the diagram by the fact that there are non-overlapping sections of the circles; that they will often tend to converge is represented by the overlapping section in the middle.

Given this understanding of the way multi-functionality of the linguistic forms of the world's languages supports a common notion of discourse transitivity, it is easy to see how a clause in discourse can be understood as more or less 'discourse-transitive' even in a language which doesn't have multi-functional forms of the type illustrated by Tongan. Even in English, for instance, a clause which has two arguments, perfective aspect, and a completely affected object can be thought of as 'more transitive' than one which is missing one or more of these characteristics. Hopper and Thompson go on to demonstrate that clauses which have many attributes associated with high transitivity share a common discourse function – that of marking the 'foreground' or event line of a narrative – whereas clauses that have fewer transitivity attributes tend to be off the event line,

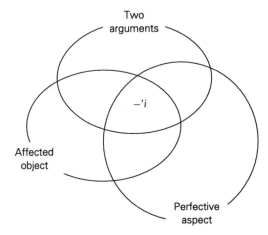

Figure 4.3   *Transitivity as a prototype category*

occurring for instance in descriptive passages. This contrast is argued to constitute the 'discourse basis' for the typological correlation among the transitivity parameters.

Lexical Classes

Another set of categories which are traditionally viewed as Aristotelian is the set of word classes or 'parts of speech' in the lexicon. Hopper and Thompson (1984) propose a prototype view of one word-class contrast, that between nouns and verbs. They argue that the primary motivation for the lexical categories 'noun' and 'verb' has to do with the need of speakers on the one hand to establish time-stable referents and track them through a discourse – the function primarily associated with nouns – and on the other hand to move events in the discourse forward through time – the function primarily associated with verbs. They argue that the morphological proper-ties associated with these two categories (such as number and noun class for nouns, tense and aspect for verbs) are motivated by these distinct discourse functions. Consequently, when nouns and verbs are associated with discourse functions other than the 'central' or 'prototypical' ones described above, these distinctive morphological markers tend to be lost.

For instance, consider the first occurrence of the word *paper* in the following excerpt from example (1) we considered above:

(17)   21 G: . . But the mayate,
         22   . . . apparently,
         23   . . it seems like he's,
         24   . . . worked in a –
    →   25 D: . . . paper company before.
         26 G: Yeah.
         27   He knows about paper.

The word *paper* in line 25 is non-referential: no specific paper is being mentioned. The fact that *paper* is not being used to track a time-stable referent in the discourse is indicated by the fact that the mention of paper in G's turn isn't a pronoun (he doesn't say 'he knows about *it*', even though both nouns arguably have the same generic referent: paper in general). Consequently, the normal morphological and syntactic attributes that are associated with nouns are lost in this context: the noun can't take articles or modifiers and can't be pronominalized.

A similar point can be made for verbs. Consider the verb *stock boost* in line 4 of the following, again taken from example (1):

(18)   1 G: . . Can you imagine man?
          2   . . . They hired summer help,
          3   . . They're paying seven fifty,
     →   4   to stock boost,

This is a purpose clause, and as such it doesn't refer to a real event that is asserted to have occurred. Because of this it is restricted to a 'stripped-down' form that doesn't allow for the normal morphological and syntactic trappings of verbs, such as tense marking, person agreement, and the expression of the subject.

Hopper and Thompson propose the term 'categoriality' for the property of being prototypical in function and having the full morphological and syntactic 'trappings' of one's category. For instance, non-referential nouns or verbs in purpose clauses can be said to be low in categoriality. The categories 'noun' and 'verb' are said to be appropriately described by a prototype structure rather than a scale, because there are different ways in which an expression can diverge from the central function of each category. A verb, for instance, can fail to move the event line forward by referring to a non-actual situation, as in the purpose clause example above, or by referring to a state rather than an event, or by being presupposed rather than asserted. These are all different ways of being low in categoriality, and they cannot be arranged along a single dimension.

As the above discussion shows, discourse-functional linguistics has used evidence from discourse variation and from typology to challenge the notion of 'grammatical category', which is at the heart of traditional approaches to grammar.

Conclusions

In the preceding sections, we have shown that a number of linguistic phenomena must be understood in terms of their functions in discourse. By establishing the discourse basis of linguistic phenomena, discourse-functional grammarians have demonstrated the importance of using natural discourse data in linguistics. In this final section, we would like to discuss several directions of research which we feel are either the most promising or the most necessary for the future of discourse and grammar research to be both fruitful and exciting.

One exciting development in discourse-functional linguistics is its recent inquiries into syntax in the most natural form of discourse: conversation. The most recent studies in this area are uncovering exactly how grammatical resources are exploited by speakers – specifically, revealing the details of how grammatical resources interact with cognitive and interactional factors. A number of these studies have found that the actual production of syntax is locally managed – that is, transpiring in real time, second-by-second, and always contingent on negotiation with the other participants in the speech event. Moreover, although the grammatical patterns resulting from this process would often be considered 'syntactically ill-formed' in traditional accounts, interactants are extremely tolerant of such constructions. This line of research is only now beginning to uncover the nature and workings of grammatical resources in actual interactional contexts, but it clearly has the potential to reshape our understanding of the fundamental categories of linguistic analysis.

Because of the focus on natural data and full context, discourse linguists find themselves using increasingly advanced technologies for collecting and analysing data. The first step is a move from the analysis of written discourse to the analysis of spoken discourse with audio tape recordings and transcriptions, using increasingly sophisticated audio equipment and richer and richer transcription systems (Edwards and Lampert, 1993). This methodology is beginning to be supplemented by a trend towards the use of video cameras, which can provide information about non-linguistic as well as linguistic context. Moreover, the use of transcriptions as the primary basis for analysis is beginning to be replaced by an emphasis on working with the audio or video recording directly, since transcriptions, no matter how rich, always sacrifice some of the information available in the context to interactants. Emerging multimedia technologies such as digitization of sound and video are being exploited to facilitate this process: digitized audio and video data can be played back endlessly without degradation of the signal, and unlike analog data, they can be stored in databases and accessed in any order.

Nearly all of the research described in this chapter is related primarily to issues of choice in grammar rather than lexicon: much attention has been paid, for instance, to how a speaker chooses between nouns and pronouns, but little to how a speaker chooses between two lexical items which could describe the same reality, such as *buy* and *sell*. The attention that has been devoted to the lexicon has focused primarily on explanations for lexical category distinctions (see earlier) rather than to choice within lexical sets. Nonetheless, linguists of all theoretical persuasions have increasingly come to realize that the lexicon is intimately intertwined with syntax, and that syntactic choice and lexical choice cannot be considered independently of each other. A handful of studies have taken on the issue of lexical selection in discourse. For instance, Downing (1980) explores how factors involving information flow and discourse structure condition the formulation of referring expressions in narrative, while Cumming (1995) discusses what semantic characteristics make a verb suitable for the discourse task of introducing new participants into discourse. However, these few studies have only begun to scratch the surface of what is potentially a vast and highly instructive area of linguistic investigation.

Finally, we would like to point out that there has not been much effort among the discourse-functional linguists whose work is described above in trying to establish a coherent overall model of human language: a model which would clarify how functional factors which have been singly and independently suggested to motivate particular linguistic forms interact with each other, and in which those interacting functional factors are incorporated with structural aspects of language in order to model the processes involved in human communication. Needless to say, such a model should include not only components covered by the traditional areas of linguistics such as morphosyntax and semantics, but also components which deal with such cognitive and interactional factors as memory, attention, empathy, and affect. Moreover, it must also incorporate those components covered by such other areas of linguistics as phonetics and phonology which have been given little attention by discourse-functional linguists. In order for discourse-functional linguistics to be considered a serious area of scientific inquiry, explicit modeling should be one of its eventual goals, and we believe the field has now reached a stage where the first steps toward this goal can be taken.

Recommended Reading

Here we list some additional works related to the issues discussed in this chapter which the interested reader can consult, arranged according to topic.

Longacre (1976), Givón (1990), and Haiman (1985) give good general overviews of the discourse-functional approach to grammar, touching on many of the issues discussed here from rather different perspectives. On the nature of the relation of context to language, see Gumperz (1982) and Auer and di Luzio (1992). There are many important studies on information flow in relation to a variety of grammatical constructions; as a representative sample, see for instance the papers in Li (1976) on subjects, Prince (1978) on clefts, Shibatani (1988) and Fox and Hopper (1994) on voice, Fox and Thompson (1990) on relative clauses, and Thompson (1990) on dative shift. On interactional factors and grammar, see Duranti and Goodwin (1992), Iwasaki (1993), Ford and Fox (1996), Fox and Jasperson (1996), Goodwin (1979; 1981), and Ochs et al. (1996). On text structure and grammar, see Haiman and Thompson (1988). On lexical categories and lexical selection, see Thompson (1988) and Cumming and Ono (1996).

Notes

The authors would like to thank Sandy Thompson, Mike Ewing and Robert Engelbretsen for their comments on a draft of this chapter.

1 This and the following example are from English conversational data collected and transcribed by Danae Paolino. The following transcription conventions are used:

1　Line breaks represent intonation units.
2　Line-final punctuation reflects intonation contour.
3　Two dots represent a short pause; three dots represent a longer pause.
4　Brackets [ ] indicate overlap between speakers.

Since there are many different systems of discourse transcription in use in the material we have drawn on for examples, with different kinds of information being notated in each system, we have simplified many of the examples by omitting non-relevant information such as timing and breath.

2 The examples in this section are taken from a transcript by Michael Ewing of an office conversation collected by Susanna Cumming. The labels above the Indonesian show the relative position of the various grammatical elements in the clause: V = verb; S = intransitive subject; A = transitive agent; O = transitive object; Obl = oblique. The following glossing abbreviations are used in the Indonesian and Malay examples: CL = classifier; EVT = eventive particle; HON = honorific pronoun; PAS = passive; PL = plural; REL = relative clause marker; TOP = topic.

3 The Classical Malay examples are taken from the *Sejarah Melayu*, a written quasi-historical narrative epic describing the history of the Malay people and the origins of their traditions.

4 For more discussion of the functions of constituent order alternation in Classical Malay and Modern Indonesian, see Cumming (1991).

5 This example is from the novelization of *Return of the Jedi* (Fox, 1987a: 169).

6 Example from Mayes and Ono (1991). Abbreviations: EMPH = emphasis; PRT = particle.

7 Example froms Duranti (1994). Abbreviations: ART = article; EMPH = emphasis; ERG = ergative marker; NEG = negative; PRED = predicate marker; PRO = pronoun; PST = past; TA = tense/aspect marker.

8 Example from Ford (1993). The transcription has been altered slightly to agree with earlier examples.

References

Auer, P. and di Luzio, A. (eds) (1992) *The Contextualization of Language*. Amsterdam: Benjamins.

Bolinger, D. (1952) *Forms of English*. Cambridge, MA: Harvard University Press.

Bolinger, D. (1986) *Intonation and its Parts*. Stanford, CA: Stanford University Press.

Bolinger, D. (1989) *Intonation and its Uses*. Stanford, CA: Stanford University Press.

Chafe, W. (1976) 'Givenness, contrastiveness, definiteness, subject, topics, and point of view', in C.N. Li (ed.), *Subject and Topic*. New York: Academic Press. pp. 25–55.

Chafe, W. (ed.) (1980) *The Pear Stories: Cognitive, Cultural, and Linguistic Aspects of Narrative Production*. Norwood, NJ: Ablex.

Chafe, W. (1984) 'How people use adverbial clauses', in *Proceedings of the Tenth Annual Meeting of the Berkeley Linguistics Society*. Berkeley, CA: Berkeley Linguistics Society. pp. 437–49.

Chafe, W. (1987) 'Cognitive constraints on information flow', in R.S. Tomlin (ed.), *Coherence and Grounding in Discourse*. Amsterdam: Benjamins. pp. 21–51.

Chafe, W. (1994) *Discourse, Consciousness, and Time*. Chicago: University of Chicago Press.

Clancy, P. (1980) 'Referential choice in English and Japanese narrative discourse', in W. Chafe (ed.), *The Pear Stories: Cognitive, Cultural, and Linguistic Aspects of Narrative Production*. Norwood, NJ: Ablex. pp. 127–202.

Cumming, S. (1991) *Functional Change: the Case of Malay Constituent Order*. Berlin: Mouton de Gruyter.

Cumming, S. (1995) 'Functional categories in the lexicon: referent introduction in Indonesian novels', *Text*, 14 (4): 465–94.

Cumming, S. and Ono, T. (1996) '*Ad hoc* hierarchy: lexical structures for reference in consumer reports articles', in B. Fox (ed.), *Anaphora in Discourse*. Amsterdam: Benjamins.

Daneš, F. (1974) 'Functional sentence perspective and the organization of the text', in F. Daneš (ed.), *Papers on Functional Sentence Perspective*. Prague: Academia. pp. 106–28.

Downing, P. (1980) 'Factors influencing lexical choice in narrative', in W. Chafe (ed.), *The Pear Stories: Cognitive, Cultural, and Linguistic Aspects of Narrative Production*. Norwood, NJ: Ablex. pp. 89–126.

Du Bois, J. (1980) 'Beyond definiteness: the trace of identity in discourse', in W. Chafe (ed.), *The Pear Stories: Cognitive, Cultural, and Linguistic Aspects of Narrative Production*. Norwood, NJ: Ablex. pp. 203–74.

Du Bois, J. (1985) 'Competing motivations', in J. Haiman (ed.), *Iconicity in Syntax*. Amsterdam: Benjamins. pp. 343–65.

Du Bois, J. (1987) 'The discourse basis of ergativity', *Language*, 63 (4): 805–55.

Duranti, A. (1984) 'The social meaning of subject pronouns in Italian conversation', *Text*, 4 (4): 277–311.

Duranti, A. (1994) *From Grammar to Politics*. Berkeley, CA: University of California Press.

Duranti, A. and Goodwin, C. (eds) (1992) *Rethinking Context: Language as an Interactive Phenomenon*. Cambridge: Cambridge University Press.

Duranti, A. and Ochs, E. (1990) 'Genitive constructions and agency in Samoan discourse', *Studies in Language*, 14 (1): 1–23.

Edwards, J. and Lampert, M. (eds) (1993) *Talking Data: Transcription and Coding in Discourse Research*. Hillsdale, NJ: Erlbaum.

Firbas, J. (1966) 'On defining the theme in functional sentence perspective', *Travaux Linguistiques de Prague*, 2: 267–80.

Ford, C.E. (1993) *Grammar in Interaction: Adverbial Clauses in American English Conversations*. Cambridge: Cambridge University Press.

Ford, C.E. and Fox, B. (1996) 'Interactional motivations for reference formulation: *He* had. *This* guy had, a beautiful, thirty-two O:lds', in B. Fox (ed.), *Anaphora in Discourse*. Amsterdam: Benjamins.

Fox, B. (1987a) 'Anaphora in popular written English narratives', in R.S. Tomlin (ed.), *Coherence and Grounding in Discourse*. Amsterdam: Benjamins. pp. 157–74.

Fox, B. (1987b) *Discourse Structure and Anaphora: Written and Conversational English*. Cambridge: Cambridge University Press.

Fox, B. and Hopper, P. (eds) (1994) *Voice: Form and Function*. Amsterdam: Benjamins.

Fox, B. and Jasperson, R. (1996) 'The syntactic organization of repair', in P. Davis (ed.), *Descriptive and Theoretical Modes in the New Linguistics*. Amsterdam: Benjamins.

Fox, B. and Thompson, S.A. (1990) 'A discourse explanation of relative clauses in English conversation', *Language*, 66 (2): 297–316.

Geluykens, R. (1992) *From Discourse Process to Grammatical Construction: On Left-Dislocation in English*. Amsterdam: Benjamins.

Givón, T. (ed.) (1983) *Topic Continuity in Discourse: a Quantitative Cross-Language Study*. Amsterdam: Benjamins.

Givón, T. (1989) *Mind, Code and Context: Essays in Pragmatics*. Hillsdale, NJ: Erlbaum.

Givón, T. (1990) *Syntax: a Functional-Typological Introduction*. Amsterdam: Benjamins.

Goodwin, C. (1979) 'The interactive construction of a sentence in natural conversation', in G. Psathas (ed.), *Everyday Language: Studies in Ethnomethodology*. New York: Irvington. pp. 97–121.

Goodwin, C. (1981) *Conversational Organization: Interaction between Speakers and Hearers.* New York: Academic Press.

Greenberg, J. (1966) *Language Universals.* The Hague: Mouton.

Grimes, J. (1975) *The Thread of Discourse.* The Hague: Mouton.

Gumperz, J. (1982) *Discourse Strategies.* Cambridge: Cambridge University Press.

Haiman, J. (1985) *Natural Syntax.* Cambridge: Cambridge University Press.

Haiman, J. and Thompson, S.A. (eds) (1988) *Clause Combining in Grammar and Discourse.* Amsterdam: Benjamins.

Halliday, M.A.K. (1967–8) 'Notes on transitivity and theme in English, parts 1–3', *Journal of Linguistics,* 3 (1): 37–81, 3 (2): 199–244, and 4 (2): 179–215.

Halliday, M.A.K. (1985) *An Introduction to Functional Grammar.* London: Edward Arnold.

Hopper, P. (1988) 'Emergent grammar and the a-priori grammar postulate', in D. Tannen (ed.), *Linguistics in Context: Connecting, Observation, and Understanding.* Norwood, NJ: Ablex. pp. 117–34.

Hopper, P. and Thompson, S.A. (1980) 'Transitivity in grammar and discourse', *Language,* 56 (2): 251–99.

Hopper, P. and Thompson, S.A. (1984) 'The discourse basis for lexical categories in universal grammar', *Language,* 60 (4): 703–52.

Iwasaki, S. (1993) *Subjectivity in Grammar and Discourse: Theoretical Considerations and a Case Study of Japanese Spoken Discourse.* Amsterdam: Benjamins.

Keenan, E. and Schieffelin, B. (1976) 'Foregrounding referents: a reconsideration of left dislocation in discourse', in *Proceedings of the 2nd Annual Meeting of the Berkeley Linguistics Society.* pp. 240–57.

Labov, W. (1972) *Language in the Inner City: Studies in the Black English Vernacular.* Philadelphia: University of Pennsylvania Press.

Li, C. (ed.) (1976) *Subject and Topic.* New York: Academic Press.

Longacre, R.E. (1972) *Hierarchy and Universality of Discourse Constituents in New Guinea Languages: Discussion.* Washington: Georgetown University Press.

Longacre, R.E. (1976) *Anatomy of Speech Notions.* Lisse: Peter de Ridder Press.

Longacre, R.E. (1985) 'Sentences as combinations of clauses', in T. Shopen (ed.), *Language Typology and Syntactic Description. Vol. II: Complex Constructions.* Cambridge: Cambridge University Press. pp. 235–86.

Mathesius, V. (1975) *A Functional Analysis of Present-Day English on a General Linguistic Basis* (trans. L. Duskova, ed. J. Vacek). Prague: Academia.

Matthiessen, C.M.I.M. and Thompson, S.A. (1988) 'The structure of discourse and "subordination"', in J. Haiman and S.A. Thompson (eds), *Clause Combining in Grammar and Discourse.* Amsterdam: Benjamins. pp. 275–329.

Mayes, P. and Ono, T. (1991) 'Social factors influencing reference in Japanese: with special emphasis on *ano hito*', *Santa Barbara Papers in Linguistics,* 3: 84–93.

Mithun, M. (1987) 'Is basic word order universal?', in R.S. Tomlin (ed.), *Coherence and Grounding in Discourse.* Amsterdam: Benjamins. pp. 282–328.

Ochs, E. (1988) *Culture and Language Development: Language Acquisition and Language Socialization in a Samoan Village.* Cambridge: Cambridge University Press.

Ochs, E., Schegloff, E. and Thompson, S.A. (eds) (1996) *Grammar and Interaction.* Cambridge: Cambridge University Press.

Ono, T. and Suzuki, R. (1992) 'Word order variability in Japanese conversation: motivations and grammaticization', *Text,* 12 (3): 429–45.

Ono, T. and Thompson, S.A. (1996) 'What can conversation tell us about syntax?', in P. Davis (ed.), *Descriptive and Theoretical Modes in the New Linguistics.* Amsterdam: Benjamins.

Payne, Doris (1990) *Pragmatics of Word Order: Typological Dimensions of Verb Initial Languages.* Berlin: Mouton de Gruyter.

Pike, K. (1954) *Language in Relation to a Unified Theory of the Structure of Human Behavior.* The Hague: Mouton.

Prince, E.F. (1978) 'A comparison of WH-clefts and It-clefts in discourse', *Language,* 54 (4): 883–906.

Prince, E.F. (1981) 'Toward a taxonomy of given–new information', in P. Cole (ed.), *Radical Pragmatics*. New York: Academic Press. pp. 223–55.

Rosch, E. (1978) 'Principles of categorization', in E. Rosch and B.B. Lloyd (eds), *Cognition and Categorization*. Hillsdale, NJ: Erlbaum. pp. 27–48.

Rumelhart, D. (1975) 'Notes on a schema for stories', in D. Bobrow and A. Collins (eds), *Representation and Understanding*. New York: Academic Press. pp. 211–36.

Shibatani, M. (ed.) (1988) *Passive and Voice*. Amsterdam: Benjamins.

Thompson, S.A. (1987) '"Subordination" and narrative event structure', in R.S. Tomlin (ed.), *Coherence and Grounding in Discourse*. Amsterdam: Benjamins. pp. 435–54.

Thompson, S.A. (1988) 'A discourse approach to the cross-linguistic category "adjective"', in J. Hawkins (ed.), *Explanations for Language Universals*. Oxford: Blackwell. pp. 167–85.

Thompson, S.A. (1990) 'Information flow and "dative shift" in English', in J. Edmondson, C. Feagin and P. Mühlhäusler (eds), *Development and Diversity: Linguistic Variation across Time and Space*. Dallas: Summer Institute of Linguistics and University of Texas at Arlington. pp. 239–54.

Tomlin, R.S. (1987) 'Linguistic reflections of cognitive events', in R.S. Tomlin (ed.), *Coherence and Grounding in Discourse*. Amsterdam: Benjamins. pp. 455–79.

Wright, S. and Givón, T. (1987) 'The pragmatics of indefinite reference: quantified text-based studies', *Studies in Language*, 11 (1): 1–33.

5

Discourse Styles

Barbara Sandig and Margret Selting

Characterization and Delimitation of the Field

What Is Style?

Strictly speaking, style can only be spoken of in the plural (Carter and Nash, 1990: Chapter 1), that is to say in respect of the range of possible variations, when formulating discourse. Styles differ from each other; we are therefore able to speak of a variety of styles. Moreover, this concept of style is not a judgement, such as that underlying remarks like *that has no style*, but rather a concept which is appropriate for identifying and describing different styles, their meaning and their relevance in discourse. This is the concept of style which will be discussed here.

Our concept of styles covers all kinds of meaningful variation in written and spoken discourse. Style includes literary styles (of different epochs, authors or genres), non-literary written styles (such as the styles of various newspapers or magazines, or variations within a newspaper such as news style, arts/review style, advertisement style and so on), as well as different styles in spoken discourse (see below; cf. Carter and Nash, 1990; Widdowson, 1992).

In the following we will try to clarify how style is formed and structured and how it contributes to different kinds of interaction.

Style Features

As members of a speech community we are all aware of a number of style features which exist because we have a variety of alternatives at hand for referring to the same object, the same process, the same fact. They are not all equal in value but are stylistically differentiated.

Lexical Style Features Our vocabulary provides a large variety of alternatives to denote the same thing, but they partially differ in meaning (Table 5.1). Such meaning 'connotations' belong to different 'stylistic levels' and indicate distinct spheres of action, activity types, topics or 'social worlds' within a speech community. And they are not randomly mixed. Mixing

Table 5.1

Colloquial	Normal/standard	Formal	Domain-specific
wolf down	eat	dine	
	always	invariably	
	for you	on your behalf	
because of your application	with reference to your application	in consideration of your application	,
	water		H_2O

these levels either results in a stylistic error or has a specific stylistic meaning.

Syntactic Style Features With respect to syntax, some characteristic stylistic choices associated with particular activity types are, for example, ellipses in headlines and slogans, or the fronting of locatives in tourist guide books (cf. Enkvist, 1981: 100).

Phonological and Graphological Style Features In the slogan *I like Ike!* the use of rhyme and sound repetition creates an overall impression in a completely different way from *I vote for Ike*. The graphical form can have an additional effect: compare *I like Ike!* with *I love Ike*, in which the rhyme is lost. The choice of the verb (*like, vote for, love*) depends on the following name. The sentence *I like Ike!* expresses the intended message in a more subtle way and, through the use of the 'familiar' name, also in a more 'committed' way than *Vote for Eisenhower!*

Figures of Style Prototypical style features as described in classical rhetoric are devices such as metaphor, parallelism, alliteration, rhyme, etc. It is for example perfectly normal to use the metaphor *a pile of money*. When, however, a large bank lost more than $6,000 million by fraud, a 'stronger' image was required. Yet, the head of the bank talked about *peanuts* to play down the damage, and people were upset. The stylistic meaning of a metaphor, which is created by the kind of relation between the denotation and the image used, suggested too much playing down in this case.

Pragmatic Style Features We can also choose between different ways of performing a speech act, for instance the salutation in letters (*Dear Barbara, Dear Madam*) and the complementary closing in letters (*Love, Sincerely yours, Respectfully*, etc.). Through the selected variants, letter writers cannot help expressing their relationship with the addressee. Even the failure to use specific parts as expected is stylistically relevant: thus a letter without salutation and closing would be 'coarse' or 'uneducated'.

Holistic Style Structures and their Functions

Single style features are always only a part of a larger holistic style structure, a *Gestalt*, which arises from the interplay of different kinds of features.

Written and Spoken Style Structures Both written and spoken styles are structures constituted by bundles of co-occurring features. For example, in texts, the global text format and typographical features used interact with the kind of lexis and syntax, sound qualities like rhyme, as well as with the choice of speech acts and their realizations, etc. In spoken discourse sequences and kinds of speech acts and their realizations, kinds of turn taking, the choice of words and syntax, as well as prosodic structures and voice quality, are particularly important. Altogether the co-occurring style features form a particular whole (*Gestalt*). Such holistic entities suggest stylistic functions which can be interpreted by recipients.

Functions of Styles: Types of Stylistic Meaning

There are some typical and recurrent meanings that are constituted by the use of stylistic variation:

1 to express one's relation towards a situation, as, for example, through the degree of formality or institutionalization of speech activities
2 to enable the self-presentation of the speaker/writer as, for example, 'involved', 'funny', 'educated', 'member of a certain class or group', 'acting in a certain role'
3 to tailor (design) activities for particular types of recipients, such as children, foreigners, in-group members
4 to define a particular (kind of) relation between speaker or writer and recipient, for example, to establish and maintain participant relations as 'polite', 'distant', 'intimate'
5 to set apart different kinds of activities in their sequence (see later); and so on (cf. Sandig, 1986b: Chapter 1.2; Selting, 1992).

Style thus makes certain kinds of meaning interpretable. Meaning achieved through the use of style does not have to be made semantically explicit. If I start a letter with *Dear Margret*, I define the relationship (for the past and the future) as 'personal', 'friendly', 'close', etc. I do not have to make this explicit. Styles are ideal means for expressing implied meanings.

Typified Styles

Genre and Activity-Type Specific Styles All of us can recognize the style of a sermon, of a telegram, of trivial literature; languages for special purposes and jargons can be looked upon as styles. For specific roles such as the nagging mother, the professor or the teenager there is a wide range of styles. One person can present herself alternatively as 'academically educated' or 'naive feminine' or 'young and up-to-date'; via style she 'contextualizes' her discourse as 'academic', 'feminine', etc. We can also change styles in discourse and thus contextualize passages of speech, such as indicate stylistically whether we are disputing or narrating (cf. Selting, 1992). However, writers or speakers can deviate from expected styles by using, for example, linguistic and paralinguistic cues from religious style in an everyday context: thus, a 'normal' everyday message can be presented like a piece of sermon.

In sum, stylistic variation is a kind of language variation that is actively and meaningfully used in order to suggest interpretive frames for the interpretation of utterances. Consider the following example:

(1) Somewhere he is leaning against the bar, tall, dark and handsome. Suddenly he sees a woman, tall, dark hair, seductively attractive. Both hold their breath, no one moves. Then she goes up to him and it is as if they have both known each other for a long time and, yet, so excitingly new. He takes her hand and slowly they walk into the setting sun.

This story contextualizes a trivial novel: *leaning against the bar* suggests a place of leisure: *he* and *a woman* are described as 'a good match' through the parallelisms *tall, dark* and *handsome/attractive*. The 'strong mutual attraction' of the two is described by doubling different spontaneous body reactions which are attributed to both of them. The interplay of explicit description and style features, which strongly and even stereotypically suggests a particular atmosphere, meets our expectations of trivial literature.

Regional and Social Style If language variation is interpreted and treated by participants in written or spoken discourse as a meaningful resource, it is of stylistic significance. In this perspective, for example, regional dialect can be used as a kind of 'regional style' symbolizing the regional identity and allegiance of its speakers, or sociolects can be deployed as 'social styles' which symbolize different social worlds and their meanings for speakers and participants in interaction. So, Dittmar et al. (1988) analyse 'Berlin wit' or 'Berlin loudmouth' (*Berliner Schnauze*). This term is a lay categorization to refer to a particular style with particular verbal, prosodic and sequential features and presentational strategies which particular story-tellers may use to dramatize their stories about situations of conflict. Similarly, the contributions in Kallmeyer (1994) analyse the formal repertoire and the functions of switching between Standard German and *Mannemer Gosch*, as the local broad dialect in the German city of Mannheim is called. This style of speaking is analysed as symbolizing urban and suburban identity for its users.

Gender Styles A vast research area concerned with styles is the study of gender roles and their relevance for related stylistic preferences in social interaction. Are there male and female styles?

Earliest research concentrated on isolated linguistic variables on the phonological and syntactic level and later on isolated features of verbal behaviour such as the use of tag questions, hedges, interruptions, recipient tokens, and topic control strategies in relation to the speaker's gender role. More recently, however, there have been some approaches which study gender-specific preferences for 'discourse style' (cf., for example, Tannen, 1990; Günthner and Kotthoff, 1991; 1992). Goodwin (1990), however, shows that the conversational strategies of boys and girls are not simply gender-specific, but vary fundamentally with conversational activities and participation framework, both genders being perfectly capable of using both cooperative and uncooperative strategies to achieve their aims in interactional sequences.

Cultural and Subcultural Styles   Tannen (1984) describes different (sub-) cultural styles used by American East Coast Jewish-identified and West Coast (and one London) raised friends who, when meeting for a Thanks-giving dinner, encountered difficulties in getting on with each other on easy terms in cross-subcultural discourse. Their styles differed most saliently in terms of pacing, grossness of humour, and story-telling (1984: 149). But nevertheless, style is not a matter of polar distinctions, and Tannen sum-marizes: 'each person used a unique mix of conversational devices that constituted individual style. When their devices matched, communication between them was smooth. When they differed, communication showed signs of disruption or outright misunderstanding' (1984: 147).

Within society the use and alternation between discourse styles co-occurs with other aspects of its members' life-styles: their housing, ways of living, clothing, taste, etc. Bourdieu's (1979) notion of *habitus* is intended to integrate all these different dimensions of style. He points out that styles are socially evaluated: members of a society use and interpret *habitus* styles according to the symbolic value attached to them in social and economic life.

The Degree of Prototypicality of Style Features

Style features can be distinguished according to their prototypicality. There are prototypical features such as the pronunciation /pai/ for /pei/ ('pay') in Cockney or the use of *trouble and strife* for *wife* as an example of Cockney rhyming slang. These features are prime cues for Cockney style. In general, these are used along with less prototypical features such as the 'h'-dropping in Cockney, and along with features which belong to standard language. All stylistic resources can be used intensively or only gradually. They are combined with other features and adapted to the specific tasks of interaction.

Producing and Interpreting Styles

Speakers use stylistic variation in order to express additional meaning relevant for interaction. Speakers can produce 'conventional' styles, that is those that correspond to our stylistic expectation. But they can also use stylistic resources creatively and even individually, thus both deviating from and exploiting our knowledge and expectations about stylistic conventions. In all cases the activity is enriched with stylistic meaning in order to perform it most effectively.

Stylistic meaning is not restricted to the author's stylistic intentions; the text, however, does provide a basis for its interpretation (Widdowson, 1992). Consider the following example taken from a 1971 article on style:

(2)   When we study a writer's style we are studying **a man** writing as well as an artist at work. Because **he** is an artist **he** has perhaps a more highly marked individuality . . .

Today, in the light of the discussion about feminism, modern women, and men sympathizing with them, interpret this text as 'old-fashioned', the writer as representing a 'macho' culture. Thus, from the background of our stylistic knowledge we can interpret the way a person talks and thus infer that s/he is old, belongs to the lower class, etc.

The Field of Linguistic Stylistics

Originally, stylistics developed out of the field of rhetoric, in particular out of the study of the *elocutio*.

Traditional Stylistics

Much work in traditional stylistics was based on structuralist approaches. On the one hand it aimed at a classification of stylistic features for a given language (Leech and Short, 1981). On the other hand styles of literary texts were analysed with structuralist methods (Jakobson and Lévi-Strauss, 1962; Riffaterre, 1966). Western European stylistics concentrated on the description of literary style, whereas Prague School stylistics attributed as much importance to it as they did to scientific style, journalistic style, administrative style and colloquial style.

More recently, in the 1980s and 1990s, stylistics profited from the development of research in neighbouring areas such as linguistic pragmatics, text linguistics, sociolinguistics and discourse analysis. (For an overview of recent trends cf. Sandig, 1995.)

Pragmatic Stylistics

Pragmatic stylistics is concerned both with the recurrent constitution of particular speech acts rather than others, and with particular features of the performance of speech acts, such as the particular wording of requests. In institutional contexts the use of 'explicit performative formulae' is common in order to constrain possible interpretations: *I hereby order you to stop*. In other contexts the implicit or 'primary performative' phrase *Stop!* is sufficient. Speech acts, however, can also be performed 'indirectly', for example when a request is packaged as a question, *Could you please stop?*, in order to express politeness (cf. Sandig, 1986b: Chapter 1.3).

Text Linguistic Stylistics

Text linguistic stylistics is, on the one hand, concerned with a particular choice of words or recurrent sentence structures (cf. Enkvist, 1981) or different kinds of sentence connections. On the other hand, it is concerned with studies of particular aspects of texts which are shown to be stylistically relevant, such as the description and comparison of the stylistic conventions of text types.

Sociolinguistic Stylistics

In sociolinguistic stylistics style is related to social categories. Levinson (1988) distinguishes between two sociolinguistic approaches which result in quite different notions of style (and register): the *alternates approach* and the *ethnographic approach*.

The alternates approach is based directly on the traditional notion of style: 'On this view, *sociolinguistics is the study of different realizations of the same meaning or function*, and the study of style and register would be the study of different ways of saying the same thing *within* a dialect, a repertoire, or other restriction' (Levinson, 1988: 167). In a now classical example Labov (1972) isolated and described contextual styles in the speech of New York City speakers. The frequency with which speakers pronounced the five phonological variables 'r', 'eh', 'oh', 'th' and 'dh' was found to vary between the following styles: careful speech in the interview situation, reading styles for continuous passages of text, reading word lists, minimal pairs.

In the ethnographic approach, '*sociolinguistics is the study of the cultural distinctiveness of speech functions*. There is no necessity for the comparison of two or more different realizations of the same function or meaning – we are interested precisely in the unique and incomparable' (Levinson, 1988: 168). Here again we can cite some of Labov's (1972) observations: he noted that his interviewees used different styles before and during the interviews, and that they also altered their styles of speaking when required to switch from more neutral to more emotive topics. Changes of topic or digressions therefrom, as well as particular topics such as talking about childhood rhymes and customs, etc., produced specific styles of speaking. Furthermore, changes in the participation framework, such as new people entering the room, resulted in style alteration. The degree of attention paid to speech in different activities such as informal conversation versus reading aloud caused the interviewee to adapt her/his style to these activities. Some interviewees used their styles of speaking for self-presentation more than others.

Interactional Stylistics

Franck (1984) incorporated ideas from conversation analysis into stylistic analysis, most prominently in the description of the recipient design and negotiation of interactional styles, for the investigation of phenomena such as differing 'politeness' or 'vagueness' in interaction. Almost simultaneously Gumperz (1982), in an approach called interpretive or interactional sociolinguistics, combined insights from the ethnography of speaking, anthropology, sociolinguistics, micro-sociology and conversational analysis to propose new ways of analysing speech styles as 'contextualization cues'. By this he meant cues that speakers use to suggest the interpretation of what is said within and in relation to particular interpretive frames for dimensions such as politeness, degree of intimacy, formality, institutionalization, etc.

Gumperz (1982) pointed out that although contextualization cues such as prosody, code-switching and style alter(n)ation are non-referential in nature, they are used in culturally specific ways. Since contextualization cues are the most implicit and unconsciously used devices which are interpreted according to one's own culturally conventionalized expectations, the misuse or the lack of knowledge of the correct use of cues can create unnoticed misinterpretations of communicative intent.

Examples of Current Research

In the following we present some sample analyses which illustrate current text linguistic and interactional stylistics. We analyse style features and typified styles, such as those discussed in the first section, which are important elements for the analysis of styles. Against the background of the stylistic conventions of text types (second section, text linguistic stylistics) we ask how individual texts are stylistically composed and what stylistic meaning is suggested by that style (cf. Sandig, 1986b: Chapter 2.1).

Text Linguistic Stylistics: Text (Type) Conventions and Styles

Part of the knowledge that we need to interpret texts stylistically is the knowledge about text (type) conventions. To manage recurrent social tasks members of speech communities have developed conventionalized or standardized solutions, that is text conventions. Conventionalized text types, such as weather forecasts or lonely hearts advertisements in a newspaper, are related to types of situations in which the problem that they are intended to solve is a recurrent one. In such a context the respective text conventions have a particular social meaning. As will be shown below, texts of this type have particular internal structures and characteristics which can be conformed with or stylistically varied by the writer, for example for purposes of self-presentation (cf. also Sandig, 1986a).

For illustration we shall analyse some lonely hearts advertisements from the personal columns of the weekly newspaper *Die Zeit*, a newspaper addressing a well-educated readership.[1]

A Conventional Ad

(3) 39 years old, presently working south of Munich and looking for a partner. Interested in music and art and nature and would like to meet a woman who also values religious faith. (*Die Zeit*, 13 December 1990)

The meaning of these ads is an attempt to come into contact with persons of the opposite sex. This request conventionally appears at the end of the text before the box number or address for replies. As an introduction to this request the writer portrays him/herself as 'looking for' a partner; he or she describes both him/herself and his/her dream partner explicitly and at the same time implicitly through the style in which the ad is written. The parallelism (or discrepancy) between explicit description and implicit stylistic meaning is stylistically relevant. This also allows the writer to avoid an all-too-explicit positive self-portrayal. Finally, the relationship between self-description and the description of the dream partner makes it possible to interpret various kinds of relationship. For example, those who go into great detail describing themselves but waste few words on the partner can be described as 'dominant'. By these standards the example given above suggests a 'tendency toward dominance over his partner' on the part of the writer. Moreover, to reduce costs, it is a general text convention of proto-typical ads to use elliptical sentences like *39 years old* in (3) and abbreviations such as 34/1.84 in (4).

An Individual Ad   For this particular text convention in the weekly paper *Die Zeit* it is prototypical to use style to present oneself as an individual as much as possible. This was not done in the above example; however, it definitely can be seen in the following.

(4) Prof with pep (34/1.84/fit) looking for a young pedalling partner with pizazz. Replies with photos appreciated. (*Die Zeit*, 29 July 1984)

Since self-description is relevant in marriage ads, we can interpret this text as follows: the person is 'self-ironical' (*prof* is a categorization of teachers by students and others and has a connotation of 'informality') and 'uncon-ventional' (*with pep* is colloquial and positive), is 'looking for a match' (*with pizazz* is synonymous with *with pep*) who, like the author himself, is environmentally aware and (somewhat) sportive (*pedalling*) and possibly also 'progressive', 'modern', 'alternative', etc. Moreover, they should both have some sense of aesthetics: this is suggested by the alliteration in *prof with pep* and *pedalling partner with pizazz*. The request for *replies with photos appreciated*, however, leaves some freedom for the partner. This ad is prototypical for an ad in *Die Zeit* as far as style is concerned but not in length: it is unusually short. That it nonetheless fulfils its function is due to its style which matches the text's explicit self-portrayal of the author as someone with *pep*.

We thus also interpret the text in relation to our knowledge about the text (type) convention. In relation to the prototypical stylistic realization of ads in *Die Zeit* the first example can be interpreted as 'non-individual' and, depending on the perspective, 'stiff' and 'humourless', but also as 'serious' and 'factual'.

There are ads in which writers refer to themselves by using the personal pronoun *I* and thereby indicate 'personal' style, whereas the writers of examples (3) and (4) appear to be 'non-involved' since they use the third person.

A Romantic Ad   Let us now finish example (1), the beginning of which was quoted in its entirety earlier.

(1a)   Somewhere . . . into the setting sun. Why not live a love story *à la* Courths-Mahler? 40 something, worldwide. (*Die Zeit*, 13 December 1990)

The writer of the ad uses the 'trivial' story as an implicit self-portrayal (*I'm longing for feelings*) and for the stylistic description of the dream partner and the desired 'parallel' relationship. The self-portrayal that is represented as a text pattern is thus inferred from the trivial story within the context of the ad. Also, in retrospect the story is explicitly interpreted as a piece of trivial literature: Courths-Mahler was a famous author of love stories around the turn of the century. This can also be interpreted as 'I am old-fashioned and looking for an old-fashioned partnership.' At the same time the writer of the ad establishes some degree of distance by switching to the impersonal rhetorical question *Why not . . .?* The latter also serves self-irony. The prototypical request for contact in marriage ads is expressed here indirectly by the rhetorical question. Thus the rhetorical question fulfils a variety of functions. The ellipses at the end do not conform to the conventional form: *40 something* is 'colloquial' in comparison with *about 40*; the information on age and geographical location corresponds to the text convention and makes the ellipses here interpretable as applying equally to both partners.

All of these three sample ads remain within the bounds of text conventions established for prototypical marriage advertisements.

An Unconventional Ad   Exactly because the following ad deviates from standard text conventions, it sets itself apart and attracts attention:

(5)   Women are the worst
       Either they cling to you, or after a catastrophic affair they nurse their reluctance to get involved in a relationship with an attitude of I-need-my-freedom, don't want a creative curly head (36) in the metropolitan area of DU – D – E, don't like the mountains, don't play tennis nor go

skiing, prefer soaking up the sun at the sea, go for macho-Italians (if only for their body), smoke like chimneys, prefer the opera to the comedy club, and they only read the personal columns for fun, but are too much of a coward to answer for once an ad with their photograph.

As I said before: Women are the worst. Or are there any exceptions?

(*Die Zeit*, 21 May 1993)

Here the prototypical speech act of 'describing' is substituted by 'complaining' and by an 'explanation' for the complaint. This complaint starts with an eye-catcher: *Women are the worst*. Within the framework of the text conventions, however, we also learn a lot about the writer and his dream partner. By expressing the negative or things that are missing, he describes himself via presuppositions: *don't want a creative curly head (36) in the metropolitan area of DU-D-E*, where abbreviations are used to describe the age and the region. Through the use of a long, complex sentence and the choice of words (*reluctance to get involved, an attitude of I-need-my-freedom*) he represents himself as an 'academic', but by the choice of colloquial expressions (*smoke like chimneys, soaking up the sun*) also as 'unconventional'.

The choice of a 'complaint' also matches the interpretation as 'unconventional' and lends stylistic weight to his explicit self-portrayal as 'creative'. Furthermore, the formation of a sound sequence with 'w' in *women are the worst* supports this self-portrayal, as does the fact that the complaint is linguistically rounded off at the end by repeating this line. The end of the ad opens up a new perspective with the question *Or are there any exceptions?* The prototypical request to include a photograph with the reply appears at the end of the ad here, as usual, but is 'individually changed' (*but are too much of a coward to answer . . . an ad with their photograph . . . Or are there any exceptions?*).

Conclusion: the Individual Text as a Holistic Gestalt   Each of the texts constitutes a unit, a *gestalt*, partly in relation to the text convention, partly through its own individual presentation. The texts achieve their effectiveness through their relation to the prototype and also to similar texts of the same type that appear in their neighbourhood. This fact can be made use of methodologically, since stylistic text analysis is often based on different methods of comparison (cf. Fix, 1991). We can describe a given text in relation to the prototype (of the text type) or compare several texts of the same type with each other (and in relation to the prototype). In all cases we use our general linguistic knowledge as a more general framework and add to this the interpretation of the relations of the selected text characteristics mentioned above. Another method of stylistic analysis is to look at 'the same' topic in different types of texts (for example, Carter and Nash, 1990: describing places, describing cars) or investigating 'the same' event in several presentations, in newspapers with different political stances, etc.

The examples (1) and (5) show that styles such as that of a trivial novel or a complaint are actively used and are adapted to the requirements of the individual writer.

Interactional Stylistics

Characteristically, studies in interactional stylistics seek to analyse the way participants in the interaction handle, negotiate and interpret styles. It is assumed that participants deploy styles of speaking and their alter(n)ation according to their tacit knowledge about conventionally or situationally evoked associations between stylistic, that is linguistic and paralinguistic, features and associated interpretive frames. The interactionist approach wants to show in detail how styles of speaking are used as a resource and (made) relevant for participants in interaction. It stresses the need to warrant the analysis by reconstructing and demonstrating that and in what way in subsequent interaction recipients react and orient to the object of study (cf. Gumperz, 1982; 1992; Tannen, 1984; the contributions in Hinnenkamp and Selting, 1989; Auer and di Luzio, 1992; Kallmeyer, 1994; etc.).

The following analysis focuses on styles of speaking. Style in conversational interaction is conceived of as a contextualization cue (Gumperz, 1982; 1992; see earlier), that is as a signalling cue that suggests particular interpretive frames for what is said. Style is assumed to be constituted by the use of bundles of co-occurring linguistic cues from, for example, lexico-semantics, syntax, prosody – in particular rhythm and intonation.

The following transcripts present some extracts from a conversational story that Mia tells her recipients to describe her friend's change from a woman who wears sloppy and scruffy clothes to one who wears very chic and fashionable clothes after a year's stay in France. (A detailed analysis of the entire story can be found in Selting, 1994: 393ff.)

In the telling of her story Mia changes styles dramatically and thereby makes the parts of her story recognizable for her recipients. In order to show how this is achieved, we need to present the spoken styles in the extracts in a detailed transcription. The following transcription conventions are most important here (cf. also Selting, 1994; 1995). If transcription lines do not represent entire utterances as in part (6a) of the transcript, they represent rhythmic cadences (Couper-Kuhlen, 1993). A rhythmic cadence is the stretch of talk that extends from the accented syllable (beat) over the following unaccented syllables up to the beginning of the next accented syllable, which is then excluded. This can be seen in part (6b) of the transcript. Capital letters are used to represent accented syllables. Cadences which are heard as rhythmically organized are placed beneath each other; they are roughly similar in length of time. In order to verify the auditive interpretation of rhythm the length of cadences was also measured with a stop watch; the average values are given in the right margin of the transcript. Beneath the text, relevant intonation, loudness, tempo and other cues are indicated.[2] All relevant parameters will be spelled out in the analysis.

Mia's Introduction to her Story

(6a)   A friend of mine – I shared a flat with her for a long time – was
       always running around in these absolutely sloppy clothes.

```
1   Mia:   ne FREUNdin von mir (.) die: (.)
                   R(   /            )        –
                   < slowly                slowly
                   a friend of mine        she
2   Mia:   m: mit der hab ich lange zuSAMMgewohnt
                       R(                /              )
                   slowly                          slowly
                   m   with her I shared a flat for a long time
3   Mia:   die: is: (.) toTAL SCHMUDdelig immer so RUMgelaufen
                           F( \          \              \   /   )
                   slowly                              slowly >
                   she was    always running around in these absolutely
                              sloppy clothes
```

The extract starts with Mia's introducing and characterizing the main
character of her story in lines 1–3. Lexically, Mia first chooses neutral words
and then, in line 3, the evaluative item *schmuddelig* 'sloppy', the hyperbolic
intensifiers *total* 'absolutely' and *immer* 'always' and the colloquial verb
rumlaufen 'run around' modified by the particle *so*. Syntactically, this is
phrased in a left dislocation and a complex full sentence which has a
parenthetical clause embedded in it. Intonationally, we find rising and falling
global pitch and rising and falling pitch accent movements (// \\\\) which
constitute normal and unconspicuous contours. As the accents do not follow
each other in rhythmic intervals, these units are not presented in rhythmic
notation.

The Point of Mia's Story   After Mia has told a pre-change story (not
reproduced here), she presents the point of her story, her friend's going to
France and returning very chic, in the following way:

(6b)   Then she went to France for half a year and came back dressed dead
       chic, dead chic.

```
27   Mia:    /   DANN isse n halbes Jahr nach    /              (1.1)
             H(↑\
                 then did she for half a year to
28   Mia:    /   FRANKreich gegangen (.)         /              (1.2)
                 ↓/                       )
                 France go
29   Mia:    /   KAM     /                                      (0.4)
             F(\
                 came
```

```
30   Mia:    /    WIEder    /                              (0.4)
                        /    )
                  back
31   Mia:    /    TO:D      /                              (0.4)
             H,F(↑\
                  dead
32   Mia:    /    SCHICK
                        \   )
                  chic
33   Eli:              ((hh))          /                   (0.6)
34   Mia:    [ /      (..)             /                   (0.6)
35   Eli:    [ ((laughs quietly))

36   Mia:    [ /    TO::D              /                   (0.7)
             [  H(↑ –
             [  <loud
             [  dead
37   Eli:    [ ((laughs quietly))
38   Mia:    /    SCHICK (.)           /                   (0.6)
                    – )
                  loud >
                  chic
```

Here, lines 27 and 28 again exhibit a relatively normal, unconspicuous style, with unconspicuous lexical items and unconspicuous syntax. Yet, pitch is globally high here, with an extra high pitch peak in the first word *DANN* 'then' with which Mia focuses on the new part of her story. Additionally, we find a rhythmic organization with albeit relatively long cadences of about 1.1 and 1.2 seconds. This part seems to prepare for the climax of Mia's story which immediately follows in lines 29–38.

For the presentation of the point of her story, her friend's return from France, Mia switches to a saliently marked emphatic style in lines 29 to 38. Here, at the lexical level we find the compound evaluative adjective *todschick*, which combines the items *tod* 'death' and *schick* 'chic', *todschick* directly contrasts with *schmuddelig*; it is a stylistically marked item that triggers an emphatic interpretive frame. Syntactically, we find elliptical constructions that give only the items that are absolutely necessary to make the point (a verb to denote the relation between the prior pre-climax story and the point to follow, an adjective to denote the friend's new look).

At the prosodic level, there are drastic changes in comparison to the prior units. We find maximally dense accentuation. Instead of the earlier alternation between accented and unaccented syllables, we find almost exclusively accented syllables. The density of accented as opposed to unaccented syllables, and the density of highly prominent primary as opposed to less prominent secondary accents, is higher in these units than in the prior units. The density increases within the three units. In the rhythmic notation we find almost only accented syllables in relatively brief cadences – first of 0.4 seconds and later of mostly 0.6 seconds. Moreover, Eli's silent laugh in line 33 and the following pause, which functions as a 'silent beat', fit into the picture of a rhythmically integrated sequence in which the salience of the prosodic marking increases throughout the sequence of units.

We also find marked intonation: high global pitch on both uses of the key word *todschick*, and additional movements to extremely high local pitch peaks in the accents on the syllable *tod*. Additionally, there is increased global loudness, a saliently elongated vowel in the syllable *tod*, and a level pitch movement in the item *todschick* in its second repeated occurrence.

Furthermore, the repetition of the word *todschick* signals emphasis. Mia pauses briefly after both utterances of this word. These pauses do not yield the floor. They are inserted for dramatic effect. As a result of the addition of marking devices in each successive unit during the sequence, the climax is heard as an 'escalation'.

Conclusion: Style as a Contextualization Cue   In sum, the first lines are presented in an unmarked and unconspicuous style, while the climax is presented in a highly marked emphatic style. Are these styles merely random choices? Are they determined by the structure of the story? For this to be true, the ways in which story-tellers present their stories are both too consistent and too different, hence the styles can be neither random choices nor determined. It is much more likely that the constitution of styles is actively used as a holistic contextualization cue which makes the speaker's structuring of the story, her preparing and constructing the climax, recognizable and interpretable for the recipient(s). Yet: how do we know that the styles are relevant at all? This can be shown by demonstrating that recipients orient to them. In our example, we can see that Eli reacts to Mia's signalling of the climax of her story by silently laughing, that is by one of the ways that recipients show their recognition and understanding of the point of a story.

Participants use co-occurring cues from lexico-semantics, syntax and prosody to constitute styles of speaking which can be actively used as flexibly and dynamically alterable resources. Thus they suggest interpretive frames for the interpretation of talk and make relevant particular recipient responses. If speakers actively use and alter(n)ate styles in the construction of activities, and if recipients can be shown to orient to this, this can be taken as evidence of the interactive and interpretive relevance of styles in interaction. (For further examples cf. Selting, 1992; 1994; 1995.)

Fields of Application

The study of style is relevant for the study of language both in the mono-lingual and in the second or foreign language classroom. In the process of learning, both first and second or foreign language learners often mix styles or registers. Typical examples are students using expressions or idioms from spoken language in their written texts, or second language learners using expressions from their first language in second language texts or contexts. Teaching can try to increase stylistic awareness in order to prevent stylistic mistakes and flaws (Hoffmann, 1988).

In all areas of international relations and intercultural communication, with respect to both written and spoken interaction, style is a relevant dimension as a possible source of difficulties and conflicts (cf. Tannen, 1985; Günthner, 1993; Kotthoff, 1994; Tiittula, 1995).

With respect to political and other public discourse, stylistic analysis can contribute to critical awareness (van Dijk, 1984). A further area of research, critical linguistics, is concerned with the ways in which different world views, predominantly with respect to phenomena such as power and status, manifest themselves implicitly and subconsciously in the style of texts (Kress, 1985; Simpson, 1993).

In therapeutic discourse the style of self-presentation, the kind of re-presentation of reality and the kind of handling of relationships is relevant and can be used for diagnosis by the analyst (Labov and Fanshel, 1977; Baus and Sandig, 1985).

Conclusions

Styles are the socially interpreted and socially meaningful ways of using language variation as a resource in written and spoken interaction. It is language variation, typically in conventionalized co-occurring structures, which is interpreted in relation to speakers, text types, communication tasks, activity types, contexts, settings, etc. Typified styles have (proto-) typical features and structures but nevertheless they are dynamic and flexible enough to be adapted according to recipient design and situational or textual exigencies.

Although holistically interpreted styles are associated with particular activity or text types, discourse types, situation types, institutional roles, cultural contexts, etc., style is *not* (only) a variety selected in unilateral dependence on these extralingual factors. As styles can be strategically used in other than their conventionally associated contexts, this shows that style is a signalling system which has to be described as a resource in its own right. Often the establishment or negotiation of style in interaction is the result of interactive processes between speakers or writers and recipients, that is an interactive achievement.

Recommended Reading

Carter and Nash (1990): explain basic terminology, analyse literary and non-literary sample texts, apply methods of style analysis and present exercises for the constitution of styles.

Franck (1984): see section here on interactional stylistics.

Gumperz (1982): develops the view of contextualization theory that influenced many modern conceptions and analyses of style.

Kress (1985): see section here on fields of application.

Labov (1972): see section here on sociolinguistic stylistics.

Stickel (1995): presents the state of the art in German and European-German stylistics.

Tannen (1984): see section here on cultural and subcultural styles.

Widdowson (1992): shows special features of literary texts and transitions between everyday texts and literary texts and encourages a creative approach to poetic texts.

Notes

We are grateful to H. Gerzymisch-Arbogast, A. Arbogast and L. Paul for their help with the translation of this chapter.

1 For reasons of conciseness only the English translation of the ads appears here. The original German texts can be found in the issues indicated at the ends of the quotations.

2 *Transcription symbols in the text line of transcripts*

aber **DA** kam	primary accented syllable(s) of a unit
aber DA kam	secondary accented syllable(s) of a unit
si:cher	lengthening of a sound
(.)	brief pause of up to about 0.5 seconds
((lacht))	para- and/or non-linguistic events
ich [gehe	simultaneous talk, overlapping utterances
[jaha	

Transcription symbols in the prosody line(s) of transcripts

Global pitch direction:	(noted before the left parenthesis)
F,R,H,M,L( )	notation of the global pitch direction before the accent sequences delimited by parentheses: F = falling, R = rising, H = high, M = mid, L = low
H,F( )	combination of global characterizations

Accent (proto-)types or unaccented local pitch movements on and after accented and/or unaccented syllables:

\	falling
/	rising
–	level

Accent modifications:

↑\, ↓/, ↑–	locally larger pitch movements than in surrounding accents, higher or lower accent peaks than usual

Other prosodic parameters:

<*loud voice*>, <*soft voice*> etc.	used with local or global extension, the extension is indicated by the position of the < >

References

Auer, P. and di Luzio, A. (eds) (1992) *The Contextualization of Language*. Amsterdam: Benjamins.

Baus, M. and Sandig, B. (1985) *Gesprächspsychotherapie und weibliches Selbstkonzept*. Hildesheim, Zurich; New York: Olms.

Bourdieu, P. (1979) *La Distinction: critique sociale du jugement*. Paris: Éditions de Minuit.

Carter, R. and Nash, W. (1990) *Seeing Through Language: a Guide to Styles of English Writing*. Oxford; Cambridge, MA: Blackwell.

Couper-Kuhlen, E. (1993) *English Speech Rhythm*. Amsterdam: Benjamins.

Dittmar, N., Schlobinski, P. and Wachs, I. (1988) 'Berlin style and register', in N. Dittmar and P. Schlobinski (eds), *The Sociolinguistics of Urban Vernaculars*. Berlin, New York: de Gruyter. pp. 44–113.

Enkvist, N.E. (1981) 'Experiential iconism in text strategy', *Text*, 1: 97–111.

Fix, U. (1991) 'Stilistische Textanalyse – immer ein Vergleich? Das Gemeinsame von Methoden der Stilanalyse – das Gemeinsame an Stilbegriffen', *Germanistische Linguistik*, 106–7: 133–56.

Franck, D. (1984) 'Stil und Interaktion', in B. Spillner (ed.), *Methoden der Stilanalyse*. Tübingen: Narr. pp. 121–35.

Goodwin, M. (1990) *He-Said-She-Said: Talk as Social Organization among Black Children*. Bloomington, IN: Indiana University Press.

Gumperz, J. (1982) *Discourse Strategies*. London: Cambridge University Press.

Gumperz, J. (1992) 'Contextualization revisited', in P. Auer and A. di Luzio (eds), *The Contextualization of Language*. Amsterdam, Philadelphia: Benjamins. pp. 39–54.

Günthner, S. (1993) *Diskursstrategien in der interkulturellen Kommunikation*. Tübingen: Niemeyer.

Günthner, S. and Kotthoff, H. (1991) *Von fremden Stimmen: Weibliches und männliches Sprechen im Kulturvergleich*. Frankfurt: Suhrkamp.

Günthner, S. and Kotthoff, H. (1992) *Die Geschlechter im Gespräch: Kommunikation in Institutionen*. Stuttgart: Metzler.

Hinnenkamp, V. and Selting, M. (eds) (1989) *Stil und Stilisierung: Arbeiten zur interpretativen Soziolinguistik*. Tübingen: Niemeyer.

Hoffmann, L. (1988) 'Intercultural writing: a pragmatic analysis of style', in W. Van Peer (ed.), *The Taming of the Text: Explorations in Language, Literature and Culture*. London, New York: Routledge. pp. 152–75.

Jakobson, R. and Lévi-Strauss, C. (1962) '"Les chats" de Charles Baudelaire', in *L'Homme: Revue française d'anthropologie*, II (1): 5–21.

Kallmeyer, W. (ed.) (1994) *Kommunikation in der Stadt. Band 1: Exemplarische Analysen des Sprachverhaltens in Mannheim*. Berlin, New York: de Gruyter.

Kotthoff, H. (1994) 'Zur Rolle der Konversationsanalyse in der interkulturellen Kommunikationsforschung. Gesprächsbeendigungen im Schnittfeld von Mikro und Makro', *Zeitschrift für Literaturwissenschaft und Linguistik (LiLi)*, 93: 75–96.

Kress, G. (1985) 'Ideological structures in discourse', in T.A. van Dijk (ed.), *Handbook of Discourse Analysis. Vol. 4: Discourse Analysis in Society*. London, Orlando, San Diego: Academic Press. pp. 27–42.

Labov, W. (1972) 'The isolation of contextual styles', in W. Labov (ed.), *Sociolinguistic Patterns*. Philadelphia: University of Pennsylvania Press. pp. 70–109.

Labov, W. and Fanshel, D. (1977) *Therapeutic Discourse*. New York: Academic Press.

Leech, G. and Short, M. (1981) *Style in Fiction*. London, New York: Longman.

Levinson, S. (1988) 'Conceptual problems in the study of regional and cultural style', in N. Dittmar and P. Schlobinski (eds), *The Sociolinguistics of Urban Vernaculars*. Berlin, New York: de Gruyter. pp. 161–90.

Riffaterre, M. (1966) 'Describing poetic structures – two approaches to Baudelaire's "Les chats"', in *Yale French Studies*, 36–37: 200–42.

Sandig, B. (1986a) 'Vom Nutzen der Textlinguistik für die Stilistik', in A. Schöne (ed.), *Kontroversen, alte und neue. Akten des VII Internationalen Germanistenkongresses Göttingen 1985*, vol. 3. Tübingen: Niemeyer. pp. 24–31.

Sandig, B. (1986b) *Stilistik der deutschen Sprache*. Berlin, New York: de Gruyter.

Sandig, B. (1995) 'Tendenzen der linguistischen Stilforschung', in G. Stickel (ed.), *Stilfragen*. Berlin, New York: de Gruyter. pp. 27–61.

Selting, M. (1992) 'Intonation as a contextualization device: case studies on the role of prosody, especially intonation, in contextualizing story telling in conversation', in P. Auer and A. di Luzio (eds), *The Contextualization of Language*. Amsterdam: Benjamins. pp. 233–58.

Selting, M. (1994) 'Emphatic speech style – with special focus on the prosodic signalling of heightened emotive involvement in conversation', *Journal of Pragmatics*, 22: 375–408.

Selting, M. (1995) *Prosodie im Gespräch: Aspekte einer interaktionalen Phonologie der Konversation*. Tübingen: Niemeyer.

Simpson, P. (1993) *Language, Ideology and Point of View*. London, New York: Routledge.

Stickel, G. (ed.) (1995) *Stilfragen*. Berlin, New York: de Gruyter.

Tannen, D. (1984) *Conversational Style*. Norwood, NJ: Ablex.

Tannen, D. (1985) 'Cross-cultural communication', in T.A. van Dijk (ed.), *Handbook of Discourse Analysis. Vol. 4: Discourse Analysis in Society*. London: Academic Press. pp. 203–15.

Tannen, D. (1990) *You Just Don't Understand: Women and Men in Conversation*. New York: William Morrow.

Tiittula, L. (1995) 'Stile in interkulturellen Begegnungen', in G. Stickel (ed.), *Stilfragen*. Berlin, New York: de Gruyter. pp. 198–224.

van Dijk, Teun A. (1984) *Prejudice in Discourse: an Analysis of Ethnic Prejudice in Cognition and Conversation*. Amsterdam, Philadelphia: Benjamins.

Widdowson, H.G. (1992) *Practical Stylistics: an Approach to Poetry*. Oxford: Oxford University Press.

6

Rhetoric

Ann M. Gill and Karen Whedbee

There is little consensus as to the meaning of the word *rhetoric*. It has been defined and redefined by scholars throughout history: 'the ability to see, in any given case, the available means of persuasion' (Aristotle, 1991: 1355b26); 'the art of speaking well – that is to say, with knowledge, skill and elegance' (Cicero, 1942: II 5); 'that art or talent by which discourse is adapted to its end' (Campbell, 1988: 1); 'the finding of suitable arguments to prove a given point, and the skilful arrangement of them' (Whately, 1963: 39); the process of 'adjusting ideas to people and people to ideas' (Bryant, 1972: 26). While some of these definitions equate rhetoric with persuasion, others define rhetoric more broadly as any type of instrumental expression. One definition identifies rhetoric with argumentation, another with eloquent language. Finally, while some definitions associate rhetoric exclusively with discourse, at least one leaves open the possibility that rhetoric may include non-discursive activities and objects.

Although definitions of rhetoric vary, two themes occur with regularity. First, the essential activities of rhetoric are located on a political stage. For example, all of the major writers on rhetoric from antiquity – Isocrates, Plato, Aristotle, Cicero, Quintilian – believed that politics was the principal locus of rhetoric, and, therefore, they designed their theories of rhetoric for use by political agents. More recent writers have suggested that rhetoric functions also in religion, science, philosophy, literature, and elsewhere; however, even these writers usually acknowledge political speaking and writing as the centerpiece of rhetorical practice.

Second, rhetoric is discourse calculated to influence an audience toward some end. Theories vary widely in their description of the end of rhetoric. Some writers describe rhetoric as a means for persuading audiences; others conceive of rhetoric as a method for reaching reliable judgments and decisions in a community; still others emphasize rhetoric as a means for inducing cooperative activity.[1] Although descriptions of the ends of rhetoric vary widely, the consistent theme is that rhetoric is a type of instrumental discourse. It is, in one way or another, a vehicle for responding to, reinforcing, or altering the understandings of an audience or the social fabric of the community.

In this chapter, we begin with a brief discussion of classical conceptions of rhetoric, which focused on the composition of rhetorical texts, and of

some themes in contemporary rhetorical criticism. We then discuss the
process of rhetorical criticism, including basic questions that can guide
contemporary critics and some of the constructs critics consider in answering those questions. Finally, we conclude with an illustration of rhetorical
critics in action.

Rhetorical Composition

Rhetoric has been the subject of uninterrupted study for at least 2,500 years
– from the time of Plato and Aristotle to the present.[2] Throughout most of
this time, writers approached the subject from the perspective of composition; that is, most of the major works on rhetoric (with a few notable
exceptions) were textbooks addressed to students. These textbooks outlined
the methods and techniques for creating effective rhetorical discourse. Until
print became a practical medium of communication, rhetoric was nearly
synonymous with political oratory; the textbooks explained to students how
to compose and deliver an effective public speech in a courtroom, before a
legislature, and at a ceremonial occasion. After the advent of print, the
scope of rhetoric expanded to include reference not only to effective
speaking but also to effective writing.

Many of these composition textbooks were structured according to the
'Roman canons of rhetoric'. These five canons, first developed in detail by
the philosopher and politician Cicero, can be described roughly as stages in
the composition and delivery of a public speech. The first canon is *invention*. In this initial stage of composition, speakers attempt to discover all
the possible arguments that can be brought in support of a thesis. Once
speakers have accumulated a variety of arguments, they next identify the
strongest arguments and organize those according to a compelling structure. The second canon, *disposition* (or arrangement), explains the most
effective ways to organize arguments in the introduction, body, and
conclusion of a speech. The third canon, *elocution*, focuses on expressing
the ideas and arguments in clear and vivid language. The textbooks
explained to students how to 'clothe' their ideas with figures of speech such
as 'schemes' (repetition, parallelism, and antithesis) and 'tropes' (metaphor,
simile, and analogy). The fourth canon, *memory*, presents various
mnemonic devices for remembering the ideas and language of the speech.
And finally, the fifth canon, *delivery*, explains the strategies for effective
verbal and non-verbal presentation, including vocal pitch, rate, and volume
as well as gestures and movement.

Another important concept included in the early textbooks on rhetoric
was 'modes of proof'. According to Aristotle, there are three modes of
proof or ways a speaker persuades an audience to accept a thesis. First,
audiences are persuaded through *ethos*, or the character of the speaker:
'[W]e believe fair-minded people to a greater extent and more quickly [than
we do others]' (1991: 1356a6). Second, audiences are persuaded through

pathos, or emotion: '[F]or we do not give the same judgment when grieved and rejoicing or when being friendly and hostile' (1356a15). And third, audiences are persuaded through the argument of the speech itself, or *logos*: we are persuaded more readily by speakers who present a thesis and then support that thesis with evidence and reasoning.

Finally, the concept of *propriety* (or, in Greek, *kairos*) played a central role in many discussions of public speaking. First developed by the Greek sophist Gorgias, propriety is a multidimensional concept. At its most basic level, propriety is the adaptation of discourse to extrinsic variables such as the setting, the audience, and the occasion for the speech. Propriety governs the choice of when to speak, when to remain silent, what to say, and how to say it. The message, its organization, and its expression must be timed so as to respond to the demands of particular audiences and situations. But also, propriety refers to the internal timing of a speech. The speaker must orchestrate the flow of ideas, the rhythm of language, and the variations of tone to create vivid and internally coherent prose. Nearly all textbooks on rhetoric emphasized that students cannot learn propriety by studying abstract rules and principles; propriety is an innate creative and perceptual ability that can be improved only by long hours of practicing public speaking and by emulating great orations of history.

Rhetorical Criticism

In the past, as we have seen, much of the activity of rhetoricians was concentrated on pedagogy – teaching students how to create effective rhetorical discourse. While the creation of discourse remains the province of contemporary rhetoric, the emphasis has shifted to include the criticism of rhetorical texts. The activities of rhetorical critics in the last thirty years have been quite varied; what they have in common is explication of the dynamic interaction of a rhetorical text with its context, that is, *how* a text responds to, reinforces, or alters the understandings of an audience or the social fabric of the community.

Earlier in this century, critics used the classical rhetorical theories as frames for analysis of historically important political texts. Thus, they looked for the ways in which texts used the Ciceronian canons, the Aristotelian modes of proof, and other concepts from theories about rhetorical composition. Contemporary criticism still draws from classical conceptions of rhetoric, but the texts appropriate for study and the frames used by critics have expanded significantly.

Not only have film, computer text, and broadcast messages been added to the category of rhetorical texts, but rhetorical criticism has responded to the contemporary view that linguistic structures or systems of discourse order and give sense to human experience (Foucault, 1972), that is, the way in which we talk about the world affects how we understand or 'see' it. If everything in human experience is constructed linguistically, then the range of texts susceptible to rhetorical analysis expands to include non-discursive items such as the Vietnam Veterans' Memorial in Washington, DC (Blair et al., 1991) and Israeli pioneering settlement museums (Katriel, 1994).

The communication revolution also has led to changing conceptions about the audience for rhetoric. Computers, for example, allow 'audience' to become author, recreating texts by breaking up narratives and choosing how much or how little information and description will be displayed on the monitor. Also, as texts, even speeches, have a life beyond their creation or first hearing, the audience for rhetoric can be a reader or viewer far removed in time and situation from the creation of a text.

Most importantly, however, rhetorical critics also confront the awareness that not all individuals or groups have equal access to channels of communication and that discourse is not benign but hegemonic; rhetoric can operate as a means of domination and oppression, such as focusing on male ways of understanding, thereby suppressing female perspectives. Every text, in focusing on some things, in making some things present to an audience, at one and the same time obscures something else (Burke, 1966; Derrida, 1982).

The specific objectives of contemporary rhetorical criticism have been named and discussed variously; however, at least two major schools of thought seem to operate simultaneously. According to one school, rhetorical criticism aims to increase appreciation of the historical importance of rhetorical texts (and especially public address). Some critics attempt to clarify the political effects of speeches and writings; others attempt to examine the inner workings and structure of canonical texts; and still others aim to recover unappreciated rhetorical texts and rhetors (speakers and writers) of the past. The second school aims to determine how rhetoric invites a construction or reconstruction of events and phenomena. Textual structures are identified, discussed, and in some cases dismantled to determine how they operate to create understandings, to sanction particular ways of viewing the world, or to silence particular people or points of view. Underlying both of these schools is at least one common goal – increasing our knowledge of how rhetoric operates. Both schools also use similar critical processes.

The Critical Process

When reading a rhetorical text, the critic brings to it a store of knowledge, including knowledge of the history of rhetoric and oratory, of theories about language (including many of the topics in these two volumes), and of writings in various disciplines, including philosophy, sociology, linguistics, and political science. These understandings form the particular 'conceptual baggage', or more positively the 'expectations and predilections', the critic brings to the text (Leff, 1980: 345). Initial experience with a rhetorical text leads a critic to ask questions of the text, questions that focus attention on particular aspects of the text and how it functions. For example, among the most basic questions the critic might ask are: what expectations are created by the context? What does the text present to an audience? What features of the text are significant? There are, of course, many more specific questions critics ask of texts.

In answering these or other questions, a critic once again draws on her particular store of knowledge; she crawls around and through a text, inspecting it from every angle, from some distance as well as up close, and she makes judgments about how it operates and what it says (and does not say). Once the critic has formulated answers to the questions she asks of the text, she conveys that understanding in another text that is itself rhetorical, representing her ideas as both warranted and enlightening.

In this section, we attempt to illustrate how rhetorical criticism functions by identifying some of the constructs used by critics in answering questions asked of a text. For this illustration, we will ask three basic questions, beginning with contextual expectations. As that activity which goes by the name *rhetorical criticism* has been largely a US phenomenon, and as detailed knowledge of the cultural context surrounding a rhetorical text is necessary for insightful evaluation, most of the examples we cite necessarily are drawn from the United States. We have attempted explanations for those readers unfamiliar with a particular text or the circumstances surrounding it.

What Expectations Are Created by the Context?

When examining the context for a text, a critic can focus on the context at the time the text was created or the context at the time a particular audience experiences (sees, hears, reads) the text. Rhetorical critics view texts as pragmatic: a rhetorical text responds to or interacts with societal issues or problems, and it produces some action upon or change in the world. In this view, rhetoric 'labors between the challenge and the fitting response, the imperfection and the remedy, the crisis and the calm' (Bitzer, 1981: 232). In short, rhetoric obtains its character as rhetorical from specific events and situations.

Imagine the following situation. A person has died. Family and friends gather to mourn and pay tribute to the deceased. Whether or not you have heard a funeral oration before, you would understand that the situation demands a specific type of utterance. A speaker cannot ignore the solemnity of the occasion, the grief of the audience, or the audience's need to make sense of mortality. Any funeral oration is generated by the situation and also is constrained by the situation. In this example, the situation is much more than a painted backdrop against which actors play out their roles; the situation directly limits and shapes the character of the speech.

Not all rhetorical situations are so easy to reconstruct as a funeral oration. On 8 August 1974, one of the largest audiences in US television history gathered to hear Richard Nixon announce his resignation from the office of president of the United States. Many in the audience expected, or at least hoped, to hear Nixon admit responsibility for the Watergate scandal that led to the downfall of his presidency. (The scandal involved members of his reelection committee breaking into the headquarters of an opposing political party and a subsequent coverup by Nixon and other high-ranking members of his administration.) Instead of addressing this situation, Nixon first justified his resignation and then attempted to reclaim and redefine the nature of his administration. He indicated that he wanted Americans to remember him for his decisive role in ending the Vietnam War, in signing the SALT I Treaty, and in renewing American relations with China.

The discrepancy between the audience's expectations and what actually occurred in the speech was dramatic. For the audience, the salient issue of the situation was the deception and corruption revealed in the Watergate scandal. Nixon, however, saw the situation in an entirely different light. The salient issue for him was that he had become the first president in US history to be forced to resign from office. For both personal and political reasons, Nixon focused his attention on the international and long-term consequences of his resignation, addressing future generations of Americans rather than the hostile viewers gathered in front of their television sets that night. By asking how Nixon viewed the situation, a critic can understand his choices of subject matter, arguments, and expression in the speech.

As the previous example illustrates, several constructs critics can use in analysing a text arise from the context: (1) *exigence*, the problem or issue to which the text is addressed; (2) *audience*, the actual people who are addressed by the rhetor; (3) *genre*, the nature of the text itself; and (4) *rhetor credibility*, the social position of the rhetor in relation to the audience addressed.

Exigence   Critics who analyse political public speeches or writings nearly always use the construct *exigence* as a part of their analysis because the historical events to which a text addresses itself or responds are central to understanding the text. For Richard Nixon, the exigence for his resignation speech was the fact that he had been forced to resign from office. His conception of the exigence shaped and constrained what he said in the speech. Nixon's immediate audience, however, perceived the exigence differently; they saw the scandal of Watergate as the pertinent issue and, consequently, their expectations for the speech were different from those of Nixon.

When US President Bill Clinton spoke in 1996 at the funeral of former US Congresswoman from Texas, Barbara Jordan, most critics would view that text in the context of a funeral held before a large audience in a black Southern Baptist Church for a national heroine. Jordan was the first African American female elected to Congress from the state of Texas, a lawyer renowned for her knowledge of the US Constitution, and a woman who had electrified national television audiences with her brilliant oratory during congressional Watergate hearings and keynote speeches at national political conventions. The exigence that caused Clinton to speak placed expectations upon the resulting rhetorical text.

Audience   Equally important to a rhetorical critic is to identify the actual audience addressed by the text. The critic must be alert to the fact that those who are in the immediate vicinity of the rhetor may or may not represent the actual audience addressed by the rhetor. Richard Nixon, for example, did not address his resignation speech to those who were gathered in front of their television sets on 8 August 1974. Instead, he projected his speech forward in time, and he addressed himself to future generations of Americans.

As should be clear, *audience* and *exigence* interact in complex ways. Lake (1983) uses both of these constructs in analysing Native American protest rhetoric from the 'Red Power' movement in the United States from 1968 to 1974. As Lake notes, most political commentators of the time maintained that the rhetoric of the Red Power movement was a failure. These commentators expressed surprise at the tactics of the movement, which seemed designed to alienate whites rather than to attract them to the Native American cause. The commentators assumed that the exigence for the Red Power movement was the injustices committed against Native Americans by whites, and they also assumed that the leaders of the Red Power movement addressed their rhetoric to white audiences. Lake challenges these assumptions; the rhetoric of the movement was intended, he argues, not to effect political changes or to persuade white audiences but instead to 'regenerate traditional Indian religious beliefs and to restore the ancient ways of life'. The exigence, according to Lake, was the concern that native traditions, rituals, and languages were being abandoned as Native Americans assimilated into white culture. The audience for Red Power rhetoric was other Native Americans. As Lake explains, this exigence and this audience imposed constraints on the rhetoric of the Red Power movement because some rhetorical modes are not open to Indians 'if they are to remain Indians'. For example, the Indian audience's distrust of written language (which 'denudes' the sacredness of the spoken word) led the Red Power movement to use other forms of rhetorical texts, such as occupation of sacred and symbolic lands (Mount Rushmore, Alcatraz Island) and traditional dancing (the Ghost Dance) (1983: 133–4).

Genre   A genre is a group of texts that share specific discursive features. For example, a genre might be created as response to a similar recurring situation, such as the funeral oration. Or, a genre might be created when texts employ similar argumentative or stylistic strategies. Hofstadter (1965), for example, identifies what he calls 'the paranoid style' – a type of rhetorical text that features argument about conspiracy theories; Campbell and Jamieson (1995) refer to a genre of 'enactment rhetoric' in which the author of the text embodies the argument and is proof of its truth.

When a speaker employs a genre, expectations are created both in the speaker and in the audience. As Bakhtin explains:

> Speech genres organize our speech in almost the same way as grammatical (syntactical) forms do. We learn to cast our speech in generic forms and, when hearing others' speech, we guess its genre from the very first words; we predict a certain length (that is, the approximate length of the speech whole) and a certain compositional structure; we foresee the end; that is, from the very beginning we have a sense of the speech whole, which is only later differentiated during the speech process. (1990: 956)

An expectation of genre establishes the rhetorical parameters of a text, determining not only its structure but also its vocabulary, syntax, argumentative moves, and narrative appeals. The speaker who oversteps these parameters, betraying audience expectations, often provokes a negative reaction. Generic classification is one of the means by which a critic or audience member establishes the standards for evaluating a rhetorical text. A generic misclassification creates expectations that the text is not designed to fulfill (Jamieson, 1973).

The importance of genre is illustrated in Lake's analysis of the rhetoric of the Red Power movement. Political commentators classified the rhetoric as 'protest rhetoric' in the same genre with the civil rights rhetoric of African Americans and Hispanic Americans. As Lake explains, that generic misclassification forced the commentators into assuming that the rhetoric was a failure. However, the Native Americans were employing genres grounded in Native American culture and chosen specifically because they were alien to white Americans.

Richard Nixon's resignation speech provides a still more complicated instance of generic misclassification. The resignation of a president was unprecedented in American history. Consequently, in one sense, the audience did not know what to expect from the speech because there was no established genre that would have shaped their expectations. On the other hand, scandal is a common event in politics. The genre politicians normally employ in response to scandal is *apologia* – a type of speech in which speakers either defend their actions or apologize for their misdeeds. The expectations of Nixon's television audience were shaped by their previous experiences with the genre of *apologia*. Nixon, however, defied these expectations; he employed a type of hybrid genre that combined elements from a campaign speech and a commemorative speech. From the perspective of the television audience, the disjunction between their expectations and the actual speech provoked condemnation – and suspicion that Nixon had lost touch with reality.

Genres are not static but dynamic; that is, generic expectations evolve. Jamieson illustrates this evolution of generic expectations in her discussion of a film about two early-twentieth-century US bank robbers who have become cultural icons – *Bonnie and Clyde*. The film by that name portrays them as attractive, appealing outlaws with whom the audience sides as they are pursued by bumbling police. The music and tone of the film are reminiscent of 'slapstick comedy'. As Jamieson notes: 'Audiences submitted to the entrapment of the film [and] laughed. A generic classification was made and reinforced.' The film ends, however, in a 'bloodbath'. Says Jamieson: 'Audiences tensed, stunned by generic betrayal.' That film changed generic expectations, according to Jamieson: 'The solicitation and entrapment of *Bonnie and Clyde* can, however, shatter generic expectations but once. Exposure sets up expectations. When other [later] films . . . blend the hilarious with the horrid, the shock is muted. A generic permutation has occurred and audiences approach specimens of it with responses conditioned by *Bonnie and Clyde*' (1973: 168).

Rhetor Credibility   The authority speakers and writers possess because of their status in government or society, previous actions, or reputation for wisdom creates expectations and affects the operation of a text. These background characteristics and qualifications to speak or write affect how a text is understood and what effect it has. Logue and Miller (1995) illustrate the operation of the position of the rhetor in their analysis of a controversy between two elderly sisters and the mayor of a small town in the southern United States. Because of a mistake made during a meter installation in 1966, the sisters were paying not only for their own water but also for their neighbor's water. That it took twenty-three years for the women to convince the town to rectify the mistake (and to reimburse them for their lost money) was due in large part, Logue and Miller argue, to the sisters' lack of rhetorical status or authority. The sisters were well known in the community as being industrious and resourceful, but also modest and respectful. Their reputation for amiability was only one rhetorical disadvantage of many: they came from a low socioeconomic class; they were women; and they were elderly. Although they were armed with ingenious and ultimately correct evidence of the town's mistake, they were repeatedly rebuffed by the mayor and the mayor's assistants.

Rhetor credibility is, of course, relevant to our other examples, as well. Any interpretation of Richard Nixon's resignation speech needs to acknowledge that, as Nixon stepped before the microphones and television cameras, his audience perceived him as a liar and a fallen leader. As well, Barbara Jordan's reputation as an extraordinary orator and a tough-minded and principled woman who demanded that the US constitutional mandates for equal opportunity be honored created expectations surrounding her rhetorical texts. Further, that Bill Clinton was both white and male created particular expectations when he rose to deliver a funeral oration for Jordan.

The second general question rhetorical critics may ask concerns what that text presents. This turns the critic's focus from the context to the text itself.

What Does the Text Present to an Audience?

Some critics determine that a text is eloquent, or persuasive, or not persuasive. Many contemporary critics, however, identify what a text presents
to a reader or listener by indicating the objects, events, or particular
understandings that are created by a text or what a text ignores or makes
absent. Among the many things a text can create are a *rhetorical persona*
for the speaker or writer, an *implied audience*, and *contextual understandings*. A text also can make things *absent* or silence particular voices.

Rhetorical Persona In literary criticism, it is common to distinguish
between the author of a literary work and a fictitious authorial persona
created in the literary work. Similarly, rhetorical critics often distinguish
between a rhetor (or speaker) and the persona created in the rhetorical text.
Consider, for example, the first sentence of US President Abraham
Lincoln's Second Inaugural Address, delivered in 1865: '"At this second
appearing to take the oath of the presidential office, there is less occasion
for an extended address than there was at the first."' As Slagell explains,
the sentence is notable for its 'impersonal tone, use of the passive voice,
and lack of self-references' (1991: 157). The text portrays Lincoln as a
captive victim of the American Civil War; he emerges from the text as
being acted upon rather than as a principal actor in the war. Contrast
Lincoln's textual persona with that of another former US President,
Franklin Roosevelt, speaking during the Great Depression in the United
States in the early part of the twentieth century:

> So first of all let *me* assert *my firm* belief that the only thing we have to fear is
> fear itself – nameless, unreasoning, unjustified terror which paralyzes needed
> efforts to convert *retreat into advance*.
>   In every dark hour of our national life a *leadership of frankness and vigor* has
> met with that understanding and support of the people themselves which is
> essential to *victory*. (Daughton, 1993: 431; emphasis added)

Whereas Lincoln emerged from the text as a captive victim of circumstance, Roosevelt emerges as a strong and vigorous leader. Moreover, as
Daughton explains, by metaphorically describing the Depression as a war
(with 'retreats and advances', and ultimately 'victory'), the role Roosevelt
assumed was 'that of military leader. The text conveys a firm, warlike
resolve to triumph over adversity, encouraging listeners to unite . . . behind
strong military leadership' (1993: 431–4).

Of course, a rhetor who occupies the role of president of the United States
has a great deal of flexibility in constructing his rhetorical persona. By
contrast, rhetors who represent oppressed groups have to negotiate an
acceptable persona in order to have their voices recognized as legitimate.
This point is illustrated by K.A. Foss (1987) in her analysis of the rhetoric of
the nineteenth-century abolitionist and women's rights lecturer Sojourner
Truth. As Foss explains, Truth represented two oppressed groups: she was
an African American and she was a woman. Truth's 'mere presence on a

public platform called into question basic beliefs of the society and typically generated considerable hostility' (1987: 387). The persona that emerges from Truth's speeches is one that was recognized by her audiences as appropriate for women – the mother figure. This persona of 'mother' was able to engage in behaviors associated with mothers – scolding and praising, for example. Foss explains: 'Inherent in scolding is a kind of superior wisdom; the one doing the scolding has seen more of life and has the right to make such judgments. Such a superior attitude is allowable, however, and even expected in the mother–child relationship and is softened by the sense of caring that accompanies it' (1987: 388). While the role of 'mother' does not allow the speaker the flexibility or degree of authority that the role of 'president', for example, would allow, Truth gained some degree of authority on a public speaking platform through this persona.

Implied Audience   Just as we distinguish between a real rhetor and rhetorical persona, we also can distinguish between a real audience and an 'implied audience'. The 'implied audience' (like the rhetorical persona) is fictive because it is created by the text and exists only inside the symbolic world of the text. McGee (1975), for example, discusses the audience implied by British philosopher John Locke's writings. John Locke's 'people' are 'perceptive in ways no philosopher could be, powerful in a way no army could match, patient in a way any behavioral scientist would envy' (1975: 238). An audience implied by a text, says McGee, becomes 'infused with an artificial, rhetorical reality by the agreement' of an actual audience 'to participate in a collective fantasy' (1975: 242).

In texts of the independence movement for Quebec, Canada's French-speaking province, Charland finds an implied audience – the *peuple québécois*, who 'do not exist in nature, but only within a discursively constituted history' (1987: 137). Charland cites Claude Morin's 'polemical history' as an example: '"Like many other peoples, Quebeckers have experienced an awakening of self-consciousness. They want to assert for themselves, not as French-speaking Canadians, but as *Québécois*, citizens who, for the moment, suffer the want of a country that is their own"' (1987: 136). As another example, the Quebec government's White Paper includes the following historical account: '"In 1760, our community was already an established society along the St. Lawrence. North American by geography, French by language, culture, and politics, this society had a soul, a way of life, traditions, that were its very own. Its struggles, its successes, and its ordeals have given it an awareness of its collective destiny, and it was with some impatience that it tolerated the colonial tie."' This text, argues Charland, creates the *peuple québécois* by rendering 'the world of events understandable with respect to a transcendental collective interest that negates individual interest' (1987: 139–40).

Contextual Understanding   A text can present a contextual understanding or a particular consciousness by naming events, objects, and other aspects of the context in a particular way. For example, Carlson (1992) argues that a feminist consciousness is created in a body of discourse. She surveyed almost thirty years (1834 to 1860) of *The Advocate of Moral Reform*, published bi-weekly by the New York Moral Reform Society, a group of women dedicated to ending prostitution. She finds this body of discourse gradually creates a feminist consciousness for readers out of what was a traditional acceptance of the male-dominated Christian social order. Early references in *The Advocate* describe prostitution as evil and such women as perpetrators. Over time the perspective shifts, and prostitutes become victims in the pages of the *Advocate*. This changed portrayal creates a sympathy binding all women as victims and as sisters, presenting a feminist consciousness.

Not only can a text operate to name the context, it also can operate to rename it. Attorney Gerry Spence is well known in the United States for his courtroom victories in high-profile cases, including winning an acquittal for white separatist Randy Weaver, who was charged with murder. Weaver, his family, and a young family friend were involved in a month-long standoff with a large number of US law enforcement officers on Ruby Ridge, Weaver's remote mountain homesite in the western state of Idaho. When shots eventually were fired (who fired them was never determined), the federal marshals called in reinforcements, and, over the next few days, Weaver's wife, son, and dog were shot and killed, as was a federal marshal. Spence's courtroom oration defending Weaver names and renames the context, that is, the events on trial, in a way that was compelling to the jury, who found Weaver not guilty of murdering the marshal.

First, Spence (1993) names the federal officers as 'they', setting them apart from ordinary Idahoans, like the jury and Randy Weaver. 'They' are people who like to start trouble; they 'got excited' on Ruby Ridge, 'because they've got a war, they can bring in their airplanes, and they can bring in their helicopters and they can bring in their snipers and their assaulters, and they can have themselves a big war up in northern Idaho' (1993: 18).

Spence's text renames Randy Weaver, not as a white supremacist but as a god-fearing family man who just wants to be left alone. He argues that the prosecution and media have 'demonized' Randy Weaver, that is, they have unfairly and incorrectly characterized him, hoping the jury will think, 'this is a man that believes different than me, this is a man that we can't trust, this is a man we don't care what happens to' (1993: 12). Spence's narrative, however, erases the demonization by renaming it and by naming all the prosecutor's mistaken characterizations of Weaver:

> [H]ow many days did you hear these people over here try to make this man a member of the Aryan Nations Church when he plainly was not, and tried to connect him in some way or another with their beliefs? And you heard horrid things that turn my stomach that he does not subscribe to at all . . . [H]e is not a white supremacist, he believes that people of different races should live separately. (1993: 40)

Furthermore, 'they'

looked to the bottom of the well for everything they could find against Randy Weaver. There isn't a thing that he ever did in his life that they didn't look up and try and smear him. If they would have found a crime they would have brought it to your attention. And this is a man who never had even a traffic accident. Never even had a traffic ticket. Never been charged with a crime of any kind, and honorably served his country. Had no history of any kind of criminal record. (1993: 48)

In addition, 'they' demonize Weaver by mistakenly naming his home. Spence says: 'The FBI people want to call it a compound. Why? Because if you kill them in the compound it's okay, but if you kill them in the house it might not be okay.' Spence renames the 'compound' – it was a ramshackle cabin and a 'birthing' shed. Thus, Spence's oration creates a familiar context for the jury, leading them to accept Spence's context for the whole case – a verdict of 'not guilty' (1993: 67).

Absence Many contemporary critics focus on what is absent from or silenced by a text. As Wander puts it, the potential of a text 'to command being' also involves the potential 'to spell out being unacceptable, undesirable, insignificant' (1984: 209). Television characters, Wander explains, 'conform to conventional standards of beauty' and are 'white or near white, fine-featured, young, well proportioned, and of average height'. Negated are elderly, extremely short or tall, fat, scarred, or limping individuals (1981: 518–19).

By using language that privileges one aspect of an event, another thereby is negated. Reese and Buckalew (1995) analysed the US televised reporting of the Persian Gulf War by studying the evening-news transcripts from 2 August 1990 to 28 February 1991 of a local television station in Austin, Texas. Prior to the bombing of Baghdad, according to Reese and Buckalew, the station covered local 'peace' activities heavily. After the bombing began, the station's news coverage operated to create community consensus of patriotic support for the war and to make absent any dissent. Reese and Buckalew note: 'The language used to describe public opinion either privileged the pro-war position, or denigrated the anti-war voices.' Among the many examples they cite are the following statements, made by either a television reporter or an anchor person:

[Regarding an anti-war protest at the University of Texas] Protestors outnumbered those supporting the war by 2 to 1, but supporters say that's only because the anti-war folks are more vocal.

[Regarding a pro-war protest] In the beginning pro-war forces were relatively quiet, now they are gaining in momentum. [Camera cuts to pictures of the rally.] Later the pro-war group *was confronted* by those opposed to the U.S. presence in the Persian Gulf.

One of the 'most important linguistic techniques' was to 'align the pro-war with the pro-troops position', according to Reese and Buckalew, who give the following example:

[Regarding school children's reaction to the war]   In the meantime the students are following through on their commitment to support not the war itself but rather the Americans in the Middle East *fighting for peace.*

This 'remarkable inversion' obliterates any possible semantic space for anti-war sentiment, as the war has become the pathway to peace (1995: 48–9).

A critic may conclude that a text is persuasive, that it creates a persona for the rhetor, an implied audience, a contextual understanding, an absence, or something else. The way in which the text operates to accomplish this is the subject of our third general question a critic can ask of a text.

What Features of the Text Are Significant?

The features that interest a critic generally are related to another judgment made by the critic. For example, if the text is deemed highly eloquent or persuasive, the features the critic identifies are those that lend the text its eloquence or persuasiveness. If the text is deemed to present a rhetorical persona, an implied audience, a contextual understanding, an absence, or so on, the critic identifies those features that create such an effect. Among the many constructs critics use in identifying significant features of a text, we discuss and illustrate *structure and temporality, argument, metaphor,* and *iconicity.* Our discussion of these features of particular texts necessarily involves their instrumental operation in what the text presents.

Structure and Temporality   Focus on the structure of texts, such as the introduction, body, and conclusion of a speech, is as old as the art of rhetoric itself. Contemporary concern with the structure of texts is related to Saussure's (1986) insight that we experience discourse in a linear fashion. Thus, the structure of a text becomes intertwined with time. Contemporary rhetorical critics make much use of temporality in evaluating texts. One focus is on chronology, as Medhurst (1987) illustrates in his criticism of the 'Atoms for Peace' speech delivered to the United Nations General Assembly by former US President Dwight Eisenhower in 1953. Medhurst observes that the speech moved 'from present danger, to past efforts toward reconciliation [with the Soviet Union], to a vision for the future'. A chronological pattern of organization, notes Medhurst, would have forced Eisenhower to begin with past failures and to 'bury the present in the middle portion of the speech' rather than featuring the warning about the ability of the Soviets to launch a preemptive strike. Also, Eisenhower would have been unable 'dramatically to juxtapose the failures of the past with his visionary plan for the future' if his organizational pattern had been chronological (1987: 208).

The placement of former US President Abraham Lincoln's famous line – 'A House divided against itself cannot stand' – in the speech he gave to the Illinois State Republican Convention (after he was nominated as its candidate for the United States Senate) enhanced the effectiveness of that phrase. It comes, notes Leff, as an interruption, at a moment in the speech when 'our expectations have been prodded in a different direction' (1983: 7–8):

> Mr. President and Gentlemen of the Convention: If we could first know *where* we are, and *whither* we are tending, we could better judge *what* to do, and *how* to do it. We are now into the fifth year, since a policy was initiated, with the *avowed* object, and *confident* promise, of putting an end to slavery agitation. Under the operation of that policy, that agitation has not only, *not* ceased, but has *constantly augmented.*
>
> In *my* opinion, it will not cease, until a *crisis* shall have been reached and passed.
>
> A House divided against itself cannot stand. (1983: 3)

The first paragraph creates a temporal and spatial setting, then develops a 'pattern of temporal progression', moving from the past to the present to the future. Says Leff, the famous fifth sentence breaks the progression, and this break is the source of part of its force (1983: 8).

Argument Rhetorical critics frequently focus on arguments within a text and do so from a variety of perspectives. As Chapter 8 in this volume (by van Eemeren, Grootendorst, Jackson and Jacobs) is devoted to the topic of argumentation, we refer readers to that account of contemporary theories of argument for a more detailed treatment of the subject. Here we will concentrate only on one of the more distinctively rhetorical forms of argument, the *enthymeme.*

First introduced in Aristotle's work *On Rhetoric,* the enthymeme is among the oldest concepts of rhetorical analysis. Many people describe the enthymeme as an abbreviated syllogism. It is 'abbreviated' because it omits a premise; the audience creates coherence in the incomplete argument by consciously or unconsciously supplying the 'missing link' from the premises in their own belief system. For example, suppose someone presents the following argument: 'It's more difficult to beat Brazil than the United States. So we're better off scheduling a football (soccer) game against the United States.' One premise and the conclusion of the argument are stated explicitly by the speaker. However, as it stands, the conclusion does not follow from the premise. To make the argument coherent, the audience unconsciously 'fills the gap' or supplies the missing premise:

> It is more difficult to beat Brazil than the United States.
> [*Of two good things, the one more easily accomplished is the better.*]
> Therefore, we are better off scheduling a game against the United States.

If an audience is to be persuaded by the argument, they must assume the italicized premise. If the audience does not assume that premise, they will reject the argument as incoherent.

The theoretical construct of the enthymeme allows the critic to examine the interaction between a speaker, a text, and an audience. In creating and responding to enthymemes, speaker and audience reveal their unstated

beliefs and values; they reveal their ideology or 'implicit philosophy' about
the nature of reality, the nature of their community, and their conception of
appropriate social relations. Fulkerson (1979), for example, illustrates how
Martin Luther King Jr, a leader of the US civil rights movement in the
1960s, used the concept of enthymeme in his 'Letter from Birmingham Jail'.
King's letter was a response to a letter written by eight Christian and Jewish
clergymen who objected to King's strategy of civil disobedience. Fulkerson
notes that King expanded the clergymen's enthymemes into syllogisms in
order to refute their arguments. For example, the clergymen argued:

[*Outsiders have no right to protest in Birmingham, Alabama.*]
King is an outsider.
Therefore, King has no right to protest.

As Fulkerson explains, King began his refutation by attacking the minor
premise; he explained that he indeed had ties to Birmingham and that he
was not an outsider. Then King attacked the implied major premise: he
cited the tradition of Christian missionary work, and he also argued that, in
an interdependent nation such as the United States, no citizen is an outsider
anywhere. In effect, King revealed that the argument of the clergymen
depended on a narrow, Southern, sectionalist mentality. This sectionalist
mentality contradicted both the ideology of Christianity and the ideology
of American nationalism. King forced the clergymen into revealing their
loyalties: were they Southerners? Or were they American clergymen? No
matter what the answer, King had succeeded in defusing the clergymen's
argument. If they responded they were American clergymen, then they had
to acknowledge that the implied premise in the enthymeme is inconsistent
with their own ideology. And if they responded they were Southerners, then
their argument lost the institutional sanction of the Church.

Olson and Goodnight (1994) analyse discourse in the social controversy
over the use of animal fur as clothing. As they note, anti-fur rhetoric
suggests that 'the claim that it is acceptable to use fur is based on the
enthymematically-supplied premises that humans may use animals so long
as such use proceeds humanely and that fur production is humane'. The
anti-fur advocates 'block completion of the "acceptable use" enthymeme,
challenging the argument's implicit premise by defining "cruelty" as any use
(humane or inhumane) of animals for the primary purpose of producing
luxury items'. The anti-fur activists similarly block completion of the
'humane use' enthymeme 'by associating fur with cruelty'. They graphically
depict the conditions of fur production, including 'traps, tiny cages, and
instruments of death' (1994: 259–60). With both discourse and pictures, the
anti-fur advocates 'disrupt the most basic, habituated enthymemes of the
fur industry' (1994: 262).

Metaphor Figures of speech, including metaphors, can be identified in
order to account for the aesthetic appeal of the text. Recent studies in
metaphor (Lakoff, 1987; Lakoff and Johnson, 1980), however, suggest that

metaphor plays a much larger role in rhetoric than merely adding ornamentation to a text. The fundamental form of human understanding is a metaphoric process; the mind grasps an unfamiliar idea only by comparison to or in terms of something already known. Thus the metaphoric language in a text presents a particular view of reality by structuring the understanding of one idea in terms of something previously understood. In this view of metaphor, it shapes human experience. For example, Lakoff and Johnson demonstrate the pervasive use of the metaphor of war when speaking of argument, making argument an antagonistic, competitive event: '[W]e don't just *talk* about arguments in terms of war. We can actually win or lose arguments. We see the person we are arguing with as an opponent. We attack his positions and we defend our own.' This metaphor 'structures the action we perform in arguing' (1980: 4). Critics seek to explain what structures or understandings metaphors create in a text.

Ivie's (1987) analysis of lectures and books by Helen Caldicott, an anti-nuclear war activist from Australia, demonstrates how a critic locates clusters of words around a single metaphor that presents a particular way of understanding events. Caldicott criticizes the United States' '"pathological reactions"' to the Soviet Union; the United States has '"engineered her own suicide"' through '"paranoid projection"' (1987: 177). Other words used frequently by Caldicott are 'crazy', 'deranged', 'madness', 'insane', 'paranoia', and so on, leading Ivie to observe that Caldicott's discourse is dominated by one metaphor, that of madness. This metaphor urges a revision of American understanding of the Soviet Union, one in which the prevailing understanding of the so-called 'Soviet threat' is undermined. In Ivie's analysis, the efforts by Caldicott and other 'Cold War idealists' did not change public opinion in the United States because the metaphoric restructuring 'promoted a reversal rather than a transcendence of the conventional image of a barbarian threat to civilization'. As 'Americans have traditionally exonerated themselves of any guilt for war', the effect of the metaphor of madness and other prevalent metaphors in Cold War idealists' rhetoric was to 'decivilize America's image rather than the enemy's' (1987: 178).

Critics also look for 'archetypal metaphors' in rhetorical texts. Archetypal metaphors operate across generations to place value judgments on the subjects to which they are associated. Osborn (1967) details how lightness and darkness work as archetypal metaphors: light relates to survival, sight, and warmth; darkness relates to fear of the unknown, vulnerability, and cold. Osborn cites former British Prime Minister Winston Churchill's frequent use of these archetypal metaphors, suggesting that, in moments of crisis, 'the speaker must turn to the ancient archetypal verities, to the cycle of light and darkness, to the cycle of life and death and birth again . . . and find them all unchanged, all still appealing symbolically to the human heart and thus reassuring one that man himself, despite all the surface turbulence, remains after all man' (1967: 339).

This gendered language foreshadows a related role of metaphor in structuring a rhetorical text to which critics are sensitive. Griffin (1993) notes that the communication strategies suggested in the writings of US feminist philosopher Mary Daly are illustrated in a commencement address delivered by the author Ursula Le Guin at Mills College, a private school for women, in 1983. As the 'foreground' of patriarchal linguistic structures and rules for language use 'oppresses and limits individuals and creates a state of ontological erasure for women', Daly describes the world created by women's communication as the 'background'. Among her many suggested strategies for women's communication is the use of metaphors to reverse the patriarchal structures created by discourse in the foreground (1993: 164–7). As Griffin notes, Le Guin illustrates this in her reversal of the archetypal light–dark metaphor. Le Guin states, 'darkness is the place that "nourishes"'. It is the 'place "where no wars are fought and no wars are won"'. By this metaphorical reversal, by making darkness the place '"to be at home there, keep house there, be your own mistress, with a room of your own"', Le Guin redescribes and reorients the world for her audience (1993: 172–3).

Iconicity   An *icon* is a sign that mimics what it represents. For example, a portrait is an icon for whoever is portrayed in the portrait. Most words are symbolic rather than iconic because the relationship between the word and what the word signifies is arbitrary; there is no resemblance between the word and the meaning of the word. We use one word rather than another simply because it is the convention adopted by users of a specified language. However, when we combine words into sentences and phrases, we create complex forms of iconicity (Hawkes, 1977: 136–40). This point is illustrated by Lakoff and Johnson who contrast the following two sentences: (1) 'He ran and ran and ran and ran'; (2) 'He ran.' The repetition in the first sentence changes its meaning without changing its semantic content. Lakoff and Johnson account for the change in meaning by noting that the length of the sentence mimics the behavior described by the sentence (1980: 127–8). If a sentence is longer, the more substance it must contain. Iconicity functions in a way that is similar to metaphor; iconicity 'rests on the intuitive recognition of similarities between one field of reference (the form of language) and another' (Leech and Short, 1981: 242).

The aesthetic importance of iconicity long has been recognized in rhetorical theory. Longinus (1965), supposed author of the ancient treatise *On the Sublime*, certainly understood the power of iconicity and illustrated its use throughout the treatise. For example, Longinus quoted a passage from a speech by Demosthenes in which an aggressor attacks a victim: 'By his manner, his looks, his voice, when he acts with insolence, when he acts with hostility, when he strikes you with his fists, when he strikes you like a slave'. As Longinus explains, Demosthenes used syntax to mimic the onslaught of the aggressor: 'The orator does just the same as his aggressor; he belabours the judges' minds with blow after blow . . . Thus all the way through, although with continual variations, he preserves the essential character of the repetitions and the asyndeta' (1965: 130).

Iconicity, however, is not just an aesthetic device; it also serves instrumental functions. As British linguists have shown, iconic composition subtly reveals and reinforces ideological structures (Fowler et al., 1979). Rhetorical critics also emphasize this point. In analysing Martin Luther King Jr's 'Letter from Birmingham Jail', Fulkerson notes that the elaborate parallelism and repetition create and reinforce a particular persona for King:

> [T]he rhythms and balance created by parallelism, especially when a series of parallel constructions is used to build to a climax, probably have an affective impact, much as they would in oral discourse but to a lesser degree. The major effect is ethical, portraying the rhetor as a man who can balance various views and who has his ideas under complete control. (1979: 134)

Rhetorical critics need to remain alert to the possibility that syntax is not just a vehicle for correct usage or for ornamentation but also may convey a message, or at least reinforce a message, to an audience.

In sum, the three questions we have examined here – What expectations are created by the context? What does the text present to an audience? What features of the text are significant? – are some of the more basic questions rhetorical critics might ask as they approach a rhetorical text. However, the reader should keep in mind that these questions are by no means exhaustive. Critics can examine texts using a variety of methods, and in doing so, they can adopt a variety of perspectives. Rhetorical critics frequently draw from some of the same writings about language that dominate scholarship in every other field listed in these two volumes, including narrative, argumentation, genre/register, pragmatics, gender, and ethnicity.

In the final section of this chapter, we attempt to demonstrate the critical process in action. We do this by giving several possibilities for what rhetorical critics might see in a single text.

The Critical Process in Action

Rhetorical critics analyze entire rhetorical texts, which range from a speech or a written document to an entire body of discourse or even the rhetorical construction of a concept such as *equality* (Condit and Lucaites, 1993) or *whiteness* (Nakayama and Krizek, 1995). Space limits do not allow us to reproduce an entire text in order to illustrate the process of critical evaluation. We, therefore, focus on one of the most well-known twentieth-century orations in the United States, Martin Luther King Jr's 'I Have a Dream' speech, delivered on the steps of the Lincoln Memorial in Washington, DC in 1963 to an audience of over 250,000 people. The speech was the culmination of the March on Washington by civil rights activists. The speech is seen as one of the most moving speeches in recent times, one which gave moral force to the civil rights movement in the United States. We begin our demonstration of the critical process by describing portions of two critics' analyses of the speech – Cox (1989) and Hariman (1989). We chose these two because they ask similar questions of the text but come to different answers and, therefore, to different evaluations of the text. Then, using some of the constructs we discussed earlier in this chapter, we suggest other possibilities for analysing this rhetorical text.

The main question Cox asks of the text is: what features are the source of the speech's moral power? In order to answer that question, Cox makes use of several of the questions we have discussed in this chapter. Specifically, in his effort to understand the contextual expectations on the speech, Cox studied the historical situation King faced. The Southern states' response to the clamor for civil rights was a policy of 'gradualism' – waiting for social change to happen in the natural course of events. Based on statements King made in his 'Letter from Birmingham Jail', Cox argues that King believed such 'gradualism' was a tragic misconception. King wrote: '"It is the strangely irrational notion that there is something in the very flow of time that will inevitably cure all ills"' (Cox, 1989: 183).

Cox argues that King's speech operates as a 'powerful critique' to the policy of gradualism (1989: 183). In the first half of the speech, King sets up the conflict between 'the promises of democracy and the state of justice delayed' (1989: 189). The speech begins with a reference to the Lincoln Memorial, which features an enormous statue of a seated Abraham Lincoln at the top of the Memorial steps upon which King and his entourage were standing:

> Five score years ago, a great American, in whose symbolic shadow we stand today, signed the Emancipation Proclamation. This momentous decree came as a great beacon of light of hope to millions of Negro slaves who had been seared in the flames of withering injustice. It came as a joyous daybreak to end the long night of their captivity.
>
> But one hundred years later, the Negro still is not free. One hundred years later, the life of the Negro is still sadly crippled by the manacles of segregation and the chains of discrimination.
>
> One hundred years later, the Negro lives on a lonely island of poverty in the midst of a vast ocean of material prosperity. One hundred years later. . . . (King, 1988: 325)

Cox argues that these words introduce the temporal frame and moral promise that guide the remainder of the address. The articulation of time prepares the audience for the significance of the March and of King's demands:

> So we have come here today to dramatize a shameful condition.
>
> In a sense we have come to our nation's capital to cash a check. When the architects of our republic wrote the magnificent words of the Constitution and the Declaration of Independence, they were signing a promissory note to which every American was to fall heir. This note was a promise that all men, yes, black men as well as white men, would be guaranteed the unalienable rights of life, liberty, and the pursuit of happiness. (1988: 325)

The metaphor of a check 'assumes . . . that a promise has been made'. The promise King cites is both moral and temporal, Cox argues, as the illocutionary act of promising 'predicates a future act'; it has a 'moral claim in subsequent time upon the one who utters the promise'. At this point, King moves to 'the temporal and moral failure' (Cox, 1989: 192–3):

> It is obvious today that America has defaulted on this promissory note insofar as her citizens of color are concerned. Instead of honoring this sacred obligation, America has given the Negro people a bad check, which has come back marked 'insufficient funds'. (King, 1988: 325)

Here, Cox identifies a break in the temporal form:

> But we refuse to believe that the bank of justice is bankrupt. We refuse to believe that there are insufficient funds in the great vaults of opportunity of this nation. So we have come to cash this check – a check that will give us upon demand the riches of freedom and the security of justice. (1988: 325)

This is an attempt, argues Cox, to 'dissociate the promise from the record of temporal failure' (1989: 193). The March becomes a resumption of the journey to see the promise fulfilled.

> We have also come to the hallowed spot to remind America of the fierce urgency of now. This is no time to engage in the luxury of cooling off or to take the tranquilizing drug of gradualism. Now is the time to make real the promises of democracy. Now is the time to rise from the dark and desolate valley of segregation to the sunlit path of racial justice. Now is the time. . . . (King, 1988: 325–6)

Says Cox: 'By framing the present in relation to the promises of democracy, King is able to bring focus to the timeliness of the choice before America' (1989: 194).

The most famous section of the speech, the 'I have a dream' passage, apparently was extemporaneous on King's part. It articulates his vision of the future and, Cox argues, completes the temporal movement of the speech begun in the promises of democracy. Then, near the end of the speech, King exhorts:

> And so let freedom ring from the prodigious hilltops of New Hampshire.
> Let freedom ring from the mighty mountains of New York . . .
> Let freedom ring from the snow-capped Rockies of Colorado.
> Let freedom ring from the curvaceous slopes of California . . .
> Let freedom ring from Stone Mountain of Georgia.
> Let freedom ring from Lookout Mountain of Tennessee.
> Let freedom ring from every hill and molehill of Mississippi, from every mountain side, let freedom ring. (1988: 327–8)

Cox argues: 'In the quasi-mythical time of this vision, past and future are reconciled; no longer is there any tension between promise and reality, or between struggle and deliverance.' This injunction is for the fulfillment of the promise, happening in the very birthplace of the racist, anti-black organization, the Ku Klux Klan (Stone Mountain of Georgia). The movement across the continent is, Cox explains, 'as much moral as geographical'. It is the 'eschatological experience of exile and the promise of deliverance' (1989: 201).

King ends the speech:

> And when this happens, and when we allow freedom to ring, when we let it ring from every village and hamlet, from every state and city, we will be able to speed up the day when all of God's children – black men, white men, Jews and Gentiles, Catholics and Protestants – will be able to join hands and to sing in the words of the old Negro spiritual, 'Free at last, free at last; thank God Almighty, we are free at last'. (1988: 328)

This, says Cox, is the 'fulfillment – within the temporal space of the text' of a 'heritage that King had articulated in the Lincolnian words of his opening sentence . . . The timing of change in the polity and eschatological time are merged. King's dream becomes an empowering vision of the fulfillment of time' (1989: 202). Cox's analysis of this speech is that King redefines public time as morally charged and urgent. The dream of a future time 'orients our action now, as instrumental to this end' (1989: 204).

Hariman asks similar questions of this text, but his analysis differs from Cox's in part because he identifies different contextual expectations to which the speech is responding. Hariman argues that King is responding not only to the policy of gradualism but also to a schism within the civil rights movement, pitting those who advocated radical change against those who favored more modest reforms. Hariman cites a different statement from King's 'Letter from Birmingham Jail' to illustrate this. King writes: '"I stand in the middle of two opposing forces in the Negro community. One is a force of complacency . . . The other force is one of bitterness and hatred, and comes perilously close to advocating violence."' After further documenting the conflict among factions within the movement, Hariman argues that, if a split occurred, 'the center would have had the most to lose' (1989: 207–9). From this perspective of the historical situation, Hariman argues that King's speech is not the triumph that Cox claims it to be; instead, the text 'reasserts a moderate voice and some of the assumptions of gradualism' (1989: 206).

This understanding of the context also leads Hariman to read the text differently than Cox read it. As one example, Hariman argues that King's use of the check metaphor does not create moral or temporal urgency but instead asserts a moderate voice, as checks take time to write and days to process. Furthermore, says Hariman, checks are part of the institutional order: they can be 'a sacred obligation only if capitalism is a religion' (1989: 210). As another example, Hariman reads King's 'time' and his 'dream' not as real but as mythical; they are part of the 'myths used to legitimate the status quo'. Also, the 'concluding coda of "let freedom ring",' says Hariman, evokes an image of church and town hall bells that toll on special occasions, with a 'ceremonial sounding'. King's speech, concludes Hariman, is 'capable of occluding the present behind a miasma of myth' (1989: 211).

Hariman says King's 'let freedom ring' stanzas can be read as transforming time into space, as they move geographically around the United
States: 'A disturbing sense of public time is being reduced to a reassuring
sense of public space,' he says, drawing on Mircea Eliade's observation that
'creating and maintaining the mythic consciousness' requires converting
time to space in order 'to escape the anxiety of living in history' (1989:
213). This evaluation leads Hariman to criticize King's speech for 'driving
competing speakers into marginality' (1989: 216) but, at the same time,
Hariman acknowledges it as 'a masterpiece' (1989: 215).

While Cox and Hariman provide us with important insights into the
internal workings of the text, many other readings of King's speech are
possible. For example, a critic might ask what makes this text a 'masterpiece', that is, what features account for the text's aesthetic appeal? One
might focus, for instance, on King's extensive use of metaphor and simile
to create vivid images of abstract principles. Many of these metaphors are
presented in pairs:

. . . a joyous *daybreak* to end the long *night* of their captivity.

. . . lonely *island* of *poverty* in the midst of a vast *ocean* of material *prosperity*.

Now is the time to *rise* from the *dark* and desolate *valley* of segregation to the
sunlit path of racial justice. Now is the time to *lift* our nation from the *quicksands*
of racial justice to the *solid rock* of brotherhood. (King, 1988: 325–6)

These paired metaphors – moving from dark to light, from low to high,
from isolation to integration – subtly reinforce King's message about the
ultimate effectiveness of non-violent protest. Further, a critic might note
King's extensive use of anaphora (repetition) and parallel sentence structure. These patterns and rhythms of the speech create expectations for the
audience; as King breaks and shifts the rhythm, he generates a sense of the
dramatic urgency of the moment.

A critic also might ask how the many metaphors of King's speech
operate to create particular understandings. Cox and Hariman provide very
different readings of the check metaphor. Another critic, with different
expectations and predilections, might focus on the familiarity of the
metaphors. While only some of the metaphors qualify as archetypal, they
all are familiar (dreams, checks, beacons, flames, joyous daybreaks, long
nights, and so on); indeed, many of the metaphors are so familiar as to risk
being tedious if not fatuous. A critic might analyse these metaphors as
reassuring in their orthodoxy. Nearly all of the metaphors originate from
biblical text, from the Protestant tradition, from the European literary
canon, and from the political tradition upon which the United States was
founded. They are metaphors designed to reinforce – not to challenge –
dominant conceptual frames. Rather than startle the audience, the metaphors lull the audience into accepting conservative and patriarchal
standards and orientations. King's challenge to the audience is carefully
mediated, and his stylistic choices contrast sharply with the choices of, for

example, Malcolm X, the leader of a more militant faction of the civil rights movement. Malcolm X insisted: 'I don't see any American dream; I see an American nightmare' (1964: 2). Malcolm X's religion (Black Muslim), countenance, and discursive style were more foreign than familiar to white America.

A critic could direct attention to King's choice of rhetorical genres. By creating the case for civil rights within the genre of a ceremonial speech rather than a political speech, King's text is reassuring and reasonable rather than radical. It is exhorting but not demanding; it is uplifting rather than condemnatory; it is full of dream and hope rather than dread and doubt. In accordance with the ceremonial genre, the speech uses impersonal and distant referents for the failures of the past. It is 'America' and not 'white Americans' who have defaulted on the promissory note. Indeed, the only specific personal condemnation is to particular residents of the South: 'Alabama, with its vicious racists, with its governor having his lips dripping with the words of interposition and nullification.' Everyone else is potentially part of the dream for tomorrow; 'we' are 'all of God's children' who will 'join hands' and sing the 'old Negro spiritual, "Free at last"' (1988: 328).

A critic might note further that, while the speech makes present the failed promises of democracy and emancipation and the hope for redemption, women are almost entirely absent from the speech. King refers to a *brotherhood* several times during this speech, and his inclusive statements refer to males:

> This note was a promise that all men, yes, black men as well as white men, would be guaranteed the unalienable rights of life, liberty, and the pursuit of happiness. (1988: 325)

> I have a dream that one day on the red hills of Georgia, sons of former slaves and sons of former slave-owners will be able to sit down together at the table of brotherhood. (1988: 325)

> . . . we hold these truths to be self evident, that all men are created equal. (1988: 327)

> . . . we will be able to speed up that day when all of God's children – black men and white men. . . . (1988: 328)

The only female presence to emerge directly from the speech are children, 'little girls':

> I have a dream that one day . . . right there in Alabama, little black boys and little black girls will be able to hold hands with little white boys and little white girls as sisters and brothers. (1988: 327)

An ironic contrast exists between King's speech – addressed to an audience that included women – and a speech delivered in 1995 by Louis Farrakhan during the 'Million Man March' on Washington, DC. In his lengthy and rambling speech, Farrakhan made an effort, at one point, to acknowledge the black women who had been excluded from the Million Man March.

Technically, women were not excluded from participation in the Civil Rights March of 1963; however, they were, in a sense, rhetorically excluded from King's speech.

Each of these perspectives on King's speech could be developed in some detail. In addition, critics could ask many other questions and analyse his text by means of many other constructs. This example, and indeed the entire chapter, are intended to illustrate rather than define the process of rhetorical criticism and the relevance of rhetoric to a student of discourse analysis.

Conclusions

These various critical approaches to King's speech and the discussion of basic questions and critical constructs are intended to demonstrate how a rhetorical critic might analyse a rhetorical text. To describe the range of critical activity is difficult, as that which critics see in or ask of a rhetorical text is as various as the expectations and predilections they bring to it. Drawing from history generally and the history of rhetoric particularly, writings about language, past rhetorical activity, and so on, critics evaluate rhetoric by reading the context and the text in a way that illuminates the operation and effects of rhetoric.

Recommended Reading

To gain a sense of the history of rhetoric, see Kennedy (1994), Conley (1990), and Vickers (1988). For a sampling of writings that have influenced the development of rhetoric, see Bizzell and Herzberg (1990). For examples of critical texts as well as suggestions for doing rhetorical criticism, see Foss (1995), Burgchardt (1995), and Leff and Kauffeld (1989). For discussion of the critical process, see Nothstine et al. (1994). For various perspectives on the critical process, see Black (1978), McKerrow (1989), Warnick (1992), and Leff (1980).

Notes

1 Two scholars (Foss and Griffin, 1995) more recently have suggested that rhetoric be viewed as invitational rather than persuasive. This description of the end of discourse may change rhetorical practice in the years to come.

2 As the English word *rhetoric* comes fom the Greek (*rhêtorikê*), tecnically the study of rhetoric begins in Ancient Greece. However, instrumental use of oral discourse is as old as language itself. Many extant ancient texts include discussion of matters that scholars now describe as rhetorical. For example, the ancient Egyptians wrote 'wisdom books' that advise how to speak in different settings, explaining, for example, how to speak effectively with one's superiors and with one's subordinates. They also include advice about how to present oral petitions and what sorts of strategies are effective and ineffective in petitions – threats, flattery, argument.

References

Aristotle (1991) *On Rhetoric: a Theory of Civil Discourse* (trans. G. Kennedy). New York: Oxford University Press.

Bakhtin, M. (1990) 'The problem of speech genres', (trans. V.W. McGee), in P. Bizzell and B. Herzberg (eds), *The Rhetorical Tradition: Readings from Classical Times to the Present*. Boston: Bedford. pp. 944–63.

Bitzer, L.F. (1981) 'Political rhetoric', in D.D. Nimmo and K.R. Sanders (eds), *Handbook of Political Communication*. Beverly Hills, CA: Sage. pp. 225–48.

Bizzell, P. and Herzberg, B. (eds) (1990) *The Rhetorical Tradition: Readings from Classical Times to the Present*. Boston: Bedford.

Black, E. (1978) *Rhetorical Criticism: a Study in Method*. Madison, WI: University of Wisconsin Press.

Blair, C., Jeppeson, M.S. and Pucci, E. (1991) 'Public memorializing in postmodernity: the Vietnam Veterans Memorial as prototype', *Quarterly Journal of Speech*, 77 (3): 263–88.

Bryant, D.C. (1972) 'Rhetoric: its function and its scope', in D. Ehninger (ed.), *Contemporary Rhetoric*. Glenview, IL: Scott, Foresman. pp. 15–37.

Burgchardt, C.R. (ed.) (1995) *Readings in Rhetorical Criticism*. State College, PA: Strata.

Burke, K. (1966) *Language as Symbolic Action: Essays on Life, Literature, and Method*. Berkeley, CA: University of California Press.

Campbell, G. (1988) *The Philosophy of Rhetoric* (ed. L. Bitzer). Carbondale, IL: Southern Illinois University Press.

Campbell, K.K. and Jamieson, K.H. (1995) 'Form and genre in rhetorical criticism: an introduction', in C.R. Burgchardt (ed.), *Readings in Rhetorical Criticism*. State College, PA: Strata. pp. 394–411.

Carlson, A.C. (1992) 'Creative Casuistry and Feminist Consciousness: a Rhetoric of Moral Reform', *Quarterly Journal of Speech*, 78 (1): 16–32.

Cicero (1942) *De Oratore*, Books I and II (trans. E.W. Sutton and H. Rackham). Cambridge, MA: Loeb Classical Library.

Charland, M. (1987) 'Constitutive rhetoric: the case of the *peuple québécois*', *Quarterly Journal of Speech*, 73 (2): 133–50.

Condit, C.M. and Lucaites, J.L. (1993) *Crafting Equality: American's Anglo-African Word*. Chicago: University of Chicago Press.

Conley, T.M. (1990) *Rhetoric in the European Tradition*. New York: Longman.

Cox, J.R. (1989) 'The fulfillment of time: King's "I have a dream" speech (August 28, 1963)', in M.C. Leff and F.J. Kauffeld (eds), *Texts in Context: Critical Dialogues on Significant Episodes in American Political Rhetoric*. Davis, CA: Hermagoras. pp. 181–204.

Daughton, S. (1993) 'Metaphorical transcendence: images of the holy war in Franklin Roosevelt's first inaugural', *Quarterly Journal of Speech*, 79 (4): 427–46.

Derrida, J. (1982) *Margins of Philosophy* (trans. A. Bass). Chicago: University of Chicago Press.

Foss, K.A. (1987) 'Sojourner truth', in B.K. Duffy and H.R. Ryan (eds), *American Orators before 1900: Critical Studies and Sources*. New York: Greenwood. pp. 385–90.

Foss, S.K. (1995) *Rhetorical Criticism: Exploration and Practice*, 2nd edn. Prospect Heights, IL: Waveland.

Foss, S.K. and Griffin, C.L. (1995) 'Beyond persuasion: a proposal for an invitational rhetoric', *Communication Monographs*, 62 (1): 2–18.

Foucault, M. (1972) *The Archaeology of Knowledge* (trans. A.M. Sheridan). New York: Pantheon.

Fowler, R., Hodge, B., Kress, G. and Trew, T. (1979) *Language as Control*. London: Routledge and Kegan Paul.

Fulkerson, R.P. (1979) 'The public letter as a rhetorical form: structure, logic, and style in King's "Letter from Birmingham jail"', *Quarterly Journal of Speech*, 65 (2): 121–36.

Griffin, C.L. (1993) 'Women as communicators: Mary Daly's hagiography as rhetoric', *Communication Monographs*, 60 (2): 158–77.

Hariman, R. (1989) 'Time and the reconstitution of gradualism in King's address: a response to Cox', in M.C. Leff and F.J. Kauffeld (eds), *Texts in Context: Critical Dialogues on Significant Episides in American Political Rhetoric*, Davis, CA: Hermagoras. pp. 205–17.

Hawkes, T. (1977) *Structuralism and Semiotics*. Berkeley, CA: University of California Press.

Hofstadter, R. (1965) *The Paranoid Style in American Politics and Other Essays*. New York: Knopf.

Ivie, R.L. (1987) 'Metaphor and the rhetorical invention of cold war "idealists"', *Communication Monographs*, 54 (2): 165–82.

Jamieson, K. (1973) 'Generic constraints and the rhetorical situation', *Philosophy and Rhetoric*, 6 (3): 162–70.

Katriel, T. (1994) 'Sites of memory: discourses of the past in Israeli pioneering settlement museums', *Quarterly Journal of Speech*, 80 (1): 1–20.

Kennedy, G.A. (1994) *A New History of Classical Rhetoric*. Princeton, NJ: Princeton University Press.

King, M.L. (1988) 'I have a dream', in L. Rohler and R. Cook (eds), *Great Speeches for Criticism and Analysis*. Greenwood, IN: Alistair. pp. 325–8.

Lake, R.A. (1983) 'Enacting red power: the consummatory function in Native American protest rhetoric', *Quarterly Journal of Speech*, 69 (2): 127–42.

Lakoff, G. (1987) *Women, Fire, and Dangerous Things: What Categories Reveal about the Mind*. Chicago: University of Chicago Press.

Lakoff, G. and Johnson, M. (1980) *Metaphors We Live By*. Chicago: University of Chicago Press.

Leech, G.N. and Short, M.H. (1981) *Style in Fiction: a Linguistic Introduction to English Fictional Prose*. London: Longman.

Leff, M.C. (1980) 'Interpretation and the art of the rhetorical critic', *Western Journal of Speech Communication*, 44 (4): 337–49.

Leff, M.C. (1983) 'Rhetorical timing in Lincoln's "House divided" speech', paper presented for the Van Zelst lecture in communication at Northwestern University, Evanston, IL.

Leff, M.C. and Kauffeld, F.J. (eds) (1989) *Texts in Context: Critical Dialogues on Significant Episodes in American Political Rhetoric*. Davis, CA: Hermagoras.

Logue, C.M. and Miller, E.F. (1995) 'Rhetorical status: a study of its origins, functions, and consequences', *Quarterly Journal of Speech*, 81 (1): 20–47.

Longinus (1965) *On the Sublime*, in T.S. Dorsch (ed., trans.), *Classical Literary Criticism*. Harmondsworth: Penguin. pp. 99–158.

Malcolm X (1964) 'The ballot or the bullet', speech delivered at Cory Methodist Church, Cleveland, OH.

Medhurst, M.J. (1987) 'Eisenhower's "atoms for peace" speech: a case study in the strategic use of language', *Communication Monographs*, 54 (2): 204–20.

McGee, M. (1975) 'In search of "the people": a rhetorical alternative', *Quarterly Journal of Speech*, 61 (3): 235–49.

McKerrow, R.E. (1989) 'Critical rhetoric: theory and praxis', *Communication Monographs*, 56 (2): 91–111.

Nakayama, T.K. and Krizek, R.L. (1995) 'Whiteness: a strategic rhetoric', *Quarterly Journal of Speech*, 81 (3): 291–309.

Nothstine, W.L., Blair, C. and Copeland, G. (1994) *Critical Questions: Invention, Creativity, and the Criticism of Discourse and Media*. New York: St Martin's.

Olson, K.M. and Goodnight, G.T. (1994) 'Entanglements of consumption, cruelty, privacy, and fashion: the social controversy over fur', *Quarterly Journal of Speech*, 80 (3): 249–76.

Osborn, M. (1967) 'Archetypal metaphor in rhetoric: the light–dark family', *Quarterly Journal of Speech*, 53 (2): 115–26.

Reese, S.D. and Buckalew, B. (1995) 'The militarism of local television: the routine framing of the Persian Gulf War', *Critical Studies in Mass Communication*, 12 (1): 40–59.

Saussure, F. (1986) *Course in General Linguistics* (eds C. Bally and A. Sechehaye, trans. R. Harris). La Salle, IL: Open Court.

Slagell, A.R. (1991) 'Anatomy of a masterpiece: a close textual analysis of Abraham Lincoln's second inaugural address', *Communication Studies*, 42 (2): 155–71.

Spence, G. (1993) Transcript of closing arguments. *United States* v. *Weaver*. Case no. CR 92-080-N-EJL, US District Court in Boise, ID.

Vickers, B. (1988) *In Defence of Rhetoric*. Oxford: Clarendon.

Wander, P. (1981) 'Cultural criticism', in D.D. Nimmo and K.R. Sanders (eds), *Handbook of Political Communication*. Beverly Hills, CA: Sage. pp. 427–528.

Wander, P. (1984) 'The third persona: an ideological turn in rhetorical theory', *Central States Speech Journal*, 35 (4): 197–216.

Warnick, B. (1992) 'Leff in context: what is the critic's role?', *Quarterly Journal of Speech*, 78 (2): 232–7.

Whately, R. (1963) *Elements of Rhetoric* (ed. D. Ehninger). Carbondale, IL: Southern Illinois University Press.

7

Narrative

Elinor Ochs

Narrative Realms

Imagine a world without narrative. Going through life not telling others what happened to you or someone else, and not recounting what you read in a book or saw in a film. Not being able to hear or see or read dramas crafted by others. No access to conversations, printed texts, pictures, or films that are about events framed as actual or fictional. Imagine not even composing interior narratives, to and for yourself. No. Such a universe is unimaginable, for it would mean a world without history, myths or drama; and lives without reminiscence, revelation, and interpretive revision.

When we think about narrative, literary forms come to mind as narrative texts *par excellence*. At least since Aristotle's *Poetics* (1962), narrative genres such as tragedy and comedy have been the preoccupation of philosophers and critics. As a fundamental genre that organizes the ways in which we think and interact with one another, however, narrative encompasses an enormous range of discourse forms, including popular as well as artistic genres. The most basic and most universal form of narrative may be the product not of poetic muse, but of ordinary conversation.

Scholars of narrative have argued that narratives are authored not only by those who introduce them but also by the many readers and interlocutors who influence the direction of the narrative (Bakhtin, 1981; 1986; Bauman, 1986; Goodwin, 1981). This co-authorship is most evident in conversational narratives, where interlocutors ask questions, comment and otherwise overtly contribute to an evolving tale (Ehlich, 1980; C. Goodwin, 1984; M. Goodwin, 1990; Jefferson, 1978; Mandelbaum, 1987; Quasthoff, 1980; Ochs et al., 1992; Sacks, 1978). The interactional production of narrative maintains and transforms persons and relationships (Miller et al., 1992). How we think about ourselves and others is influenced by both the message content of jointly told narratives and the experience of working together to construct a coherent narrative.

Our species is fortunate to have access to several communicative modalities available to create a narrative. Narratives can be produced through spoken, written, kinesthetic, pictorial, and musical modes of representation. Spoken and written narratives are commonplace. Dramatic enactments of events through body movements and facial expressions may be even more basic a narrative vehicle, given the historicity, ubiquity, and enticement of performance (Aristotle, 1962). Indeed Kenneth Burke (1973: 103) harkens back to ritual drama 'as the Ur-form, the "hub", with all other aspects of *human* action treated as spokes radiating from this hub'. And every picture tells a story in the form of a more or less compressed narrative. Indeed the history of art is in part a history of narrative representation (Adorno, 1984; Berger, 1972; Dissanayake, 1988; Marsack, 1991). In some cases, a narrative is communicated through a series of depictions, as in certain forms of cave art or certain medieval illustrated manuscripts. In other cases, the sequence of events is compressed into a single representation, requiring the viewer to untangle the storyline from different elements in the scene. From one point of view, minimalist art places heavy demands on viewers by inviting them to create a narrative from highly abstract and elusive forms and juxtapositions. From another point of view, minimalist liberates the viewer from having to discern a single, authoritative narrative scripted by artist or patron. Rather, the viewer is free to construe a range of possible narratives suggested or inspired by the visual forms (Capps et al., 1993).

The range of narrative interpretation that characterizes paradigms of visual art also characterizes other narrative modes, particularly music. Instruments, tonality, and melodic leitmotifs may more or less explicitly, more or less iconically, build characters and move them through emotional and actional realms. The ethnomusicologist Steven Feld (1982) describes how the Kaluli people of Papua New Guinea relate the melodic contours of bird songs to particular forms of human sentiment, activity, and states of being. Certain pitches, for example, convey sadness and weeping, which in turn may evoke loss and abandonment. Kaluli reproduce these melodic contours in sung narrative performances to arouse strong feelings from those listening (Schieffelin, 1976).

While a narrative may be crafted through a single modality, more often narrators intertwine a multiplicity of modalities. Narrators may quote or make reference to a narrative excerpt from a book or newspaper, blending oral and written instrumentalities. Or demonstrations involving artifacts may be incorporated, as when children in American schools engage in a narrative activity called 'sharing time' in which they tell a story through both words and displays of objects brought from home (Michaels, 1981). Similarly, narrating may involve tellers talking about, looking at, and pointing to visual representations. This is seen in courtroom narration, where witnesses and lawyers piece together a plausible narrative, using objects and images they construct as evidence (Goodwin, 1994). Scientific narratives also rely on graphs, diagrams and other figures. While sometimes scientists merely refer to a figure, in the throes of working through a scientific problem they may construct a narrative account from the perspective of being a symbolic object *within* a figure (Ochs et al., 1994). At these moments, scientists use the figure as a frame of reference as they gesturally and vocally narrate changes in physical states along symbolic points within the figure. Picture books also interweave images with linguistic text, inviting readers to pursue a narrative line across these two modalities. And theatrical drama can be enacted through a variety of modalities including pantomime, voice, written text, visual image, and musical instrumentation.

In some cases, the interpenetration of communicative modalities is evoked rather than actualized. Rather than using different modes of communication, the narrator implies these modes through stylistic variation. For example, when authors shift from descriptive prose to direct quotation, they imply a shift to speech. In so doing, they transform the reader into an (over)hearer as well. These interpenetrations produce intertexts or hybrid modes of discourse (Bakhtin, 1981; 1986). The intermingling of implied modalities is especially prevalent in the novel, where authors craft not only spoken dialogue but also inner silent forms of communication in a literary format. The play of communicative channels weaves a complex relationship between author, character, and reader/(over)hearer. If well wrought, such complexity yields meanings that render the author an artist and the product a work of art.

As this discussion implies, narrative plays host to a range of genres. In the course of telling a narrative, speakers may engage in a wide range of language activities. For example, they may embed an argument within a narrative, as in the following exchange[1] among family members narrating a story:

Mom: = We didn't <u>laugh</u> believe me.
Rhoda: [Yes you did – you st[arted to <u>laugh.</u>
Corky: [*((shaking head no))* [hh
            ((Mom looks to Corky for confirmation of memory))
Mom: I don't think we did – I [had to go-
Rhoda: [YES YOU DI:D!
                        (from Family Dinner Corpus: Ochs, 1986–90[2])

In this example, Rhoda accuses her family of laughing at her during an embarrassing incident. When an interlocutor is the butt of a narrative, he or she often disputes the account of events. Gossip, a form of narrative in which a breach in cultural norm is recounted, is characteristically contentious (Brenneis, 1984; Haviland, 1977; Goodwin, 1990). The highly confrontative nature of gossip is captured in Goodwin's (1990) account of this activity among African American girls. These pre-adolescents engage in complex, conflict-laden narratives called 'He-said-she-said', wherein one girl tells another/others about what a third girl said about her/them (such as 'They say y'all say I wrote everything over there'). This reported accusation is refuted (*'UH* UH. = *THAT* WAS VINCENT SAID.'), in turn triggering lengthy public discussion.

Not only can narrative house other language activities, it can itself be incorporated into a larger genre or activity. For example, not only can a narrative house a dispute, it can also be housed within an ongoing dispute, as when someone launches a story to illustrate a point he or she is advocating. Narratives can also appear as a part of a prayer. In the following example, a child begins to say grace at the dinner meal, but in the midst of a formulaic thanksgiving, she launches a narrative about events in her day:

```
Laurie:   =kay – Jesus? – plea:?se – um – help us to love
          and .hh um – Thank you for letting it be a n:ice day
          and for taking a (fine/fun) nap?
          .hh – a:nd – for (letting) Mommy go bye
          and I'm glad that I cwied today?
          cuz I like cwying [.hh and
Annie?:                      [((snicker))
Laurie:   I'[m glad (that anything/everything) happened today=
Roger?:   [((snicker))
Laurie:   =in Jesus name
          ((claps hands)) A:-MEN!
                              (from Family Dinner Corpus: Ochs, 1986–90)
```

In this example, Laurie's story about crying at school when 'Mommy go bye' is framed within the saying of grace. However, grace does not function simply as a set of bookends for Laurie's narrative, as visualized below:

Grace | Narrative | Grace

Rather, features of the genre of grace seep into the telling of the story:

G r N a ARRA c TIVE e

In particular, a defining feature of grace is an expressed sentiment of thankfulness. This sentiment organizes Laurie's narrative when she recounts 'I'm glad that I cwied today' and 'I like cwying'. Events like crying, which are normally associated with sadness, are imbued with a sensibility appropriate to the occasion of giving thanks for a meal. In this fashion, narratives become organized by the contexts in which they are constructed.

When we think about written narratives, many of us envision them as different from Laurie's narrative. Delimited by titles and typographical spacing, perhaps even a book cover, written texts appear to have defined boundaries. However, even written texts can be part of an ongoing communicative interaction – for example, a dispute or a supplication or a political agenda – that in subtle and profound ways shapes the narrative text. Kenneth Burke (1973: 1) notes: 'Critical and imaginative works are answers to questions posed by the situation in which they arose. They are not merely answers, they are *strategic* answers, *stylized* answers.' Scholars ranging from Burke to Russian formalists (Bakhtin, 1981; Todorov, 1984) to proponents of cultural studies (Williams, 1982; 1983) implore interpreters of narrative to embed such texts in the social and historical dialogues in which they participate.

Given the variety of modes and genres that realize narrative activity, it is an enormous task to consider how narrative is rooted in cultural systems of knowledge, beliefs, values, ideologies, action, emotion, and other dimensions of social order. Typically cultural analyses of narrative focus on a particular context of narrative activity, for example spoken or sung narrative performances (Bauman, 1986; Becker, 1979; Briggs, 1992; Feld, 1982; Hymes, 1971; Jacobs, 1959; Scollon and Scollon, 1981a; E.L. Schieffelin, 1976; Tedlock, 1972; Watson-Gegeo and Boggs, 1977; Witherspoon, 1977), mythic tales (Lévi-Strauss, 1955; B. Schieffelin, 1984), conversational narratives of personal experience (Miller et al., 1990; 1992; Morgan, 1991; Ochs and Taylor, 1992b), reading stories (Heath, 1983), writing stories (Scollon and Scollon, 1981b), gossip (Besnier, 1993; Brenneis, 1984; M. Goodwin, 1990; Haviland, 1977), or classroom narrative events (Cazden and Hymes, 1978; Michaels, 1981; Ochs et al., 1994; B. Schieffelin, forthcoming). Narrative in each of these contexts is rendered meaningful *vis-à-vis* some property of local ethos – for example, an orientation towards autonomy or intervention, explicit moralizing, sacredness of text, facticity of text, imagined selves, social asymmetries, and so on. To date no study examines narrative activity as it is variously construed across modes, settings, and participants within a single speech community. As such, we need to be cautious in positing broad generalizations that identify a culture with one narrative style.

Narrative and Time

The term 'narrative' is used either in a narrow sense to specify the genre of story or in a broad sense to cover a vast range of genres, including not only stories but also reports, sports and news broadcasts, plans, and agendas among others. What holds these diverse modes of narrative together? Regardless of the contexts in which they emerge, the modalities through which they are expressed, and the genres laminated within them, all narratives *depict a temporal transition from one state of affairs to another*. This attribute does not uniquely define narrative. We may think of this temporal attribute as a necessary but not sufficient characterization of narrative. As will be discussed later, narratives depict far more than an ordering of events.

Literary philosopher Paul Ricoeur (1988) refers to the temporal property of narrative as the 'chronological dimension'. This transition is captured linguistically by a sequence of two or more clauses which are temporally ordered (Labov, 1972). This characterization encompasses narratives that are captivating as well as those that are dull. It includes accounts of enigmatic events as well as those that are predictable. A narrative can be a simple chronicle of events or an account that contextualizes events, by attempting to explain them and/or persuade others of their relevance.

Narratives may concern past, present, future, hypothetical, habitual, or other culturally relevant mode of reckoning time. Narratives that are primarily concerned with *past events* include broad genres such as stories, histories, and reports concerning either professional or personal matters. Livia Polanyi (1989: 17), for example, notes that 'stories and past time reports are specific, affirmative, past time narratives which tell about a series of events which took place at specific unique moments in a unique past time world.' William Labov and Joshua Waletzky (1968: 287) refer to personal stories as 'narratives of personal experience' and characterize them linguistically as 'one method of recapitulating past experience by matching a verbal sequence of clauses to the sequence of events which (it is inferred) actually occurred'. Both of the narratives excerpted above, about Rhoda's embarrassment and Laurie's crying, are narratives of personal experience.

Narratives can also be primarily concerned with sequences of events taking place in *present* time, for example, sports broadcasts in which commentators narrate actions, strategies, and reactions of players and their audiences. Alternatively, narratives may focus on the *future*, as with event sequences such as agendas, prescriptions, advice, suggestions, instructions, forecasts, warnings, threats, and planning generally. In the following excerpt, a young girl narrates a series of suggestions, forming a plan for her birthday party:

Sally: Mommy! I know what I'munna do for my birthday? –
          Could we paint our face for our birthday?
Mom: If you want,

          .
          .

Sally: *((counting on her fingers as she speaks))*
          Mommy, paint our face, number one –
          Okay, now. go to the park, number two,
          Daddy has to play monster, number three,
          U:m: – number !FOU:?:r! go to miniature golf
          And number five go to UCL pool –
          And number SIX? – kiss Mommy,
          Ha-ha I'm just kidding,
                              (from Family Dinner Corpus: Ochs, 1986–90)

Narratives about *hypothetical* worlds can concern hypothetical past, present, future, or generic time and include such genres as plans, science fiction, and narratives of personal experience. For example, the following segment of hypothetical narrative is constructed by a principal investigator (PI) and a student who are planning how to resolve a scientific problem:

PI: If you take your li:ne there (0.2) and you-
          temperature [quench (0.5) down to:: where I have
                [((*Student looks at board*))
          that word [long range order,
                    [((*Student rises, goes to board*))

Student: Yeah,
PI: will you see any dynamics at all down there?,

(Ochs et al., forthcoming)

In this excerpt, the principal investigator uses a figure on the blackboard to take the student and himself on an imaginary narrative journey (Ochs et al., 1994; forthcoming). The principal investigator posits a sequence of hypothetical moves, and elicits from the student a consequential generic event.

While scientific narratives (such as experimental reports) reckon time primarily in terms of scientific units of measurement, autobiography and other genres of personal narrative reckon time in terms of a person's apprehension of time. As noted by Ricoeur (1988), narrative time is human time, not clock time. Ricoeur's approach to narrative draws on the philosophy of Martin Heidegger (1962), who distinguishes physical time from existential time. In *Being and Time*, Heidegger suggests that humans experience time as a fusion of past, present, and future. We experience ourselves in the present time world, but with a memory of the past, and an anxiety for the future. A property of our species is that we have human cares; and these cares lead us to contextualize the present in terms of the past and future, the past in terms of the present and future, and the future in terms of the past and present.

It is our cares about the present and especially about the future that organize our narrative recollections of past events. Narrative serves the important function of bringing the past into the present time consciousness. That is, narrative provides a sense of continuity of self and society. But perhaps even more importantly, narrative accounts of past events help us to manage our uncertain future. In Heidegger's framework, when we construct narratives about the past, we apprehend them in terms of what they imply for the present and future.

For these reasons, narratives that touch on past events are always about the present and future as well (Ochs, 1994). In some cases, narratives provide new models, open up novel possibilities, for the shape of our lives to come. In other cases, narratives about the past touch off a concern about the present or future. For example, in 'He-said-she-said' narratives told by African American girls, gossip about the past 'instigates' one of the interlocutors (the accused) to defend herself in the present and posit how she will redress the offense in the future (Goodwin, 1990: 271):

Barbara: Well you *t*ell her to come say it in
          front of my fa:ce. (0.6) and *I*'ll *p*ut
          her somewhere.

In conversational narrative, a concern for the present and future may crop up at any point in the telling. Co-narrators wander over the temporal map, focusing on the past then relating it to the present and future and then returning to another piece of the past. For example, after Laurie recounts (during grace) how she cried when her mother left her at school, the family returns to Laurie's predicament to help her face tomorrow (Ochs, 1994: 129):

Mother: but honey? – I only work –
              this – it was only this week that I worked there all
              week? because it was the first week? of school
              [but –
Annie: [she <u>cried</u> at three o'clock too
              (0.2)
Mother: but after this? – it – I only work one day a week? there
              and that's Tuesday

The family narratively ricochets from relevant bits of the past:

Mother: Laurie? – you didn't take yer ((*shaking head no*)) –
              blanket to school either did you.
Laurie: No I (for)<u>got</u> it ((*petulant*)).

to strategies for conquering the future:

Mother: We'll hafta get it out of the closet –
              and put it over there with the <u>lunch</u> stuff.
              (2.0)
Jimmy: yes – so you could – bring it (with/to) school.

What is the import of experienced time (human time) for understanding narrative? One implication is that different narrative genres, such as stories and plans, organize the same text. The compression of different temporal domains within a single stretch of discourse in turn suggests that genre is best understood as a *perspective* on a text rather than as a *kind* of text (Ochs, 1994). Rather than mapping particular genres on to different narrative sequences, we examine the same stretch of talk or writing or music or visual representation for different genre properties. Rather than asking, 'What genre is this text?', we ask, 'How (if at all) is this text organized as a story? a plan? a broadcast? a forecast?' And so on. The task of the narrators and scholars is to pursue the generic threads that run through a text and fathom their interconnections.

For the remainder of this chapter, the discussion will focus on characteristics of one narrative genre, namely stories. We will pursue the linguistic, psychological, and sociological structuring of such narratives.

Narrative Point of View and Plot Structure

While narratives can in principle recount utterly predictable events, usually stories concern noteworthy events. Something happened that the storyteller finds surprising, disturbing, interesting, or otherwise tellable (Labov and Waletzky, 1968; Chafe, 1980). Stories normally have a point to make, which organizes the construction of the narrative itself. Often the point is a moral evaluation of an occurrence, an action, or a psychological stance related to a set of events.

Stories are not so much depictions of facts as they are construals of happenings. Kenneth Burke (1962) looks at stories as *selections* rather than as *reflections* of reality. And Erving Goffman notes:

> A tale or anecdote, that is, a replaying, is not merely any reporting of a past event. In the fullest sense, it is such a statement couched from the personal perspective of an actual or potential participant who is located so that some temporal, dramatic development of the reported event proceeds from that starting point. A replaying will therefore incidentally be something that listeners can empathetically insert themselves into, vicariously reexperiencing what took place. A replaying, in brief, recounts a personal experience, not merely reports on an event. (1974: 504)

Ricoeur (1981: 278) calls point of view the *configurational* dimension of narrative. Aristotle introduced the term *mythos* or 'plot' to characterize how events and emotions are interwoven to form a coherent narrative. It is plot that distinguishes a list of events from a history of events or a story of events (Frye, 1957; Ricoeur, 1981; White, 1981). In creating a plot, historians and storytellers give structure to events within a sense-making scheme. The plot knits together circumstantial elements such as scenes, agents, agency (instruments), acts, and purposes into a coherent scheme that revolves around an exceptional, usually troubling, event (Burke, 1962).

The plot can be seen as a theory of events in the sense that it provides an explanation of events from a particular point of view (Feldman, 1989; Ochs et al., 1992). In this sense, stories are akin to scientific narratives. While scientific narratives de-emphasize agents and motives (Latour, 1987), they share with story narratives the property of recounting something out of the usual – an enigma, a discrepancy, an oddity, a challenge, an upset that disturbs the equilibrium. Further, both scientific and personal narratives try to shed light on that problem by placing the problem within a sequence of cause–effect events and circumstances.

The capacity to create and decipher plots is a quintessential faculty of the human species. Jerome Bruner (1990) has proposed that narrative is a basic instrument of folk psychology. Stories are cultural tools *par excellence* for understanding unusual and unexpected conduct. In storytelling, narrators intertwine two domains of behavior, what Bruner calls 'dual landscapes': (1) situational circumstances and protagonists' actions, and (2) protagonists' mental states. Often, for example, narrators explain an unusual and unexpected action in terms of a protagonist's thoughts and feelings. In so doing, narrative serves to 'render the exceptional comprehensible' (1990: 52). Because stories recount events that depart from the ordinary, they also serve to articulate and sustain common understandings of what the culture deems ordinary. For this reason among others, narrative is a powerful means of socializing children and other novices into local notions of situational appropriateness. Co-narrators often comment on how they would behave in the reported events and how others should have conducted themselves. As participants to these narrative interactions, children come to understand what is expected, normal, and appropriate.

Building a Narrative

How are story narratives constructed? How are they initiated and developed, and how do they come to completion?

When we see a printed text, a title or other visible feature may initially identify the text as a possible story. While stories told in conversation do not have titles, they do often have *story prefaces* (Sacks, 1992). Instead of abruptly beginning a story, a teller transitions into it with the co-operation of other interlocutors. This activity is accomplished through story prefaces such as 'You want to hear a story?', wherein interlocutors indicate an intention to tell a relevant story and elicit a go-ahead to do so from others. Tellers of stories in conversational interaction often have an additional task: not only do they let others know that a story is coming up (which will occupy the floor for more than one utterance), they also need to link their story at least vaguely to current talk. This goal may be accomplished through repetition of some portion of the prior talk, as in the following example (Jefferson, 1978: 221):

Roger: Speakin about *for*ties. I worked on a k-o:n Morga*nel*li's
          Forty.

Sometimes story prefaces are introduced by someone other than the person who eventually initiates the story. For example, women sometimes preface and forward a story to their husbands to tell (C. Goodwin, 1986; Mandelbaum, 1987). In the excerpt below, Phyllis prefaces a story in a way that retains her husband Mike as its principal teller (C. Goodwin, 1986: 298):

Phyl: *M*Iike siz there wz a big *f*ight down there las' night,
Curt: Oh rilly?
         (0.5)
Phyl: Wih *K*eegan en, what.
         Paul [de Wa::*ld*?]
Mike: *P*aul de Wa:l d. Guy out of . . .

Once a story is launched, it assumes a particular structure. The elements that comprise a story have been analysed by philosophers, folklorists, literary critics, and discourse analysts at least since Aristotle. Aristotle (1962) described in some detail the architecture of tragedy and comedy. He characterized tragedy in terms of principles of plot, character (moral habits), language, thought, spectacle (manner), and melody. For Aristotle, the soul of tragedy is the plot, and character is of secondary importance. A plot must have a beginning, a middle, and an end, but this progression is not as obvious as it might first appear:

> A beginning is that which does not come necessarily after something else, but after which it is natural for another thing to exist or come to be. An end, on the contrary, is that which naturally comes after something else, either as its necessary sequel or as its usual (and hence probable) sequel, but itself has nothing after it. A middle is that which both comes after something else and has another thing following it. A well-constructed plot, therefore, will neither begin at some chance point nor end at some chance point, but will observe the principles here stated. (1962: 52)

Literary studies such as Vladamir Propp's *The Morphology of the Folktale* (1986), Northop Frye's *The Anatomy of Criticism* (1957), Paul Ricoeur's *Time and Narrative* (1988), and Roland Barthes's *The Semiotic Challenge* (1988) continue to draw on these Aristotelian principles in analysing the structure of story narratives.

William Labov's (1972) linguistic analysis of narratives of personal experience also harks back to Aristotle's notion of the narrative essentials of a beginning, middle and end. Rather than analysing written narratives, Labov gathered oral narratives of purported lived experiences in the course of interviewing a population of speakers in New York City. The narratives were produced in response to the interview question, 'Were you ever in a situation where you were in serious danger of being killed?' Examining these narratives, Labov comments that some 'are complete in the sense that they have a beginning, a middle, and an end', but other more fully formed narratives display the following structural features of personal experience narratives (1972: 363): (1) abstract (for example, 'My brother put a knife in my head'), (2) orientation ('This was just a few days after my father died'), (3) complicating action ('I twisted his arm up behind him . . .'), (4) evaluation ('Ain't that a bitch?'), (5) result or resolution ('After all a that I gave the dude the cigareete, after all that'), and (6) coda ('And that was that').

These elements are echoed in 'story grammars', which, somewhat parallel to Propp's morphology of Russian folktales, articulate a syntax of story narratives (Mandler and Johnson, 1977; Mandler, 1979; Stein and Glenn, 1979; Stein and Policastro, 1984). In these analyses, stories have grammatical constituents, which in turn are composed of internal constituents. The constituents and the rules that order them are seen as reflecting our tacit knowledge of story structure. In Stein and Glenn (1979), major story constituents include: (1) a setting, either (2) an initiating event or (3) an internal response, (4) an overt attempt, (5) a consequence. Stein and Policastro (1984) add a sixth story component: a reaction to (3), (4), or (5). Jean Mandler and Nancy Johnson (1977) include as well an 'ending' component, and make a further distinction between stories that are goal-oriented and those that are not. Those that are goal-oriented parallel the

Stein and Glenn model. Stories that are not goal-oriented consist of (1) a setting, (2) a beginning, (3) a simple reaction – either an emotional response or an unplanned action – and (4) an ending. All constituents comprising a story episode, and with the exception of the setting, are seen as invariantly ordered.

The concept of *setting* is common to literary, linguistic, and psychological models of narrative. Story grammars and linguistic conceptualizations of setting define setting in terms of the physical, social, and temporal context of protagonists' conduct. Literary analyses of stories and cultural psychological approaches (Bruner, 1990; 1991; Feldman, 1989) emphasize that setting goes beyond time and space and social circumstance to encompass the psychological climate that anticipates a beginning narrative event. The historical rise of the novel and other narrative genres is linked to greater attention to what Bruner (1990) calls the 'mental landscape', including the emotional states, morality, perspectives, and motives of protagonists as they enter a crucial narrative event. It is the psychological climate that colors protagonists as tragic hero/heroines or comedic fools. Aristotle notes, for example, that a tragedy rests on establishing that the protagonist is of high moral fiber and that the protagonist is an unwitting victim of circumstances. This psychological context is established in settings.

While pieces of the setting appear at the start of stories, narrators may also delay revealing crucial aspects of the setting until much later in the story. There are many reasons for this. One is that the narrator may wish to slowly disclose vital elements of the context to build suspense. If the narrator were to reveal all the relevant background initially, the story loses its dramatic tension. Another reason is that narrators themselves are not always aware of important details of the story setting at the start of the storytelling. It is only when the story is under way that storytellers make a connection between a prior circumstance and the troublesome event of concern in the narrative. In conversational storytelling, a narrator may be reminded of such circumstances by co-narrators participating in the interaction (Ochs et al., 1989). In therapeutic conversations, the psychotherapist is often instrumental in evoking unmentioned states of mind, actions, or conditions that may render a narrative event more meaningful (Capps and Ochs, 1995a; 1995b).

Yet another reason for late revelations of settings is that narrators at first try to present themselves in the best light as protagonists (Ochs et al., 1989). They build settings in such a way that their emotions and actions seem reasonable and worthy of an interlocutor's empathy. However, sometimes the best laid plans of mice and men run amok, when other co-narrators bring out undisclosed pieces of the setting that unravel this positive self-portrayal. Such dissembling occurs in the narrative excerpt to follow. The story opens with nine-year-old Lucy complaining about how her school principal inadequately punished a girl who pulled up her friend's dress in front of the boys:

Lucy: I don't think Mrs. um Andrew's being fair because um

         .

         .

         When we were back at school um –
         this girl? – she pulled um – Vicky's <u>dress</u> *((puts hand to knee))*
         up t'here *((gestures with hand high on chest))* in front of the boys
Mom: mhm?
Lucy: she only – all she did was get a <u>day</u> in de<u>ten</u>tion

Her family sympathizes with Lucy's perspective. Then, unexpectedly, her six-year-old brother Chuck introduces a piece of the setting unbeknownst to her parents: Lucy herself had been punished by the principal and for the same length of time (one day) as the girl who embarrassed her friend:

Chuck: Lucy? – you only went to it <u>once</u> – right?=
Father: =*((clears throat))*
         (1.0) *((Lucy arches her back, eyes open wide, looks shocked, starts shaking her head 'no' once, father looking at her))*
Mother: (<u>You</u>' [ve been in it/<u>You</u> can tell us can't you?)
Father: [I'm lis?tening)
Lucy: *((low to Chuck)* (thanks)
         (0.4)
Lucy: *((louder))* [<u>yeah</u> – that – (was   )
Mother: [(She was in it) once?
         (0.6)
Lucy: Once.

                                                        (Ochs et al., 1992: 47)

Lucy's plight is a common one in conversational storytelling. When we tell stories among intimates such as family members and friends, we are vulnerable to their knowledge of our lives. They can at any moment introduce background information that undermines the point we as narrators are trying to convey.

All characterization of stories specify *a key event that disrupts the equilibrium of ordinary, expected circumstances.* For example, the notions of 'complication' (Aristotle, 1962), 'trouble' (Burke, 1962), 'deviation from the ordinary' (Bruner, 1990), 'complicating action' (Labov, 1972), 'initiating event' (Stein and Glenn, 1979), and 'inciting event' (Sharff, 1982) all concern an unpredictable or unusual or problematic event on which a narrative episode focuses. In the story that Laurie tells while saying grace, for instance, she focuses on the problematic event of 'Mommy go bye.' In Lucy's story, the focus initially is on the problematic conduct of a schoolmate: 'this girl? – she pulled um – Vicky's <u>dress</u> up t'here in front of the boys.'

In many stories, the key troublesome event is seen as provoking *psychological responses* and *actions* that attempt to reinstate a sense of equilibrium. In Mandler and Johnson's (1977) framework, these are goal-directed stories. For example, in Laurie's story, 'Mommy go bye' is seen as inciting Laurie to cry. In Lucy's story, the schoolmate's transgression is seen as inciting the principal to punish the transgressor with one day's detention.

These psychological and actional responses in turn have *outcomes*, which in turn may engender *further psychological responses and actions*. For example, in Lucy's story, Lucy becomes upset when she discovers that the principal gave the schoolmate only one day's detention. She tells her family that the principal is not fair; and when her mother asks her, 'You think she should have gotten suspended?', Lucy responds, 'At LEAST!'

In a study of the narrative construction of agoraphobia, Lisa Capps and Elinor Ochs (1995a; 1995b) found that the narratives of panic experience told by an agoraphobic woman consistently delineate a series of spiraling problematic events, wherein one problem leads to another. For example, a traffic jam is seen as inciting heightened awareness. This realization in turn incites panic, which then incites the protagonist to initiate a series of attempts to mitigate panic that fail, inciting further panic until eventually the protagonist communicates her distress and escapes the situation. In stacking problem upon problem, the narrator constructs a world in which she is helpless and driven by panic.

When storytellers recount that a problematic event incited psychological responses or actions, the story appears to be capped in past time. As discussed earlier, however, stories have a way of edging into the future, and storytellers often frame an inciting event, a psychological response or an attempt to handle that event as *still* unresolved, *still* problematic at the time of the telling. For example, in Laurie's story, while Laurie herself treats the problematic event of 'Mommy go bye' as finished business ('I'm glad (that anything/everything) happened today in Jesus name A:-MEN!'), her mother does not. Laurie's mother treats both 'Mommy go bye' and Laurie's response as *current* problems, which provoke her to propose a set of future actions to help. In the case of panic stories, the sufferer of agoraphobia consistently frames panic as not only a past problem but also an ongoing problem with debilitating consequences. Indeed a hallmark of agoraphobia is the tendency to ruminate about the consequences of past panic episodes for future life experiences. The storied past becomes a rationale for the here-and-now and beyond (Capps and Ochs, 1995a; 1995b).

Many narratives appear to be motivated by narrators' current dissatisfaction with how they or some other protagonist handled a situation, as in Lucy's complaint about the response of her school principal to a school problem. Indeed one motivation for narrators to initiate stories is to work through with other interlocutors how they currently feel or should feel about some element of a past situation. The writer Vaclav Havel notes in his *Letters to Olga* (1989) that this motivation is part of an all-encompassing quest to relate our personal lives to a broader horizon of relationships, places, objects, ideologies, values, and other human concerns. Our experiences are full of enigmas, and we tell stories to probe with others these mysteries and frustrations. While the character of co-narration varies, the activity offers an opportunity and a potential for communal reflection not only on the meaning of particular experiences but also on the meaning of life on historical, cultural and cosmological planes.

In many communities, the activity of problem-solving through collaborative narration is emblematic of friendship, collegiality, or family membership. Unfortunately, members of these communities are not always able to enjoin familiars to narratively work through problems. Even in close physical proximity of family and friends, persons may feel awkward or incapable of presenting an unresolved narrative. In the absence of informal problem-solving encounters of this sort, would-be narrators may bring their stories to community practitioners. In a number of societies, these practitioners are said to engage in 'disentangling' (Watson-Gegeo and White, 1990), and in others, 'psychotherapy'.

Narrative Identities

Narrative is not only a genre of discourse, it is also a social activity involving different participant roles. Both Bakhtin (1981) and Goffman (1974) distinguish the narrative role of author (or, in Goffman's words, principal) from that of narrator (or, in Goffman's words, animator). As noted earlier, Bakhtin also inspired the perspective that narrative audience plays a key role in the construction of narrative (see Duranti, 1986; C. Goodwin, 1986). The audience is a co-author of narrative form and meaning.

Jennifer Mandelbaum (1987) suggests that audience involvement varies in storytelling. She distinguishes between teller-driven and recipient-driven stories. Teller-driven stories resemble Erving Goffman's description of a story: 'Sometimes [the participant] will sustain his story across several consecutive turns, the interposing talk of others largely taking the form of encouragement, demonstrations of attentiveness and other "back channel" effects' (1974: 509). In recipient-driven storytelling, recipients take a more active role: 'teller and recipient together work out what a storytelling is "about" and how it is to be understood' (Mandelbaum, 1987: 238). Recipient-driven storytelling characterizes situations in which the recipient is also a story protagonist, especially when the recipient is the butt of a story. This observation resonates with Marjorie Goodwin's (1990) study of 'He-said-she-said' interactions, where the primary story recipient is both the object of accusation and highly active in structuring the ensuing story.

Charles Goodwin (1986) points out that story recipients vary in their knowledge and expertise concerning story details. In storytelling interactions among adult Americans, recipients who are more knowledgeable tend to contribute more to the ongoing telling. Their knowledge can be viewed as an entitlement to narrate (see also Shuman, 1986). Knowledge is not always a basis of narrative rights, however. Carolyn Taylor's (1995a;

1995b) study of family storytelling suggests that American children often don't get to tell stories about themselves, but rather are expected to listen as one or both parents assume this right. In parallel fashion, the medical anthropologist Basil Sampson writes an article called 'The sick who do not speak' (1982) in which he portrays how persons who have been sick or injured in Australian aborigine communities do not have the right to tell the story of their illness. The sick are thought to be not themselves in this condition and therefore unable to portray events. Instead those who cared for the sick person retain this right.

The assignment of the roles of teller and audience, or teller and recipient, to whole narratives ultimately breaks down in conversational storytelling in which many participants construct the story. Particularly where storytelling includes close friends and family members, the telling can be widely distributed. Particularly in these cases it makes better sense to assign the roles of teller and audience/recipient turn-by-turn as the storytelling evolves. At one moment a participant may be teller and the next a recipient.

In examining family storytelling, Ochs et al. (1992) found it useful to consider all family members present as co-tellers in that telling routinely shifted from one family member to another in the course of a story. We distinguished an *initial teller*, someone who introduces a story, from *other tellers*, those who contribute to the telling of a story once introduced. Rather than assuming a minor role, family members as other tellers contributed substantially to story construction, including supplying pieces of the setting, positing psychological responses, and attempting to resolve the central story problem. For example, after Lucy as initial teller introduced the story about the schoolmate who gets only one day of detention, her mother continues the story by suggesting Lucy's psychological response to the schoolmate's offensive actions:

Lucy: she only – all she did was get a <u>day</u> in deten<u>tion</u>
Mother: mhm? – <u>you</u> think she should have gotten suspended?
         (0.6)
Lucy: at <u>LEAST</u>

         .
         .
         .

Mother: (cuz Lucy) was <u>really</u> embarrassed
         ((*nodding yes, talking while eating*))
         (1.6)
Mother: (I mean you/Lucy really) would have liked to kill the – the
         girl – huh?
Lucy: [(*(nods yes slowly, as she chews, fork in mouth)*)
Mother: [(cuz) you were upset with her –
         (*(speaking very fast)*) but you were held back
         because you (thought) your school was goin' to do it
         and the school didn't do it and you feel up<u>set</u>

Other family members also chime in as co-tellers. Lucy's younger brother Chuck, for example, suggests that he would give more detention as punishment:

Chuck: I <u>think</u>? she should – <u>be:</u> in there for a h- <u>whole</u> MONTH? or
          so=
?:   =(well maybe)
          (0.6)
Chuck: <u>each</u> day she('d) hafta go there – <u>each</u> day <u>each</u> day <u>each</u> day
          even if? . . .

And as noted earlier, it is Chuck who takes the story in a radically different direction when he discloses that Lucy herself was in detention.

Narrating Lives

When those involved in narrative interactions actively participate as both tellers and recipients, they exercise their entitlement to co-author a narrative. When that narrative concerns a lived experience, co-authors impact the understanding of that experience. It is not only a narrative but a life or a history that is collaboratively constructed. Narrative is a sense-making activity; it is also a primary vehicle for retaining experiences in memory. Entitlement to co-tell a narrative is then a powerful right, encompassing past, present, future, as well as imagined worlds.

As co-tellers draft a story, they script one or more narrative messages. The message may concern what happened, discerning *truth* status of events. Hence telling a story becomes, for better or for worse, a means of establishing a sense of reality in memory. On the other hand, the narrative message may concern what should have happened, discerning the *moral* status of events (Duranti, 1994; Ochs et al., 1992). Indeed, because narratives have at least one point of view, they inherently convey judgments. All of the narratives illustrated in this chapter communicate strong moral messages, but perhaps the most striking is the story of Lucy and the girl who got one day's detention in school. Everyone in the family throws in their moral judgment first about the girl and then about Lucy. Very often, story narratives are vehicles for socializing values of a family or a public institution such as a school or a community at large.

Messages about truth and morality contribute to *causal explanation*s that narratives routinely construct. Because they present a point of view and because they frame an event as provoking responses, story narratives in particular allow co-tellers to build explanations about situations (Ochs et al., 1992). In some cases, co-tellers work together to build a compatible account of events. In these cases, collaborative storytelling helps to create solidarity – for example, a coherent family, institution, or community culture.

However, in other cases, co-tellers challenge one another's explanations of emotions, actions, and circumstances. This often happens when stories are narrated among those who share a history with one another and with the protagonists in a story narrative. In societies such as mainstream America, those privy to background relevant to an unfolding story may introduce elements that radically alter the storyline. For example, in the story about school detention, Lucy's younger brother's revelation of her detention experience undermines Lucy's explanation of why the school principal is not fair. Whereas Lucy had based her sense of injustice on the gravity of the schoolmate's transgression, her brother provides an alternative basis for Lucy's judgment: the principal was not fair to give Lucy and the schoolmate equal amounts of detention. Co-narration that involves challenging and redrafting storylines is akin to academic and legal challenging and revision of explanations for events. In both cases, challenges recast a narrative account as a *version* of experience rather than as fact. As such, collaborative storytelling of personal experiences is a province for socializing intellectual skills demanded in professional worlds (Ochs and Taylor, 1992a; Ochs et al., 1992).

Challenging how another is telling a story, like all human actions, is socially organized. There are expectations concerning which stories are challengeable. For example, Heath (1983) notes that the white working families in her study discouraged challenging written narratives. Similarly, family, institutional and community cultures may structure who assumes the role of challenger. In many communities, for example, adults more than children are given this entitlement (Heath, 1983; Goody, 1978; Ochs and Taylor, 1992b; Ochs and Taylor, 1994). In the white middle-class American families studied by Ochs and Taylor, mothers challenged more than twice as often and fathers more than three times as often as did children in collaborative narrative interactions. Because narrative activity is ubiquitous in these households, the recurrent narrative roles of family members help to constitute their family identities. When a family member routinely assumes the role of challenger, this narrative role becomes part of their family identity. In middle-class American families, challenging narrative accounts is a routine social action that contributes to the identity of parent but especially the identity of father. The predilection for parents, especially fathers, to challenge is well understood by young children, who in turn display a predilection to sabotage or only minimally comply with parental efforts to elicit their stories. Familiar to these households are exchanges of the type: 'What did you do at school today?' 'Nothing.' Children in these families are loath to have their stories problematized and redrafted by authoritative co-narrators.

Conclusion

Narrative activity in these ways is at once a discursive medium for collective probing and problem-solving and a tool for instantiating social and personal identities (Mumby, 1993). Narrative activity allows members of communities to represent and reflect upon events, thoughts and emotions, but this opportunity may be asymmetrically allocated, granting reflective rights to some more than to others. Crucial to the construction of a self, an other, and a society, co-narration crafts biographies and histories; yet the meaning of experience and existence – what is possible, actual, reasonable, desirable – tends to be defined by some more than others. To these ends, narrative has the capacity to limit, indeed imprison, or to expand and transform the human psyche.

Recommended Reading

Bakhtin (1981)
Bruner (1990)
Duranti (1986)
Goodwin (1984)
Goodwin (1990)
Heath (1983)
Labov and Waletzky (1968)
Miller et al. (1990)
Ochs et al. (1992)
Ricoeur (1988)
Sacks (1992)
Stein and Policastro (1984)
White (1981)

Notes

I am indebted to Lisa Capps and Teun van Dijk for their careful reading of earlier drafts and their suggestions. This work is partly supported by the Spencer Foundation for Educational Research.

1 Transcription conventions

.hhh	inbreath
hhh	outbreath
underline	emphatic stress
:	sound stretch
(0.2)	pauses in seconds and fractions of seconds
(.)	micropause (less than 0.2 seconds)
((comment))	non-vocal action or transcriber's comment
.	falling (final) intonation
?	rising (final) intonation
,	continuing (final) intonation
?,	slightly rising (final) intonation
bolded text	phenomenon of focus
[	overlapping talk or actions
( )	doubtful hearings
bu-	cutoff sound or syllable
°you°	low in volume
>well<	speeded up speech
CAPS	loud volume
^	sudden pitch rise
*	vocal fry

204 Discourse as Structure and Process

2 Many of the examples used in this review are drawn from the Family Dinner Corpus gathered during 1986–90 as part of a larger project 'Discourse Processes in American Families', supported by the National Institute of Child Health and Development (grant no. 1 ROH HD 20992-01A1). Members of the research team included principal investigators Elinor Ochs and Tom Weisner, and research assistants Maurine Bernstein, Dina Rudolph, Ruth Smith, and Carolyn Taylor.

References

Adorno, Theodor (1984) *Aesthetic Theory*. London: Routledge and Kegan Paul.

Aristotle (1962) *Poetics* (trans. James Hutton). New York: W.W. Norton.

Bakhtin, Mikhail (1981) *The Dialogic Imagination: Four Essays* (ed. M. Holquist, trans. C. Emerson and M. Holquist). Austin, TX: University of Texas Press.

Bakhtin, Mikhail (1986) *Speech Genres and Other Late Essays* (trans. Vern W. McGee). Austin, TX: University of Texas Press.

Barthes, Roland (1988) *The Semiotic Challenge*. New York: Hill and Wang.

Bauman, Richard (1986) *Story, Performance, and Event*. Cambridge: Cambridge University Press.

Becker, Alton L. (1979) 'Text-building, epistemology, and aesthetics in Javanese shadow theatre', in Alton L. Becker and A.A. Yendoyan (eds), *The Imagination of Reality: Essays in Southeast Asian Coherence Systems*. Norwood, NJ: Ablex. pp. 211–43.

Berger, John (1972) *Ways of Seeing*. London: BBC and Penguin Books.

Besnier, Niko (1993) 'Reported speech and affect on Nukulaelae', in Jane H. Hill and Judith Irvine (eds), *Responsibility and Evidence in Oral Discourse*. Cambridge: Cambridge University Press. pp. 161–81.

Brenneis, Donald (1984) 'Grog and gossip in Bhatgaon: style and substance in Fijian Indian conversation', *American Ethnologist*, 11: 487–506.

Briggs, Charles L. (1992) '"Since I am a woman, I will chastize my relatives": gender, reported speech, and the (re)production of social relations in Warao ritual wailing', *American Ethnologist*, 19: 337–61.

Bruner, Jerome (1990) *Acts of Meaning*. Cambridge, MA: Harvard University Press.

Bruner, Jerome (1991) 'The narrative construction of reality', *Critical Inquiry*, 18: 1–21.

Burke, Kenneth (1962) *A Grammar of Motives and a Rhetoric of Motives*. Cleveland and New York: Meridian Books.

Burke, Kenneth (1973) *The Philosophy of Literary Form*. Berkeley, CA: University of California Press.

Capps, L., Bjork, R. and Siegel, D. (1993) 'The meaning of memories', *UCLA Magazine*, 4 (4): 8–10.

Capps, L. and Ochs, E. (1995a) 'Out of place', *Discourse Processes*, 19 (3): 407–40.

Capps, L. and Ochs, E. (1995b) *Constructing Panic*. Cambridge, MA: Harvard University Press.

Cazden, Courtney and Hymes, Dell (1978) 'Narrative thinking and storytelling rights: a folklorist's clue to a critique of education', *Keystone Folklore*, 22 (1–2): 21–35.

Chafe, Wallace (ed.) (1980) *The Pear Stories: Cognitive, Cultural, and Linguistic Aspects of Narrative Production*. Norwood, NJ: Ablex.

Dissanayake, Ellen (1988) *What Is Art For?* Seattle: University of Washington Press.

Duranti, Alessandro (1986) 'The audience as co-author: an introduction', *Text*, 6 (3): 239–47.

Duranti, Alessandro (1994) *From Grammar to Politics: Linguistic Anthropology in a Western Samoan Village*. Berkeley and Los Angeles: University of California Press.

Ehlich, K. (ed.) (1980) *Erzahlen im Alltag (Storytelling in Everyday Life)*. Frankfurt: Suhrkamp.

Feld, Steven (1982) *Sound and Sentiment: Birds, Weeping, Poetics, and Song in Kaluli Expression*. Philadelphia: University of Pennsylvania Press.

Feldman, Carol (1989) 'Monologue as problem-solving narrative', in K. Nelson (ed.), *Narratives from the Crib*. Cambridge, MA: Harvard University Press.

Frye, Northrop (1957) *The Anatomy of Criticism*. Princeton, NJ: Princeton University Press.

Goffman, Erving (1974) *Frame Analysis: an Essay on the Organization of Experience*. New York: Harper and Row.

Goodwin, Charles (1981) *Conversational organization: Interaction between Speakers and Hearers*. New York: Academic Press.

Goodwin, Charles (1984) 'Notes on story structure and the organization of participation', in M. Atkinson and J. Heritage (eds), *Structures of Social Action*. Cambridge: Cambridge University Press. pp. 225–46.

Goodwin, Charles (1986) 'Audience diversity, participation and interpretation', *Text*, 6 (3): 283–316.

Goodwin, Charles (1994) 'Professional vision', *American Anthropologist*, 96 (3): 606–33.

Goodwin, Marjorie Harness (1990) *He-Said-She-Said: Talk as Social Organization among Black Children*. Bloomington, IN: Indiana University Press.

Goody, E. (1978) *Questions and Politeness: Strategies in Social Interaction*. Cambridge: Cambridge University Press.

Havel, Vaclav (1989) *Letters to Olga*. New York: Henry Holt.

Haviland, John Beard (1977) *Gossip, Reputation, and Knowledge in Zinacantan*. Chicago: University of Chicago Press.

Heath, Shirley Brice (1983) *Ways with Words: Language, Life and Work in Communities and Classrooms*. Cambridge: Cambridge University Press.

Heidegger, Martin (1962) *Being and Time* (trans. John Macquarrie and Edward Robinson). New York: Harper and Row.

Hymes, Dell (1971) 'The "wife" who "goes out" like a man: re-interpretations of a Clackamas Chinook myth', in P. and E.K. Maranda (eds), *Structural Analyses of Oral Traditions*. Philadelphia: University of Pennsylvania Press.

Jacobs, Melville (1959) *The Context and Style of an Oral Literature*. Chicago: University of Chicago Press.

Jefferson, Gail (1978) 'Sequential aspects of storytelling in conversation', in J. Schenkein (ed.), *Studies in the Organization of Conversational Interaction*. New York: Academic Press. pp. 219–48.

Labov, William (1972) *Language in the Inner City: Studies in the Black English Vernacular*. Philadelphia: University of Pennsylvania Press.

Labov, William and Waletzky, Joshua (1968) 'Narrative analysis', in W. Labov et al. (eds), *A Study of the Non-Standard English of Negro and Puerto Rican Speakers in New York City*. New York: Columbia University. pp. 286–338.

Latour, Bruno (1987) *Science in Action*. Cambridge, MA: Harvard University Press.

Lévi-Strauss, Claude (1955) *Tristes Tropiques*. Paris.

Mandelbaum, J. (1987) 'Recipient-driven storytelling in conversation'. Unpublished PhD dissertation, University of Texas at Austin.

Mandler, J.M. (1979) 'Categorical and schematic organization in memory', in C.K. Puff (ed.), *Memory Organization and Structure*. New York: Academic Press.

Mandler, J.H. and Johnson, N.S. (1977) 'Remembrance of things parsed: story structure and recall', *Cognitive Psychology*, 9: 111–51.

Marsack, Alexander (1991) *The Roots of Civilization*. Mount Kisco, NY: Moyer Bell.

Michaels, Sarah (1981) '"Sharing time": children's narrative style and differential access to literacy', *Language in Society*, 10: 423–42.

Miller, P., Mintz, J., Hoogstra, L. and Fung, H. (1992) 'The narrated self: young children's construction of self in relation to others in conversational stories of personal experience', *Merrill-Palmer Quarterly*, 38: 45–67.

Miller, P., Potts, R., Fung, H., Hoogstra, L. and Mintz, J. (1990) 'Narrative practices and the social construction of self in childhood', *American Ethnologist*, 17 (2): 292–311.

Morgan, Marcyliena (1991) 'Indirectness and interpretation in African American women's discourse', *Pragmatics*, 1 (4): 421–51.

Mumby, Dennis (1993) *Narrative and Social Control*. London: Sage.

Ochs, E. (1994) 'Stories that step into the future', in D.F. Biber and E. Finegan (eds), *Perspectives on Register: Situating Language Variation in Sociolinguistics*. Oxford: Oxford University Press. pp. 106–35.

Ochs, E., Jacoby, S. and Gonzales, P. (1994) 'Interpretive journeys: how physicists talk and gesture through graphic space', in M. Biagoli, R. Reid and S. Traweek (eds), *Located Knowledges: Intersections between Cultural, Gender, and Science Studies*, special issue of *Configurations*, 2 (1): 151–72.

Ochs, E., Smith, R. and Taylor, C. (1989) 'Dinner narratives as detective stories', *Cultural Dynamics*, 2: 238–57.

Ochs, E. and Taylor, C. (1992a) 'Science at dinner', in C. Kramsch (ed.), *Text and Context: Cross-Disciplinary Perspectives on Language Study*. Lexington, MA: D.C. Heath.

Ochs, E. and Taylor, C. (1992b) 'Family narrative as political activity', *Discourse and Society*, 3 (3): 301–40.

Ochs, E., Taylor, C., Rudolph, D. and Smith, R. (1992) 'Story-telling as a theory-building activity', *Discourse Processes*, 15 (1): 37–72.

Ochs, E. and Taylor C. (1994) 'Mothers' role in the everyday reconstruction of "father knows best"', in K. Hall (ed.), *Locating Power: Proceedings of the 1992 Berkeley Women and Language Conference*. Berkeley, CA: University of California Berkeley.

Ochs, E., Gonzales, P. and Jacoby, S. (forthcoming) '"When I come down, I'm in the Domain State": talk, gesture, and graphic representation in the interpretive activity of physicists', in E. Ochs, E. Schegloff and S.A. Thompson (eds), *Interaction and Grammar*. Cambridge: Cambridge University Press.

Polyani, L. (1989) *Telling the American Story: a Structural and Cultural Analysis of Conversational Storytelling*. Cambridge, MA: MIT Press.

Propp, Vladimir (1986) *The Morphology of the Folktale*. Austin, TX: University of Texas Press.

Quasthoff, U.M. (ed.) (1980) *Erzahlen in Gesprachen (Storytelling in Conversations)*. Tubingen: Narr.

Ricoeur, Paul (1981) *Hermeneutics and the Human Sciences*. Cambridge: Cambridge University Press.

Ricoeur, Paul (1988) *Time and Narrative* (trans. Kathleen Blarney and David Pellauer). Chicago: University of Chicago Press.

Sacks, Harvey (1978) 'Some technical considerations of a dirty joke', in J. Schenkein (ed.), *Studies in the Organization of Conversational Interaction* (ed. Gail Jefferson from four lectures delivered at the University of California, Irvine, Fall 1971). New York: Academic Press. pp. 249–69.

Sacks, Harvey (1992) *Lectures on Conversation*. Cambridge, MA: Blackwell.

Sampson, Basil (1982) 'The sick who do not speak', in D. Parkin (ed.), *Semantic Anthropology*. New York: Academic Press. pp. 183–95.

Schieffelin, Bambi (1984) 'Ade: a sociolinguistic analysis of a relationship', in John Baugh and Joel Sherzer (eds), *Language in Use: Readings in Sociolinguistics*. Englewood Cliffs, NJ: Prentice-Hall. pp. 229–43.

Schieffelin, Bambi (forthcoming) 'Creating evidence: making sense of written words in Bosavi', in Elinor Ochs, Emanuel Schegloff and Sandra Thompson (eds), *Interaction and Grammar*. Cambridge: Cambridge University Press.

Schieffelin, Edward L. (1976) *The Sorrow of the Lonely and the Burning of the Dancers*. New York: St Martin's Press.

Scollon, R. and Scollon, S. (1981a) *Narrative, Literacy, and Face in Interethnic Communication*. Norwood, NJ: Ablex.

Scollon, R. and Scollon, S. (1981b) 'The literate two-year-old: the fictionalization of self: abstracting themes: a Chipewayan two-year-old', in R.O. Freedle (ed.), *Narrative, Literacy and Face in Interethnic Communication*. Norwood, NJ: Ablex. pp. 57–96.

Sharff, Stefan (1982) *The Elements of Cinema: toward a Theory of Cinesthetic Impact*. New York: Columbia University Press.

Shuman, A. (1986) *Storytelling Rights: the Uses of Oral and Written Texts by Urban Adolescents.* Cambridge: Cambridge University Press.

Stein, N. and Glenn, C.G. (1979) 'An analysis of story comprehension in elementary school children', in R.O. Freedle (ed.), *New Directions in Discourse Processing.* Norwood, NJ: Ablex. pp. 53–120.

Stein, N. and Policastro, M. (1984) 'The concept of a story: a comparison between children's and teacher's viewpoints', in H. Mandl, N. Stein and T. Trabasso (eds), *Learning and Comprehension of Text.* Hillsdale, NJ: Erlbaum.

Taylor, Carolyn (1995a) '"You think it was a fight?" Co-constructing (the struggle for) meaning, face, and family in everyday narrative activity', *Research on Language and Social Interaction,* 28 (3): 283–317.

Taylor, Carolyn (1995b) *Child as Apprentice-Narrator: Socializing Voice, Face, Identity, and Self-Esteem amid the Narrative Politics of Family Dinner.* Unpublished PhD dissertation, University of Southern California.

Tedlock, Dennis (1972) *Finding the Center: Narrative Poetry of the Zuni Indians.* New York: Dial Press.

Todorov, Tzvetan (1984) *Mikhail Bakhtin: the Dialogical Principle* (trans. Wlad Godzich). Minneapolis: University of Minnesota Press.

Watson-Gegeo, Karen and Boggs, Stephen T. (1977) 'From verbal play to talk story: the role of routines in speech events among Hawaiian children', in Susan Ervin-Tripp and Claudia Mitchell-Kernan (eds), *Child Discourse.* New York: Academic Press. pp. 67–90.

Watson-Gegeo, Karen and White, Geoffrey (eds) (1990) *Disentangling: Conflict Discourse in Pacific Societies.* Stanford, CA: Stanford University Press.

White, Hayden (1981) 'The value of narrativity in the representation of reality', in W.J.T. Mitchell (ed.), *On Narrative.* Chicago: University of Chicago Press.

Williams, Raymond (1982) *The Sociology of Culture.* New York: Schocken Books.

Williams, Raymond (1983) *Writing in Society.* London: Verso.

Witherspoon, Gary (1977) *Language and Art in the Navajo Universe.* Ann Arbor, MI: University of Michigan Press.

8

Argumentation

Frans H. van Eemeren, Rob Grootendorst, Sally Jackson and Scott Jacobs

What is Argumentation?

Argumentation uses language to justify or refute a standpoint, with the aim of securing agreement in views. The study of argumentation typically centers on one of two objects: either interactions in which two or more people conduct or have arguments such as discussions or debates; or texts such as speeches or editorials in which a person makes an argument (O'Keefe, 1977). An adequate theoretical approach to argumentation should have something to say about both the process of argumentation and the arguments produced in that process. Consider the following passage, adapted from a syndicated newspaper story (Associated Press, 1993):

(1) A recent study found that women are more likely than men to be murdered at work. 40% of the women who died on the job in 1993 were murdered. 15% of the men who died on the job during the same period were murdered.

The first sentence is a claim made by the writer, and the other two sentences state evidence offered as reason to accept this claim as true. This claim-plus-support arrangement is what is most commonly referred to as an argument.

But arguments do not only occur as monologic packages; an argument may also be built in the interaction between someone who puts forward a standpoint and someone who challenges it, as in the following exchange between a young female patient and a middle-aged male therapist (from Bleiberg and Churchill, 1977; see also Jacobs, 1986). (In transcriptions of conversation, square brackets are commonly used to indicate points at which one person's speech overlaps another's, as when the doctor begins talking before the patient ends. A period in parentheses indicates a short pause.)

(2) 1 Pt: I don't want them to have anything to do with my life, except (.)
             [security(?)
     2 Dr: [You live at home?
     3 Pt: Yes.

4 Dr: They pay your bills?
5 Pt: Yeah.
6 Dr: How could they not have anything to do with your life?

In turn 1 the patient's statement that she does not want her parents ('them') to have anything to do with her life seems to commit her to the standpoint that it is possible for her parents to have nothing to do with her life. The therapist calls out and challenges this standpoint by asking a series of questions whose answers can be seen to support a contradictory position: it is not possible for the patient's parents not to have anything to do with her life.

Examples (1) and (2) illustrate features central to the concept of argumentation. First, a characteristic inferential structure can be extracted from both cases: propositions put forward as claims and other propositions (reasons) put forward as justification and/or refutation of those claims. Second, the arguments in both examples are about an issue which has two sides and which provides for two opposing communicator roles: a protagonist who puts forward a claim and an antagonist who doubts that claim, contradicts it, or otherwise withholds assent. For the newspaper story, the antagonist is a skeptical audience projected or imagined as needing proof to be convinced of the claim; for the therapy session, the antagonist is the therapist who challenges the patient's position and puts forward a contradictory standpoint. Third, these examples point to the way in which arguments are embedded in acts and activities. In the newspaper story, the writer does not openly make the claim or the argument for the claim that women are more likely than men to be murdered at work; the writer reports what claim and supporting argument are made by 'a recent study', thereby avoiding any personal responsibility for the truth of what is argued. In the therapy session, the argument for the therapist's standpoint is secured through questions that elicit concessions by the patient that commit her to an inconsistent position, forcing her to back down from her initial standpoint. The argument emerges from this collaborative activity. Moreover, the patient's initial standpoint occurs in the act of expressing a wish, and it is the therapist who seems to pin on the patient the further claim that such a wish is a realistic possibility.

These two arguments have another feature in common: both involve questionable means of building a case. In (1), the conclusion seems plausible only because of a very serious flaw in reasoning that, by its nature, is difficult to notice. Women are in fact much less likely than men to be murdered at work. While the statements contained in the support may be true, their truth does not guarantee the truth of the conclusion, for reasons we will explore shortly. The problem with the argument in (2) is not so much with the truth of what is said or with the reasoning itself as with the aggressive method by which the therapist pushes forward. The rhetorical question in turn 6 and the brusque, declarative form of the other questions amount to a 'put-down' of the patient that discourages her from advancing serious defense of her standpoint. The analysis of such inadequacies (generally termed fallacies) is among the most long-standing concerns of the study of argumentation.

A Brief History of the Study of Argumentative Discourse

The tradition of argumentation study has a very long history that can be traced back to ancient Greek writings on logic (proof), rhetoric (persuasion), and dialectic (inquiry), especially the writings of Aristotle. Since argumentation's function is to convince others of the truth, or acceptability, of what one says, the enduring questions addressed in the theory of argumentation have had to do with matters of evaluation: what it takes for a conclusion to be well supported, what criteria should govern acceptance of a standpoint, and so on. Historically, the study of argumentation has been motivated by an interest in improvement of discourse or modification of the effects of that discourse on society. Aristotle treated argumentation as a means to expose error in thinking and to shape discourse toward a rational ideal.

Central to Aristotle's logic was a distinction between form and substance. Rather than giving a particularistic analysis of the strengths and weaknesses of individual arguments, Aristotle's logic identified argument patterns that could lead from statements already known to be true to other statements whose truth was yet to be established. These patterns applied universally, so that any contents could be substituted for any other contents with the same result. Consider the following argument:

(3)   Some child molesters are teachers.
       Some teachers are women.
       Therefore, some child molesters are women.

In arguments of this sort (called 'categorical syllogisms'), the first two sentences (the premises) refer to three categories, each premise stating a relationship between two of the three categories. The third sentence (the conclusion) states a relationship between the two categories not paired in the premises. The conclusion is likely to be accepted as true by most people, as are the two premises offered in its support. But the conclusion is not in fact justified by the two premises, as can be seen by abstracting from the argument just the formal relationships asserted to hold among the three categories mentioned. By convention, we use S to stand for the category that appears as the subject of the conclusion, P to stand for the category that appears in the predicate of the conclusion, and M to stand for the 'middle' term that connects S and P by being paired with S in one premise and with P in the other. We can eliminate the complication of substance by substituting S for 'child molesters', M for 'teachers', and P for 'women', so as to exhibit the form of the argument as follows:

(4) Some *S* are *M*.
     Some *M* are *P*.
     Therefore, some *S* are *P*.

The flaw in this argument is that the *S* category may be completely contained in the portions of *M* that are not *P*, so that it is possible that no *S* are *P*. So, while the conclusion is possibly true, it is not necessarily true. It may be true that some child molesters are women, but this is not assured by the truth of the premises. When an argument's form guarantees that the conclusion will be true any time the premises are true, the form is said to be 'valid'. But if the conclusion may be false even though the premises are true, the form is said to be 'invalid'.

People rarely present their arguments in the form of complete syllogisms. Nevertheless, these forms do have an intuitive grounding in everyday reasoning, as can be seen in the following exchange between an uncle and his four-year-old nephew:

(5) ((Curtis runs into the kitchen and crashes into his uncle))
     Uncle: Curtis, what are you doing?
     Curtis: I'm a spaceman.
     Uncle: You can't be a spaceman. You're not wearing a helmet.
     Curtis: Han Solo doesn't wear a helmet.
     Uncle: Yeahhhh.
     Curtis: He's a spaceman. (.) As you can see, not all spacemen wear helmets.
     ((Curtis races off into the living room))

By filling in the suitable missing premise and paraphrasing each expression to fit a certain standard form, the uncle's argument can be made to correspond to a valid form of syllogism. The missing premise is that helmet-wearing is a necessary property of being a spaceman, ordinarily expressed as 'All spacemen wear helmets.' In standard syllogistic form, all statements express a relationship between two categories, so we further paraphrase the premise as 'All spacemen are helmet-wearers.' To represent the uncle's argument in the standard form of a syllogism, the subjects and predicates of all statements must be treated as general categories. So 'Curtis' must be considered a category with a single member, in which the explicitly stated premise 'You are not wearing a helmet' can be rewritten as 'All Curtisses are non-helmet-wearers', or, by a relation called 'obversion', rewritten into the logically equivalent form 'No Curtis is a helmet-wearer.' Substituting in the abstract category labels *P*, *M*, and *S* for 'spacemen', 'helmet-wearers', and 'Curtis', we get the movement from ordinary conversational expression to abstract categorical representation show in Table 8.1. Notice that whether we choose this particular translation or some other similar translation (for example, allowing 'non-helmet-wearers' as a category), we get a form in which, if the premises are true, the conclusion

Table 8.1

Conversational expression	Categorical paraphrase	Categorical abstraction
All spacemen have helmets.	All spacemen are helmet-wearers.	All P are M.
Curtis does not have a helmet.	No Curtis is a helmet-wearer.	No S are M.
Therefore, Curtis is not a spaceman.	Therefore, no Curtis is a spaceman.	No S are P.

Table 8.2

Conversational expression	Categorical paraphrase	Categorical abstraction
Han Solo does not have a helmet.	No Han Solo is a helmet-wearer.	No P are M.
Han Solo is a spaceman.	All Han Solos are spacemen.	All S are M.
Therefore, not all spacemen are helmet-wearers.	Therefore, some spacemen are not helmet-wearers.	(Assuming that there is at least one member of S) Some S are not P.

cannot be false; this is the defining feature of a valid form, and this property transfers to any 'substitution instance' of the form.

Though the argument is valid, that does not mean that the truth of the conclusion is beyond doubt; one or both premises may be false. The conclusion that Curtis is not a spaceman follows given the truth of the premises, but one may still challenge the truth of the conclusion by challenging the truth of one of the premises, and in the dialogue itself this is what occurred. Curtis inferred the syllogistic requirement that his uncle must be assuming that all spacemen wear helmets, and he concentrated on rebutting that inferred premise. In this case we substitute S for 'spacemen', P for 'helmet-wearers', and M for 'Han Solo' (again treating a specific individual as a category with just one member), as seen in Table 8.2. The conclusion of Curtis's syllogism contradicts the first premise of his uncle's syllogism, which was never actually stated but which is nevertheless necessary to represent the form and content of the uncle's reasoning. Given the existence of Han Solo, Curtis infers a proposition that in classical syllogistic logic is called the 'contradictory' of his uncle's proposition. One of the two propositions must be true and one must be false.

From Aristotle's logic, the study of argumentation has taken a tradition of analysing the form of argumentative inference independently of its content. The development of modern symbolic logic is a direct response to the concern for formally representing the inferential structure of seemingly acceptable or unacceptable arguments.

Classical rhetoric has to do with effective persuasion: with principles that lead to assent or consensus. Aristotle's rhetoric bears little resemblance to modern-day persuasion theories, which are heavily oriented to analysis of attitude formation and change but largely indifferent to the problem of the invention of persuasive messages (O'Keefe, 1990; Eagly and Chaiken, 1993). In Aristotle's rhetoric, the emphasis was on production of effective argumentation for an audience where the subject matter did not lend itself to certain demonstration. Whereas the syllogism was the most prominent form of logical demonstration, the enthymeme was its rhetorical counterpart. Enthymemes were thought of as syllogisms whose premises are drawn from the audience. They are usually only partially expressed, their logic being completed by the audience. The failure of the uncle's argument in (5) is an enthymematic failure of his audience (Curtis) to accept an implied premise (though Curtis does recognize the premise). The enthymematic quality of everyday ('marketplace') arguments leads to one of the enduring problems of argumentation analysis: how to represent what is left implicit in ordinary argumentative discourse.

Also important for the subsequent study of argumentation was the analysis of fallacies (what were first termed 'sophistical refutations' or 'sophisms', after the Sophists, a group of ancient theorist-practitioners who were accused of equating success in persuasion with goodness in argumentation). Among the sophisms Aristotle identified were argument forms that have a false appearance of soundness, such as the fallacy of equivocation, a reasoning error that arises from an unnoticed shift in the meaning of terms used within an argument.

The argument about on-the-job murder rates in (1) contains a fallacy of equivocation. The equivocation is between two possible concrete meanings for 'probability' or 'likelihood'. The conclusion refers to the probability of a woman (or man) being murdered on the job calculated by comparing the number of women (or men) who are murdered on the job in proportion to all working women (or men). The conclusion suggests that this proportion is higher for women than for men. But the grounds for the conclusion define probability quite differently, as a proportion calculated by comparing the number of women (or men) who are murdered on the job against the number who die on the job. The conclusion of the story would follow from these grounds only if men and women had similar overall rates of death on the job. But the same article reports that men account for 93 percent of all workplace fatalities. The difference this makes is very pronounced: based on other statistics reported in the story, one can calculate that there were 849 men murdered on the job, but only 170 women murdered, even though (as the article also reports) men and women today are fairly evenly represented in the American workforce (55 percent and 45 percent respectively). The grounds for the conclusion are true: comparing only men and women who die on the job, the probability that a male death is due to murder is lower than the probability that a female death is due to murder. Nevertheless, comparing all employed men and women, the probability of a male worker being murdered is much higher than the probability of a female worker being murdered.

Over the long history of argumentation theory, one mainstay has been the cataloguing and analysis of fallacies (Hamblin, 1970). The work involved in this form of theory will apparently never be completed, as the invention of new forms of argumentation (such as probabilistic reasoning) creates new opportunities for fallacies to emerge and new opportunities to identify them and explain why they are fallacious.

To complete the overview of Aristotle's contributions to the study of argumentation, the Aristotelian concept of dialectic is best understood as the art of inquiry through critical discussion. Dialectic is a way of putting ideas to critical test by attempting to expose and eliminate contradictions in a position: a protagonist puts forward a claim and then provides answers to a skeptical questioner (an antagonist). The exchange between the therapist and patient in (2) captures the structure of such a method, if not its cooperative spirit. While the paradigm case of dialectic is the question and answer technique of the Socratic dialogues, a pattern of assertion and assent may also be employed, as in (5). The adequacy of any particular claim is supposed to be cooperatively assessed by eliciting premises that might serve as commonly accepted starting points, then drawing out implications from those starting points and determining their compatibility with the claim in question. Where difficulties emerge, new claims might be put forward that avoided such contradictions. This method of regimented opposition amounts to the pragmatic application of logic, a collaborative method of putting logic into use so as to move from conjecture and opinion to more secure belief.

While Aristotle outlined duties for the roles of questioner and answerer and the types of questions and answers allowed, the dialectical conception of argumentation has, until recently, been largely ignored in the development of argumentation theory. Notions like burden of proof, presumption, or *reductio ad absurdum* proof have developed in argumentation theory without much notice of their dialectical echo. The recent rediscovery of dialectical conceptions of argument marks a decisive shift in attention for argumentation theory and research.

Contemporary Perspectives

The turning points for the contemporary study of argumentation were Perelman and Olbrechts-Tyteca's *La Nouvelle Rhétorique* (in English, *The New Rhetoric*), and Toulmin's *The Uses of Argument*, both published in 1958. Toulmin argued for a new, non-formal conception of rationality, tied to substantive discourse contexts ('fields') that varied in their normative organization. Perelman and Olbrechts-Tyteca's new rhetoric reintroduced the audience to argumentation and provided an inventory of effective argumentation techniques. Most important for contemporary argumentation study were the start toward an interactional view of argument and the move away from formal logic. Both Toulmin and Perelman took judicial argument as a model for argumentation generally, focusing attention on the interchange between two opposing arguer roles. These landmark works took the first steps toward studying argumentation as a linguistic activity.

The principal contribution of the new rhetoric has been to return argumentation to a context of controversy in which some audience is to be addressed. Rhetoric has often been understood as anti-rational or as a departure from a rational ideal. But in contemporary rhetorical theory there is a striking retreat from a hard distinction between rhetoric, the study of effective techniques of persuasion, and dialectic, long associated with ideals of reasonableness, rationality, and tendency toward truth. The distinctive theme in these modern re-examinations of rhetoric is the situated quality of argumentation and the importance of orientation to an audience. The central theoretical questions are how opposing views come to be reconciled through the use of language and how actual audiences may be brought through rhetoric itself to more closely approximate the stance of an ideally rational audience.

This tendency toward dialectification is even more explicit in the philosophical work of Hamblin (1970). In his detailed critique of the 'standard treatment' of fallacies, Hamblin built the case for seeing argument as a dialectical process organized around disputants' efforts to convince one another of their respective standpoints. Important features of Hamblin's approach are the emphasis on rules defining speaker commitments and regulating interactional moves rather than an emphasis on logical forms as the generative mechanism for argumentation as well as the recognition of the self-constituting and self-regulating character of argumentation. Hamblin's interest in the formal analysis of dialogue is a direct precedent for many of the most interesting current trends in argumentation theory.

Although it is possible to approach dialectic formally and non-contextually, the dialectical approach to argumentation tends to be accompanied by an interest in 'real' arguments as they arise in the back and forth of real controversies. Because of concerns with the problems of assessing the adequacy of ordinary argumentative cases, with the conditions of ordinary argument, and with the communicative and interactional means by which argumentation is conducted, dialectical approaches have tended to align themselves with pragmatic approaches to discourse and conversational interaction.

Accompanying a broad trend toward dialectification has been an equally influential trend toward functionalization and contextualization. Central to this trend has been Toulmin's work (1958; 1970). In broad outline, Toulmin theorized that regardless of substantive context, argument could be seen as the offering of a claim together with answers to certain characteristic questions, but that standards for judging the adequacy of arguments are variable from one argument field to another. The question of what a speaker has 'to go on' gives rise to what Toulmin called 'grounds' – roughly equivalent to the premises of classical logic. The question of what

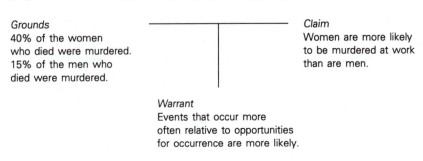

Grounds
40% of the women
who died were murdered.
15% of the men who
died were murdered.

Claim
Women are more likely
to be murdered at work
than are men.

Warrant
Events that occur more
often relative to opportunities
for occurrence are more likely.

Figure 8.1

justifies the inference from these grounds to the claim gives rise to the 'warrant' or 'inference license' – better understood as a kind of reasoning strategy or rule than as another premise. 'Backing' for the warrant might take the form of substantive information similar in kind to the 'grounds', so that the structure nowadays called 'the Toulmin model' differs from a classical description of argument in focusing not on the formal relationships among parts of an argument but on the functional relationships.

Consider how we might 'diagram' the arguments in (1) and (3). In diagramming such arguments, we often find that we must add elements not actually stated but necessary to represent the speaker's reasoning. In example (1), we must add an assumption about how one computes and compares probabilities, as in Figure 8.1

Example (3) is much more complicated, despite its apparent simplicity, because to diagram it adequately we must treat it as two arguments, one of which builds the grounds for the other. As with example (1), we must add content left implicit. Specifically, we must atttribute to the uncle the belief that having a helmet is a necessary feature for a spaceman, not just a property that happens to be shared by all spacemen. This implicit belief can be partitioned into a factual proposition about properties of the category 'spacemen' (appearing in Figure 8.2 as backing for an assumption about category membership requirements) and a reasoning rule that specifies conditions under which something may be treated as a member of a class. Factual materials specific to the individual case provide the grounds for the conclusion or the backing for the warrant; reasoning rules and other similar elements serve as warrants, as shown in the diagram in Figure 8.2.

These diagrams not only help to explain how the various parts of the arguments are related, but also help to locate problems in each argument. In the upper diagram, the problem is easily recognized as having to do with what is considered an 'opportunity' for each event to occur; the probability of a woman's being murdered on the job is reasonably measured not as the proportion of deaths that are murders but as the proportion of all working women murdered on the job, a much lower figure. In the lower diagram, the fault is in the unstated part of the backing for the warrant: the apparently mistaken belief that all spacemen have

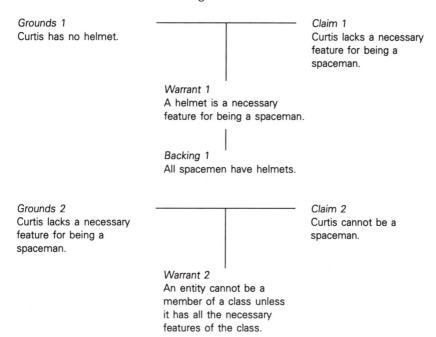

Grounds 1
Curtis has no helmet.

Claim 1
Curtis lacks a necessary feature for being a spaceman.

Warrant 1
A helmet is a necessary feature for being a spaceman.

Backing 1
All spacemen have helmets.

Grounds 2
Curtis lacks a necessary feature for being a spaceman.

Claim 2
Curtis cannot be a spaceman.

Warrant 2
An entity cannot be a member of a class unless it has all the necessary features of the class.

Figure 8.2

helmets and the correspondingly faulty assumption that having a helmet is a necessary feature of being a spaceman.

The embeddedness of argumentation in substantive discourse contexts is also foreshadowed in Toulmin's work, especially in the idea that standards for evaluation of argument are 'field-dependent' and in the still more fundamental idea that the field-independent elements of argumentation (claim, grounds, warrant, etc.) can be understood as answers to the questions of an idealized interlocutor. Although the style of analysis inspired by Toulmin's work (diagramming of arguments as completed units) may seem to focus more on argument form and content than on interactions, the argument structure is really the product of an interaction with each part of the argument defined in terms of some specified interactional function – as answers to particular questions or challenges to the initial claim.

One thread leading from Toulmin's work forward is the 'informal logic' movement (Govier, 1988; Johnson and Blair, 1983). Although the name suggests otherwise, informal logic is not a new kind of logic. Rather, it is a normative approach to argumentation in everyday language that is broader than the formal logical approach. The informal logician's objective is to develop norms, criteria and procedures for interpreting, evaluating and construing argumentation that are faithful to the complexities and uncertainties of everyday argumentation. A common theme in informal logic is that formally invalid arguments are often quite reasonable as bases for practical decisions.

According to Blair and Johnson's (1987) program, the cogency of argumentation is not identical to formal validity in deductive logic. They argue that the premises for a conclusion must satisfy three criteria: (1) relevance, (2) sufficiency, and (3) acceptability. With relevance, the question is whether there is an adequate relation between the contents of the premises and the conclusion; with sufficiency, whether the premises provide strong enough evidence for the conclusion in the face of objections and counterargumentation; with acceptability, whether the premises are true, probable or otherwise reliable.

A step further toward a functional, interactional view of argument is taken by pragmatic argumentation theories such as the pragma-dialectical theory of van Eemeren and Grootendorst (1984; 1992; van Eemeren et al., 1993; see also Walton, 1989; 1995). The pragma-dialectical theory begins with the assumption that the purpose of argumentation is to resolve a difference of opinion, so that the opposition of argumentative roles is a characteristic feature of argumentative discourse. Argument is seen as a kind of interaction that arises in the context of other interactional business, when something said, implied, or otherwise conveyed makes plain that there is a difference of opinion between two parties. This description is necessarily abstract, since argumentation can take any form from a single, written text by an author addressing an unknown audience to a heated back-and-forth debate between two people talking face to face. But the important, defining feature of argument is that it occurs as a means of addressing – and attempting to resolve – a difference of opinion by means of exploring the relative justification for competing standpoints. The writer envisions an audience to be persuaded by means of arguments offered to support the writer's views or to refute the audience's own views. Arguers in conversation with one another allow their respective positions to unfold in direct response to each successive move by their partners. But in both cases, the organization of the argument depends on the existence of opposing roles and on the arguer's understanding of the issues that must be resolved to overcome the opposition.

Reflecting broad trends toward dialectification, functionalization, and contextualization of argument, pragma-dialectical theory offers a model of argumentative discourse not in terms of form and content but in terms of discussion procedure. In place of a set of standards to be applied to individual units of proof, the pragma-dialectical model offers rules for argumentative interaction and associated preconditions having to do with such things as participant abilities, attitudes, and power.

Argumentation is seen within the pragma-dialectical view as a discourse device for the regulation of discourse itself. It falls within the class of devices known as 'repair mechanisms' and its function is to locate and resolve differences of opinion (Jackson and Jacobs, 1980). The view of argumentation as a form of repair (pre-emptive or *post hoc*) is important, because it calls attention to the embeddedness of argument within other sorts of interactional business. In other words, the analysis of any particular argument – including such arguments as those occurring in the newspaper story about murders on the job and in the spaceman conversation – is relativized, placed within some broader discourse context that guides the analysis by defining what is at stake.

To say that argumentation comes about as a form of repair is also to say that the organization of argument must be understood in terms of general interactional principles. In the pragma-dialectical view, insights from speech act theory (Searle, 1969) and Grice's (1989) theory of conversational implicature are used as a bridge between the special organization of argumentation and the general principles that organize discourse and interaction (van Eemeren et al., 1993, especially Chapters 1 and 5).

Case Study: Critical Analysis of Advertorials

Dialectical theories of argumentation have their most transparent application to argumentative discussion, that is to direct exchange of views between two disputants. Many published analyses of such materials can be found (for example, van Eemeren et al., 1993; Chapters 5–7). We have chosen for a case study a more challenging set of materials: a series of monologic texts representing just one side of a discussion. What makes our analysis 'dialectical' is not that its object is dialogue but that it places any argumentative text into the context of one party's effort to convince another of a standpoint by answering doubts and objections and by grounding conclusions in mutually acceptable starting points. The trick is to see that these short monologues reflect an image of an author as protagonist (here, RJR Tobacco) but also project an image of an addressee as antagonist or skeptical interlocutor (here, a young person considering whether to smoke).

The two texts presented in examples (6) and (7) originally appeared as editorial advertisements (or 'advertorials') published in American magazines during the period 1984–6 and paid for by the R.J. Reynolds Tobacco Company. The two advertorials are ostensibly acts of advice urging young people not to smoke. They make particularly interesting cases for reconstruction because of the way in which these advertorials exploit and subvert the very standards of open and cooperative discussion they seem to promote. The *appearance* of a good faith effort as reasonable argument only serves to disguise the fallacious design.

(6) 1   Some surprising advice to young people
     2   from RJ Reynolds Tobacco.
     3   Don't smoke.
     4   For one thing, smoking has always been an adult custom. And even for adults, smoking has
     5   become very controversial. So even though we're a tobacco company, we don't think it's a good idea
     6   for young people to smoke.

7   Now, we know that giving this kind of advice to young people can sometimes backfire.

8   But if you take up smoking just to prove you're an adult, you're really proving just the

9   opposite. Because deciding to smoke or not to smoke is something you should do when you don't have

10   anything to prove.

11   Think it over. After all, you may not be old enough to smoke. But you're old enough to think.

12   *R.J. Reynolds Tobacco Company*

(7) 1   Some straight talk about smoking
     2   for young people.

3   We're R.J. Reynolds Tobacco, and we're urging you not to smoke.

4   We're saying this because, throughout the world, smoking has always been an adult custom.

5   And because today, even among adults, smoking is controversial.

6   Your first reaction might be to ignore this advice. Maybe you feel we're talking to you as if

7   you were a child. And you probably don't think of yourself that way.

8   But just because you're no longer a child doesn't mean that you're already an adult. And if you

9   take up smoking just to prove you're not a kid, you're kidding yourself.

10   So please don't smoke. You'll have plenty of time as an adult to decide whether smoking is

11   right for you.

12   That's about as straight as we can put it.

13   *R.J. Reynolds Tobacco Company*

While one can readily sense that something is amiss, the problem is how to bring the argument to account for the offenses committed. Argument reconstruction is an analytic tool that may serve such a critical function. What we will try to show in this section is that the arguments provided are so weak as to be virtually self-defeating. The arguments in these advertorials invite the conclusion that there are no good arguments why young people should not smoke. How this communicative effect is achieved in texts that *seem* to argue against young people smoking can be shown through a reconstruction of the arguments.

Considered dialectically, the advertorials must be seen as contributions to a broader public debate concerning the role of tobacco and the tobacco industry in American society. By 1984, public attitudes toward smoking had shifted dramatically, leading to unprecedented restrictions on smoking in restaurants, hotels, government buildings, trains, and airlines. Congressional hearings were scheduled to consider, among other things, further restrictions on the advertising of cigarettes. Part of the call for the hearings was the argument that cigarette companies were advertising to children to replace the growing number of adult smokers who were quitting or dying. So, even though the two advertorials appear to be self-contained rhetorical acts simply directed toward young people, we should expect broader circumstances to motivate the way in which arguments are selected and fashioned. Not coincidentally, these two advertorials were followed by a third, entitled, 'We don't advertise to children.' As part of the proof of this claim, the third advertorial argued: 'First of all, we don't want young people to smoke. And we're running ads aimed specifically at young people advising them that we think smoking is strictly for adults.'

At least on the surface, the arguments in (6) and (7) have the appearance of reasonable efforts at dialectical engagement. Both advertorials begin with seemingly plain and direct justifications for why young people should not smoke (lines 4–5). First, smoking has always been an adult custom. Second, even for adults smoking is controversial. These arguments define a kind of disagreement space in which protagonist and antagonist engage not so much over the issue of whether or not smoking is a bad idea in general, but over an issue that might plausibly be raised by a young reader considering smoking: if (as RJR Tobacco must believe) it is okay for adults to smoke, why is it a bad idea for young people to smoke?

The reactions of a young interlocutor are then more openly anticipated and addressed in both ads. In lines 7–11 of (6) the tobacco company anticipates that somehow giving this kind of advice might backfire, provoking young people to try to prove they are adults by doing exactly what is being advised against. The nature of the problem is more explicitly anticipated in lines 6–9 of (7): this kind of advice might be rejected because it might seem condescending (by talking to the reader as if they were a child). In both cases RJR argues that rejecting the advice by taking up smoking will not prove that a young person is an adult or not a kid.

Finally, both advertorials lay claim to the special credibility of 'disinterested' argumentation. In (6), RJR implies that they are arguing against their own self-interest as a tobacco company, calling their advice 'surprising' and then asserting that they don't think it is a good idea for young people to smoke 'even though we're a tobacco company' (line 5). In (7), the advertorial opens and closes by characterizing its message as 'straight'.

So far, we have described the arguments more or less informally, restricting ourselves to claims and reasons that closely parallel material presented in the texts. The two primary arguments for not smoking could be presented as follows:

(8) *Claim*:   Young people should not smoke.
   Reason 1: Smoking has always been an adult custom.
(9) *Claim*:   Young people should not smoke.
   Reason 2: Smoking is controversial even among adults.

Like most naturally occurring arguments, the texts themselves are incomplete as outlines of the underlying reasoning. This does not mean that the arguments are inferentially defective or that the reasons fail to give any adequate justification for the claim, but only that we have to fill in what has been left implicit.

Intuitively, people understand more in these arguments than is being said explicitly. Some set of tacitly shared beliefs and meanings are taken for granted in building these arguments, and the assumption of these beliefs and representation of these meanings allow the reasons to stand in a justifying relation to the claim. This is the characteristic feature of enthymematic argument. But what are these tacit beliefs? And by what principles would a satisfactory representation be constructed? This is the problem of unexpressed premises, and can be usefully seen as a special instance of the problems of coherence and inference in discourse generally.

One way to handle the problem is to try to identify assertable propositions which, though unexpressed, could still be treated as premises to which the arguer is committed in making the argument. We presume that RJR Tobacco is attempting to make a cooperative contribution to the debate and, following Grice's (1989) theory of implicature, we should look for propositions which, though unstated, are mutually available and would be recognized by reasonable people to make the argument acceptable if they were stated. At a minimum, a reasonable arguer should be held to be committed to an inferential pattern that is valid and whose premises are true, or at least, plausible. One such pattern would be the following:

(10) *Premise 1*: If smoking has always been an adult custom, then young people should not smoke.
Premise 2: Smoking has always been an adult custom.
Conclusion: Young people should not smoke.
(11) *Premise 1*: If smoking is controversial even among adults, then young people should not smoke.
Premise 2: Smoking is controversial even among adults.
Conclusion: Young people should not smoke.

In each case, a premise has been added that fits a deductively valid pattern of inference called *modus ponens*. *Modus ponens* is a form of reasoning about propositions; its 'elements' are propositions rather than categories. Using p and q as propositional variables (symbols that can stand for any proposition), we can represent the abstract form of (10) as follows, where p is the proposition 'smoking has always been an adult custom' and q is the proposition 'young people should not smoke':

(12) If p then q.
p.
Therefore, q.

Notice that although the advertorials do not state the 'if p then q' premise, the protagonist (RJR) is nonetheless committed to its truth by virtue of offering *p* as a reason for accepting *q*. Since the argumentative functions of the 'reason' and 'claim' in (8) and (9) are more or less transparent, so is the commitment to the added premise in (10) and (11).

But explicating such a premise as a step in reconstruction is rather pointless unless it helps us to find the substantive grounds that the premise itself stands in for. Adding a premise that asserts in effect 'If reason then claim' can be done with any two statements that appear in an argumentative relation. This does nothing more than state that inferring the one statement from the other is permitted. While such a premise satisfies logically minimal criteria for valid inference, it does not really answer the question of why one might think the one assertion is good reason to claim the other. Where possible, one should search for unexpressed premises that are informative in this way and not substantively vacuous. Thus, in (5), the unexpressed premise in the uncle's argument is better seen as something like 'All spacemen wear helmets' than as the trivial 'If you're not wearing a helmet then you can't be a spaceman.' What is wanted, then, is a more informative alternative to premise 1 or a more informative unpacking of its basis.

Let us first consider the reasoning in (10): what does smoking being an adult custom have to do with why young people should not smoke? R.J. Reynolds builds into its arguments the assumption that whether or not to smoke is something that adults are entitled to decide for themselves ('deciding to smoke or not to smoke is something you should do when you don't have anything to prove', (6) lines 9–10; 'You'll have plenty of time as an adult to decide whether smoking is right for you', (7) lines 10–11). This is at least part of what it means to assert that something is an adult custom.

And we can also readily extract from both advertorials the proposition that young people are not adults. In (7), it is supposed that young people probably do not think of themselves as children. And RJR answers by denying that this shows they are an adult (lines 8–9). In both (6) and (7), young people are projected as trying to prove they are adults – an attempt which, according to the advertorial, only proves they are not adults. But so what if young people are not adults? Why is showing this pertinent to the claim that young people should not smoke?

Because to assert that something is an adult custom means not just that adults have a right to practice it, but that *only* adults are entitled to do so. If someone is not an adult, they are not entitled to practice it ('smoking is strictly for adults').

So, we can unpack the argument in (10) as being grounded in the following line of reasoning. Only a person who is an adult is entitled to practice an adult custom. (If a person is an adult, that person is entitled to practice an adult custom. If a person is not an adult, that person is not entitled to practice an adult custom.) Young people are not adults. It follows from this that young people are not entitled to practice an adult custom. Since smoking is an adult custom, young people are not entitled to smoke. And, since it is safe to assume that people should not do what they are not entitled to do, it can be concluded that young people should not smoke.

The substance of this reasoning is certain to be rejected by young people who are considering smoking, but it is all that the advertorials offer as grounds for their advice. And here is where we begin to see the troublesome weakness of the arguments in these advertorials. No matter how we wiggle around trying to find a substantive basis for connecting the stated reasons to the claims, we consistently find a chain of reasoning that seems only to presume and reassert the adult entitlement, adult privilege, and adult authority to restrict children's choices.

RJR Tobacco is defending a position that only adults are entitled to smoke, and young people are excluded from this category. But *why* are young people excluded? Here, we should notice that the categories of 'adult' and 'child' are primarily moral, not biological classifications. Adults have *rights* that children do not have. And exercise of these rights requires a capacity for mature decision-making. Now, it is a widely taken for granted assumption that children are incapable of making wise decisions about health issues and are therefore in need of protection from their own bad choices. Both ads do allude to childish, immature reasoning by young people (in (6): 'But if you take up smoking just to prove you're an adult, you're really proving just the opposite'; in (7): 'if you take up smoking just to prove you're not a kid, you're kidding yourself'). But RJR pointedly blocks an assumption that this is the basis for excluding young people from adult classification. Example (6) concludes by urging young people to 'Think it over' and by asserting that they 'may not be old enough to smoke. But [they]'re old enough to think.'

Actually, no real argument is ever put forward to think that young people are different in any important respect from adults. Both ads anticipate that a young reader will reject classification as non-adult (and will attempt to prove adult status by smoking), but neither ad substantively defends the premise. In (7), RJR does not justify withholding adult status from young people; they only deny that the fact that the reader is not a child does not mean the reader is an adult (line 8). In (6), RJR defends the claim that young people are not adults through a kind of circular reasoning that Fogelin and Sinnott-Armstrong (1992) call a self-sealing argument: by pushing the burden of proof on young people to prove that they are adults (and attributing a motive that a young reader is highly likely to disavow), the tobacco company guarantees that young people cannot be adults because adults are persons who do not have anything to prove. In both cases, what looks like substantive refutation and counterargument is really a refusal to mount a defense. By failing to accept the burden of justifying its classification of young people, the advertorials leave this issue at an impasse.

Also noticeably withheld is any real justification for why smoking is a restricted activity. Yet this is presumably the basis for the controversy in the first place: young people do not recognize the legitimacy of the restriction to adults. The advertorials merely yoke their claim that young people should not smoke to the presumption by custom that they are not entitled to smoke until they become adults. Invoking the force of presumption is what is done by saying that smoking has 'always' been an adult custom, and that this is so 'throughout the world'.

The lack of genuine substantive support is particularly noticeable since the advertorials do not make use of the seemingly strongest available arguments against smoking: cigarettes are a lethal, addictive drug, especially so for young people. One might think that the argument reconstructed in (11) alludes to these substantive objections to smoking; but in saying that smoking is controversial really nothing more is conveyed than that some people approve of smoking and others do not. The argument functions only to bolster the presumption of exclusion.

To see this, we must first unpack the meaning of 'controversial.' To say that something is controversial is to say that there are two sides to the issue, neither of which is clearly correct, so that the issue is contested but essentially undecided. To say that 'smoking is controversial' means that it is neither clearly right to smoke nor clearly wrong to smoke. And in the absence of a decisive conclusion, the position with the presumption wins so that adults should be entitled to smoke if that is what they choose to do.

But there is another sense of 'controversial' that especially applies to issues where one position enjoys a presumption – the sense of a position being strongly challenged. To preface the reason in (9) with the qualification 'even among adults' conventionally implicates that smoking is more 'controversial' for some group other than adults. Presumably young people form this contrast group since it is the status of smoking for this group that is at issue in the advertorials. If smoking is controversial among adults, it must be more so among young people. And here the meaning is that for young people, smoking is even more questionable, more challengeable. That is, the case that smoking should not be permitted is stronger for young people than it is for adults.

But what makes the case stronger? No substantive basis for challenge or contrast is provided in either advertorial. The only difference is that adult smoking has customary presumption – something that does not apply to young people.

The paradoxical quality of the arguments is pernicious, working to undermine the credibility of the very advice they offer while simultaneously resisting critical examination. The advertorials appear to openly engage the doubts and challenges of young people with substantive argumentation and frank refutation, but in fact consistently refrain from advancing serious arguments. They appear to provide arguments that are disinterested, balanced, and objective, yet the manner and content of argument are subtly crafted to maintain a strategic consistency with the position that smoking by adults is a legitimate, mature, and reasonable decision. Most importantly, the advertorials offer advice, but do it in a fashion paradoxically adapted to young people: adapted not by selection of premises the audience is likely to accept but by selection of premises the audience is almost sure to reject.

Practical Applications of Argumentation Study

To understand the whole field of argumentation study, it is first necessary to imagine three (or more) distinct scientific objectives. The first objective is prescriptive: to arrive at a set of principles that tell people how to argue well. This altogether practical interest was the first to emerge and is clearly embodied in centuries of writings on rhetoric, dialectic, and logic. The second objective is descriptive: to arrive at an empirically correct model of argumentative discourse, analogous in form and compatible in substance to models of such phenomena as talking on topic, managing the floor in conversation, or negotiating social identities. Obvious examples of descriptive argumentation research can be found within conversation analysis and related streams of work (Coulter, 1990; Goodwin, 1983; Jacobs and Jackson, 1982; Schiffrin, 1984). Modern formal logic and cognitive science have also taken a recent turn toward description of natural inferential processes, as in efforts to model such long-neglected phenomena as the use of heuristics and the structure of 'default reasoning'. The experimental study of social influence also offers a form of descriptive argumentation research, heavily oriented to identifying what factors actually influence people when presented with argumentative texts (Eagly and Chaiken, 1993; O'Keefe, 1990). The third objective is critical: to develop a framework for the evaluation and improvement of actual argumentative practices, treating the practices both as phenomena to be explained and as opportunities for intervention – that is, for attempts to bring about social change (Goodnight, 1982).

Each of these aims has some form of practical spinoff, for the study of argumentation has from classical times been a practical business concerned with the improvement of reasoning and reason-giving discourse. Contemporary argumentation study, with its emphasis on substantive discourse practices and discourse contexts, embodies this practical component a little differently than have more traditional approaches. In the broad interdisciplinary domain of argumentation research, there are two principal sorts of applications.

Pedagogical Applications: the Cultivation of Argumentative Competence

The first sort of application is most obviously connected with the centuries-old rhetorical tradition: the development of critical capability. In the study of argumentation, one objective is to cultivate competence in analysis and critical inquiry. The study of fallacies is, in its best pedagogical embodiments, the cultivation of a critical sense that makes the student a better participant in argumentative discourse: better not in the sense of being able to win in debates, but better in the sense of being able to advance discussion toward a rational resolution. So, for example, in teaching students to recognize self-interest as a potential threat to rationality, we create antagonists for views that should be opened to inspection. Case studies such as our analysis of tobacco industry advertorials, for example, serve not only as potential contributions to an ongoing discourse, but also as exemplars for critical thinking about public persuasion.

But to say that contemporary pedagogical applications have close ties to classical rhetoric is not to suggest that these contemporary applications merely recycle the achievements of the past. On the contrary: since discourse practices themselves evolve along with other social conditions, critical analysis will necessarily face new challenges related to changing practices. For example, in contemporary public discourse, the extremely pervasive use of public opinion polls as a tool for the management of public opinion creates some distinctively modern forms of fallacy that require careful theoretical analysis and systematic pedagogical attention (for example, Harrison, 1996).

Interventions: the Design of Discourse Processes

The second sort of application, associated conceptually with pragmatically oriented approaches such as Willard's (1982; 1989) interactionist theory and with our own pragma-dialectical theory, centers on the design of discourse processes. Human societies have always designed communication systems, but an explicit and detailed attention to the design features of particular systems is a recent development stimulated by broader social changes such as the explosion of communication and information technology. As we have pointed out elsewhere (van Eemeren et al., 1993: Chapter 8), the blending of descriptive and normative concerns supports not just the individual-level pedagogical applications long associated with argumentation study, but also social- or institutional-level applications that take the form of proposals for how to conduct discourse.

How might we think about interventions for the case study we have been examining? Probably the first lesson is that in a world of advertorials, infomercials and docudramas, where talk radio serves as a public forum, and the quality of jury decisions in murder trials is judged against the results of public opinion polls, what the public needs is not just more or better information about the content of issues but more and better information about the way in which information is being provided. What is so insidious about messages like the R.J. Reynolds Tobacco advertorials is not so much the deceptive content of their arguments, as the disarming frame in which the arguments are presented. It is unlikely that any set of regulations or procedures for critical discussion can anticipate or prevent their own subversion and exploitation. Rather, what needs to be provided for is the self-regulating capacities of the argumentation process itself. The only effective way to control fallacious argumentation is with counter-argumentation that points out what is going on.

And this leads to another lesson. There is no natural argumentative forum for reasoned opposition to 'paid' editorials like those published by R.J. Reynolds. An argumentative solution to the problem presented by this case might require not only the development of text to rebut text but also the design of structures to support the activity of rebutting (such as government grant programs for development of anti-smoking educational campaigns).

The design features of disputation structures – whether they are adversarial or non-adversarial, how they provide for balanced competition among views, what endpoints they recognize as resolutions, and so on – are properly within the domain of argumentation study. Of special interest from a pragma-dialectical perspective is the way in which the design of disputation can correct for obstacles to rational discussion encountered in real-life circumstances.

Recommended Reading

To follow up an interest in such practical issues as including composition or analysis of arguments, handbooks taking a language- or discourse-centered approach include van Eemeren and Grootendorst (1992), Fisher (1988), Fogelin and Sinnott-Armstrong (1992), Walton (1989), and Woods and Walton (1982).

Empirical analysis of argumentative discourse is discussed thoroughly by van Eemeren et al. (1993) as well as Jacobs and Jackson (1982).

Good starting points for theoretical study of argument may be found in van Eemeren et al. (1996) or Willard (1989), and any serious theoretical study of argumentation will also include Perelman and Olbrechts-Tyteca (1958; 1969) and Toulmin (1958).

References

Associated Press (1993) 'Women are more likely to be murdered at work than men, study finds', *Arizona Daily Star*, 2 October: A5.

Blair, J.A. and Johnson, R. (1987) 'Argumentation as dialectical', *Argumentation*, 1: 41–56.

Bleiberg, S. and Churchill, L. (1977) 'Notes on confrontation in conversation', *Journal of Psycholinguistic Research*, 4: 273–8.

Coulter, J. (1990) 'Elementary properties of argument sequences', in G. Psathas (ed.), *Interaction Competence*. Washington, DC: International Institute for Ethnomethodology and Conversation Analysis, and University Press of America. pp. 181–203.

Eagly, A.H. and Chaiken, S. (1993) *The Psychology of Attitudes*. Fort Worth, TX: Harcourt Brace Jovanovich.

Fisher, A. (1988) *The Logic of Real Arguments*. Cambridge: Cambridge University Press.

Fogelin, R. and Sinott-Armstrong, W. (1992) *Understanding Arguments: an Introduction to Informal Logic*, 4th edn. San Diego, CA: Harcourt Brace Jovanovich.

Goodnight, G.T. (1982) 'The personal, technical, and public spheres of argument: a speculative inquiry into the art of public deliberation', *Journal of the American Forensic Association*, 18: 214–27.

Goodwin, M.H. (1983) 'Aggravated correction and disagreement in children's conversations', *Journal of Pragmatics*, 7: 657–77.

Govier, T. (1988) *A Practical Study of Argument*, 2nd edn. Belmont, CA: Wadsworth.

Grice, H.P. (1989) *Studies in the Ways of Words*. Cambridge, MA: Harvard University Press.

Hamblin, C.L. (1970) *Fallacies*. London: Methuen.

Harrison, T. (1996) 'Are public opinion polls used illegitimately? 47% say yes', in S. Jackson (ed.), *Argument and Values: Proceedings of the Ninth SCA/AFA Summer Conference on Argumentation*. Annandale, VA: Speech Communication Association.

Jackson, S. and Jacobs, S. (1980) 'Structure of conversational argument: pragmatic bases for the enthymeme', *Quarterly Journal of Speech*, 66: 251–65.

Jacobs, S. (1986) 'How to make an argument from example in discourse analysis', in D.G. Ellis and W.A. Donohue (eds), *Contemporary Issues in Language and Discourse Processes*. Hillsdale, NJ: Lawrence Erlbaum. pp. 149–67.

Jacobs, S. and Jackson, S. (1982) 'Conversational argument: a discourse analytic approach', in J.R. Cox and C.A. Willard (eds), *Advances in Argumentation Theory and Research*. Carbondale and Edwardsville, IL: Southern Illinois University Press. pp. 205–37.

Johnson, R. and Blair, J.A. (1983) *Logical Self-Defense*. Toronto: McGraw-Hill.

O'Keefe, D.J. (1977) 'Two concepts of argument', *Journal of the American Forensic Association*, 13: 121–8.

O'Keefe, D.J. (1990) *Persuasion: Theory and Research*. Thousand Oaks, CA: Sage.

Perelman, C. and Olbrechts-Tyteca, L. (1958) *La Nouvelle Rhétorique: traité de l'argumentation*. Brussels: University of Brussels.

Perelman, C. and Olbrechts-Tyteca, L. (1969) *The New Rhetoric: a Treatise on Argumentation* (trans. J. Wilkinson and P. Weaver). Notre Dame, IN: University of Notre Dame Press.

Schiffrin, D. (1984) 'Jewish argument as sociability', *Language in Society*, 13: 311–36.

Searle, J.R. (1969) *Speech Acts*. Cambridge: Cambridge University Press.

Toulmin, S.E. (1958) *The Uses of Argument*. Cambridge: Cambridge University Press.

Toulmin, S.E. (1970) *An Examination of the Place of Reason in Ethics*. Cambridge: Cambridge University Press.

van Eemeren, F.H. and Grootendorst, R. (1984) *Speech Acts in Argumentative Discussions*. Dordrechts-Holland: Foris.

van Eemeren, F.H. and Grootendorst, R. (1992) *Argumentation, Communication, and Fallacies: a Pragma-Dialectical Perspective*. Hillsdale, NJ: Lawrence Erlbaum.

van Eemeren, F.H., Grootendorst, R., Jackson, S. and Jacobs, S. (1993) *Reconstructing Argumentative Discourse*. Tuscaloosa, AL: University of Alabama Press.

van Eemeren, F.H., Grootendorst, R., Snoeck Henkemans, F., Blair, J.A., Johnson, R.H., Krabbe, E.C.W., Plantin, C., Walton, D., Willard, C.A., Woods, J. and Zarefsky, D. (1996) *Fundamentals of Argumentation Theory*. Hillsdale, NJ: Lawrence Erlbaum.

Walton, D.N. (1989) *Informal Logic: a Handbook for Critical Argumentation*. Cambridge: Cambridge University Press.

Walton, D.N. (1995) *A Pragmatic Theory of Fallacy*. Tuscaloosa, AL: University of Alabama Press.

Willard, C.A. (1982) *Argumentation and the Social Grounds of Knowledge*. Tuscaloosa, AL: University of Alabama Press.

Willard, C.A. (1989) *A Theory of Argument*. Tuscaloosa, AL: University of Alabama Press.

Woods, J. and Walton, D. (1982) *Argument: the Logic of the Fallacies*. Toronto: McGraw-Hill.

9

Genres and Registers of Discourse

Suzanne Eggins and J.R. Martin

Definition and Delimitation of Topic

This chapter introduces register and genre theory (R&GT), a label which can be applied to a range of linguistic approaches to discourse which seek to theorise how discourses, or texts,[1] are like and unlike each other, and why. The kinds of questions R&GT ask can be outlined by comparing the following texts:

Text 1
Although the term postmodern had been in cultural circulation since the 1870s, it is only in the 1960s that we see the beginnings of what is now understood as postmodernism. In the work of Susan Sontag and Leslie Fiedler we encounter the celebration of what Sontag calls a 'new sensibility', a new pluralism following the supposed collapse of the distinction between high and popular culture. It is a sensibility in revolt against the normalising function of modernism; its rebellion is an attack on the canonisation of modernism's rebellion, an attack on modernism's official status as the high culture of the modern capitalist world. What these critics oppose is not so much the project of modernism as its canonisation in the museum and the academy

Text 2
Most of this stuff I can't really comment on because I don't understand a word of it. If I understand 2% I think I'm doing pretty well . . . Post Modernism is a big fad in intellectual life right now. It's intriguing as an intellectual phenomenon. I don't think there's much in the way of intellectual substance to it. It offers people a device to be careerist, and go to conferences and get cushy jobs and write a lot of articles and be very wealthy and live in big hotels, and keep totally disengaged from any human activity that matters, and meanwhile be more radical than thou.

As register and genre theorists, our concern when confronted with these two texts is to describe and explain both how the texts are alike and how they are different. The similarities in this case are confined to topic: both texts are 'about' the intellectual movement which has come to be known as postmodernism. The linguistic evidence of this similarity is in the use of the key lexical item: *postmodernism*.

The differences between the texts, however, are more marked than their similarities. In non-technical terms, we could describe text 1 as 'heavier' or more formal, more technical, and more factual than Text 2, which sounds more chatty, accessible, and opinionated. The first step in an R&G analysis would be to *describe* the linguistic patterns (words and structures) in the two texts which created such different effects. There are three main areas of difference between the texts: the degree of formality of the language used, the amount of attitude/evaluation expressed by the text-producer, and the background knowledge drawn on in the texts. In text 1, for example, we find:

Textual formality

(a) Use of standard unabbreviated syntax.
(b) No references to the writer.
(c) Thematic prominence (first position in the clause) given to the concept of postmodernism or to generic groups of participants: for example, *Although* the term postmodern; it *is a sensibility*; these *critics*.
(d) Frequent use of embedding, where units of clause structure are filled by elements which are themselves clauses; for example, *what is now understood as postmodernism*; *the celebration of what Sontag calls a 'new sensibility'*; *What these critics oppose*.
(e) Lexically dense noun phrase structures with heavy post-modification: for example, *a sensibility in revolt against the normalising function of modernism*; *an attack on the canonisation of modernism's rebellion*; *an attack on modernism's official status as the high culture of the modern capitalist world*.
(f) Nominalized vocabulary (action meanings expressed as nouns): *circulation, beginnings, work, celebration, sensibility, pluralism, collapse, distinction, revolt, rebellion, canonisation, attack*.
(g) Use of 'elevated' vocabulary: *sensibility, the project of modernism, the academy*.

Expression of attitude

(a) Sparse use of minimizing or intensifying adverbs: only *in the 1960s*.
(b) Sparse and oblique use of attitudinally loaded vocabulary: *the* supposed *collapse*.

Assumed knowledge

(a) Use of terms which have specialized technical meanings within academe: *pluralism, high and popular culture, canonisation, modernism, capitalist*.
(b) References to scholars without biographical details being presented: *Sontag, Fiedler*.

Text 2, on the other hand, displays the following patterns:

Textual formality
(a) Frequent references to the writer, who is grammatically the subject: for example, *I can't really comment on; I don't think.*
(b) Thematic position filled either by the writer (*I don't think there's much in . . . it*) or simple unnominalized noun phrases naming postmodernism: *most of this stuff, it.*
(c) Use of contractions and idioms: for example, *can't, don't, understand a word of it.*
(d) Low level of nominalization: *activity.*
(e) Frequent use of action verbs: *go to conferences, get cushy jobs, write a lot of articles.*

Expression of attitude
(a) Frequent use of intensifying or minimizing adverbs: *really, pretty, very, totally, more.*
(b) Frequent use of attitudinally loaded lexical items ('snarl' words): *stuff, fad, intriguing, device, cushy, radical.*

Assumed knowledge
(a) Rather than technical lexis, everyday vocabulary is used: *stuff, people, cushy, a lot of.*
(b) Indirect reference to the Bible: *more radical than thou.*

Note that to complete this first step of R&G analysis, the specification of language differences, we need to be able to draw on a detailed description of grammatical and discourse patterns in English.

The second step in an R&G analysis is to try to *explain* the linguistic differences enumerated in the first step. One obvious explanation for the differences is that each text must have happened in a very different social context. And of course that is true: text 1 comes from a textbook, and so occurs in a written, academic context; text 2 is an excerpt from a public speech, a face-to-face encounter with a generalist audience.[2]

Our explanation has highlighted a very important observation about text: that each text appears to carry with it some influences from the context in which it was produced. Context, we could say, gets 'into' text by influencing the words and structures that text-producers use.

We can push our explanation further by trying to specify just what dimensions of social context appear to have an impact on the language of texts. With texts 1 and 2 we can note that choices of vocabulary and structure are influenced by three main contextual dimensions. Firstly, the difference in the formality between the texts can be related to the degree of feedback that was possible between the text-producer and his audience, the principal contrast being between spoken and written situations. If we analysed a large sample of written language and compared that with a large sample of spoken language, we would find differences similar to those we have noted for texts 1 and 2: written language will use fewer personal references, greater nominalized vocabulary, fewer action verbs, with meanings packed densely into complex noun phrases. We refer to this dimension of the context as the *mode*.

Our second cluster of linguistic differences (the absence/presence of attitudinal and evaluative choices) relates to the roles being played by each text-producer: in text 1 the role taken on by the writer is that of 'educator' and in text 2 it is that of 'social commentator/radical critic'. The language of the texts illustrates the discourse roles to which these social roles give access: social critics express attitudes and judgements, while educators (in our culture) must limit their expression of attitude or express it in disguised ways. This role dimension of context is referred to as the *tenor* of a situation.

Finally, the contrast between technical and everyday vocabulary can be related to the degree of familiarity with the topic that each text-producer is assuming in his audience. As we saw above, this is expressed partly through the choice of words which have very precise, technical meanings within the field of the textbook (cultural studies). Assumed knowledge is also realized through the 'other contexts and other texts' to which the audience is assumed to have access: in the first text, the audience is assumed to know who Susan Sontag and Leslie Fiedler are, whereas in the second text, the only assumed shared text is that of the Bible. Thus, both technicality of lexis and sources of intertextual references are significant indicators of what we call the *field* of the discourse.

Thus, we can find in the immediate situational contexts dimensions which help to explain why each text uses the linguistic patterns that it does. The analysis of these two texts has demonstrated that linguistic differences between texts can be correlated with differences in the contexts in which the texts were produced.

It is significant that we identified not just one, but several, clusters of patterns that differentiated the texts. Similarly, we identified not just one, but several contextual dimensions that had 'got into' the texts. This plurality suggests that a text is the weaving together simultaneously of several different strands of meanings. If we ask, for example, what text 1 'is about' (that is, what it means), we need to recognize that it is about more than one thing at a time. On the one hand, the text makes meanings about a reality (what postmodernism is, who was involved in its development, etc.). But these *ideational* meanings are not the only meanings the text is making. In addition, the text is also saying something about the writer's attitudes to his topic and his role relationship with his readers. These are the *interpersonal* meanings of the text. Finally, through its strand of *textual* meanings, the text is saying something about how it is organized as a linguistic event (that is, that it is a written text, and should be read as such).

It is these notions of the strands of meanings in text, and their correlation with contextual dimensions, that give approaches to R&GT

their two common themes. Firstly, they focus on the detailed *analysis* of variation in linguistic features of discourse: that is, there is explicit, ideally quantifiable, specification of lexical, grammatical and semantic patterns in text. Secondly, R&GT approaches seek to *explain* linguistic variation by reference to variation in context: that is, explicit links are made between features of the discourse and critical variables of the social and cultural context in which the discourse is enacted. *Register* and *genre* are the technical concepts employed to explain the meaning and function of variation between texts.

The concept of *register* is a theoretical explanation of the common-sense observation that we use language differently in different situations. More technically, contextual dimensions can be seen to impact on language by making certain meanings, and their linguistic expressions, more likely than others. We can say that context places certain meanings 'at risk'. The notion of 'at risk' can be demonstrated initially with the example of meals. When it comes to what to eat, those of us in the affluent West are generally faced with options to choose among. But dimensions of the mealtime context, principally what time of day it is and who we will be eating the meal with, will make certain choices more or less likely. Thus, if it is morning and you are in your ordinary domestic context, you are more likely to reach for the cereal and toast than to whip up a quick pavlova or put a chicken in the oven to roast. This relationship is probabilistic rather than deterministic: while certain foods are more likely to be chosen than others given the context, there is nothing to stop you from eating roast chicken and pavlova for breakfast if you so decide.

Similarly with language, key dimensions of the social context (such as whether the interactants can see and hear each other or not, whether they share the same background knowledge, and whether they have strong attitudes to express) will make certain meanings more likely to be made. Thus, in face-to-face context most university lecturers are more likely to begin their classes with 'Well, now today we're going to have a look at some ideas about an intellectual movement that's come to be called post-modernism', whereas they are more likely to begin Chapter 1 of a textbook with 'In this book it will be suggested that the intellectual movement known as postmodernism'. However, again the relationship is probabilistic not deterministic: some lecturers do in fact begin their face-to-face encounters with students by announcing that 'It will be suggested in this lecture that the intellectual movement known as postmodernism', making linguistic choices that the flagging interest of their students might suggest to them are more appropriate in a different context.

Theorizing the language/context relationship (just what dimensions of context matter to text, and how context gets 'into' text) is a central concern of register theorists. In subsequent sections we review formulations that range from the relatively 'weak' position of ethnographers such as Hymes (1972; 1974), who posit that a rather disparate number of dimensions of context have an *impact* on text, to the 'strong' position, associated with

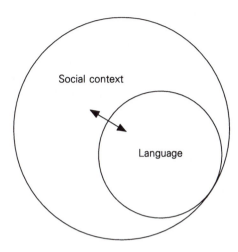

Figure 9.1   *Register theory: relating language to context*

social semiotic approaches (for example, Halliday, 1978; 1985a) which claim that texts are in fact the *realization* of a finite and very limited number of critical contextual dimensions. It is the interactive nature of this realizational relationship between social context and language that will be developed throughout this chapter, as we gradually elaborate on the simple model captured in Figure 9.1.

Given that texts are semantically multidimensional (are making more than one meaning at a time), discourse analysts need also to offer an explanation of the coherence most texts achieve. If we return to texts 1 and 2, we can note that one of the devices which helps to weave the three strands of meanings together into a coherent whole is the writer's use of the cohesive resources of the language. Choices of demonstrative articles and pronouns which co-refer to participants (people, places, things) introduced by noun phrases earlier in the text (for example, *it, these critics*), and the use of conjunctions to stamp logical relations between parts of the text (*although, if*), give the texts *cohesion* (Halliday and Hasan, 1976; Martin, 1992). But a further significant device which enables each text to function as a semantic unit comes from the *generic structure* being enacted by the texts.

For in addition to register variation, texts may also exhibit variation in terms of *genre*. The term 'genre' is most familiar as it is used in traditional literary studies, where it refers to 'types of literary productions', with short stories, poems, novels, and plays being the principal different genres recognized, each genre in turn being sub-classified so that we have the range of genres we might find in a bookshop (spy novels, crime novels, romance novels, etc.) or in an anthology (ballads, epics, lyrics, etc.). The use of genre as a concept in R&GT differs from this traditional use in two important respects. Firstly, linguistic definitions of genre draw on Russian literary theorist Bakhtin's (1986) identification of speech genres as 'relatively stable types' of interactive utterances. This broadens genre to include everyday as well as literary genres, in both written and spoken modes. Thus, a transactional encounter such as buying meat at the butcher's is a genre, as is a recipe in a magazine or a staff meeting in the workplace. Secondly, linguists define genres functionally in terms of their social purpose. Thus, different genres are different ways of using language to achieve different culturally established tasks, and texts of different genres are texts which are achieving different purposes in the culture.

Genre provides further explanation of the differences between texts 1 and 2. While text 1 is fulfilling the cultural purpose of 'tertiary education', text 2 is fulfilling a very different cultural purpose of 'delivering social commentary', or perhaps more accurately 'stirring'. We can see these differences of purpose reflected both in the way the texts achieve coherence and in the way each text unfolds dynamically. Thus, in the way the types of meanings of the text co-occur we recognize a pattern typical of a particular genre. With text 1, for example, we recognize that to write in an objective way about a technical topic taking on the role of educator is quite consistent with the cultural task of 'making a textbook'. We also recognize a text's genre by the sequence of functionally distinct stages or steps through which it unfolds. In text 1 the writer moves us through the stages: date the term, give direct definition from early source, unpack and elaborate on definition, and summarize early uses of term. Text 2, on the other hand, has very different stages: it begins with a stage of personal difficulties with concept, then offers a definition, followed by a dismissal of concept, and justification of dismissal. Each text is in turn an excerpt only, taken from complete texts which have clearly different staging structures: text 1 is from Chapter 7 of a text which stages its content by moving chronologically through different academic movements, culturally a very familiar staging structure for a textbook.

Thus, the major linguistic reflex of differences in purpose is the staging structure by which a text unfolds. Genre theory suggests that texts which are doing different jobs in the culture will unfold in different ways, working through different stages or steps. Again, this relationship between context and text is theorized as probabilistic, not deterministic: an interactant setting out to achieve a particular cultural goal is most likely to initiate a text of a particular genre, and that text is most likely to unfold in a particular way – but the potential for alternatives is inherent in the dialogic relationship between language and context.

R&GT is, then, a theory of functional variation: of how texts are different, and the contextual motivations for those differences. A useful R&GT is one that will allow for both textual *prediction* and contextual *deduction*. That is, given a description of the context, it should be possible to predict the meanings that will be at risk and the linguistic features likely to be used to encode them. Alternatively, given a text, it should be possible to deduce the context in which it was produced, as the linguistic features selected in a text will encode contextual dimensions, both of its immediate context of production and of its generic identity, what task the text is achieving in the culture.

For prediction and deduction to be possible, analysts must be able to relate categories of context to the detailed specification of language patterns. That is, R&GT must provide a methodology for textual analysis, *and* it must provide an account of how situational and cultural context are expressed systematically in language choices. Thus, a fully developed R&G theory involves both a detailed account of language, *and* a theory of context and the relationship between context and language.

In this chapter we will concentrate on outlining the systemic functional approach to register and genre analysis. The systemic approach not only provides a detailed description of the functions and structures of English (cf. Halliday, 1985b), but goes further and relates the contextual dimensions of register to the semantic and grammatical organization of language itself. This results in a coherent, functional explanation of why particular dimensions of context are important and others not. Similarly, the systemic approach has been developing detailed specifications of the staging structures and realization features of different genres, as well as accounts of how genres can relate to and evolve into other genres, thus providing replicable and functionally motivated accounts of different genres in our culture.

A further dimension of the systemic approach which space allows us only to touch on briefly in this chapter is that it takes contextual explanation one step further, by recognizing that the differences between texts are also the reflection of a more abstract contextual dimension that we could call *ideology*. Ideology refers to the positions of power, the political biases and assumptions that all social interactants bring with them to their texts. Thus, while text 1 tacitly takes up and supports the positions of academic ideology (seeking to trace development of the concept, withholding personal opinion, etc.), text 2 introduces an ideology of humanistic morality. In each case, the ideological perspectives have functional motivations: they tell us something about the interests of the text-producers. Thus, the text-producer in text 1 wants us to recognize him as a good teacher, and so adheres to traditional academic ideology, whereas in text 2 the speaker's interests are served by debunking the 'myths' of an academic movement which may represent a challenge to his own preferred perspective.

At this point we will look briefly at the work of linguists who have worked on modelling social context.

Brief History

Within the various European traditions, the most influential body of work on register[3] stems from what we might refer to as 'British contextualism'

(Monaghan, 1979). This work was influenced by the anthropologist Malinowski and his discussions of meaning in context. For Malinowski (1923; 1935), this included the more 'immediate' context of situation of an utterance and the more 'global' context of culture. These ideas inspired Firth (1957a; 1957b) to build context into his model of language (alongside grammar, morphology, lexis, phonology and phonetics). Firth (1957b/1968: 176–7) outlined a provisional schema for application to 'typical repetitive events in the social process':

1   The participants: persons, personalities and relevant features of these.
    (a)   The verbal action of the participants.
    (b)   The non-verbal action of the participants.
2   The relevant objects and non-verbal and non-personal events.
3   The effect of the verbal action.

Firth's students and their colleagues developed this framework in various directions. Halliday's reworking of the schema is outlined below (taken from Halliday, 1985a/1989: 12; for closely related neo-Firthian schemata see Ellis and Ure, 1969; Gregory, 1967; Gregory and Carroll, 1978; Ure and Ellis, 1977):

1   *Field, the social action*: what is happening, the nature of the social action that is taking place: what it is that the participants are engaged in, in which the language figures as some essential component.
2   *Tenor, the role structure*: who is taking part, the nature of the participants, their statuses and roles: what kinds of role relationship obtain among the participants, including permanent and temporary relationships of one kind or another, both the types of speech role that they are taking on in the dialogue and the whole cluster of socially significant relationships in which they are involved.
3   *Mode, the symbolic organization*: what part language is playing, what it is that the participants are expecting the language to do for them in the situation: the symbolic organization of the text, the status that it has, and its function in the context, including the channel (is it spoken or written or some combination of the two?) and also the rhetorical mode, what is being achieved by the text in terms of such categories as persuasive, expository, didactic, and the like.

One of the attractions of this particular model of context for Halliday's theory is that it fits nicely with his model of the organization of language itself. Beginning in the 1950s, his work on Chinese and, later, English grammar led him to the observation that choices for meaning are organized into three main components, which he refers to as *ideational, interpersonal* and *textual* metafunctions. As previewed in the first section, the ideational metafunction is concerned with mapping the 'reality' of the world around us (who's doing what to whom, when, where, why, how). The interpersonal metafunction is concerned with organizing the social reality of people we interact with (by making statements, asking questions, giving commands;

Table 9.1   *The functional organization of language in relation to categories for analysing context*

Metafunction (organization of language)	Register (organization of context)
Interpersonal meaning (resources for interacting)	Tenor (role structure)
Ideational meaning (resources for building content)	Field (social action)
Textual meaning (resources for organizing texts)	Mode (symbolic organization)

saying how sure we are; saying how we feel about things). The third metafunction, the textual, is concerned with organizing ideational and interpersonal meanings into texts that are coherent and relevant to their context (what we put first, what last; how we introduce characters and keep track of them with pronouns; what we leave implicit and what we spell out).

Halliday (for example, 1978) makes the important point that a model of language of this kind can be 'naturally' related to the organization of context, with ideational meaning used to construct field (the social action), interpersonal meaning used to negotiate tenor (the role structure) and textual meaning used to develop mode (symbolic organization). This resonance between the functional organization of meaning in language and Halliday's model of context is outlined in Table 9.1. As far as we know, British contextualism is the only tradition that suggests this kind of direct correlation between the functional organization of language and the organization of context. Ghadessy (1988; 1993) provides useful collections of studies within this general framework. For illustrative work on one specific register (scientific English), see Halliday and Martin (1993).

Among the American traditions, the most comparable work is that evolving out of the anthropological linguistics inspired by Sapir and Whorf (Hymes and Fought, 1981). Schiffrin (1994), in her introduction to American discourse analysis, surveys this work under the heading of 'ethnography of communication' (see also Saville-Troike, 1982).[4] The best known schema for analysing context deriving from this tradition is Hymes's (1972) SPEAKING grid (Table 9.2). A grid of this kind would function as a kind of ethnographer's check-list, as they observe the ways in which speakers make sense of what counts as a communicative event. This knowledge about how to communicate was glossed by Hymes (for example, 1974) as *communicative competence*. One of the best known studies in this tradition is that of Heath (1983), who studied communicative events involving literacy in an Appalachian community.

Within the various European traditions, a major strand of work on genre staging[5] again derives from British contextualism (Monaghan, 1979). Mitchell (1957) is the classic Firthian study and examines the language of

Table 9.2 *Hymes's SPEAKING grid for the analysis of the components of communicative events*

S	Setting	Physical circumstances
	Scene	Subjective definition of an occasion
P	Participants	Speaker/sender/addressor
		Bearer/receiver/audience/addressee
E	Ends	Purposes and goals
		Outcomes
A	Act sequence	Message form and content
K	Key	Tone, manner
I	Instrumentalities	Channel (verbal, non-verbal, physical)
		Forms of speech drawn from community repertoire
N	Norms of interaction and	Specific properties attached to speaking
	interpretation	Interpretation of norms within cultural belief system
G	Genre	Textual categories

buying and selling in the Moroccan marketplace. His analysis involved setting up text structures of the following kind for market auction and market transaction contexts (in the formula, ^ stands for the typical sequence of realization, although Mitchell notes that some variability and overlap is found):

Market auction
Auctioneer's Opening ^ Investigation of Object of Sale ^ Bidding ^ Conclusion

Market transaction
Salutation ^ Enquiry as to Object of Sale ^ Investigation of Object of Sale ^ Bargaining ^ Conclusion

The most exemplary 'neo-Firthian' study is Sinclair and Coulthard's (1975) analysis of classroom discourse. The distinctive feature of this study is its attempt to build up generic structure, beginning with the smallest units of analysis, the act, and proceeding through moves, exchanges and trans-actions to the largest unit, the lesson. Developments in this tradition are surveyed in Coulthard and Montgomery (1981) and Coulthard (1992).

Australian work on genre staging was initially inspired by Hasan (1977; 1984; 1985; Halliday and Hasan, 1980). Hasan introduces the notion of *generic structure potential* to generalize the range of staging possibilities associated with a particular genre. Her analysis of staging in service encounters and nursery tales is outlined below, along with a key interpreting the structural conventions in the formula:

Service encounter
[(Greeting) (Sale Initiation) ^] [(Sale Enquiry$_n$) {Sale Request ^ Sale Compliance}$_n$ ^ Sale ^] Purchase ^ Purchase Closure (^Finis)

Nursery tale
[(#Placement# ^) Initiating Event$_n$ ^] Sequent Event$_n$ ^ Final Event [^
(Finale) (Moral)]

Key
(X)	optionality
X ^ Y	sequence
X Y	order
[X Y]	domain of order
X$_n$	iteration
[X ^ Y]$_n$	enclosed elements proportionately iterative
#X# Y	enclosed element interspersed/included in Y

Among the American traditions, the most comparable work[6] is that developed by variation theorists, particularly Labov (Labov and Waletzky, 1967; Labov, 1972). Work on narrative of personal experience has been particularly influential. Labov and Waletzky's analysis is outlined below, making use of the conventions introduced above:

Narrative of personal experience
(Abstract) ^ [(#Orientation#) ^ Complication] ^ [#Evaluation# ^ Resolution] ^ (Coda)

For further discussion of narrative genres, see Ochs in Chapter 7 of this volume.

Current State of Theories

The previous section outlined similarities and differences in approaches to register and genre analysis within European and American traditions. In this section we will concentrate on presenting recent developments to the European approach, mainly from the perspective of systemic functional linguistics.[7]

As noted above, Halliday's approach to register emphasizes systematic links between the organization of language and the organization of context. The relationship between the language components (the ideational, interpersonal and textual metafunctions) and context variables (field, tenor and mode) is termed *realization*. Read from the perspective of context, realization refers to the way in which different types of field, tenor and mode condition ideational, interpersonal and textual meaning; read from the perspective of language, realization refers to the way in which different ideational, interpersonal and textual choices construct different types of field, tenor and mode. This relationship is outlined in Figure 9.2, which maps metafunctions onto the model of language (the inner circle) and social context (the outer circle) presented in Figure 9.1.

When applying this model, systemic linguists typically draw on Halliday's (1985b) detailed functional-semantic description of the grammar of English

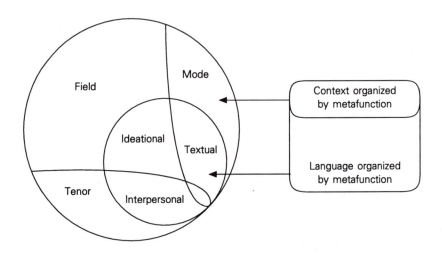

Figure 9.2   *Context and language in the systemic functional model*

Table 9.3   *Relationship between context, strata, and systems in the systemic functional model*

Context		Language	
Register variable	Type of meaning 'at risk'	Discourse-semantic patterns (cohesion)	Lexico-grammatical patterns
Field	Ideational	Lexical cohesion Conjunctive relations	Transitivity (case) Logico-semantic relations (taxis)
Tenor	Interpersonal	Speech function Exchange structure	Mood, modality, vocation, attitude
Mode	Textual	Reference (participant tracking)	Theme, Information structure Nominalization

and Halliday and Hasan's (1976) and Martin's (1992) work on cohesion and discourse analysis. Some of the variables typically considered are outlined in Table 9.3.

As a result of applying these delicate descriptions of language systems to a range of texts, new ways of characterizing field, mode and tenor variables have evolved. Martin (1992) for example offers a description of the mode of a situation in terms of two distance continua: (1) a continuum of spatial distance, referring to the amount of immediate feedback available between interactants in a discourse, and (2) a continuum of experiential distance, referring to the distance between language and the event in which it is

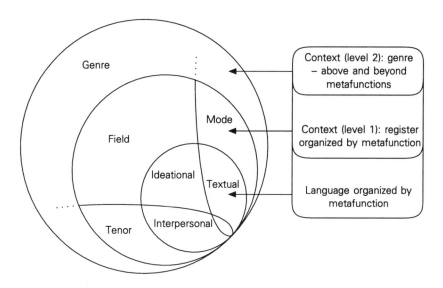

Figure 9.3   *Genre in relation to register and language*

involved (that is, whether language is accompanying or constituting the interactive event). Poynton (1985) offers a clarification of tenor as involving three continua of (1) power (ranging from equal to unequal), (2) frequency of contact (ranging from frequent to occasional), and (3) degree of affective involvement (ranging from high to low). Work on the register variable of field has concentrated on exploring the differences between contexts ranging from 'everyday/common-sense' to 'technical/specialized' (Halliday and Martin, 1993; Chapter 9; Rose et al., 1992). For examples of register analysis using the tools outlined in Table 9.3, see Halliday, 1985b/1994: Appendix 1; Eggins, 1994: Chapter 10; Martin, 1992).

Another major step in the development of a model of context along these lines has been the suggestion by Martin and colleagues (for example, Ventola, 1987; Martin, 1992) that two layers of context are needed – with a new level of genre posited above and beyond the field, mode and tenor register variables described above. Analysis at this level has concentrated on making explicit just which combinations of field, tenor and mode variables a culture enables, and how these are mapped out as staged, goal-oriented social processes. A great deal of this research has been pursued in educational contexts where it has formed the basis of Australia's distinctive genre-based literacy programs (Christie, 1991a; 1991b; 1994; Cope and Kalantzis, 1993; Hagan et al., 1993; Hasan and Williams, 1996; Martin, 1993). An outline of this stratified model of context is presented in Figure 9.3, which adds the level genre to the model outlined in Figure 9.2.

The following section provides an illustration of how this model of language and context is used in text analysis.

Analysis

To demonstrate the application of R&GT, we will compare and contrast the following two texts, taken from the first two pages of a booklet about dog obedience training provided free to residents by an inner-city council:[8]

Text 3: Introduction
(1a)All dogs are, by instinct, pack animals (b)and must have a leader – (c)as the dog's owner that should be you. (2a)To earn your dog's respect (b)you must possess or develop the leadership qualities of authority, consistency, kindness and patience. (3a)You must instil confidence (b)and be firm but never harsh. (4a)He will from time to time test your leadership, (b)so you must make sure from the beginning (c)that you are consistent. (5a)Dogs are like people (b)in that if you do not earn their respect (c)you will get very little in return (d)and this is where problems can arise.

(6a)As the dog's trainer you must have fundamental training knowledge and the ability to impart that knowledge to your dog. (7a)To achieve this (b)simply follow the home training method as set out in this booklet.

(8a)Dogs are the only animals that have complete affinity with people. (9a)They will give unconditional devotion and loyalty. (10a)They will protect you and your family, (b)asking nothing in return except responsible leadership and perhaps the occasional beef bone as a much coveted addition to their diet. (11a)A dog cannot reason as a human does (b)but they are highly intelligent. (12a)It is the dog owner's responsibility to teach him acceptable social behaviour. (13a)Your dog's acute senses and desire to please make the training process extremely simple. (14a)Dogs also have an excellent memory (b)which is a great help.

(15a)Dogs have a limited understanding of vocabulary – (b)so don't waste words. (16a)Each command must be a single syllable if possible (b)and be accompanied by the dog's name, (c)which should also be of a single syllable for preference, (c)or reduced to a single syllable for training. (17a. . .)For example, ((b)for the purposes of the program we will call our dog 'Sam') (. . .17a)the commands would be 'Sam Sit', 'Sam Down', 'Sam Stay'. (18a)Every command must be completed. (19a)If you command your dog to sit, (b)he must sit. (20a)Then he must be dismissed with a consistent, permanent word such as 'Relax'. (21a)This sequence is important, (b)the dog must know (c)that a lesson is only finished with your permission.

(22a)By following this program, (b)not only will you enjoy the rewards of a more responsive and controllable dog, (c)but you will build a lasting trust and friendship that otherwise may not have transpired.

Text 4: Message from Council
(1a)Marrickville Council believes (b)that the education of dog owners about their responsibilities is preferable to prosecutions and fines. (2a)To that end

the Council endorses all efforts to make dog owners aware of the Laws regarding their dog and the reason behind them. (3a)To assist in promoting increased dog awareness, (b)Council is supplying this booklet (c)as a tool for dog owners to become better equipped in the day-to-day management and care of their pet.

(4a)Dogs should be taught social behaviour at the earliest opportunity (b)so that they do not interfere with the quality of life of your neighbours and the general public.

(5a)Council is receiving an ever increasing number of reports of wandering dogs and barking dog incidents. (6a. . .)For the safety and protection of all, dogs, both large and small, (b)as well as those considered tame by their owners, (. . .6a)must be kept restricted to the confines of your property and (c)when in public places, (. . .6a)under effective control by means of a chain, cord or leash.

(7a)Another growing problem is animal faeces in public areas. (8a)There is a never ending outcry from residents (b)about dogs littering their front lawns and nature strips with faeces. (9a)Parks, foreshores and other public places are areas where people want to relax and enjoy life (b)and they should not have to tolerate dog droppings on their shoes or their children's hands. (10a)It is crucial that dog owners be aware of their responsibility to remove dog droppings in public areas.

(11a)The Council is hopeful (b)that by making dog owners aware of their responsibilities (c)and making it possible for them to undertake effective training of their dogs in their own homes, (d)the public will enjoy better facilities. (12a)Council Rangers are patrolling (b)and 'on-the-spot' Penalty Notices will be issued to owners who neglect their responsibilities.

Both texts seek to persuade readers to comply with a directive, and yet they do so in very different ways. Technically, the texts are from the same genre (directive), but exhibit variation in register (field, tenor, mode). We will now briefly explain the linguistic features which realize these contextual dimensions, and suggest reasons for the differences between the texts.

Our justification for claiming that both texts are directives comes from an analysis of generic structure in each text, for which we draw on Iedema's (1995, 1997) analysis of administrative texts. The directive or regulatory purpose of text 3 is achieved principally through the obligatory stage of command. To identify the command stage we refer to Halliday's (1985b/ 1994: 341ff) notion of *grammatical metaphor*, where he distinguishes *congruent* and *metaphorical* grammatical realizations of semantic choices. With metaphorical realizations there is a tension between meanings and wordings. For example, with indirect speech acts there is a mismatch between grammar and discourse function (such as the use of modalized interrogatives to realize commands). With congruent realizations the meanings match the wordings. For example, the most congruent grammatical form in

Table 9.4   *Schematic structure stages in text 3*

Functionally labelled stages of schematic structure	Clause domain	Purpose of stage	Key linguistic realizations
Enablement 1: facilitation	1–6	To explain one aspect of what is necessary if you are to successfully follow the command	Relational ('be') processes describing dogs as generic class; modulations of obligation
Command	7	To state the core directive motivating the text	Direct imperative; purpose clause (*to achieve this*)
Legitimization 1: reason	8–14	To justify compliance by explaining the nature of dogs	Positive evaluative lexis (*affinity, devotion, loyalty, desire to please*); dogs as Subject/Theme
Enablement 2: command specification	15–21	To clarify how to follow the method	'Dogs' Subject in relational processes describing their abilities; reader as Subject in clauses with modulations of obligation
Legitimization 2: purpose	22	To reinforce positive outcomes of following training method	Cause–consequence logical relations: positive lexis (*rewards, trust, friendship*); contrastive relation to negated situation (that otherwise may not have transpired)

which to realize the semantic act 'command' is the imperative. In text 3 the command is realized in paragraph 2: *To achieve this simply follow the home training method as set out in this booklet.* This direct imperative is the most congruent realization of the directive purpose of the text (of course, reinforcing meanings of obligation associated with this command stage are expressed prosodically throughout the text; imperatives and declaratives modulated with *must* occur in all paragraphs except the last). The other paragraphs of the text support this obligatory stage in two ways: either with enablements, stages which provide necessary information or procedures for the achievement of the command; or with legitimizations, which offer incentives and justifications for complying. Table 9.4 summarizes these stages as they appear in text 3.

We can state the schematic structure of text 3 in linear form as follows:

Enablement 1 ^ Command ^ Legitimization 1^ Enablement 2 ^ Legitimization 2

Table 9.5 *Schematic structure stages in text 4*

Functionally labelled stages of schematic structure	Clause domain	Purpose of stage	Key linguistic realizations
Enablement 1: orientation	1–3	To orient the reader to the purpose of the text	Thematizing of Council as agents in promoting/ supplying information; sets up lexis of 'awareness', 'punishment' (*prosecutions/ fines*)
Command	4	To direct readers to control their dogs' behaviour	Modulated declarative; purpose clause of justification
Legitimization 1: reason 1:	5–6	To offer a first reason for compliance with the command: so their dogs don't roam around wild	Modulated declarative, with nominalized abstracts (*safety and protection*) in purpose circumstance; manner circumstance (*by means of*)
Legitimization 2: reason 2:	7–10	To offer a second reason for compliance: so dogs don't poo everywhere	Thematizing of argument structure: (*another . . . problem*); modulated declaratives (*should not, it is crucial that*)
Legitimization 3: threat	11–12	To inform readers of sanctions associated with non-compliance	Lexis of punishment (*penalty, neglect*); manner clause (*by making dog owners aware*); institutionalized modulation (*responsibilities*)

Despite its very different 'tone', text 4 is also a directive text. The core command is expressed in the text in clause 4a: *Dogs should be taught social behaviour at the earliest opportunity*. The realization of this command involves two types of grammatical metaphor. One is interpersonal metaphor, that is tension in the relationship between speech act and clause mood; here the use of a modulated declarative rather than an imperative clause. The other is ideational metaphor, that is incongruence in the realization of actions and doings, typically their nominalization; so for example what has to be taught is the abstract concept *social behaviour*. A more congruent realization of this command involves unpacking the noun *behaviour* into its congruent process form (*to behave*), and as a consequence inserting the readers as elided actors, as in *You must teach your dogs to behave socially* (more congruently: *Teach your dogs to behave socially*).

Table 9.6 *Register variables in texts 3 and 4*

Register variable	Text 3	Text 4
Field: social action	Positive attributes/nature of dogs and rewards for owners	Negative dog behaviours and institutional punishments
Mode: symbolic organization	Lower experiential and interpersonal distance (closer to spoken language)	High experiential and interpersonal distance (written language)
Tenor: role structure	Power difference constructed on expertise: writers assert knowledge of dogs	Power difference constructed on institutional identity: power to punish is with the writers

Again, as with text 3, the command is supported by both enablement and legitimizations giving reasons, with an additional stage of threat occurring at the end of the text. The stages are summarized in Table 9.5.

Expressed linearly, the schematic structure of text 4 is:

Enablement 1 ^ Command ^ Legitimization 1 ^ Legitimization 2 ^ Legitimization 3

While the texts share the common stages of command, enablement and legitimization, text 3 shows a preference for enablements (a positive stage), while text 4 orients more to providing justifications for compliance, with the negative threat stage standing in contrast to text 3's positive enticement in the final enablement. This positive/negative distinction is also realized within the support stages. In text 3 support for the command stage is drawn from two sources: (1) ideas about dogs (their limitations and their positive responsive behaviour) and (2) implications for dog owners (as needing to display leadership). In a congruent form, then, text 3 is arguing: *you need to train your dog because this is what dogs are like!* In text 4, on the other hand, the supports for the command stage are largely negative: the enumeration of the problems dogs cause, and the punishments dog owners face for non-compliance. The message of text 4, then, is: *train your dogs – or else!*

These differences in the way dog owners are positioned to comply with the directives are encoded in different values for each of the register variables, as summarized in Table 9.6.

We will now briefly review the major linguistic patterns which realize these register differences.

Field

Differences in field are realized through both transitivity selections and lexical choices. In text 3, 'dogs' are the most frequent participants, and their natures are described through relational ('being') processes which describe or define them (1a, 5a, 8a, 11b), or possessive processes which enumerate their attributes (8a, 14a, 15a).

Dog owners are encoded both as needing certain attributes, in (2b)*you must possess or develop the leadership qualities of authority, consistency, kindness and patience*; and as actors in verbal and action processes, in (7b)*simply follow the home training method as set out in this booklet,* (19a)*If you command your dog to sit.*

In text 4, the major participant is the Council, which is represented as involved in several processes of consciousness: (1a)*Marrickville Council believes,* (11a)*The Council is hopeful.* The Council is also encoded as a benevolent actor: it *endorses, assists, supplies* and *receives.* By contrast, members of the Council's jurisdiction act only very obliquely, as the implied sources of the reports in (5a)*Council is receiving an ever increasing number of reports of wandering dogs and barking dog incidents*; as circumstantial to an existential process in (8a)*There is a never ending outcry from residents*; or as an amorphous group of 'people' in (9a)*Parks, foreshores and other public places are areas where people want to relax and enjoy life.*

Dog owners appear either as indirect participants (in prepositional phrases), as in (6a. . .)*For the safety and protection of all, dogs, both large and small,* (b)*as well as those considered tame by their owners*; or as people who act as a result of initiative from Council, for example they *become better equipped* or are *made aware.*

The apparent 'topic' of the text, *dogs,* never occur as the 'active' participants in any major clauses, only featuring once as actors in a non-finite dependent clause: ((8a)*There is a never ending outcry from residents* (b)*about dogs littering their front lawns and nature strips with faeces.* At other times dogs appear in the texts even less directly, through nominalized references to *dog droppings.* Thus dogs are encoded as non-initiatory, but under the control (and responsibility) of their owners.

The repeated reference to dog owners' *awareness* (3a, 11b) is an interesting strategy by which the regulative function of the text becomes disguised: rather than the text appearing to be about telling dog owners what to *do,* it becomes a text which merely helps dog owners to *think* about a problem. This allows the coercive and punitive role of the Council to be encoded very obliquely.

The main semantic domains developed by each text are seen through the lexical relations. In text 3 the main lexical strings are: (1) personal qualities (*leadership qualities, consistency, kindness, patience, confidence, respect*); and (2) control (*authority, firm, harsh, training, method, program, command, permission*). In text 4 the main lexical strings are: (1) awareness (*education, make aware, better equipped*); (2) control methods (*prosecution, fines, Laws, management, safety, protection, restricted, confines, control, responsibility, training, Penalty Notices, neglect, responsibilities*). While the strings in text 3 construe the relevant field as that of dog training, the strings in text 4 recontextualize dog training as an aspect of bureaucratic regulation.

Tenor

Differences in tenor are realized through (1) mood and (2) Subject choice. In text 3, the command function of the text is realized either congruently through direct imperatives (such as 7b, 15b), or through modulated declaratives (2b, 3a, 18a, 20a). The serial repetition of these command speech acts in which 'you', the reader, is Subject, enacts in a very direct way the power/status difference between writers and readers. High certainty modalities in text 3 (4a, 9a, 10a) encode the writers' position as experts.

In text 4, however, interpersonal metaphor is used to 'bury' the commands and displace the intended addressee (you, the reader), through modulated declaratives in which *dogs* are made subject and their owners either ellipsed or grammatically demoted to possessive pronoun status:

(4a)*Dogs should be taught social behaviour at the earliest opportunity* (b)*so that they do not interfere with the quality of life of your neighbours and the general public*;

(6a. . .)*For the safety and protection of all, dogs, both large and small . . . must be kept restricted to the confines of your property . . .*

The most frequent Subject in text 4, however, is the institutional entity, *the Council*, source of the directive. Assertions of obligation are encoded indirectly, as for example in: (10a)*It is crucial that dog owners be aware of their responsibility to remove dog droppings in public areas.* Congruently: *Remove your dog droppings!*

Mode

Differences in mode are realized through (1) nominalization and (2) Theme choice. The nominalizations in text 3 concern the qualities possessed by dogs (*affinity, desire to please*) and (good) dog owners (*leadership, authority, consistency, kindness, patience, confidence, training knowledge, training method, responsibility*, etc.). These nominalizations tend to construe specific types of behaviour as desirable qualities of the pet/owner relationship. The nominalizations in text 4 include: *education, responsibilities, prosecutions, fines, efforts, increased dog awareness, management, care, social behaviour, reports, barking dog incidents, safety, protection, confines, control*. These nominalizations tend to construe various aspects of the management process as institutional entities. One effect of these nominalizations is to increase the lexical density of the text (a higher proportion of the words are content-carrying rather than grammatical). Nominalizations also 'dress up' rather prosaic events in language more appropriate to constructing institutional authority. Thus, instead of saying that 'people complain frequently about other people's dogs barking', the text refers to *barking dog incidents*.

In addition, the ideational nominalizations work closely with the interpersonal incongruence noted above to enable the writers to construct distance between themselves and readers, as well as between themselves and the concrete events dealt with in the text. These effects can be demonstrated by a congruent rewrite of paragraph 4:

> Residents complain all the time that dogs shit on their front lawns and nature strips. People want to relax in parks, foreshores and other public places, but other people let their dogs shit there. Dogs should not shit there because then people get dog shit on their shoes and their kids pick it up in their hands. When your dog shits in a public place, you must clean it up.

Patterns of theme choice further support the dogs versus institution focus. Text 3 presents the dogs and the addressees as Theme most frequently and uses no marked Themes at all, while in text 4 the Council dominates as Theme.

While the positioning of dependent clauses as Theme in both texts is a realization of their written mode, the lower nominalization and more repetitive Theme in text 3 lessen both the interpersonal and experiential distance between reader and writers. Combined with the tenor choices discussed above, these features make the text sound more 'spoken' than text 4, which employs textual and interpersonal resources to maintain authoritarian distance.

To sum up this abbreviated genre and register analysis, we might conclude that text 3 directs by providing dog owners with some friendly advice about their beloved pet, whereas text 4 directs by constraining dog owners as rational subjects of reasoned bureaucratic control.

Summary and Conclusion

In this chapter we have explained how R&GT views text, and therefore the lexical, grammatical and semantic choices which constitute it, as both encoding and construing the different layers of context in which the text was enacted. The terms *register* (context of situation) and *genre* (context of culture) identify the two major layers of context which have an impact on text, and are therefore the two main dimensions of variation between texts. Within the approach outlined here, register and genre variation are two realizational planes in a social semiotic view of text. This view is inherently dialogic and interactive: text is both the realization of types of context, and the enactment of what matters to cultural members in situations. Just as texts are not neutral encodings of a natural reality but semiotic constructions of socially constructed meanings, so the task of R&GT is not merely the description of linguistic variation between texts. It must also involve analysts in exposing and explaining how texts serve divergent interests in the discursive construction of social life – including the interests of the discourse analysts themselves.

Recommended Reading

Bakhtin (1986), Cranny-Francis (1990): Bakhtin's paper is a good introduction to his thinking, which has been extremely influential in contemporary critical theory; Cranny-Francis exemplifies a social and historical orientation with respect to the evolution of feminist genre fiction. For further reading in the area of critical discourse analysis and register/genre theory, see Halliday (1978), Bernstein (1990), Fairclough (1992), Fuller (forthcoming), Kress (1985), Kress and Hodge (1988), Thibault (1991), Lemke (1995); the area of language and gender is foregrounded in Poynton (1993), Iedema and Eggins (1997); for the extension of R&GT to the analysis of other semiotic domains, see Kress and van Leeuwen (1990), O'Toole (1994).

Bazerman (1988), Swales (1990): Bazerman's discussion of Newton's writing is an excellent introduction to rhetorical approaches to genre, complementing in interesting ways Halliday and Martin (1993). Swales extends this work in his detailed study of scientific research articles. See also Bhatia, 1993.

Biber (1988), Labov (1972): Biber's book is a good introduction to quantitative approaches to register analysis, and complements Halliday's (1985c) qualitative analysis of mode. The Labov paper is his well-known study of the narrative of personal experience genre. For examples of quantitative studies based on systemic functional text analysis, see Eggins (1982), Horvath (1985). For recent work on probabilistic grammar see Halliday (1991; 1992a; 1992b; 1993).

Heath (1983), Schiffrin (1994): Heath provides an excellent example of ethnographic approaches to speech events. Schiffrin places this study within a spectrum of mainstream American approaches to discourse.

Mitchell (1957), Halliday and Hasan (1980), Halliday (1985c), Halliday and Martin (1993): Mitchell's paper is the outstanding example of Firthian approaches to context. Halliday and Hasan introduce systemic functional perspectives on register and generic structure. Halliday focuses on mode, while Halliday and Martin gather together a series of studies on the register and genres of scientific English. For collections of systemic-based register and genre studies, see Ghadessy (1988; 1993); for detailed work on casual conversation see Eggins and Slade (1997); for a closely related approach to register see Leckie-Tarry (1995).

Eggins (1994), Martin (1992), Matthiessen and Bateman (1991), Ventola (1987): Eggins provides a clear introduction to recent Australian perspectives on register and genre in relation to functional grammar. Martin develops discourse semantics as an interface between functional grammar and work on register and genre. Matthiessen and Bateman provide an introduction to systemic linguistics in a computational context, including consideration of less synoptic approaches to register issues (see also Bateman, 1989; Bateman and Paris, 1991; Paris, 1993). Ventola applies this model in an in-depth study of service encounters. See also Iedema et al., 1994 on media discourse. For recent developments in this tradition see Christie and Martin (1997).

Notes

1 For further discussion of the definition and identification of text in a systemic approach, see Halliday and Hasan (1976; 1980/1985: 10–11), Eggins (1994).

2 Text 1 is taken from Storey (1993: 155). Text 2 is from a speech by Professor Noam Chomsky (1995: 3).

3 In order to simplify the discussion, we will pass over the important work of the Prague School (see Garvin, 1964; Vachek, 1966); recently, their work on 'intellectualization' (see Havránek in Garvin, 1964) has been influential in Philippines' language planning (for example, Gonzalez, 1988).

4 Schiffrin (1994) explores the work of Gumperz and Goffman in a related chapter on 'interactional sociolinguistics'; Brown and Levinson's (1987) work in this tradition has been extremely influential.

5 There is of course a considerable body of relevant 'continental' work on narrative staging, including Barthes (1966), Propp (1968) (see Chapter 7 of this volume); Toolan (1988) provides an excellent overview.

6 For relevant tagmemic work on genre structure see Pike (1967; 1982), Pike and Pike (1983); and for important analysis of relationships among genres see Longacre (1974; 1976).

7 For a general introduction to systemic functional linguistics, see Eggins (1994). For a more detailed discussion and exemplification of points outlined in this section, see Halliday (1985b), Martin (1992).

8 Source: *Dogs: Non Aggressive Basic Obedience Training*, a booklet provided by Marrickville Council, Sydney, Australia, 1995, pp. 1, 2. Text 3 written by B.F. and S. Daly. Text 4 written by an unidentified council employee. Text is divided into ranking clauses.

References

Bakhtin, M.M. (1986) 'The problem of speech genres', in M.M. Bakhtin, *Speech Genres and other Late Essays* (trans. V. McGee). Austin, TX: University of Texas Press. pp. 60–102.

Barthes, R. (1966) 'Introduction to the structural analysis of narratives', *Communications*, 8. Reprinted in R. Barthes, *Image-Music-Text*. London: Fontana, 1977. pp. 79–124.

Bateman, J. (1989) 'Dynamic systemic-functional grammar: a new frontier', in *Systems, Structures and Discourse: Selected Papers from the Fifteenth International Systemic Congress. Word*, 40 (1–2): 263–86.

Bateman, J. and Paris, C. (1991) 'Constraining the deployment of lexicogrammatical resources during text generation: towards a computational instantiation of register theory', in E. Ventola (ed.), *Functional and Systemic Linguistics: Approaches and Uses*. Berlin: Mouton de Gruyter. pp. 81–106.

Bazerman, C. (1988) *Shaping Written Knowledge: the Genre and Activity of the Experimental Article in Science*. Madison, WI: University of Wisconsin Press.

Bernstein, B. (1990) *Class, Codes and Control. Vol. 4: The Structuring of Pedagogic Discourse*. London: Routledge.

Bhatia, V.K. (1993) *Analysing Genres: Language Use in Professional Settings*. London: Longman.

Biber, D. (1988) *Variation across Speech and Writing*. Cambridge: Cambridge University Press.

Brown, P. and Levinson, S. (1987) *Politeness*. Cambridge: Cambridge University Press.

Chomsky, N. (1995) 'Writers and intellectual responsibility', speech at NSW Writers' Centre, Sydney, 23 January. *Newswrite*, February: 3.

Christie, F. (1991a) 'First and second order registers in education', in E. Ventola (ed.), *Functional and Systemic Linguistics: Approaches and Uses*. Berlin: Mouton de Gruyter. pp. 235–56.

Christie, F. (1991b) 'Pedagogical and content registers in a writing lesson', *Linguistics and Education*, 3: 203–24.

Christie, F. (1994) *On Pedagogic Discourse*. Final Report of a Research Activity funded by the ARC, 1990–2. Melbourne: Institute of Education, University of Melbourne.

Christie, F. and Martin, J.R. (eds) (1997) *Geures and Institutions: Social Processes in the Workplace and School*. London: Cassell (Open Linguistics Series).

Cope, W. and Kalantzis, M. (1993) *The Powers of Literacy: a Genre Approach to Teaching Writing*. London: Falmer.

Coulthard, M.C. (ed.) (1992) *Advances in Discourse Analysis*. London: Routledge.

Coulthard, M.C. and Montgomery, M. (eds) (1981) *Studies in Discourse Analysis*. London: Routledge and Kegan Paul.

Cranny-Francis, A. (1990) *Feminist Fiction: Feminist Uses of Generic Fiction*. Cambridge: Polity.

Eggins, S. (1982) 'The primary school description study: a quantitative analysis of variation in texts'. Unpublished BA thesis, Linguistics Department, University of Sydney.

Eggins, S. (1994) *An Introduction to Systemic Functional Linguistics*. London: Pinter.

Eggins, S. and Slade, D. (1997) *Analysing Casual Conversation*. London: Cassell Academic.

Ellis, J. and Ure, J. (1969) 'Language varieties: register', in A.R. Meetham (ed.), *Encyclopedia of Linguistics: Information and Control*. Oxford: Pergamon. pp. 251–9.

Fairclough, N. (1992). *Discourse and Social Change*. Cambridge: Polity.

Firth, J.R. (1957a) 'Ethnographic analysis and language with reference to Malinowski's views', in R.W. Firth (ed.), *Man and Culture: an Evaluation of the Work of Bronislaw Malinowski*. London. pp. 93–118. Reprinted in F.R. Palmer (ed.), *Selected Papers of J.R. Firth, 1952–1959*. London: Longman, 1968. pp. 137–67.

Firth, J.R. (1957b) 'A synopsis of linguistic theory, 1930–1955', in *Studies in Linguistic Analysis* (special volume of the Philological Society). London: Blackwell. pp. 1–31. Reprinted in F.R. Palmer (ed.), *Selected Papers of J.R. Firth, 1952–1959*. London: Longman, 1968. pp. 168–205.

Fuller, G. (forthcoming) 'Cultivating science: negotiating discourse in the popular texts of Stephen Jay Gould', in J.R. Martin and R. Veel (eds), *Reading Science: Critical and Functional Perspectives on Discourses of Science*. London: Routledge.

Garvin, P. (ed.) (1964) *A Prague School Reader on Esthetics, Literary Structure and Style*. Georgetown: Georgetown University Press.

Ghadessy, M. (ed.) (1988) *Registers of Written English: Situational Factors and Linguistics Features*. London: Pinter.

Ghadessy, M. (ed.) (1993) *Register Analysis: Theory and Practice*. London: Pinter.

Gonzalez, A. (1988) 'The intellectualization of Filipino: agenda for the twenty-first century', *Philippine Journal of Linguistics*, special issue *Setting a Research Agenda for the Intellectualization of Filipino*, 19 (2): 3–6.

Gregory, M. (1967) 'Aspects of varieties differentiation', *Journal of Linguistics*, 3: 177–98.

Gregory, M. and Carroll, S. (1978) *Language and Situation: Language Varieties and their Social Contexts*. London: Routledge and Kegan Paul.

Hagan, P., Hood, S., Jackson, E., Jones, M., Joyce, H. and Manidis, M. (1993) *Certificate in Spoken and Written English*, 2nd edn. Sydney: NSW AMES and NCELTR.

Halliday, M.A.K. (1978) *Language as a Social Semiotic: the Social Interpretation of Language and Meaning*. London: Edward Arnold.

Halliday, M.A.K. (1985a) 'Context of situation', in M.A.K. Halliday and R. Hasan (eds), *Language, Context and Text*. Geelong, Vic.: Deakin University Press. pp. 3–14. Republished by Oxford University Press, 1989.

Halliday, M.A.K. (1985b) *An Introduction to Functional Grammar*. London: Edward Arnold. 2nd edn 1994.

Halliday, M.A.K. (1985c) *Spoken and Written Language*. Geelong, Vic.: Deakin University Press. Republished by Oxford University Press, 1989.

Halliday, M.A.K. (1991) 'Towards probabilistic interpretations', in E. Ventola (ed.), *Functional and Systemic Linguistics: Approaches and Uses*. Berlin: Mouton de Gruyter. pp. 39–61.

Halliday, M.A.K. (1992a) 'Language as system and language as instance: the corpus as a theoretical construct', in J. Svarrtvik (ed.), *Directions in Corpus Linguistics: Proceedings of Nobel Symposium 82, Stockholm, 4–8 August 1991*. Berlin: Mouton de Gruyter. pp. 61–77.

Halliday, M.A.K. (1992b) 'The act of meaning', in J.E. Alatis (ed.), *Georgetown University Round Table on Languages and Linguistics 1992: Language, Communication and Social Meaning*. Washington, DC: Georgetown University Press.

Halliday, M.A.K. (1993) 'Quantitative studies and probabilities in grammar', in M. Hoey (ed.), *Data, Description, Discourse: Papers on the English Language in Honour of John McH. Sinclair (on his Sixtieth Birthday)*. London: HarperCollins. pp. 1–25.

Halliday, M.A.K. and Hasan, R. (1976) *Cohesion in English*. London: Longman.

Halliday, M.A.K. and Hasan, R. (1980) *Text and Context: Aspects of Language in a Social-Semiotic Perspective*. Tokyo: Graduate School of Languages and Linguistics and the Linguistic Institute for International Communication, Sophia University. New edition published as *Language, Context, and Text: Aspects of Language in a Social-Semiotic Perspective*. Geelong, Vic.: Deakin University Press, 1985. Republished by Oxford University Press, 1989.

Halliday, M.A.K. and Martin, J.R. (1993) *Writing Science: Literacy and Discursive Power*. London: Falmer, and Pittsburg: University of Pittsburg Press.

Hasan, R. (1977) 'Text in the systemic-functional model', in W. Dressler (ed.), *Current Trends in Textlinguistics*. Berlin: Walter de Gruyter. pp. 228–46.

Hasan, R. (1984) 'The nursery tale as a genre', *Nottingham Linguistic Circular*, special issue *Systemic Linguistics*, 13: 71–102.

Hasan, R. (ed.) (1985) *Discourse on Discourse*. Canberra: Applied Linguistics Association of Australia, Occasional Papers 7.

Hasan, R. and Williams, G. (eds) (1996) *Literacy in Society*. London: Longman (Applied Linguistics and Language Study).

Heath, S.B. (1983) *Ways with Words: Language, Life, and Work in Communities and Classrooms*. Cambridge: Cambridge University Press.

Horvath, B. (1985) *Variation in Australian English: the Sociolects of Sydney*. London: Cambridge University Press.

Hymes, D. (1972) 'Models of the interaction of language and social life', in J. Gumperz and D. Hymes (eds), *Directions in Sociolinguistics: the Ethnography of Communication*. New York: Holt, Rinehart and Winston. pp. 35–71.

Hymes, D. (1974) *Foundations in Sociolinguistics: an Ethnographic Approach*. Philadelphia: University of Pennsylvania Press.

Hymes, D. and Fought, J. (1981) *American Structuralism*. The Hague: Mouton. (Janua Linguarum, Series Maior 102.)

Iedema, R. (1995) *Literacy of Administration (Write it Right Literacy in Industry Research Project – Stage 3)*. Sydney: Metropolitan East Disadvantaged Schools Program.

Iedema, R. (1997) 'The language of administration: the organising of human activity in formal institutions', in F. Christie and J.R. Martin (eds), *Genres and Institutions: Social Processes in the Workplace and School*. London: Cassell Academic.

Iedema, R. and Eggins, S. (1997) 'Gender, semiosis and women's magazines', in R. Wodak (ed.), *Gender and Discourse*. London: Sage.

Iedema, R., Feez, S. and White, P. (1994) *Media Literacy Industry Research Monograph 2*. Write it Right Project. Disadvantaged Schools Program, Metropolitan East, Sydney.

Kress, G. (1985) *Linguistic Processes in Socio-Cultural Practice*. Geelong, Vic.: Deakin University Press.

Kress, G. and van Leeuwen, T. (1990) *Reading Images*. Geelong, Vic.: Deakin University Press (Sociocultural aspects of language and education). (revised 1996 as *Reading Images: the Grammar of Visual Design*. London: Routledge).

Kress, G. and Hodge, R. (1988) *Social Semiotics*. London: Polity.

Labov, W. (1972) 'The transformation of experience in narrative syntax', in W. Labov (ed.), *Language in the Inner City*. Philadelphia: Pennsylvania University Press. pp. 354–96.

Labov, W. and Waletzky, J. (1967) 'Narrative analysis', in J. Helm (ed.), *Essays on the Verbal and Visual Arts. Proceedings of the 1966 Spring Meeting of the American Ethnological Society*. Seattle: University of Washington Press. pp. 12–44.

Leckie-Tarry, H. (1995) *Language and Context: a Functional Linguistic Theory of Register* (ed. D. Birch). London: Pinter.

Lemke, J.L. (1995) *Textual Politics: Discourse and Social Dynamics*. London: Taylor and Francis.

Longacre, R.E. (1974) 'Narrative vs other discourse genre', in R. Brend (ed.), *Advances in Tagmemics*. Amsterdam: North-Holland.

Longacre, R.E. (1976) *An Anatomy of Speech Notions*. Lisse: Peter de Ridder.

Malinowski, B. (1923) 'The problem of meaning in primitive languages', Supplement I to C.K. Ogden and I.A. Richards (eds), *The Meaning of Meaning*. New York: Harcourt Brace and World. pp. 296–336.

Malinowski, B. (1935) *Coral Gardens and their Magic*, vol. 2. London: Allen and Unwin.

Martin, J.R. (1992) *English Text: System and Structure*. Amsterdam: Benjamins.

Martin, J.R. (1993) 'Genre and literacy: modelling context in educational linguistics', *Annual Review of Applied Linguistics*, 13: 141–72.

Matthiessen, C.M.I.M. and Bateman, J. (1991) *Text Generation and Systemic Linguistics: Experiences from English and Japanese*. London: Pinter.

Mitchell, T.F. (1957) 'The language of buying and selling in Cyrenaica: a situational statement', *Hesperis*, 26: 31–71. Reprinted in *Principles of Neo-Firthian Linguistics*. London: Longman, 1975. pp. 167–200.

Monaghan, J. (1979) *The Neo-Firthian Tradition and its Contribution to General Linguistics*. Tübingen: Max Niemeyer.

O'Toole, M. (1994) *The Language of Displayed Art*. London: Leicester University Press.

Paris, C. (1993) *User Modelling in Text Generation*. London: Pinter.

Pike, K.L. (1967) *Language in Relation to a Unified Theory of the Structure of Human Behaviour*, 2nd edn. The Hague: Mouton.

Pike, K.L. (1982) *Linguistic Concepts: an Introduction to Tagmemics*. Lincoln: University of Nebraska Press.

Pike, K.L. and Pike, E.G. (1983) *Text and Tagmeme*. London: Pinter.

Poynton, C. (1985) *Language and Gender: Making the Difference*. Geelong, Vic.: Deakin University Press. Republished Oxford University Press, 1989.

Poynton, C. (1993) 'Grammar, language and the social: poststructuralism and systemic functional linguistics', *Social Semiotics*, 3 (1): 1–22.

Propp, V. (1968) *The Morphology of the Folktale*. Austin, TX: University of Texas Press.

Rose, D., McInnes, D. and Korner, H. (1992) *Scientific Literacy (Write it Right Literacy in Industry Research Project – Stage 1)*. Sydney: Metropolitan East Disadvantaged Schools Program.

Saville-Troike, M. (1982) *The Ethnography of Communication*. Oxford: Blackwell.

Schiffrin, D. (1994) *Approaches to Discourse*. Oxford: Blackwell.

Sinclair, J.McH. and Coulthard, R.M. (1975) *Towards an Analysis of Discourse: the English Used by Teachers and Pupils*. London: Oxford University Press.

Storey, J. (1993) *An Introductory Guide to Cultural Theory and Popular Culture*. Athens, GA: University of Georgia Press.

Swales, J.M. (1990) *Genre Analysis: English in Academic and Research Settings*. Cambridge: Cambridge University Press.

Thibault, P. (1991) *Social Semiotics as Praxis: Text, Social Meaning Making and Nabakov's 'Ada'*. Minneapolis, MN: University of Minnesota Press.

Ure, J. and Ellis, J. (1977) 'Register in descriptive linguistics and linguistic sociology', in O. Uribe-Villas (ed.), *Issues in Sociolinguistics*. The Hague: Mouton. pp. 197–243.

Toolan, M.J. (1988) *Narrative: a Critical Linguistic Introduction*. London: Routledge.

Vachek, J. (1966) *The Linguistic School of Prague*. Bloomington, IN: Indiana University Press.

Ventola, E. (1987) *The Structure of Social Interaction: a Systemic Approach to the Semiotics of Service Encounters*. London: Pinter.

10

Discourse Semiotics

Gunther Kress, Regina Leite-García and Theo van Leeuwen

Definition and Delimitation of the Field

The common-sense notion that language is *the* medium of representation and communication is still deeply entrenched in Western literate societies. It is common sense both in theory and in the lives of our everyday. In the humanities nothing matches the prestige of the academic disciplines founded on language or concerned with its investigation. They resist even now considering non-language materials as essential sources and materials for their activities.

Over the last two decades or so this common sense has come under sustained attack from two sources, one theoretical and one empirical. The former originated in the broad field of postmodernism, with the writings of Jacques Derrida (1976) particularly important. Feminist theory has launched a sustained attack on 'logocentrism', as a major effect of and support for the structures of patriarchy. The name of Julia Kristeva (1980) figures prominently here. The second has come from everyday communicational practices; it is simply the case that the communicational and representational landscape, the *semiotic landscape*, has changed in far-reaching ways over the last 40 years or so in the so-called developed countries. The visual is now much more prominent as a form of communication than it has been for several centuries, in the so-called developed world at least. This change is having effects on the forms and characteristics of texts. Not only is written language less in the centre of this new landscape, and less central as a means of communication, but the change is producing texts which are strongly *multi-modal*. That is, producers of texts are making greater and more deliberate use of *a range of representational and communicational modes* which co-occur within the one text. One effect of this change is that it has become impossible to read texts reliably by paying attention to written language alone: it exists as one representational element in a text which is always multi-modal, and it has to be read in conjunction with all the other semiotic modes of that text.

Multi-modality is not a new phenomenon; it has always been the case that a text was realized through a number of modes of representation and communication. Indeed it is impossible for that to be otherwise. As a medium of representation and communication, language exists only in its realizations; but from the moment when it is realized – whether in speech or in writing – it is *material*, substantial; and in this *substance* it is necessarily multi-modal. Written language, for instance, has to have a material of inscription, whether rock or clay, paper or plaster, brass or plastic. This material has specific meanings in particular cultures. A decision has to be made by a writer about the shape, 'the style' of letters which she or he wishes to use; about spacings; about the spatial display, the layout of this graphic substance on the material of inscription. The naturalization of logocentrism, which has characterized the last few centuries of Western alphabetical cultures, had obscured this always present multi-modality, and had allowed the entrenching of a belief in language as such. It is as this amaterial, abstracted and idealized form that language has been studied in the mainstream of linguistics during this century. The effects of that common sense still persist, in theory more than in practice.

The focus of this chapter is the development of ways of understanding the characteristics of multi-modal texts. That concern entails two independent but related projects. One is the analysis of the major modes of representation through which a particular text is realized, and in which it is produced. The second is an attempt to understand the culturally and historically produced potential of any one semiotic mode for making meaning. Our assumption is that specific modes – the visual, the gestural, sound, etc. – have potentials for making meaning and have limitations. This project necessitates attempts to discover the manner in which different modes are brought together, their respective contributions in the reader's making of meaning and, importantly, regularities of reading practices for (communities of) readers.

With this move from language to all the modes of representation invoked in the production of a text comes a necessary move from linguistics to semiotics – the systematic investigation of human semiosis in all modes employed in a cultural group, written and spoken language included.

This is a new concern. Discourse analysis has, on the whole, focused on the linguistically realized text. In the multi-modal approach the attempt is to understand all the representational modes which are in play in the text, in the same degree of detail and with the same methodological precision as discourse analysis is able to do with linguistic text. And although screen theory and studies of popular culture, for instance, have all dealt variously with multi-modal texts there has not, we insist, been a similar attempt to focus on the particular regularities of each semiotic mode, on the regularities of their combination, or on their respective valuation in a given culture.

Ours is not a conventional semiotic analysis. It differs from established analyses of images in advertising, as for instance in the work of Judith Williamson; it is not film analysis, or art criticism, even though we draw inspiration from many of these. Our focus is on textuality, on the social origins and production of text as much as on the reading of text. We call this practice social semiotics to draw attention to all forms of meaning making as a social activity, set in the field of politics; in structures of power; and subject therefore to the contestations arising out of the differing interests of the makers of texts. This leads to one telling difference between social semiotics and conventional forms of semiotics. We assume that the *interests* of the maker of a sign lead to *a motivated relation between signifier and signified*, and therefore to motivated signs. The maker of the sign seeks to produce the most apt representation of her or his meaning. The sign-maker's *interest* is therefore coded directly in the formal means of representation and communication. This is in total contrast to the usual assumptions in Saussurian semiotics, where that relation has been treated as an arbitrary one in most instances (Saussure, 1983). Ideology is thus a factor of all the modes involved. In this we differ also from analysts who have treated visual representations as outside ideology, the visual being treated as transparently representational, though open to ideological uses in communication.

This assertion may seem paradoxical given the emphasis in many analyses on ideological issues, exploitation through sexist practices, for instance. Yet in these, the visual is treated as a transparent medium: whether in the use of representations of women's bodies; of symbols of unspoilt nature; or of visions of family life; all are treated as transparently 'there', so that meaning can be read off, unproblematically, from the overt 'content' of images. Our emphasis, by contrast, is on the systematic structuring of the visual, on a 'visual syntax' rather than as hitherto on a visual lexis.

The Development of the Field

In this chapter we focus on two aspects of multi-modal texts: the visual, and written language. Our reasons for this are theoretical and methodological: we want to provide generally applicable ways of thinking, and some instances of description, rather than a coverage of a wide range of semiotic modes. So we do not discuss sound – whether as speech, as music, or as 'soundtrack'. We do not discuss the body as a medium of representation – whether as dance, as ballet, or as sign-language; and so on. We take as given the advances in discourse analysis, which for us includes all work in the theory of text, as they are documented in this and its companion volume, and therefore focus on developments in the study of the visual mode, on many of which our own ideas in this area are founded. Concerns with the visual span many quite distinct areas, from the psychology of perception to the study of fine art, from an interest in advertising texts to the development of textbooks, from theorizations of photography to concerns in design, and importantly, in this century particularly, the study of film.

In this section we provide very brief indications of work in photography, in art criticism, in the analysis of advertising images, and in film theory, as examples of kinds of work which have been done. We give somewhat more space to a discussion of classical semiotics in the form of the work particularly of Roland Barthes.

Two distinctions will help to focus more closely on previous work. While our ideas on the organization of visual representation are strongly indebted to the writings of scholars such as Ernst Gombrich and Rudolf Arnheim, our interests are not focused on aesthetic aspects of visual representation. Our interest, including images classified as aesthetic, is from the point of view of representation and communication, rather than from that of 'expression', as it has usually been in relation to works of art. Consequently while many of our insights come from art theory, our terminology generally does not. We are less concerned with 'volumes' and 'placement', with 'balance' and with 'weight', than with 'informational structure', with 'modal effects', with 'transitivity relations', with the expression of interpersonal, social, and attitudinal meanings.

Secondly, in our view, much work on the visual has remained at the level of 'vocabulary', to use an analogy. Of course, in the aesthetic vocabulary of Arnheim there is attention to a syntax of the visual aesthetic. However, in much analysis of advertising, or of images in textbooks, there has been a preoccupation with the visual equivalent of lexis: what is represented? How is it represented? A typical example would be a discussion of the use of a representation of the female body to 'connote' aspects of femininity, of sexuality, of eroticism, transferred to a particular commodity. Similarly with other 'lexis': whether of pine forests to suggest freshness, tall grass to suggest 'naturalness'. For us, such interests are analogous to content analysis. We refer to this 'lexical' aspect as the iconography of the visual (analogous to 'lexicography'). Our interest, however, lies specifically in the analogue of grammatical/syntactic structures of visual representations. Here little theory or description of a plausible kind exists.

'Classical Semiotics': Christian Metz and Roland Barthes

That judgement might seem dismissive of the work of at least two semioticians who have written widely on this: the Parisian semioticians Christian Metz (1971) and Roland Barthes (1973; 1977; 1984). The former's work on descriptions of filmic text in particular constitutes a sustained development of a set of terms, a metalanguage, and a methodology for the analysis and description of that medium (at least in his earlier work, before his psychoanalytic period). From our perspective the problem with the work of Metz lies in its reliance on categories developed in linguistics, taken as an adequate descriptive language for the multi-modal filmic text. This misses precisely the inherent constraints and possibilities of a particular mode, by transposing theoretical and descriptive categories developed in relation to one multiple mode (spoken and written) *language*, to another, *film*.

Our difficulty with Barthes is different, though related. Barthes provided, over a period of three decades, a range of analytic writings dealing with the whole spectrum of human semiosis – food, fashion, entertainment, art, music, photography, etc. – and established, whether in his theoretical writing, in his literary analyses, or in his journalistic commentary on the mundane, evidence of the systematicness and connectedness of meaning in a multiplicity of cultural modes. Wherever he turned his analytical eye, he provided precision and sharpness of insight. Yet in his writings language remains the 'mastercode', the form of representation which provides the central means of thinking about and comparing other modes of representation: it remains the most fully articulated form of human representation and communication. We by contrast assume always that language is one of a (large) number of modes of communication which are in play; it may be the mastercode, as it is in this text now, or it may not, as when adolescents are engaged with an electronic game; or when a film director *envisages* a shot or a scene, and gets a whole range of other participants to *enact*, to perform – mostly non-verbally – that envisaged scene as a text.

What we retain from the works of Barthes and Metz is their insistence on the need for developing a single, comprehensive means for talking about the differing modes used in representation and communication. In our view, all systems of human communication must serve three requirements:

1 to represent and communicate relevant aspects of the social relations of those who are engaged in communication
2 to represent and communicate those events, states of affairs, perceptions, which the communicator wishes to communicate
3 to enable the production of messages which have coherence, internally as a text, and externally with relevant aspects of the semiotic environment (the 'context', so-called).

These requirements correspond closely to Michael Halliday's (1978; 1985) three metafunctions of language: the interpersonal, the ideational, and the textual metafunction. We might be thought therefore to fall into the same error as the Paris School semioticians, in taking over categories developed for the description of language and extending them to a different mode. However, our assumption is that Halliday's categories can be used as abstract and general categories applicable to all human social semiosis, and not specific to language alone. The representational and communicational potentials of a particular mode, and their cultural and historical development in a particular society, then need mode-specific descriptions.

For instance, the potentials of gesture have been developed into fully articulate representational and communicational systems, which need to be understood and described in terms of that mode and not, as has been the case until quite recently, in terms borrowed from an amalgam of the distinct modes of spoken and written language.

Roland Barthes's extensive writing on the visual spans a period of some 20 years, from the early 1960s ('The third meaning') to his late *Camera Lucida* (1984). Barthes focused on the question whether the visual, and photography in particular, was a fully semiotic mode of representation. The question for him was whether the photographic/visual was an analogic mode, directly and transparently representing events and objects in the world, or whether it was a culturally formed medium and therefore transformative in its effects in representation. He gradually moved from an initial position which saw photography as unmediated, as a direct, analogue representation in which only under special circumstances some element is transformed and thereby drawn into semiosis (his 'third meaning' in the early article of that name), to a later position in which photography is seen as generally transformative, but where under certain circumstances one element in a photograph may escape the transformative effects of semiosis, and may remain beyond the conscious semiotic determination of the maker of a photographic image. This is the 'punctum' of *Camera Lucida*.

Barthes's question is central from the point of view of this chapter. If some communicational and representational modes are not entirely culturally and socially formed, and therefore enable unmediated representations of some external entity, 'an analogon of reality' in Barthes's words, then there is not much need to theorize the multi-modal text, other than perhaps its readings in terms of preferences of readers' practices. If all other modes are socially and culturally formed, and *not* transparent, then there is the need for a project of the kind we envisage.

Over the last two decades theoretical trends in this respect have been somewhat confused and even contradictory. Many analyses of texts of popular culture both stress the importance of visual elements and yet at the same time treat them as relatively unproblematically 'readable'. So in Judith Williamson's (1978) detailed study of images in advertising, the issue is to describe the effects and meanings of conjunctions of visually represented icons – a female figure with a bottle of fragrance, a pair of hands with a packet of cigarettes, etc. Both the visually represented icon, and the *conjunction* of icons, are treated as transparently readable. At the same time much effort has gone into pointing out the constructedness of images, whether through the posing of subject-matter, the cropping of a news photograph, or the recontextualization of images within a larger text. But here too the internal structure of images has received little attention. At the same time, the widespread recent scepticism towards Marxist notions of mystification has undercut the public legitimacy of readings for ideology; in many contemporary accounts of televisual or filmic texts readers are treated as able to (re)read texts highly productively, so that the text's form or its ideological force is not seen as imposing its message on the reader in any real sense.

As an example of the ideological forces and effects of visual representation we offer a simple example in Figure 10.1. This is a map, drawn by an amateur map-maker living in the village which is here (partially) mapped together with the area surrounding it. The map is meant as an aid

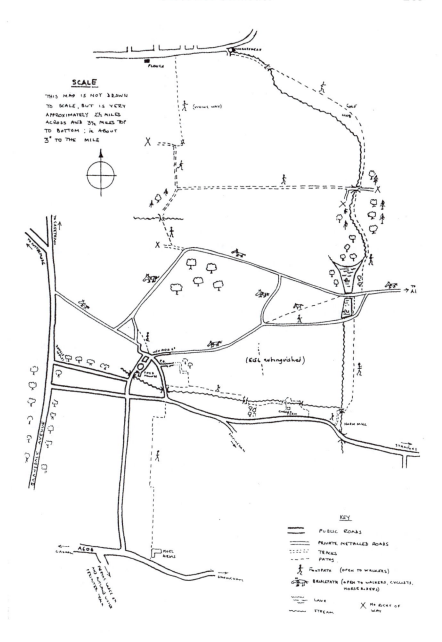

Figure 10.1 *Map of Rights of Way*

for people who wish to enjoy the countryside by walking on 'public footpaths'. These footpaths are a characteristic of the English countryside, and are a result of often very ancient histories, and of systems of land-ownership. Some of the footpaths go back for five or six millennia, others for centuries, as paths connecting regions, towns, villages and farms before the age of canals, railways and more modern roads. The 'public' retains a legal right to walk on these, a right which is often contested by the landowners whose land is crossed by these paths. This map is therefore a highly political object, particularly in this village which is still subject to what are in effect continuations of feudal patterns of landownership by the local aristocratic landowner, and many attendant social and economic relations.

A brief perusal of the map reveals an area immediately to the east of the village where a dashed line marks a former footpath, here indicated by the word 'extinguished'. No indication is given as to the use or occupancy of this land. Only close local knowledge will document that this is the 'park of the stately home' of the local aristocratic family.

The map is the result of semiotic work in a complex social context. Ideological work has been done in the production of the map: on the one hand making potentially controversial knowledge available, and on the other hand withholding it by deleting from this public record any possibility of gaining other relevant knowledge which could be used in questioning the agency of 'extinguished'. Whether we regard this as 'negation', as 'mystification', as 'rewriting', etc. is here not the point. Our point is that this visual representation and communication has social and ideological motivations and effects. Our hypothesis is that this is equally the case for all semiotic modes.

As a second example of ideological structuring in visual images, consider the drawing in Figure 10.2. This drawing, of an actual house in Sydney, is within a recognizable genre, one which romanticizes (and aestheticizes) domestic buildings of a certain period, the later Victorian period. Broadly, the genre turns certain suburbs of Sydney into 'romantic, historical Sydney': the genre is a part of the heritage industry. The material mode of representation – pencil or ink drawing – is significant for a number of reasons. Where photography might document 'decay', the drawing represents 'charm'; the line drawing can be used to select architectural features and ignore or suppress others – peeling plaster, or ugly extraneous features. In this particular instance, certain features have been suppressed, such as a tree in the front garden which otherwise obscured a frontal view of the house; the ironwork railing on the first-floor balcony is drawn to make it appear as authentic Victorian wrought-iron 'lace-work', when it was in fact a cheap substitute; and so on.

If we now reveal that the drawing was commissioned by an estate-agent, as a means of advertising the house for sale, the ideological interest for the choice of the material mode of representation as well as of the genre becomes clear. Houses of a different, more recent, period, and in other suburbs, are represented by another visual mode, that of colour photographs.

Visual representations exist within culturally and historically formed systems of representations, which, like that of language, are available for the socially motivated use by individuals with their specific interest.

Figure 10.2   *'Emoh ruo', Sydney, 1991*

Art Criticism, Art History, Art and Society

The major figures for us are Gombrich (1960; 1963), Panofsky (1939; 1955) and Arnheim (1954; 1971). Their interests focus on images within the canon of fine art, though in order to arrive at fuller understandings of these, they habitually move in their discussion between canonical works and more mundane objects, such as technical or scientific drawings, sketches done by architects, and so on. The focus of their interest is broad, ranging from establishing principles of aesthetics, and aesthetic judgement, to under-standings of the interrelations of art and society, art and culture, that is, art seen as having cultural and social origins and motivations, and therefore part of social history. They do not ignore the relations of art and brain, so that psychological, cognitive, and affective concerns appear constantly. Beyond this they share an interest in establishing means of analysis and description of visual representations within the Western canon of visual art.

The categories in these 'grammars' range across a variety of interpretative frameworks drawn (explicit or implicit) from psychological, perceptual approaches, for instance through terms such as *focus*, *salience*, or *weight*; or from aesthetic discourses, such as *balance*, *harmony*, or *spatial distribution*. These are set within broader frameworks, whether social, cultural or historical; affective, developmental or psychological. This analytic is focused through attention to 'movements' in art; to significant historical periods and developments; always contextualized within art historical movements; and within a larger social and scientific background (developments in the sciences, for instance, or in religion). Aesthetic values and, through these, social and cultural values and understandings, are at the centre. So whereas in our scheme *communication* is in the foreground, *expression* may be said to be foregrounded in the former.

Our condensed formulation of course does not do justice to the richness of insights offered in the writings of these scholars, insights into the aesthetic systems of a social group, its cultural values, and those of particular individuals; as well as the systematicness of modes of representation. In the case of another writer who has been highly influential for us as for others, John Berger (1972), the focus is much more specifically on the relatively direct representational relation between forms of visual representation, and the forms of economic and social arrangements experienced and perceived by a particular artist. In the case of other writers the focus is on more abstract considerations, more focused on formal arrangements which might be characteristic of aesthetic objects in the visual domain, and on philosophical issues arising in the domain of the visual.

Our own understanding draws in substantial ways on the work of these scholars. In general we consider that their forms of analysis lean more towards the iconographical than the syntactic, whether their orientation is social, psychological, philosophical, or aesthetic. The central question of this chapter, that of multi-modality, that is, the question of the use and valuation of visual representation in the overall semiotic landscape, is not an issue for these scholars. The place of language in that landscape remains unchallenged in their work.

Advertising

It is impossible to study advertising in contemporary Western societies without attention to the role of images. At the same time it is instructive to realize how until quite recently studies of advertising were able to focus on language alone; for instance in the work of Hawthorn (1987). One of the most influential accounts of images in advertising is that we have mentioned before, Judith Williamson's *Decoding Advertisements* (1978). It is a semiotic (and to some extent psychoanalytic) account of the structure of advertisements, of the structural relations between images, and, less focally, of the relations of image and text. Theoretical categories such as metaphor and metonym, syntagm, connotation and denotation, are at the centre of the description and of the theory underlying it. As with our comments on the work of Barthes (and Metz), Williamson on the whole focuses on relations between iconographic elements (analogous to relations between lexical items in spoken or written text), though she also pays attention to the syntagmatic relations between visual elements.

The book establishes characteristic types of such relationships. It does not overtly address either the question of the place and value of the visual in relation to verbal modes of communication, or the issues of the internal organization, the grammar of images. In a sense images, as well as (blocks of) text, are taken relatively unproblematically as givens; what is in focus is the meaning of the relationships they contract.

In some more recent work that relationship has itself become a focus of attention. So while for instance in Guy Cook's *The Discourse of Advertising* (1992) language is still the centre of attention, there is a constant awareness of the function of images as part of a more complex text. This is even more the case in Greg Myers's *Words in Ads* (1994), which, despite its title (perhaps itself an indication of older approaches), pays extensive attention to visual aspects of advertising texts, now seen as complex semiotic entities.

Film Studies and Screen Theory

The situation in this area in relation to the study of multi-modality is complex. On the one hand it is impossible to give even a thumbnail sketch of the work done in this field; it is simply too vast. On the other hand, numerous studies have focused on the structure of images (particularly from the point of view of 'shots', or of *mise-en-scène*), on sound-track, on the musical score, on lighting, and so on; and on particular effects of their combination. Yet the issue of multi-modality as we wish to pose it – presupposing both a detailed description of the semiotic organization and potential of a particular mode, *and* an account of the interrelations of the various modes to each other – has not been in focus for screen theory.

Instead there has usually been attention on specific features of the filmic text: lighting; character; diegesis; the influence of the director; aspects such as montage, editing, camera work generally; etc. Yet, paradoxically, despite this plethora of attention to detailed aspects of the filmic text or of its production, an impression remains in reading film theory that film has often been taken as though it were a single mode. The attention to details of set, lighting, staging, characterization, photography, tends to be obscured by the single word *film* as the name of a hugely composite and complex set of modes, which is nevertheless discussed as though it were not.

David Bordwell's excellent book *Narration in the Fiction Film* (1985) may stand as a representative of this complex, detailed and yet unified mode of analysis, dealing with the multiple array of semiotic modes involved in filmic text, picking out significant contributions of each, yet without problematizing either the inherent structuring of any one mode, or the question of just how they come together as a multi-modal text. The book moves from theories of cognition and perceptions, to theories of narrative and genre, to considerations of temporality and spatiality in film, to details of shots and their structure and sequencing, and so on. In discussing one sequence of shots in the film *Sunrise*, Bordwell (1985: 120–5) invokes categories such as perspective, trajectory, kinds of shot, internal structures of particular shots, vectorial lines, depth cues, volumes, camera movement (panning, tracking, transformation, velocity), psychological states (anticipation, cognitive (in)consistency), etc.

In his description both 'narration' and 'camera' take on independent agency ('the camera strikes out on its own', 'the camera . . . departs from the husband'; 'this camera-movement heightens the narration's self-consciousness', 1985: 124), indicating that we as readers are in the specialized fictive world of film criticism *per se*. The social production of this multi-modal text is here lost sight of, even if only temporarily, in an animated world of theory/fiction.

Other Areas of Interest

It is not possible here to be comprehensive in relation to all work of relevance. Clearly work which bears on the concerns of discourse analysis that goes beyond verbal text are around photography (such as Victor Burgin's collection *Thinking Photography*, 1982; Susan Sontag's provocative *On Photography*, 1979) and discussions of the use of images in print media, including the use of photographs (Hall, 1982).

The work of J.J. Gibson (*The Ecological Approach to Visual Perception*, 1986) provides stimulating insights for a rethinking of the *semiotic landscape*.

A Social Semiotic Account of Multi-Modal Texts

Some types of texts illustrate this revolution in the landscape of public communication particularly well: newspaper front pages, for instance, or the pages of school textbooks. Even 20 years ago most tabloid newspapers were covered in print. Many of the same newspapers today have hardly any written language on their front pages; those which do, have a vastly reduced amount. A profusion of images and of colour, of bold screamer headlines, characterizes the once uniformly print-covered black and white newspapers. Science textbooks tell the same story, as do textbooks in history or in geography.

Characteristics of Multi-Modal Texts

A social semiotic account of multi-modal text starts from a number of assumptions. We have discussed three of these already:

1   A number of semiotic modes are always involved in any textual production or reading.
2   Each mode has its specific culturally produced yet mode-inherent representational and communicational potentials.
3   An understanding is required as to how to read these texts, as coherent in themselves.

These need to be put together with several further principles of a social semiotic account of multi-modal texts:

4   Both producers and readers have power in relation to texts.
5   Writers and readers make complex signs – texts – which arise out of the *interest* of the producer of the text.
6   *Interest* describes the focusing of a complex of factors: social and cultural histories; present social contexts; including assessments by the sign-maker about the communicational environment.
7   *Interest* in apt representations as much as in effective communication means that makers of signs choose apt signifiers (forms) to express signifieds (meanings), so that the relation of signifier to signified is not arbitrary but motivated.

Writing as Making of Texts and Reading as Making of Text

This means that texts are saturated with the meanings of their makers represented directly, in every aspect of its form. Texts must therefore be read with the greatest attention. A text requires at least an equal degree of work from the reader as from the maker; even when the text is seemingly taken, uncritically, as transparent. Writing is the making of a new sign externally – a text – with resources available to the writer; reading is the making of a new sign 'internally' with the resources available to the reader, of which the text that is being read is the focal element.

This view of text as significantly determinative of readings and as resistant to certain rereadings is not a currently fashionable position. It means that the power of the reader is constrained by the forms of the text which is being read, just as the power of the writer is limited. In this view readers make signs in their reading (this is in accord with C.S. Peirce's, 1965, category of the *interpretant*) just as writers do in their writing. Semiotically speaking, writing and reading are both acts of making signs: writing is the act of making outwardly visible, communicable signs; reading is the act of making inwardly perceptible and non-communicative signs. Reading is therefore active and transformative, like writing. Reading is subject to constraints, because like writing it is constrained by the available means for making signs, and by the constraints of the scope of the readers' reading in their active semiotic reconstruction of all the systems of signs in the environment – usually referred to as 'the context'.

Reading and writing differ in the possibilities of communication, and the attendant cognitive cultural and social consequences. If my potentials for communication are more constrained than those of others around me, then my opportunities for full participation in social and cultural and political life are limited. More importantly, I am prevented from participation in the culturally and socially transformative action of remaking the means of representation of my community. Consequently the meanings of the dominant will remain dominant for me, and it is they who shape, more than I can, the representational resources of my community and thereby the means of my making of meaning. Cognitively, psychically, and *affectively*, I am in the position of making meanings through means of making meaning developed by others – precisely those who dominate my world. This is a semiotic account, precisely, of the dictum of Marx and Engels in their *Communist Manifesto*.

The concepts of social semiotics and of multi-modality put more conventional notions of text into crisis. If humans make and communicate meanings in many modes, then language alone no longer suffices as the focus of attention for anyone interested in the social making and remaking of meaning. If texts are always multi-modal then the question of the boundary of a text becomes a central issue. With any page, it becomes highly problematic to read only the linguistically carried meaning.

In Figure 10.3 language and image jointly carry the information. The student readers are expected to make sense of this page out of the totality of meaning produced by a reading of the page as a multi-modal text. Our contention is that this is (now) a normal condition of reading, whether of a textbook page, of any page of a newspaper, or of a television screen.

Once the seemingly firm boundaries which constituted a 'frame' for the text are loosened through asking what meanings of which message unit are expressed in what mode, then it is difficult to insist on closure for any textual unit. On a newspaper page, distinct meanings are communicated through photographs; these may relate in a number of ways to the written text, and rarely just as an illustration of it – as was the case in older forms of multi-modality. For some readers the photographic medium may constitute the main mode of communication, with language serving some ancillary, secondary function. Some readers may read all elements of the page together; though this leaves precisely the two questions of (1) the order of reading (which may be nothing like the order of composing of the page), and (2) the means by which meanings in the different modes are brought into a meaningful relation with each other.

In our main example (Figure 10.6) we consider a message unit which figures in no handbook of discourse analysis or text linguistics, let alone in any description produced in any mainstream linguistic account. It is a two-

12·9 Electronics

Circuits

In your first circuits you used torch bulbs joined with wires. Modern electrical equipment uses the same basic ideas. But if you look inside a computer there are not many wires or torch bulbs. The wires and bulbs have been replaced by electronic devices like transistors, chips and light-emitting diodes.

Transistors and chips are examples of *semi-conductors*. They are made from special crystals like silicon. Transistors work because they only conduct electricity in the right conditions. They are useful because they can turn on and off very fast, and they need very little electricity.

An electronic light

● You can make electronic circuits with wires like the circuits you made before. The difficulty is that the contacts are poor, and sometimes things do not work. It is far better to *solder* the components.

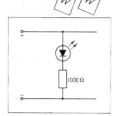

Here is a simple circuit to operate a light-emitting diode (LED).

This design shows the same circuit soldered on matrix board. The board is cheap and can be re-used.

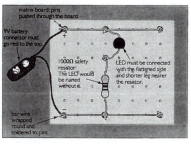

Transistors

A transistor is a special semi-conductor. It has three connections: a base, a collector and an emitter. When a small current is put on the base, it lets a much larger current flow between the collector and the emitter. So a tiny current can control a much larger one.

● Try this water-detector circuit.

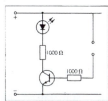

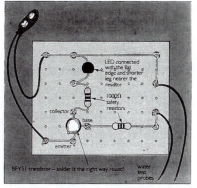

When the probes touch something wet, a very small current goes from the battery through the water to the base of the transistor. This current is big enough to make the transistor work, so the LED lights up.

Figure 10.3 *Page from Mike Coles, Richard Gott and Tony Thornley,*
Active Science No. 2. *London: HarperCollins*

page unit in a magazine, the left-hand page given over to verbal text and the right-hand page to an advertisement. (Of course this unit is likely to figure as a technical/pragmatic category in courses on newspaper and magazine layout.) It is our contention that at some level most readers of this magazine, and indeed of any others, will read the two pages together, as one unit; that is, they will bring the meanings of the visual text into conjunction with the written text, and produce for themselves a single, relatively coherent reading, even if that activity does not come into full consciousness for them.

We chose this example because here, unlike in many other instances, the principle of coherence is not at first sight strongly apparent, and the ideological message is therefore not transparently there – other than, as we said, in the 'lexicography' of the visual text: new car = wealth, glamour. The two modes which we focus on are written language (though we provide no analysis of this here) and visual images. They are brought together via the code of *layout*.

Before moving to a brief sketch of our framework of analysis, we give an instance of what we think is a genuinely multi-modal text; although it is worth pointing out that in common sense as in existing theories it would not be treated as such.

The example (Figure 10.4) is a five-year-old girl's representation of a 'newspaper'. We assume that by that she meant probably both 'newspaper' and 'newspaper page', the two being for her at this age undifferentiated. (The caption was read by her to her parent.) This image represents her assessment, her 'readings' of what newspapers are; it is an outward production of a sign based on inwardly produced prior signs, and as such the only real available evidence of the sense that she makes at this age of the notion of the newspaper. From our point of view, our reading of her sign is that she takes a newspaper page to be multi-modal, that is, to have language and image as modes of representation, in a relation of equality: neither is more important than the other. She has placed the image at the bottom, in the space we treat as meaning 'real', and language at the top, in the space we treat as meaning 'ideal'. We cannot know whether she has as yet made for herself that particular bit of the Western visual semiotic. It is the case that this placement does not reproduce a 'standard' form of the relation of image to written text in the Western newspapers that we have studied (from Australia, Britain, the USA, Austria, Germany and to a lesser extent some others). It is her own remaking of that system.

It is our strong contention that she does not see the relation of image and verbal text as one of 'illustration', that is, first producing the verbal text and then illustrating it; or as one of 'relay' or 'anchorage' (using Barthes's terminology), where either the verbal text is extended by the visual, or the visual receives its ontological anchoring from the verbal. All of these represent former ways of conceptualizing this relation; they have language at the centre. Rather we see this as entirely multi-modal, where two modes are used simultaneously to convey a complex message in the most apt form.

To treat this, as it might be in school, as an instance of 'illustration' would be to misunderstand this child's semiotic action. It would be replicating present valuations of written language as the central and definitive medium of representation, communication, and rationality, and thereby reintegrating the child's advanced notion back into a conservative state of the semiotic landscape.

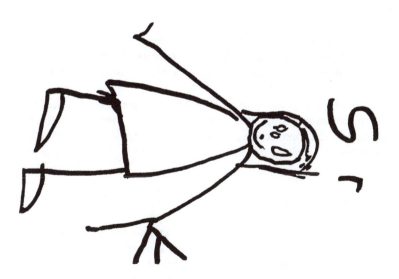

Figure 10.4   *'In John Princes Street someone got dead'* *(Emily Kress, 1993)*

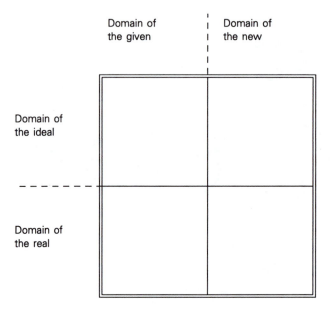

Figure 10.5   *Visual space in Western visual semiotics*

A Framework for Analysis

While we do not have space to give a detailed framework here, it may be helpful to provide an outline sketch. We refer readers who are interested in this aspect of our work to *Reading Images: a Grammar of Visual Design* (Kress and van Leeuwen, 1996).

Our assumption is that each semiotic mode has the potential for representing and communicating meanings, that is, for forming motivated signs, in respect to the three communicational tasks mentioned above. Here are some fundamental categories in the visual mode.

The Social Semiotics of the Visual Space

With respect to the task of forming coherent texts, we are here pointing to a use of the visual space (the page, a part of the ground, a wall, a rockface, a plaque, etc.) such that regular meanings attach to parts of that space. In relation to the 'page' in Western alphabetical cultures, with a left to right, top to bottom, reading direction (and with the history of the visual/ aesthetic culture of Western Europe), we posit a left–right, bottom–top distinction, such that four quadrants are formed, as in Figure 10.5.

To the bottom section of an image we assign the value *real*; to the top section the value *ideal*. Each of these may be given particular meanings in certain contexts, for instance *ideal* may mean distant in time, whether 'of the past' or 'in the future': 'an ideal form', 'a wish', etc. *Real* may have the specific meanings 'here and now', 'empirically so', etc.

The left–right distinction has a different meaning: left, as the starting point (in reading across a line), tends to have meanings such as (what is taken as) *given*, 'taken for granted', 'assumed to be the case', etc. Right, as the finishing point, tends to have meanings such as 'what is *new*', 'what is an instance (of the taken for granted)', etc. In other words, the top–bottom distinction relates to ontological judgements; the left–right distinction to the status of information.

The placement of the horizontal and vertical division between real and ideal, and between given and new, is relative to the interest of the maker of the image (or page). Similarly, what kinds of materials are placed there is both culturally shaped and determined by the interest of the maker of this structure. What is stable is the meaning of these divisions: material placed in the bottom left quadrant will be given and real, etc.

Other distributions of the space are possible and are in use in different cultures: for instance, a distribution of *centre* versus *margin*, where what is central has a different valuation to what is marginal. Different cultures have differential uses. Within a pluricultural society therefore quite different dispositions may be in use, though some may be dominant in relation to others.

The Social Semiotics of States of Affairs in the Represented World

With respect to the task of communicating about events (and their internal structures), objects, events, states of affairs, etc., we assume a use of visual elements which indicate both what are treated as major elements, and their relations. In a diagram, for instance, two elements may be connected by an arrow, so signalling one as the origin/originator/cause, and the other as recipient, goal, effect. The famous communication model of

is one such instance (except that this has three elements). It might be read as: a message M originates with S; it passes to R, where it comes to rest. Images with realist or figurative elements, for instance a person passing something to another or a person looking at another, fit easily into this scheme.

At the same time there are images which do not represent (inter)action, but rather represent states of affairs. A picture of an Antarctic explorer in a textbook shows in schematic form what he needs to wear: fur hood, heavy mittens, fur-lined coat, boots. Or there may be an image of a scientific instrument objectively represented. Images of this latter kind are quite as common as the former; usually there is some indication of a focal element, but not necessarily so. The car in our main example is a good instance of this type.

The Social Semiotics of the Social Relations of Viewer and Image

Lastly, with respect to the task of representing and communicating about the social relations of the viewer of the image to the image (a relation which parallels that of the maker of the image to the represented object), we assume a use of visual elements which indicate a set of social relations judged to be significant in that society. For instance, indications of social distance may be coded by the size of the element represented, or by its coded distance from the viewer: attitudinal relations may be coded by the viewer's lateral position in relation to an element (such as 'front on', 'to the side of', 'from the margin'). Relations of power are coded by the position of the viewer in vertical relation to the object: if the object is more powerful we look up to it; if we are more powerful, we look down on it; and so on. Forms of 'factuality' may be coded by kinds of realism, so that in relation to our main example we might say that the mode of representation is in a hyper-realist form (perhaps a surrealist form) of everyday realism.

Clearly, this is merely an indication of a grammar, which may in its simplification be misleading. Readers should use the much fuller description available in Kress and van Leeuwen (1996). Here we simply want to indicate that there are regularities of structure, and to use this skeletal framework in our analysis of the following example.

Analysis

We begin with a critical, distanced reading of the first page of the example which we have chosen to analyse, the double-page spread at the end of the Brazilian journal *Veja* (Figure 10.6). We then show that our aim to treat this as a single text is not just justified but necessary; and that not to do so would be to miss essential aspects of the meaning of (all parts of) this text. We begin with a reading of the feature article, provided by one of the authors (R. L.-G.) of this chapter. We then show how our analytic readings apply. We wish to show that readers use precisely the features we have outlined for their readings, and then to see how categories and reading match, and how one may illuminate the other. A translation of the feature article and the advertisement can be found at the end of the chapter.

A Critically Distanced Reading of the Feature Article

We have on the left side 'Point of view' written by a Brazilian conservative MP, whose constituency is located in the north-east of Brazil, a region where the discrepancies between rich and poor are most accentuated. He belongs to an elite that historically used to take their holidays in Europe, where they would spend their (not always their) money on the *dernier cri*. His past can be identified in his discourse against the cellular phone. He is against it, for the others – although he himself has one.

His discourse is ambiguous. For him, cellular telephones are good for an elite. For the people, public telephones are enough. As for the ascendant middle class, the *nouveau riche*, they must learn how to behave, before being able to have and use cellular phones – properly, of course. The important thing is not so much to have one, but to learn how to behave in the use of it. In reality he is talking about habitus from the point of view of the upper class which has historically put up barriers for protecting itself from the invasion of the parvenus. A certain way of being, of acting, of talking, of dressing denotes the belonging to the elite. It is a distinction of class. When someone is presented in a TV programme, for example, we know his origins. Not only the geographical place, but the social place. It is easy to identify his or her social class, at what kind of school and university he or she has studied, and what are his or her ideological affinities and cultural background.

The discourse of our personage is an elite discourse. It is a class discourse that uses irony to ridicule those who could eventually approximate and menace those who still have the power. But at the same time it is a populist discourse, for it can be read by those who guarantee his place as MP. His supporters are the immense majority of poor people from the north-east who vote for him, as they were taught that 'only gentlemen are capable of governing' and 'ignorant people aren't fit for being elected president'. Dominant classes have always created and devised an ideology which maintains them as dominant. The ambivalence of the discourse is due to his class background (an unconscious or hidden discourse) and at the same time his political imprisonment (the conscious or overt discourse).

But whatever the reasons why the author of 'Point of view' wrote the article, we can analyse the two pages of the review and identify the contradiction between the two texts. One is a conservative discourse and, we may say, anti-modernity. It defends the status quo, the privileged, the maintenance of the social gap.

Right beside it, the other text is an invitation to modernity. One presents modernity as unattainable, the other presents modernity as something accessible to anyone (without specifying who is the *you*). The beautiful, modern, elegant car 'of your dreams' can be bought or rented easily. It is only necessary to ask for assistance from the manager of the bank. The car is so bright that even its reflection on the roadway shines as a diamond. It is a car that makes the owner feel young (only young people can afford the wind and the sun in a convertible). It is a convertible in a country where wealthy people are using armour plated cars to protect themselves from being attacked by gangs from the slums, or from being kidnapped by organized crime.

On the left side we read an article whose intention is to limit desires (only a few are able to use a cellular phone, the majority must accept public

PONTO DE VISTA

Abaixo o telefonismo celular

O velho ditado "quem nunca comeu melado quando come se lambuza" cai como uma luva para uma praga nascida com o advento do telefone celular. No Brasil, é o telefonismo celular, uma mania, uma doença. O telefonismo é resultado do deslumbramento das pessoas diante da inovação do telefone celular. O mal vem aos poucos, é detectável em todo canto, e apenas a terapia preventiva pode contê-lo. É gente usando o celular em casa, quando poderia usar o telefone comum. É mãe dando celular para o filho ir à escola e de lá falar com amiguinhos. É filhinho de papai levando celular nas festas para impressionar as garotinhas. É casal indo fazer compra no supermercado com o celular pregado na orelha. Só falta agora alguém ligar seu celular numa secretária eletrônica portátil ou num fax. Ou ainda, por petulância suprema, usar dois celulares. E, quando atender ao segundo, responder com um insuportável "só um momentinho que estou na outra linha celular".

•

Aprecio como ninguém os confortos da vida moderna. Por isso, tenho também um celular em Brasília. Ele é um recurso extra que me permite estar acessível 24 horas por dia em momentos especiais e decisivos. Se estou no carro e é marcada uma reunião do PFL de última hora, só posso ser achado pelo celular. Um recado urgente da minha família, que mora em Pernambuco, às vezes só pelo celular. Mas é preciso ter cuidado com o exagero. Não é possível que no universo celular só existam assuntos urgentes. Ainda na semana passada vi um colega conversando com a patroa pelo celular em seu gabinete, bem ao lado do telefone comum. E, ao desligar, recebeu o chamado celular de um correligionário. Isso escraviza. Se Charles Chaplin fosse vivo e filmasse seu *Tempos Modernos* hoje, talvez não se enfiasse nas grandes engrenagens das máquinas de antigamente e preferisse se pendurar num desses neurotizantes aparelhinhos.

•

A engenhoca está virando uma porta aberta para a invasão da privacidade das pessoas. Um abuso. Os donos de telefone celular são alcançados na sua intimidade como se estivessem sendo monitorados pelo *big brother*, o ditador

> *"Enquanto os orelhões são depredados, o telefone celular serve ao exibicionismo"*
>
> **RICARDO FIÚZA**

de *1984*, de George Orwell. O diabo toca na cama, no banho, no carro, na academia, no cinema, no teatro e no restaurante. Vamos com calma, gente. Há ainda o inconveniente do barulhinho desagradável emitido pelo aparelho quando chamado. É comum o embaraço causado pelo celular tocando durante um show, no cinema ou no teatro.

•

Ser contra o telefone celular é ser contra a luz elétrica e a água encanada. Mas, da mesma forma como não dormimos com a luz acesa nem deixamos a torneira aberta o tempo todo, o celular não foi desenvolvido para transformar o indivíduo num posto de atendimento 24 horas. E essa é a neurose chapliniana do telefonismo. Alguns exibidos, em vez de pendurar uma melancia no pescoço, partiram para o celular. Além da utilização estúpida do aparelho como forma de exibir status, muito comum com qualquer novidade, os usuários afoitos estão transformando o celular numa arma contra eles mesmos.

Há também uma questão social nessa história toda. Celular não é necessariamente sinal de evolução. Possuir um aparelhinho desses pode levar seu proprietário a imaginar que finalmente vive num país moderno. Bobagem. Enquanto o seleto clube celular pinta e borda com seus brinquedinhos aqui e ali, boa (e bota boa nisso) parte dos brasileiros não

tem telefone em casa, daqueles com fio mesmo. E maior parte ainda não pensa sequer em possuir telefone porque não tem dinheiro para pagar, primeiro, a linha e, depois, a conta. Para esses resta o orelhão. Quando não está quebrado, é claro. Ou depredado. A prioridade, no Brasil, deve ser o velho telefone — barato — para o povo.

O celular é um eletrodoméstico como o forno de microondas. Mas ninguém cozinha feijão no microondas, inventado para a preparação de refeições rápidas, o descongelamento de alimentos etc. Para feijão há o fogão a gás. O telefone celular deve ter a mesma filosofia de uso. Ele não passa de um bip de luxo. Um bip que ouve e fala, mas um bip. E, como os bips, o celular foi criado para passar recados. Não podemos ser escravos da tecnologia. Ela é que existe para nos dar conforto e nos servir. Vamos deixar que apenas os deslumbrados se lambuzem com a novidade até que, pela saturação, passem a ver no celular aquilo que ele é: apenas um telefone.

Ricardo Fiúza
é deputado federal

Figure 10.6   *Feature article by Ricardo Fiúza and advertisement from* Veja *(6 October 1993) pp. 134–5*

phones as their only possibility of using a telephone). On the right page we see an advertisement whose function is to create desires, to show how it is simple and easy to realize dreams of consumerism and to materialize those dreams. People can even buy marvellous cars without having money. They can choose how they are going to pay: it can be in the national and official currency (cruzeiros) or in the money forbidden by law (dollars). It is the

COM UM FINANCIAMENTO OU UM LEASING SAFRA VOCÊ VAI COMPRAR O CARRO DOS SEUS SONHOS.

OU UM ATÉ MELHOR.

No Safra, as condições são tão boas que você vai perceber que poderia ter sonhado mais longe. Por isso o Safra é um dos líderes em leasing e no financiamento para compra de carros nacionais ou importados. Tudo com o que você mais sonha está no Safra: crédito rápido, prazos de até 36 meses, taxas competitivas, operações em cruzeiro ou dólar, além das vantagens fiscais da menor tributação. Tudo rapidamente decidido com o gerente.
Escolha o carro nos revendedores e procure o Gerente Safra. Você nem sonha com o bom negócio que o está esperando.

É MUITO FÁCIL COMPRAR O SEU CARRO

Banco Safra
Tradição Secular de Segurança

offering of an audacious car for audacious people by an audacious bank that uses an audacious advertising design. It even insinuates the possibility of cheating and not paying taxes for the buying of this car. On the left we read the criticism of consumerism; on the right, the invitation to consumerism.

And as one of the several conclusions we may state that the press survives with the money of the state (the MP linked to the government is asked to write on an important page of an important magazine), and with the money of advertising (an important bank buys a whole page of an important magazine). And the readers of the important magazine believe they are part of the group of important people who read the important magazine. They feel up-to-date, for they read the matters that are going to be the themes of discussions at political meetings, at business reunions, at dinner or cocktail parties.

In this game of buying and selling of opinion everybody is happy, but the public is more and more intoxicated with an ideology that can be identified only by those who have really learned the deeper meaning behind the words and the images.

In a way the elite fears the *arrivistes* for their audacity. The latter laugh off the former's silences about the new things they can do and buy. They denounce with their happiness and spontaneity the power relation in society, which those who have always been in power try to hide! They play the same role as Rabelais's laughter when they mime the elite's habits. And as they mime, they caricature the elite and ridicule the blasé attitude of those who were born with privileges that they did not earn but received as inheritance. They show with their laughter who is the conqueror in the present and who is becoming the past and has no future. Unlike the Rabelaisian laughter, which had only a moment of liberation of its cathartic energy during Saturnalia, that of the new rich has not been licensed but is conquering, and not just for a moment but as a process of conquest whose eventual aim might be to replace the ancient elite in power. The laughter of the Saturnalia could only ignore the hierarchic distinction during the carnival moment, to break down traditional values and to subvert the relationship between master and slave. But the suspension of the distance was temporary, and both master and slave knew it. The difference, concerning the relationship between the old elites and the *nouveaux riches*, is that the latter laugh without being allowed to do so. And they laugh with no possibility of control; the only control which the elites try to impose is, in the end, etiquette. The laughter studied by Bakhtin had a licensed liberty; the 'new rich' laughter exercises an undesired liberty. That's why they represent a menace to the traditional elites.

Some of the elites understand the situation they face and confuse power by imposing their differences. Others, overcome by the desire to ape the new model, mime the other to become the other, and in doing so lose their revolutionary impulse, as well as their identity. They learn the code with its interdiction and the image disappears. They can't laugh anymore. From that moment on, they just smile as Leonardo's Gioconda. They are no longer Rabelaisian personages. They have entered the world of Proust.

On the left page we can see the image of the establishment. The author of the article, who speaks for his social class, personalizes the ruling classes in Latin America, in our case Brazil. And especially north-east Brazil, where historical oligarchies maintain the majority of the people in a state of ignorance and extreme poverty, to maintain their privileges. He represents tradition in its most cruel sense.

His image suggests a Brazilian saying, 'Do you know to whom you are talking?' It means: do you know your place in the hierarchy of society? Do you know the distance between you and me? Do you know I'm naturally superior and you are naturally inferior, and so it must be? His photograph was taken in the parliament, where power is present and exercised in the form of laws. It is one of the major powers of the nation. *He* represents this power – the power to decide the destinies of the whole population and of the country as such. He knows that, he's proud of it and he plays the role perfectly.

His posture is that of a serious man. And ironically, in the same photo we may see the object of his criticism: a man (another MP) with a cellular phone. The author occupies almost all the space of the photo; the other is his shadow, stands behind him, is less important than he is, or, we may suggest, illustrates his discourse.

We may say he has *le physique du rôle*. He is properly dressed: he wears a dark and well-cut suit, an elegant tie, discreet but visible cuff-links. His hair is styled in the manner of middle-aged upper-class men in Latin America. And of course, he has a moustache. His hands are posed in a way that gives the impression of tranquillity but, at the same time, of authority. On the left hand, a wedding ring announces a serious married man: his wedding ring confirms his discourse of the importance of the family. He frowns slightly, his eyebrows pretending to have preoccupations. He is a man preoccupied with the destiny of his country. But if we look more accurately, we can catch a certain malice in his eyes.

A Social Semiotic Reading

Our social semiotic reading is not an attempt to demonstrate that critical reading is impossible without this kind of analysis. Rather our assumption is that critical reading depends on the reader occupying a coherent, distanced, differentiated position, whether theoretically articulated or not. Our social semiotic analysis can hope to achieve several things: to elucidate what features of a text may give rise to readings of various kinds; to show that any reading relies on cues from all semiotic modes; to demonstrate how these modes may have been utilized, in specific ways, in the production of the text; and lastly, through an elucidation of the systematic character of the visual code, to bring to the fore readings which may not easily be articulated given the ignorance of the visual mode in the mainstream of Western semiotic, representational and communicational practice.

Our attention is on the two-page spread, consisting of a feature article and an advertisement. Our intention is to read that as a single text – an act which is in itself a subversion of everyday *and* of theoretically sanctioned reading practices. We deploy, below, the sketched framework of analysis developed earlier.

The Social Semiotics of the Visual Space   The feature article occupies the left position, the advertisement the right. This is not an inevitable positioning; in the magazine as a whole 15 of the 27 whole page advertisements are placed on the left. Positioning is a matter of choice, so significance attaches to it. The left-hand position carries meanings of the kind 'taken for granted', 'starting point', 'given or assumed information'; the right-hand position carries meanings of the kind 'presented as new', 'the completion of a (two-part) structure','an instance of', 'new information', 'not previously known', etc. This immediately lends a particular meaning to the placement of feature and advertisement: 'feature' as expressing that which is (here) presented as taken for granted, as the starting point, a comment by a member of the elite on lifestyle; and advertisement as an instance of, a completion of this structure. The fact that there is a deep contradiction in the meanings presented in each, as we have pointed out in our commentary, is in an important sense both the point and beside the point. It is precisely this kind of contradiction which this semiotic structure manages to cancel, for a moment at least, in order to establish a common sense which works for both the feature and the advertisement, and importantly, as far as the magazine is concerned, for the reader/consumer.

Other magazines make other use of this meaning potential and use other distributions of advertisements and written text; always, we hypothesize, for specific cultural/ideological reasons. A magazine for a female reader from a somewhat lower class position than the readership of *Veja* (an instance we have studied is the Australian magazine *Australian Women's Weekly*) generally puts advertisements on the left. But they tend to be advertisements for essentials of a family's daily life and not for commodities which are means of establishing lifestyle. Even in *Veja* the distribution varies, as we pointed out above. Of a total of 47 whole-page or double-page advertisements, 20 are double page, 15 single page on the left, and 12 single page on the right. An analysis of any textual part of this magazine needs to be set in the full context of the semiotics of this distribution, which we will not attempt here. Such an analysis would pay attention to sequencing within the magazine (is the page in an earlier section, the middle section, later in the magazine?), to the relation between subject-matter and types of placement, etc. One point which it is essential to make, however, is that out of the magazine's total of 135 pages, 47 pages are given over to full- (or double-) page advertisements; many pages have half-page advertisements. This allows us to see what deeper content the magazine is establishing; how information, comment, documentary, news, opinion, are all tightly interwoven into and perhaps determined by consumerism; and how all of these have their role in the formation of the readers' habitus.

The structure of each separate page of the two-page unit is more strongly oriented on the vertical than on the horizontal axis, although the advertisement uses the left–right distinction, as well as a strongly emphasized centralized element. The car, the central element literally, *is* the centre of attention, from every point of view, and from everyone's point of view. At the top, on the left, is the statement *With a loan or a leasing Safra you can buy the car of your dreams*. The slogan, which offers the means of achieving the ideal, the dream, the wish, is located in the spot which semiotically is both *ideal* (the top of the page) and 'taken for granted', 'the starting point' (the left side of the structure).

The bottom of the page is concerned with the real: the information concerning the loan or the leasing arrangements, the real means of attaining the dream. The bottom section has itself a strong tripartite structure. The centre is taken by the information; the left by the slogan *or one even better* (that is, 'even better than your dreams', indicating that the reading direction is meant to be from the top left corner down, as in a printed page). The right is itself divided into top, middle, and bottom: logo plus slogan; shield or coat of arms; name of the firm plus slogan. This structure as a whole suggests that it is taken for granted that one wants to achieve more than one's dream, for that is the starting point; the information necessary to do so is central; and the information about the firm that offers the means for that achievement is the *new*, in the rightmost position.

The left-hand page has a structure which also utilizes these spatial features. A box in the centre of the top half of the page contains the 'essence of the words' of the author, in the form of a quote. This is matched by a box in the same position in the bottom half, which contains his photograph, 'the essence of his person', so to speak. This establishes a strong real–ideal structure, in which the person is the empirical real, the guarantor of the text, and the quote is the discursive ideal, the essence of the text.

The Social Semiotics of the Social Relations of Viewer and Image Some pronounced features of the interpersonal structuring of this text are the angles which position the viewer *vis-à-vis* both 'objects' – the car and the author. Both images are produced with strong low to high angles, making the objects dominant, more powerful, in each case: the one as a writer who is a member of the elite, the other as the commodity which is the object of desire. In looking at the car we are so low we can nearly see the underside of the chassis. In relation to both the author and the car we might be on our knees, looking up, adoringly. In terms of involvement, by the maker of the photograph and therefore the viewer (who necessarily occupies the position of the maker of the image), both the car and the writer are photographed side on, indicating a certain marginality on the viewer's part. It is not clear whether the author turned away from us, or not fully towards us. Similarly with the car, where our position is not fully front on. Given that the photograph is 'posed', involvement is mystified, is made ambivalent.

Involvement as signalled here is a strong signal, even if a highly ambivalent one, in each case. The coded distance of the viewer from the object is a further semiotic feature. Both images position us relatively close to the object; clearly the object of desire in the advertisement must be close to us physically and therefore affectively; clearly too, the author must be close, yet not too intimate (as in a close-up): here he is not too distant and yet he is not one of us. Both photographs position us as viewers, physically and socially, quite precisely in relation to a number of significant social and interpersonal factors: power; proximity; distance; involvement.

A further social positioning of the reader/viewer occurs through the overall modality of each of the images. By this we mean that the text constructs for us a complex representation of the world in relation to realism: what we as readers are meant to take as 'real' in the world produced for us in a particular representation. Colour (photography) is used as one means of establishing 'realism': in that respect the photograph of the author is a fully naturalistic version of this realism, the realism of the everyday. Here it is a guarantee – though hardly noticed precisely because it is naturalized – of the 'factualness' of the feature-article, or at least of the writer's persona. The photograph of the commodity on the other hand is a hyper-real version of this realism: an exaggeration or intensification of certain features into the direction of the extravagantly real, the hyper-real. For instance, the glossy sheen on the car; the sparkling reflections; the overall colour scheme, which merges the car with the background of the colour of the night. This is not the world of the everyday but the world of dreams, invoked explicitly and implicitly by all parts of this advertisement. If the modality of the photograph of the author establishes for the viewer the social world of the everyday through its realism, then the modality of the advertisement places the viewer into an equally constructed social world of the hyper-real, the dream-world, of consumer capitalism. In this respect too, the distribution along the left–right dimension is important: the hyper-real world of consumer capitalism as the 'new', as 'the instance' of the everyday world presented in the feature article.

The Social Semiotics of States of Affairs in the Represented World As a final part of our analysis, a brief word on the world of events, of states of affairs, represented here – the transitivity relations which are invoked. In the advertising image there is simply the represented object: no action is indicated, although the way the car is pointed, the way its front wheels are turned and the reflection lines on the ground, are suggestive of (potential) movement, speed. In our terms that suggestion is 'lexically' or iconographically coded, and thus part of the semiotics of states of affairs. However, action (or dynamism) is not coded through the grammar of transitivity as it could have been. Transitively, it is the world of *a state of being*: the car simply *is* there. The focus is on its existence, its presence. When we read the two-page text together, we as readers perform a movement, from feature article to advertisement, which has some of the semiotic force of *transaction* moving from the one to the other. Both the figure of the author, and of the car, point in the same direction, thus suggesting a movement of that kind. It may be that structures such as this two-page unit are weakly coded (and not overtly understood); although our action as readers implicates us in the transactional meanings, which it seems that we have produced.

To return to our earlier question: what does a reading of this kind add to the reading performed without this analysis? Readers do read, for vastly varying purposes, with totally varying commitments, with differing positions. Our analysis promises no magic insight; and we certainly do not claim that without it (critical) readings are not possible. However, our mode of analysis decisively alters the theoretical field in which reading is conceptualized. Our insistence, for instance, on the left–right structure of the visual unit enables us, or forces us, to consider what the relevant textual units are. The page or the two-page unit is not a unit in any form of text linguistics, or in various kinds of discourse analysis. This is a theoretical change with far-reaching consequences. It may have been possible before for a reader to consider the kind of unit which we have considered here: but it was not a practice legitimated by any textual theory. Now it is a necessary move, and theoretically legitimate.

Does our analysis reveal more about the culture than about the structure, form, and meaning of the text? We think so, and we also think that in any social theory of text that is precisely what an analysis should reveal. We need to be as explicit as it is possible to be about textual organization, form, meaning. But in our case the purpose of that explicitness is to explain personal, social, cultural, political and therefore ideological organization. In the simple feature of left–right, bottom–top organization of the visual space of the two-page text, deep cultural meanings are revealed. What has what kind of value? What is taken for granted, given, what is new? Here the speech, the spoken/written words of the author are *given*. The established habitus of a group is expressed linguistically. The *new*, the habitus of another group (of other groups – all the groups implicated in global consumer capitalism), is expressed visually. The commodity is shown as the new; and whether this instantiates, or whether it realizes the values of the group which speaks the established values through the feature article, is an open question here.

We do not claim that there is a single reading here, and that this form of analysis provides access to it. But our focus on the two-page unit as a single textual structure focuses precisely on a difference of social-cultural position among groups located within the elites of consumer capitalism. The position of one, a conservative, group is expressed through the conservative medium of written language, with minimal space and attention given to the visual mode. The position of another, an advanced (?) group, is expressed through the 'advanced' medium of the visual, with lesser use of the conservative medium of language. Desire is activated verbally on one page, and visually on the other. The means of fulfilling that desire are given verbally. How this tension is read and resolved by readers will have to do with their social positioning and their habitus, for they are active in making their motivated signs out of their interests in their reading of this two-page unit.

The given–new structure of the two-page unit puts these two positions into a structure of implied equivalence, and thus promises to resolve, even if only temporarily, a deep tension. Other features which we have briefly pointed to all play their part in establishing this temporary resolution, and to facilitate certain readings rather than others, in ways which we have suggested.

With these issues we have moved into social, political, and ideological domains. In this, the possibility of the use of the social semiotic repertoire for the contested, partial, *interested* use of a particular group, or a constellation of groups in a society, is the central issue. As we have said, in our view that is what a social semiotic analysis should be about.

Conclusion and Prospect

If the underlying assumptions of this chapter are correct, a vast new field for urgent research opens up. If the communicational landscape of the coming decades becomes more intensely multi-modal, demands for specific knowledge in this area will arise: whether in relation to school curricula, which cannot remain focused on language alone, or to the design of forms of public communication, nationally and globally. The social·consequences are far-reaching; new valuations of available modes will be accompanied by new possibilities of skewing communication in power relations among groups within a society, and internationally. The cognitive, cultural and political potentials of different modes will need to be understood, as will the economic and technological potentials.

The concept of multi-modality raises questions which have so far not been overtly or systematically addressed: for instance, is the enterprise of science better conducted in the visual or in the verbal mode? If information overload characterizes the present, still logocentric world, will a world oriented more towards the visual find a resolution to that problem in this potentially more effective medium? Will the new technologies, the newer forms of production, the new economies, develop out of and in interdependence with the potentials of the multi-modal and perhaps dominantly visual text?

Within the enterprise of social semiotics some of these questions can find partial answers: the required new theories of reading and of text production will have effects on forms of subjectivity. And the field will be a site of contestation, as always when there are resources to be used either for common benefit, or for narrowly bound exploitation.

Recommended Further Reading

We have chosen most articles and books here for their usefulness as examples of approaches in which image and verbal text are presented in an integrated fashion, or in which the visual mode is treated as a systematic form of communication. Some we have chosen because they are genuinely thought-provoking in relation to the concerns of our chapter.

Examples of the first are many of the writings of Roland Barthes: *Mythologies* (1973), *Image-Music-Text* (1977). John Berger's *Ways of Seeing* (1972) is stimulating in a similar way. Robert Hodge and Gunther Kress's *Social Semiotics* (1988) deals with a wide range of semiotic modes, and attempts to provide systematic ways of thinking about these. David Olson's *The World on Paper* (1994) is a highly readable account of writing as a medium in the visual mode.

Some works are more specialized, either in terms of the domain of practice or in terms of the semiotic mode. For the latter, some of the works in the theory of art stand out: as we mentioned, the works of Rudolf Arnheim (1954; 1971), Ernst Gombrich (1960; 1963), and Erwin Panofsky (1939; 1955). In many ways most of the issues of multi-modality have been either raised or already dealt with, though usually not as the main focus, and not as semiotic systems. For the discussion of particular modes there is again Barthes's *Camera Lucida* (1984), as well as his earlier writing on photography in *Image-Music-Text* (1977). Susan Sontag's *On Photography* (1979) is a well-written, thoughtful and provocative examination; Victor Burgin's edited volume *Thinking Photography* (1982) gives an interesting range of essays from a more (post)structuralist and psychoanalytic perspective.

Advertising has, for the last four decades at least, produced texts which combine overtly and deliberately the visual, verbal and other modes. Greg Myers's *Words in Ads* (1994) is, despite its title, an account which constantly pays attention to both modes and their interrelation. Judith Williamson's *Decoding Advertising* (1978) is more focused on visual images, but is a most worthwhile study of the use of images and their interrelations. One representative of film theory which is from our point of view highly suggestive, full of insight and interest, is David Bordwell's *Narration in the Fiction Film* (1985). The work of two of the authors is represented in Gunther Kress and Theo van Leeuwen's *Reading Images: a Grammar of Visual Design* (1996), and in their forthcoming *The Multi-Modal Text* (1997).

Appendix: Translation of Figure 10.6

Feature Article

Point of View: Down with Cellular Telephones

'At the same time as public telephones are destroyed, cellular telephones are a form of exhibitionism' Ricardo Fiúza

The old saying 'he who never ate molasses, when tries becomes sticky' is perfect for a plaque commissioned with the advent of the cellular telephone.

In Brazil, the cellular telephone is a mania, an illness. Telephonism is the result of the astonishment of people faced with the innovation of cellular telephones. The evil creeps slowly, can be seen everywhere, and only preventive therapy can stop it. Some people use it at home, when they could use normal telephones. Some mothers give one to their sons to take to school and talk to their friends with it. Some mummy's boys take cellular phones to parties just to impress the girls. Some couples go shopping at the supermarket with the cellular phones in their ears. One of these days someone is going to connect his/her cellular phone to a portable answerphone or to a fax. Or even more of a supreme arrogance, they may use two cellular phones. And when they answer the second one they will say, 'hold on a moment, I'm on the other cellular phone'.

•

I love as nobody else the comforts of modern life. That's why I have a cellular phone in Brasilia. It is an extra help that makes me accessible 24 hours a day at special and decisive moments. If I am in the car and my political party organizes a meeting at the last moment, I can be found only by cellular phone. An urgent message from my family, which lives in Pernambuco, sometimes can only be received by cellular phone. But we have to be careful of exaggeration. It's not possible that in the cellular universe there can be only urgent matters. Last week I saw a colleague talking with his wife by cellular phone from his office right beside the normal telephone. And as he switched off he received a cellular phone call from a member of his party. That is slavery to technology. If Charlie Chaplin was alive and made *Modern Times* again, perhaps he wouldn't put himself in the large machine of old times and would rather put himself in one of those neurosis inducing gadgets.

•

The gadget is becoming an open door for the invasion of privacy. It's too much. The privacy of the owners of mobile phones is invaded as if they were being monitored by Big Brother, the dictator in George Orwell's *Nineteen Eighty-Four*. It's in bed, in the bath, in the car, in the academy, in the cinema, in the theatre and in the restaurant. Go easy, people. There is also the inconvenience of the disagreeable noice when it rings. It's embarassing when the cellular phone rings during a show or cinema or theatre performance.

•

Being against mobile phones is the same as being against electric light or running water. But as we don't sleep with the light on or leave the tap on all the time, cellular phones weren't designed for the individual to become a 24-hours attendance office! And that is the Chaplinian neurosis of the cellular phone. Some show-offs, instead of hanging a melon round their neck, hang a phone. Besides being a silly exhibition of status, very common when the new arrives, the users are transforming the mobile phone into a weapon against themselves.

There is also a social problem in this story. Mobile phones are not necessarily a sign of evolution. To have one may lead the owner to imagine he lives in a modern country. Stupidity. At the same time that a few people play with their cellular toys the majority of Brazilian people don't have a regular phone at home. And among these, the majority don't even think of having a telephone because they can't afford to pay for the line, and afterwards for the bill. For these, only the public telephones are possible. When they are not broken, of course. Or destroyed. The priority in Brazil must be the old cheap telephone – for the people.

The cellular phone is a domestic electronic aid like the microwave. But nobody cooks black beans in a microwave, as it was designed for rapid meals, for defrosting food, etc. For black beans there is the gas stove. The mobile phone must have the same philosophy of use. It is nothing but a luxury bip. A bip that hears and speaks, but a bip. And as all bips, it was created to transmit messages. We can't be slaves of technology. Technology exists to give us comfort, to serve us. Let's leave only silly people to be excited with this novelty. Until the day comes when, saturated, they may see cellular phones as they really are: just a telephone.

© Photograph caption
Ricardo Fiúza is a federal deputy

Advertisement

With a Loan or a Leasing Safra You Can Buy the Car of Your Dreams.

Or One Even Better. With Safra, the conditions are so good that you will understand that they are beyond your wildest dreams. That's why Safra is one of the leaders in leasing and in financing the buying of national or imported cars. Everything you dream is encompassed in Safra: rapid credit, repayment over 36 months, competitive rates, operations in cruzeiros or in dollars, in addition to the fiscal advantages of low tax burden. Everything is rapidly decided with the manager. You choose the car at the dealer and look for the Safra Manager. You can't even dream how good is the business waiting for you.

Financing or Leasing Safra

It's very easy to buy your car.

Banco Safra Secular Tradition of Security

Notes

We wish to thank Paul Mercer, Rumiko Oyama, Teun van Dijk, and the participants of a course on 'Social semiotics and the multi-modal text' at the Congress of the Brazilian Society for Applied Linguistics (Campinas, September 1995) for their most helpful comments. And special thanks to Judy Benstead for bravery under fire in her work on the typescript.

References

Arnheim, R. (1954) *Art and Visual Perception*. Berkeley, CA: University of California Press.
Arnheim, R. (1971) *Visual Thinking*. Berkeley, CA: University of California Press.
Barthes, R. (1973) *Mythologies*. London: Paladin.
Barthes, R. (1977) *Image-Music-Text*. London: Fontana.
Barthes, R. (1984) *Camera Lucida*. London: Flamingo.
Berger, J. (1972) *Ways of Seeing*. London: BBC.
Bordwell, D. (1985) *Narration in the Fiction Film*. London: Methuen.
Burgin, V. (ed.) (1982) *Thinking Photography*. London: Macmillan.
Cook, G. (1992) *The Discourse of Advertising*. London: Routledge.
Derrida, J. (1976) *Of Grammatology* (trans. G. Spivak). Baltimore: Johns Hopkins University Press.
Gibson, J.J. (1986) *The Ecological Approach to Visual Perception*. Hillsdale, NJ: Lawrence Erlbaum.
Gombrich, E. (1960) *Art and Illusion*. Oxford: Phaidon Press.
Gombrich, E. (1963) *Meditations on a Hobby Horse*. Oxford: Phaidon Press.
Hall, S. (1982) 'The determinations of news photographs', in S. Cohen and J. Young (eds), *The Manufacture of News*. London: Constable.
Halliday, M.A.K. (1978) *Language as a Social Semiotic*. London: Edward Arnold.

Halliday, M.A.K. (1985) *Introduction to Functional Grammar*. London: Edward Arnold.

Hawthorn, J. (ed.) (1987) *Propaganda, Persuasion and Polemic*. London: Edward Arnold.

Hodge, R.I.V. and Kress, G.R. (1988) *Social Semiotics*. Cambridge: Polity Press.

Kress, G.R. (1993) 'Against arbitrariness: the social production of the sign as a foundational issue in critical discourse analysis', *Discourse and Society*, 4 (2): 169–91.

Kress, G.R. and van Leeuwen, T. (1996) *Reading Images: a Grammar of Visual Design*. London: Routledge.

Kress, G.R. and van Leeuwen, T. (1997) *The Multi-Modal Text*. London: Edward Arnold.

Kristeva, J. (1980) *Desire in Language*. New York: Columbia University Press.

Metz, C. (1971) *Language et cinéma*. Paris: Larousse.

Myers, G. (1994) *Words in Ads*. London: Edward Arnold.

Olson, D. (1994) *The World on Paper*. Cambridge: Cambridge University Press.

O'Toole, M. (1994) *The Language of Displayed Art*. London: Pinter.

Panofsky, E. (1939) *Studies in Iconology*. New York: Doubleday.

Panofsky, E. (1955) *Meaning in the Visual Arts*. New York: Doubleday.

Peirce, C.S. (1965) *Collected Papers*. Cambridge, MA: Belknap Press.

Saussure, F. de (1983) *Course in General Linguistics*. London: Duckworth.

Sontag, S. (1979) *On Photography*. Harmondsworth: Penguin.

Williamson, J. (1978) *Decoding Advertisements*. London: Marion Boyars.

11

Cognition

Arthur C. Graesser, Morton A. Gernsbacher and Susan R. Goldman

When people comprehend discourse, the speech or printed messages are not merely copied into their minds. Instead, the human mind actively constructs various types of *cognitive representations* (that is, codes, features, meanings, structured sets of elements) that interpret the linguistic input. These cognitive representations may incorporate words, syntax, sentential semantics, speech acts, dialogue patterns, rhetorical structures, pragmatics, real and imaginary worlds, and many other levels discussed in this volume. Each type of cognitive representation is functionally important during the processes of comprehending and producing text and talk.

During the last 25 years, cognitive psychologists have explored how the human mind represents the information in various types of cognitive representations. Cognitive psychologists have discovered that some of these cognitive representations are not equivalent to the symbolic representations that have been proposed by many formal linguists, logicians, and computer scientists. For example, suppose that a husband and wife are in the middle of a heated argument and the wife dramatically exclaims, 'If you don't leave, my clothes are going to Boston!' A traditional logician would construct a 'truth table' that specifies the truth values of all combinations of the husband's leaving versus not leaving, and of the clothes going versus not going to Boston. In an effort to 'comprehend' this speech act, a computer program would expend some processing time sorting out exactly which clothes might end up going to Boston. Both the logician and the computer program would miss the important inference that the wife would also be going to Boston (if the husband doesn't leave). In contrast, the meaning representations constructed by humans would not include the entire truth table and the precise set of clothes, but they probably would include the inference that the wife would be leaving. The meaning representations in the human mind are quite elaborate because they are anchored in a rich body of experiences and background world knowledge (which varies from person to person). At the same time, the meaning representations frequently are fragmentary (rather than complete), vague (rather than precise), redundant, open-ended, and sketchy. And yet, with all this apparent slop in the system, writers/speakers manage to construct messages that frequently can be recovered by readers/listeners with impressive accuracy.

Cognitive psychologists also investigate the mental processes that construct the cognitive representations. Some of these cognitive processes include *accessing* words in the mental lexicon, *activating* concepts in long-term memory, *searching* for information, *comparing* structures that are available in working memory, and *building* structures by adding, deleting, rearranging, or connecting information. Some cognitive processes are executed automatically and unconsciously, at lightning speed (measured in milliseconds). The execution of other cognitive processes is deliberate, conscious, and slow (measured in seconds). Of course, there is a continuum between these two extremes.

How do cognitive psychologists know whether humans actually construct these cognitive representations and perform these cognitive processes? Psychologists test hypotheses about cognition by conducting experiments and collecting data from humans. For example, there are a number of ways to test whether a reader constructs a particular representation. A group of readers might recall a text after they finish comprehending it. The content that is recalled should to some extent resemble the cognitive representations. If a theory predicts that text statement A is more central to the cognitive representation than statement B, then the likelihood that readers later recall A should be higher than that of B. As an alternative method, a series of test statements would be presented after comprehension and readers would decide whether each test statement was explicitly stated in the text. Readers should answer 'yes' when making these decisions to the extent that the test statements match cognitive representations. 'Yes' decisions should frequently occur when a test statement matches an inference that was never stated explicitly. Other tasks that unveil cognitive representations include summary protocols, true/false judgments about test statements, importance ratings for test statements, ratings on the extent to which two statements are conceptually related, and question answering.

It is possible to trace the dynamic process of constructing the cognitive representations 'on-line' during comprehension. One way we do this is by interrupting the reader and collecting data. For example, comprehenders may be asked to 'think aloud' while reading a text. The ideas that come to mind while reading include much of the content that enters the reader's consciousness at particular points in the text. The unconscious mind can also be tapped with experimental tasks. For example, readers might be periodically interrupted during comprehension and be presented test words to name as quickly as possible. The time that it takes to name a test word should be quick if the word closely matches a representation that is active in the reader's unconscious mind. There are experimental tasks that are less disruptive of comprehension than the think aloud task and the word naming task. In eye tracking studies, the researcher records the eye movements and the amount of time that the reader gazes on particular words. Alternatively, self-paced reading times are collected by having readers comprehend text at their own pace; readers press a response button that advances successive text segments one at a time, for example, word by word or sentence by sentence. Reading times for the various text segments are the data to be explained in these self-paced reading time tasks. Cognitive psychologists have devised dozens of experimental tasks that test for the existence of cognitive representations and 'on-line' cognitive processes.

The ultimate goal of the cognitive enterprise is to develop theories that specify how the cognitive representations are constructed and used. These theories are typically complex, given that discourse involves multiple levels and processing components. Moreover, psychological theories of discourse comprehension and production must be grounded in general theories of cognition. A general theory of cognition would explain memory, learning, decision making, problem-solving, and other cognitive faculties in addition to language and discourse. When theories of discourse processing become complex and sophisticated, cognitive psychologists simulate the mechanisms by developing computer models. A good computer model generates output that closely matches the data collected in psychology experiments.

Background and Development of the Cognitive Approach

Early cognitive theories of discourse were inspired by theories of discourse in other fields, such as text linguistics (van Dijk, 1972; Halliday and Hasan, 1976), artificial intelligence (Schank and Abelson, 1977), and pragmatics (Grice, 1975; Searle, 1969). Cognitive researchers explored whether the representations and claims about discourse in these sister fields provided psychologically plausible accounts of representations and processes in humans. Thus, cognitive researchers appropriately sought the wisdom and insights of other fields. As one might expect, some contributions from these sister fields proved to be valid when tested in psychology experiments, whereas other contributions ended up being blind alleys.

Propositional representations attracted the attention of researchers in early psychological theories of discourse (Clark and Clark, 1977; Kintsch, 1974). A *proposition* is a theoretical unit that contains a *predicate* (for example, main verb, adjective, connective) and one or more *arguments* (for example, nouns, embedded propositions), with each argument having a functional role (for example, agent, patient, object, location). A proposition refers to a state, an event, or an action and frequently has a truth value with respect to a real or an imaginary world.

In order to illustrate a propositional representation, consider the excerpt in Table 11.1 from the novel *Einstein's Dreams* by Alan Lightman (1993). A propositional segmentation for the first sentence is presented below the excerpt in Table 11.1. The single sentence contains seven propositions. The predicates in these propositions include verbs (lift, place, pinken), adjectives (brown, mushy), and connectives (and, [in order] to). The arguments

Table 11.1 *Excerpt and propositional representation*

Excerpt from Einstein's Dreams (Lightman, 1993: 102)
A mushy, brown peach is lifted from the garbage and placed on the table to pinken. It pinks, it turns hard, it is carried in a shopping sack to the grocer's, put on a shelf, removed and crated, returned to the tree with pink blossoms. In this world, time flows backward.

Propositional representation for the first sentence
Predicates are placed to the left of parentheses; arguments are placed within parentheses. Arguments have functional roles, such as agent, object, and location. PROP stands for proposition.

PROP 1: lift (AGENT = X, OBJECT = peach, SOURCE = from garbage)
PROP 2: brown (OBJECT = peach)
PROP 3: mushy (OBJECT = peach)
PROP 4: place (AGENT = X, OBJECT = peach, LOCATION = on table)
PROP 5: pinken (OBJECT = peach)
PROP 6: [in order] to (PROP 4, PROP 5)
PROP 7: and (PROP 1, PROP 4)

---

include objects (peach, garbage, table), an unidentified person (X), and embedded propositions (for example, propositions 4 and 5 are embedded in proposition 6). The arguments occupy various functional roles: agent, object, source, location.

Propositions were regarded as the primary functional units for segmenting text. It is important to note that some features of discourse are not explicitly captured in the propositional representations, such as tense, aspect, voice, and the determinacy of nouns. For example, the fact that the example sentence is in the passive voice rather than the active voice is not captured. These auxiliary linguistic features were regarded as comparatively unimportant in the meaning representation of text (Kintsch, 1974).

Cognitive psychologists conducted experiments to test the psychological plausibility of propositional representations. Kintsch (1974) reported that reading times increase as a function of the number of propositions in the text. This trend persists even when there is control over the number of words in the text and many other factors that potentially increase reading times (Haberlandt and Graesser, 1985). Kintsch (1974) reported that recall is better for those propositions that are structurally superordinate (that is, high in a hierarchical tree structure) than those that are comparatively subordinate. For example, propositions 2 and 3 in Table 11.1 are subordinate to proposition 1 because they modify the argument *peach* in proposition 1. Proposition 1 would therefore be recalled more often than propositions 2 and 3; readers would sometimes forget that the peach was brown and mushy.

One challenge for those who advocated propositional theories of discourse was to specify how the propositions are interrelated in a coherent fashion. Obviously, there is an important difference between texts with propositions that fit together conceptually (that is, high coherence) and texts with propositions that are unrelated (that is, no coherence). Kintsch and van Dijk developed psychological models that identified different types of coherence. Their models specified how coherent text structures are constructed in a working memory with limited capacity (Kintsch and van Dijk, 1978; van Dijk and Kintsch, 1983). It was widely acknowledged that the working memory of humans is limited in capacity. Only a handful of propositions and arguments are available in working memory at any one point in time during comprehension.

One level of coherence, called the text *microstructure* (Kintsch and van Dijk, 1978), connects explicit text propositions by argument overlap and other conceptual criteria. Two propositions are linked by *argument overlap* if they share a common argument. For example, propositions 1 and 4 are connected because they share two arguments (X and peach). Sometimes bridging inferences are needed to match arguments of propositions. For example, the pronoun it in the second sentence of Table 11.1 refers to *peach* in proposition 1, so there would need to be a bridging inference to capture the overlap: refers-to (it, peach). The process of constructing this bridging inference takes extra processing time to complete (Haviland and Clark, 1974). Although argument overlap was found to be an important criterion for establishing local coherence in many psychological experiments, argument overlap is not the only criterion for connecting propositions at the level of text microstructure (van Dijk and Kintsch, 1983). Local connections are also established by virtue of the situation described by a text, that is the mental microworld. For example, propositions may be connected by relations that convey temporality (proposition A occurred before proposition B), causality (A caused or enabled B), and other dimensions of the microworld. Local connections are established by various types of functional relations between propositions, such as comparison, contrast, generalization, example, and explanation (see Meyer, 1975). These relations, together with argument overlap, provide local text coherence at the microstructure level.

A second level of coherence consists of text *macrostructure*. Text macrostructure interrelates larger segments of text by virtue of world knowledge and genre schemata. For example, a schema for FRUIT DISTRIBUTION would connect many of the events in the example excerpt. One interesting property of this text is that the events are presented in an order that is opposite to the order of events in FRUIT DISTRIBUTION. The reversed ordering is explained by the major point that time flows backward in the imaginary world. The rest of the story shows how this backward flow of time provides illuminating insights about life and reality.

The global schemata at the macrostructure level were vigorously investigated by cognitive psychologists because they were an important key to solving the problem of text coherence. Indeed, text microstructure was hardly sufficient for establishing coherence between propositions. Some global schemata consisted of natural packages of generic world knowledge, such as person stereotypes, object concepts, and scripts (Schank and

Abelson, 1977). A RESTAURANT script, for example, contains knowledge about typical actors (for example, customer, waitress, cook), props (table, menu, food), goals (customer get food, waitress get money), actions (customer sits down, customer orders food, waitress brings food to customer, customer eats, etc.). The generic RESTAURANT script would have tentacles to many propositions in a text about a restaurant and would thereby provide global coherence. The script would supply the world knowledge that is needed for the reader to generate expectations, interpret incoming propositions, and generate inferences. Typical script content is filled in inferentially, which makes it difficult for the comprehender to determine whether a typical script proposition was explicitly stated or merely inferred by default (Bower et al., 1979; Graesser et al., 1979). According to the recognition memory experiments reported by Graesser et al. (1979), adults are entirely unable to discriminate whether a very typical script action (such as eating food) is explicitly stated or merely inferred by virtue of the RESTAURANT script.

Another class of global schemata is associated with particular text genres. Texts can be broadly classified into four different genres: descriptive, narrative, expository, and persuasive. There are various subclasses within these broad categories, and some texts are hybrids of multiple genres. Cognitive psychologists initially spent most of their efforts analysing expository texts (Kintsch, 1974; Meyer, 1975) and simple stories (Mandler and Johnson, 1977; Stein and Glenn, 1979). For example, the schema for a simple folktale has a set of components (for example, characters, setting, plot, episodes, resolution) and permissible orderings of these components (for example, the setting comes before the plot).

A different foundation for analysing text coherence addresses a *given–new* distinction (Haviland and Clark, 1974). An incoming sentence in a text contains both *given* information (that is, a proposition or argument already mentioned in the text) and *new* information. When the incoming sentence is interpreted, the comprehender first searches the previous passage context for information that matches the given information. If a match is found, the new information is appended structurally to the old proposition or argument. It takes a longer time to *reinstate* a proposition that was read several sentences earlier than to refer to a proposition that is resident in working memory. If no match is found, then a new structure needs to be built. Later in this chapter we will discuss a more recent model, called the structure building framework (Gernsbacher, 1990), that expands the given–new distinction.

Early cognitive models of discourse had a heavy emphasis on properties of the explicit text. That is, researchers proposed a quasiformal system for segmenting and organizing text, and then investigated whether these representations explained data in psychology experiments. By the early 1980s, cognitive researchers had identified some limitations with this preoccupation with the explicit text. They seriously acknowledged the importance of the reader and the constraints of general cognition. Comprehension came to be viewed as an active, flexible, strategic process rather than a passive, inflexible translation of explicit code (Graesser, 1981; van Dijk and Kintsch, 1983). It was important to consider the goals and background knowledge of the reader. Why was the reader comprehending the text? Was it read for entertainment, for a later memory test, or for proofreading? What did the reader know about the topic being discussed? Was the reader an expert or a novice about the topic? These reader characteristics profoundly influenced the cognitive representations constructed by comprehenders (Spilich et al., 1979). Although cognitive psychologists were always aware that meaning did not reside exclusively in the text *per se*, it was time to consider the reader characteristics more seriously. There was an increasing concern for the representation of the world knowledge that was activated by the text and for knowledge-based inferences (Graesser and Bower, 1990).

So far, our discussion of early psychological research on discourse has focused on reading (rather than talking) and has ignored the fact that most discourse is designed to communicate ideas in a social context. In fact, however, cognitive psychologists were quite aware of the communicative, social, and pragmatic dimensions of discourse (Bates, 1976; Clark and Clark, 1977). It was widely acknowledged that discourse comprehension and production are embedded in a communication system with three components: the writer/speaker, the reader/listener, and the text/talk. The speakers and listeners are visible, specific, and co-present in conversations. The speech acts in conversations occur in a specific context, situation, location, and time span. The speech participants have some sense of what knowledge they share (called common ground or mutual knowledge) and what goals they are attempting to achieve in the conceptually rich, situated context (Clark and Schaefer, 1989). In contrast, the writers, readers, and written texts are normally *decontextualized*. That is, the writer is invisible to the readers and the readers are invisible to the writer. Written text is produced at a different context, situation, location, and time than the comprehension of the text. The writer and reader are not always privy to what each other knows and what their separate goals are. However, in spite of these differences between text and talk, discourse is still embedded in a communication system with the three components.

Speech acts were the basic unit of linguistic analysis for those psychologists who concentrated on conversation analysis. According to the speech act theories, the stream of conversation is segmented into speech acts (D'Andrade and Wish, 1985; Searle, 1969). The representation of each speech act is a complex description that varies somewhat among speech act theorists. A speech act description might specify the speaker, the addressee, the literal propositional content, the speech act category (for example, assertion, question, promise, threat, request), and the intended meaning. For example, consider once again the wife expressing the following speech act to her husband: 'If you don't leave, my clothes are going to Boston!' The speaker is the wife, the addressee is the husband, and the speech act category is that of a threat. The literal propositional content is the conditional expression (if–then), with two embedded propositions (one about the husband not leaving and the other about the clothes going to Boston). The intended meaning stipulates that the wife plans on leaving if the husband doesn't leave.

It is important to note that there does not need to be a high semantic similarity between the literal meaning of a speech act (that is, its propositional content) and the intended meaning of the speech act (Searle, 1969). Suppose that you are at a dinner table and a person asks, 'Could you pass the salt?' This speech act is intended as an *indirect request* for you to pass the salt, even though it is literally expressed as a question about your salt passing abilities. Suppose that there is an angry storm outside and a friend of yours comments, 'Lovely weather outside.' This is an *ironic* utterance because the literal meaning is opposite of the intended meaning.

Clark and Lucy (1975) once proposed a two-stage model to account for the time-course of comprehending speech acts that involved discrepancies between the intended meaning and the literal meaning. The speaker first constructs the literal meaning and then, after detecting problems with the literal meaning, constructs the intended meaning. Therefore, extra processing time is needed to construct the intended meaning. Subsequent research challenged the two-stage model. Extra processing time was not necessarily needed to recover the intended nonliteral meaning. Instead, intended meanings can be constructed quickly (Glucksberg et al., 1982). One of the lively contemporary debates addresses the process of constructing intended meanings of speech acts on the basis of context plus the explicit text (Gibbs, 1994).

Current Directions, Theories, and Phenomena Investigated

Cognitive studies of discourse have flourished during the last 25 years. Researchers have published dozens of books and hundreds of articles in approximately a dozen different journals. Space limitations in this chapter do not permit a comprehensive treatment of all of the exciting research trends, phenomena, and theories. We instead focus on those topics that have received substantial attention in cognitive psychology and that also intersect our own programs of research. Consequently, this chapter covers text comprehension to a greater extent than text production and conversational discourse.

Cognitive Models of Discourse

Cognitive psychologists have been quite persistent in building sophisticated models of cognitive mechanisms. These models specify the representations, processing components, and interactive mechanisms in enough detail that patterns of empirical data can be simulated. Computational models simulate cognitive mechanisms on a computer. Mathematical models quantify precise patterns of processing times, memory scores, ratings, and other psychological data. These computational and mathematical models exist in the arena of discourse (Britton and Graesser, 1995; Just and Carpenter, 1992; Kintsch, 1988; Weaver et al., 1995), just as they do in other areas of cognitive psychology. It should be noted that modeling efforts are useful even when the simulated output fails to match human output. An understanding of why such discrepancies occur unveils new insights about the limitations of existing models and provides some direction for further research.

Psychological models of discourse have been greatly influenced by two major cognitive theories: symbolic theories and connectionist theories. In symbolic theories (Anderson, 1983), there is a working memory (as discussed earlier) and a vast storehouse of concepts, propositions, schemata, and production rules. A *production rule* has an 'IF [conditions] THEN [action]' format. When the conditions are met, the production is 'fired' (that is, activated) and the action (or action sequence) is performed. For example, the following simple production rule occurs frequently in most households:

IF [a telephone rings and a person is near the telephone]
THEN [the person picks up the telephone and says 'hello']

Production rules may involve cognitive actions rather than physical actions:

IF [the letter sequence h-e-r-o is perceived]
THEN [activate the concept of HERO in working memory]

A production system has thousands of these production rules. The production rules are continually being evaluated during each cycle of comprehension. According to some models, there are dozens or hundreds of these cycles of comprehension during a mere second. As new input enters working memory, all production rules are evaluated in parallel, but only a few of the production rules are fired, namely those that have their conditions satisfied. As new production rules are fired, and the information in working memory changes, verbal or physical actions are produced as output. The information in working memory dynamically changes over time, from cycle to cycle, as dictated by perceptual input and the knowledge base in long-term memory. The system learns from these dynamic changes in working memory. The process of learning creates new facts and production rules in long-term memory.

In connectionist theories (McClelland and Rumelhart, 1986), representations and processes are distributed among a large set of simple units. The units are often called *neural units* because there is a metaphor with neurons in the brain. Intelligent activity is believed to emerge from a large, interconnected mass of simple neural units. Each word, proposition, concept, schema, or rule has a corresponding ensemble of neural units. The activation level of each unit fluctuates dynamically over time, as comprehension proceeds. The units are connected by *weights*, thereby forming a *neural network.* The weight that connects one unit to another unit may be either excitatory (positive weight), inhibitory (negative weight), or zero. In a fully connected network, each unit is connected to every other unit (including itself). Therefore, if there are N units, there would be $N \times N$ weights in the *weight space.* The knowledge in long-term memory consists of the set of units and the weights in the weight space. When learning occurs, there is a change in one or more of the weights in the weight space.

So what happens during a particular comprehension cycle? A set of units is initially activated, namely those that capture the context and the per-ceived input. These units then excite or inhibit their neighboring units, according to the weights in the weight space; the neighbors then activate or inhibit their neighbors, and so on. Eventually, stability is achieved in the network when there are minimal changes in the activation values of the units: the network settles into a stable *pattern of activation.* The meaning representation at a particular point of comprehension consists of the pattern of activation values for all units. In this sense, meaning is said to be *distributed* throughout the network. In contrast, in a symbolic system, meaning is localized to one or a few symbolic expressions.

Although there have been a few bona fide connectionist models of text and discourse (for example, St John, 1992), most models are hybrids of the symbolic and connectionist theories (Britton and Graesser, 1995; Golden and Rumelhart, 1993; Goldman and Varma, 1995; Just and Carpenter, 1992; Kintsch, 1988). At this point, we will briefly describe the two most influential models of comprehension in cognitive psychology: the construction-integration model (Kintsch, 1988) and the collaborative activation-based production system model (Just and Carpenter, 1992).

Construction-Integration (CI) Model Kintsch's (1988) CI model distin-guishes three levels of representation: the surface form, the propositional textbase, and the referential situation model. The surface form preserves the exact words and syntax of sentences, whereas the textbase is similar to the propositional microstructure that was described earlier (see Table 11.1). The situation model integrates the text information with the reader's world knowledge and refers to the unique world that is conveyed in the text.

The CI is a hybrid model that combines symbolic expressions and connectionistic weights. The symbolic expressions include the content words (that is, nouns, main verbs, adjectives), the explicit text propositions, and world knowledge relevant to the text (which also comprises word and proposition expressions). For example, in the case of the text in Table 11.1, the first sentence would include 10 word units (lift, brown, mushy, place, pinken, [in order] to, and, peach, garbage, table), 7 proposition units, and 2 or more units referring to relevant world knowledge (for example, FRUIT DISTRIBUTION, grocer, other information that will not be specified here). These 19 units (10 + 7 + 2) are connected by a set of 19×19 weights, in the spirit of connectionist models. The weights are specified theoretically according to the constraints of the surface form, the textbase, and world knowledge. Consider the theoretical weight space corresponding to the textbase. Proposition 1 would have a positive weight connecting to proposition 2 by virtue of argument overlap; however, proposition 6 would not be directly connected to proposition 1 because there is no direct argument overlap in that case. Consider the weight space that involves the situation model. There would be a positive weight between grocer and proposition 1, signifying that grocer is the likely agent that lifts peaches from the garbage; there would not be a positive weight between grocer and proposition 5. Therefore, the CI model has a separate weight space for the surface form, the textbase, and the situation model. Each weight space has the same 19 nodes (and of course others that we will not bother mentioning).

The CI model simulates the dynamic fluctuation of activation values for the units in the network. These values change as comprehension proceeds, word by word, proposition by proposition, and sentence by sentence. At each cycle of comprehension, new words activate some of the units, activation spreads through the network, and the pattern of activation values for units eventually stabilizes. Then a new cycle of comprehension occurs and the process starts all over again. As a consequence, one can observe the activation value of each unit as a function of the sequence of comprehension cycles.

The *construction* phase of the CI model consists of the creation of the units corresponding to the explicit text and the associated world knowledge. These units, plus units from the prior discourse, are activated to varying degrees. The *integration* phase is the process of settling on a stable pattern of activation values. On the average, the units that have positive connection weights to many other units will settle on high activation values; units that are detached from other units will have low activation values. Therefore, coherence among the units is achieved in a systematic manner, but the connections have strength values rather than being discrete (that is, all-or-none).

Working memory plays an important role in the CI model. The CI model assumes that there are limitations on the amount of information that can be active in working memory at any point in time. Working memory holds the current sentence being processed and a set of propositions that is carried over from the previous comprehension cycle. The number of propositions carried over is designated as parameter s (designating size). The selected propositions are those that have the highest activation value. The value for s has been 2 in most of Kintsch's simulation efforts, but in principle this value could vary. The important assumption is that there is a fixed-capacity buffer. Those propositions that are *not* carried over in working memory still remain in long-term memory. However, these stored propositions can be reinstated in working memory if they are activated once again in a subsequent comprehension cycle.

The CI model predicts patterns of data in psychology experiments (Goldman and Varma, 1995; Kintsch, 1988; Haenggi et al., 1995). For example, when readers are asked to recall the text after comprehension, the likelihood of recalling the various propositions differs substantially. These recall likelihoods are positively correlated with their average activation values across the comprehension cycles. In some experiments, readers are stopped at the end of a sentence and presented with a letter string that either does or does not form a word (for example, grocer versus croger); readers decide as quickly as possible whether the test string does or does not form a word by pressing one of two buttons. The speed of these *lexical decisions* is correlated with a word's activation value, as computed by the CI model. For example, the lexical decision speed for 'grocer' would be facilitated even though it was never explicitly mentioned; it would have been activated in the situation model

Collaborative Activation-Based Production System (CAPS) Model The CAPS model is also a hybrid between the symbolic and connectionist theories (Just and Carpenter, 1992). There are symbolic expressions, such as words, phrases, propositions, schemata, and production rules. The information in working memory dynamically changes as production rules are fired in response to input. Unlike many other production systems, however, the conditions of production rules can exist at varying degrees of activation rather than being present versus absent (that is, all-or-none). The condition for a production rule is satisfied if the total activation value meets or exceeds some threshold. Consider the earlier production rule that activated the concept of HERO in working memory when the letters h, e, r, and o were registered as four elements in the condition. Suppose that the overall threshold for activating the rule is 100 units of activation in the condition. The production rule would fire if the activation values for h, e, r, and o are 40, 40, 0, and 40, respectively, because the total activation is 120, which exceeds the threshold. Thus, it would not be essential to detect all four letters in order to fire the production rule. Like all production rules, when the production rule is fired it performs the specified physical or cognitive processes.

The CAPS model captures the fact that working memory is limited in capacity and this limitation influences comprehension (Daneman and Carpenter, 1980; Whitney et al., 1991). CAPS assumes that there is a limit on the total amount of activation available for working memory elements, called the *cap*. When fired production rules request more activation than is available, the cap has been reached. Processing at the cap results in an overall system slowdown and a graceful loss of those working memory elements that are not participating in the processing. When an element falls below a minimum level of activation, it is no longer functional in working memory and cannot participate in processing.

Just and Carpenter have used the CAPS model to simulate reading times for individual words as readers comprehend sentences in text. The word reading times have been measured by collecting eye tracking data or by collecting self-paced word reading times. Longer reading times are predicted at points in the sentence when the cap is reached. Longer reading times are also predicted when the interpretation of an incoming word requires several microcycles of processing. Just and Carpenter have reported that the reading times for individual words are sometimes sensitive to the working memory spans of individual readers and that CAPS can account for the different patterns of reading times in high- versus low-span readers (Just and Carpenter, 1992; Millis and Just, 1994).

CI and CAPS Together Goldman and Varma (1995) developed a model that combines features of the CI model and the CAPS model. The fixed-buffer working memory of the CI model was replaced with a CAPS method of allocating activation in working memory. As a consequence, instead of carrying over only s propositions to the next comprehension cycle (as in the CI model, where s is normally 2), there is a more complex and judicious selection of proposition units to carry over. The improved model by Goldman and Varma provided a longer passage history, more inter-connections among propositions, and an enhanced formation of global macrostructures than did the CI model. Goldman and Varma's augmen-tation of the CI model with the CAPS model corrected one of the disappointing features of the CI model: local microstructure features of the text tended to dominate processing so the simulated reader frequently ended up losing the big picture. One other advantage of Goldman and Varma's hybrid model is that it integrated the goals and strategies of the reader into the comprehension mechanism. It was beyond the scope of the CI model to handle the systematic repercussions of particular reader goals and strategies.

Interactive Processing of Multiple Levels of Discourse and Knowledge

Everyone agrees that discourse comprehension involves multiple, highly interactive components. However, there have been some heated debates about the nature and timing of these interactive processes. For example, suppose that the reader encounters the word *he* in the middle of a novel. The process of resolving the referent of the pronoun would be influenced by sentence syntax, local semantic constraints, and the protagonists that exist in the discourse focus. Would syntax, semantics, or discourse focus have the most robust impact on fetching the correct referent for *he*? Which levels of analysis would be executed most quickly?

According to *modularity theory* (Fodor, 1983), there is an autonomous module for processing syntax and this module is more quickly executed than local semantics and discourse components. Discourse and semantics may subsequently override the syntax module, but it is syntax that reigns supreme early in the processing stream. For example, suppose that a reader encounters the sentence 'The thief stopped the girl with the dress.' According to a highly regarded hypothesis about syntax, called the *minimal attachment hypothesis* (Frazier and Fodor, 1978), there is a preference to construct syntactic structures that add a small number of new nodes to the syntactic representation. The theory predicts that the syntactic component would have an initial bias to interpret 'with the dress' as an instrumental prepositional phrase that elaborates the activity of 'stopping'. The local semantic context would later override this interpretation by assigning 'with the dress' the status of a relative clause that modifies 'girl'. So syntax is always executed first, even though semantics and discourse later prevail.

According to *interactive theories*, however, modules are highly interactive (rather than autonomous) and there is no intrinsic ordering of syntax before semantics and discourse (Just and Carpenter, 1992). Sometimes the constraints of discourse reign supreme and have a swift impact on the processing of a word, compared to the impact of local semantics and syntax (Hess et al., 1995). At other times, the local semantic context reigns supreme because it is more constraining. In addition to the modularity and interactive positions, there are a host of other models that specify inter-actions among lexical, syntactic, semantic, and discourse components (Perfetti, 1990).

Nevertheless, cognitive researchers do agree that comprehension is not a completely bottom-up process. It is not the case that syntax is initiated and entirely completed before semantics begins, or that semantics is completed before discourse processes are initiated. Instead, partial analyses evolve at all levels until the final representation is achieved. A computational model is *not* psychologically plausible if it requires a complete and accurate analysis of one component N before proceeding to another component M.

On-Line Construction of Coherent Representations

Cognitive researchers have investigated the process of constructing coherent representations at different levels of discourse during on-line comprehension (Gernsbacher, 1990; Lorch and O'Brien, 1995; Zwaan et al., 1995). Comprehension time for an incoming proposition is comparatively fast if it matches a proposition in working memory (an explicit proposition or an inference) and a bit longer if it appends new information to a proposition in working memory. Comprehension time increases if the reader needs to reinstate information mentioned earlier in the text and that no longer resides in working memory. Comprehension time increases to the extent that inferences must be made to connect the incoming sentence to prior text. A proposition takes a long time to comprehend if it is not related to any information in working memory and the previous context; in these instances, the reader builds a new structure and sometimes regards the information as irrelevant.

Strata of Meaning While reading a story, coherence is potentially monitored on several strata of meaning. These include: (1) the overlapping arguments in propositions, (2) the spatial locations of entities, (3) the causal flow of events, (4) the goals and plans of protagonists, (5) the temporal chronology of episodes, (6) the main point or theme, and (7) the purpose of the author in expressing a particular proposition. Cognitive psychologists have investigated the process of constructing representations at each of these strata, but particularly argument overlap (Kintsch and van Dijk, 1978), spatiality (Haenggi et al., 1995; Morrow et al., 1987; Rinck and Bower, 1995), causality (Fletcher and Bloom, 1988; Myers et al., 1987; van den Broek and Lorch, 1993), the goals and plans of characters (Dopkins et al., 1993; Long et al., 1992; Trabasso and Suh, 1993), and temporality (Zwaan et al., 1995).

Under what conditions do comprehenders monitor these various strata? Cognitive psychologists are divided on the answer to this question. According to McKoon and Ratcliff (1992), argument overlap among propositions is a critical stratum to monitor; coherence and elaborative inferences are monitored at the other strata only if there is break in argument overlap or if the reader has comprehension goals that are tuned to a particular stratum. According to other researchers, however, lack of argument overlap is neither necessary nor sufficient for relations to be constructed at the other strata (Albrecht and O'Brien, 1993; van den Broek and Lorch, 1993; Zwaan et al., 1995). Instead, several strata are simultaneously monitored.

Structure Building Framework   Gernsbacher (1990) proposed this model to account for the process of building coherent cognitive representations on-line. The process of building structures involves a number of subprocesses. First, comprehenders *lay foundations* for the mental structures. Next, comprehenders develop the structures by *mapping on information* when that information is related to the previous information. When the incoming information is less coherent or related, comprehenders employ a different process: they shift to *initiate a new substructure*. Therefore, most representations have several branching substructures.

The building blocks of the mental structures are called *memory nodes*. These nodes are activated by incoming stimuli and they transmit processing signals to other nodes. The processing signals either enhance (boost) or suppress (dampen) the activation levels of other nodes, much in the spirit of connectionist models. Memory nodes are enhanced when the information represented is necessary for further structure building. Nodes are suppressed when they are no longer necessary for building the multi-leafed structures.

Gernsbacher (1990) and her colleagues have extensively investigated the three subprocesses of structure building: (1) laying a foundation, (2) mapping relevant information onto the foundation, and (3) shifting to initiate a new substructure. The first two processes explain a persistent empirical phenomenon called the 'advantage of first mention'. That is, participants mentioned first in a sentence are more memorable than participants mentioned later. For example, after comprehending the sentence 'Tina beat Lisa in the state tennis match', Tina would be more memorable and quicker to access than would Lisa. The first participant is normally the discourse topic and lays the foundation of the mental structure. In a series of experiments, Gernsbacher ruled out potential extraneous explanations of this empirical finding, such as the fact that Tina is an agent and the syntactic subject. The empirical finding occurs even in those languages, such as Spanish, where the order of words is less constrained than in English.

The occurrence of processes 1 and 3 explains a second persistent empirical phenomenon, called the 'advantage of clause recency'. That is, information in the most recent clause in a sentence is more memorable and accessible than information from an earlier clause in the sentence. For example, the word 'oil' is more accessible immediately after comprehending sentence 1 than sentence 2:

1 Now that artists are working fewer hours, *oil* prints are rare.
2 Now that artists are working in *oil*, prints are rare.

Comprehenders represent each clause of these two-clause sentences in its own mental substructure. While building a clause-level substructure, comprehenders have the greatest access to information in that substructure. However, after a comprehender has finished building a representation for the most recent clause, information from the first clause becomes more accessible becasue it is the foundation for the entire sentence. Consequently, the advantage of first mention is a long-lived phenomenon whereas the advantage of clause recency is short-lived.

Gernsbacher identified some of the discourse cues that encourage the second process of mapping. The explicitness of a referring expression is an important cue for signaling coherence, as has been observed by linguists (Givón, 1993; Halliday and Hasan, 1976). *A big bad wolf* is an indefinite noun-phrase so it would signal a new structure. In contrast, *the wolf* would probably signal a mapping of information onto an existing structure and the pronoun *it* would signal mapping rather than shifting. Causal coherence involves mapping (rather than shifting) and is frequently signaled by connectives, such as *because*, *so*, and *in order to*. Temporal mapping is frequently signaled by the tense and aspects of verbs. It should be noted that surface codes and function words in a clause become less accessible whenever there is a shift to a new substructure during process 3.

Gernsbacher and her colleagues have examined the processes of enhancing and surpressing nodes during comprehension. When comprehenders encounter homographs (such as 'spade'), multiple meanings are immediately activated (for example, garden tool versus card suit) even though one meaning is appropriate for the context (such as 'He dug in the garden with a spade'). However, within a half a second, only the contextually appropriate meaning is available. What happens to the contextually inappropriate meanings? According to the structure building framework, they do not receive lower activation by mere decay or by competitive inhibition among alternative meanings. Instead, they are actively suppressed by the signals transmitted by memory nodes that represent the syntactic, semantic, and pragmatic context. Less skilled readers have problems suppressing the inappropriate meanings of words whereas skilled readers have efficient suppression mechanisms (Gernsbacher, 1993). Comprehension skill is predicted by the quality of the suppression mechanism but not by the enhancement mechanism.

Constructing Inferences and Situation Models

As discussed earlier, van Dijk and Kintsch (1983) contrasted three levels of representation: the surface form, the propositional textbase, and the refer-ential situation model. The situation model refers to the people, setting, states, events, and actions of the mental microworld that the text describes. For example, in the text in Table 11.1, the reader would imagine the process of the peaches ripening and being distributed, but in reversed order, much like a videotape going backward. Situation models have been difficult to investigate systematically for several reasons. First, world knowledge plays a central role in building situation models, yet world knowledge is imprecise, open-ended, vague, and minimally visible to the investigator. Second, situation models are unique representations that embody the idiosyncratic constraints of the particular text. It is difficult to identify general mechanisms when the representations are so idiosyncratic. Third, there is no sophisticated theory from any field that both specifies how situation models are constructed and also is psychologically plausible. Psychologists have been forced to discover the mechanisms on their own. This has presented a stimulating challenge to many cognitive psychologists. There have been lively debates over what classes of inferences are generated during reading and the construction of situation models (Graesser and Bower, 1990; Graesser et al., 1994; McKoon and Ratcliff, 1992).

Narrative text has received the most attention in studies of inference generation and situation model construction. This is because narrative texts embody episodes that resemble everyday experiences and that activate an extensive mass of world knowledge. In contrast, expository texts typically inform the reader about topics that the reader is unfamiliar with. Therefore, cognitive researchers have examined whether different classes of inferences are generated on-line during the comprehension of narratives. These classes of inferences include character traits, the knowledge and beliefs of characters, the goals and plans that motivate character actions, the manner of executing actions, the spatial setting and layout, the causes of events, emotional reactions of characters, and expectations about future episodes in the plot. To a lesser extent, researchers have explored the inferences associated with the pragmatic interaction between writer and reader, such as inferences about the attitudes of the writer and appropriate emotional reactions of the reader. Although all of these classes of inferences could potentially be generated in an elaborate analysis of a story, only a subset of the inferences is generated on-line during an initial reading of a text. A

Table 11.2   *The czar story and example inferences*

The Czar and his Daughters

Once there was a czar who had three lovely daughters. One day the three daughters went walking in the woods. They were enjoying themselves so much that they forgot the time and stayed too long. A dragon kidnapped the three daughters. As they were being dragged off, they cried for help. Three heroes heard their cries and set off to rescue the daughters. The heroes came and fought the dragon and rescued the maidens. Then the heroes returned the daughters to their palace. When the czar heard of the rescue, he rewarded the heroes.

Inferences when comprehending 'The dragon kidnapped the daughters'

SUPERORDINATE GOAL: *The dragon wanted to eat the daughters.*

   A goal that motivates an agent's intentional action.

SUBORDINATE GOAL/ACTION: *The dragon grabbed the daughters.*

   A goal, plan, or action that specifies how an action is achieved.

CAUSAL ANTECEDENT: *The dragon saw the daughters.*

   An event or state on a causal chain that bridges an explicit proposition to the previous passage context.

CAUSAL CONSEQUENCE: *Someone rescued the daughters.*

   A physical event or action on a forecasted causal chain that unfolds from an explicit proposition. Emotional reactions in characters are not included.

EMOTIONAL REACTION: *The daughters were frightened.*

   An emotion experienced by a character in response to an explicit event, action, or state.

STATE: *The dragon has scales.*

   An ongoing state, from the time frame of the story plot, that is not causally linked to episodes in the plot. These include character traits, properties of objects, and spatial relationships among entities.

---

good theory should be able to discriminate inferences generated on-line versus off-line.

Table 11.2 presents an example story about a dragon kidnapping three daughters and being saved by heroes. There are definitions and examples of six classes of inferences: *superordinate goals* that motivate characters' actions, *subordinate goals* that specify how actions are achieved, *causal antecedents* of events, *causal consequences*, *emotional reactions* of characters, and ongoing *states*. These example inferences are *extratextual* inferences rather than *text-connecting* inferences. Text-connecting inferences specify that two or more explicit propositions are connected conceptually. Extratextual inferences embellish the situation model by copying or deriving information from world knowledge. An investigation of the inferences illustrated in Table 11.2 has provided informative tests among different models of inference generation. The models make different predictions about which classes of inferences are generated on-line.

Explicit Textbase Position   This position is compatible with early models of text comprehension that focused on the explicit text (Kintsch, 1974; Mandler and Johnson, 1977). According to this position, the explicit text-base reigns supreme in shaping the cognitive representation of discourse, not the situation model. The only inferences that are constructed on-line are the referential inferences that bind explicit arguments and propositions in text (for example, linking pronouns to previous arguments, establishing argument overlap). None of the extratextual inferences in Table 11.2 are constructed on-line according to this first position.

Minimalist Hypothesis   McKoon and Ratcliff (1992) proposed this hypothesis to account for those inferences that are automatically (versus strategically) encoded during comprehension. The only inferences that are encoded automatically during reading are those that make text statements locally coherent. Situation-based inferences are encoded only when there is a break in local coherence (specifically, argument overlap) or when the reader has a goal to construct a particular class of inferences (for example, the goal of tracking the spatial locations of characters and objects). Causal antecedent inferences are the only inferences in Table 11.2 that are important for establishing local text coherence; readers need to construct causal antecedents in order to causally bridge an incoming story event with the prior passage context. Therefore, the minimalist hypothesis predicts that causal antecedent inferences should have the highest strength of encoding during comprehension and that the other inferences are sporadically generated on-line.

Current-State Selection Strategy and the Causal Inference Maker Model
These models specify the process of constructing causal connections between explicit actions and events in stories (Fletcher and Bloom, 1988; van den Broek and Lorch, 1993). According to these two models, only two classes of extratextual inferences are reliably generated on-line: causal antecedents and subordinate goals. However, it is beyond the scope of this chapter to describe the mechanisms that supply these predictions.

Constructionist Theory   Graesser et al. (1994) developed a constructionist theory that has three major assumptions. The *reader goal* assumption states that comprehenders construct inferences that address the comprehenders' goals. This first assumption does not offer any discriminating, invariant predictions about the on-line status of the inferences in Table 11.2, but it does offer context-sensitive predictions that consider the idiosyncratic goals of the reader. The second assumption, the *coherence* assumption, states that comprehenders attempt to construct a meaning representation that is coherent at both local and global levels. Whereas causal antecedents are important for establishing local coherence, superordinate goals and emotional reactions of characters are important for establishing global plot coherence in stories. It should be noted, however, that attempts to construct global coherence constitute an effort, not necessarily an achievement. If the text is choppy, meandering, and pointless, readers will give up trying to construct a globally coherent meaning representation. According to the third, *explanation* assumption, comprehenders attempt to explain *why* actions, events, and states are mentioned in the text. Inferences that answer such why-questions include causal antecedents and superordinate goals (Graesser, 1981). In summary, the constructionist theory predicts that three classes of inferences are reliably constructed on-line when individuals comprehend stories: causal antecedents, superordinate goals, and emotional reactions of characters. The other three classes of inferences in Table 11.2 are elaborations that are not normally constructed on-line: causal consequences, subordinate goals, and states.

Prediction-Substantiation Model   This model asserts that comprehension is expectation-driven in addition to explanation-driven (Bower et al., 1979; Schank and Abelson, 1977). Expectations are formulated when a higher-order knowledge structure is activated (such as a script); the content of the global structure supplies the expectations. The only classes of inferences in Table 11.2 that would *not* be generated on-line are subordinate goals and states. It should be noted that the previous models resisted the possibility that expectation-based consequence inferences are generated on-line. This is because (a) there are too many future plots that could conceivably unfold, (b) it takes a large amount of working memory resources to construct even a single hypothetical plot, and (c) most expectations end up being disconfirmed in the face of subsequent discourse (Graesser, 1981; Kintsch, 1988).

Promiscuous Inference Generation   This extreme position predicts that all six classes of inferences are generated on-line, as long as the reader has the prerequisite world knowledge. Comprehenders build a complete, lifelike situation model by fleshing out all of the details about the characters, props, spatial layout, actions, events, and so on. The meaning representation is akin to a high-resolution mental videotape of the narrative, along with complete information about the mental states of characters. It would be difficult to find a researcher who seriously advocates this position, but it nevertheless is an interesting extreme position to consider.

Tests of the Models of Inference Generation   An adequate test of the above models would need to assure that comprehenders have the prerequisite background knowledge to generate the extratextual inferences. It would be pointless to assess whether a class of inferences is generated on-line if few readers had the critical world knowledge. Therefore, some researchers have collected 'think aloud' protocols or question answering protocols from a sample of readers in order to extract potential inferences that may (or may not) be generated on-line during comprehension (Graesser, 1981; Trabasso and Suh, 1993). These verbal protocols are collected as the sample of readers comprehend the text, sentence by sentence. If an inference is manifested in these protocols, there is some assurance that the reader has the prerequisite knowledge to make the inference. However, more rigorous experimental tests are needed to assess whether the inference is truly made on-line during normal comprehension (that is, when verbal protocols are not collected).

One type of experimental test involves interrupting the comprehender at critical points in the text and collecting word naming data or lexical decision data. Suppose that the reader of the story in Table 11.2 is interrupted after reading the explicit statement 'The dragon kidnapped the daughters.' The alternative test words to name would come from the six inference classes: *eat*, *grab*, *see*, *rescue*, *fright*, and *scales*. Of course, the words selected in tests of the various inference classes would be equated on word frequency, syntactic category, number of letters, and a host of other extraneous factors.

Graesser et al. (1994) examined evidence from several dozen experiments on inference generation in order to evaluate the above theoretical positions. They argued that most of the existing evidence supports the constructionist theory rather than the other positions. For example, readers generate superordinate goals on-line but not subordinate goals (Long et al., 1992). They generate causal antecedents but not causal consequences (Magliano et al., 1993; Potts et al., 1988). They generate character emotions (Gernsbacher et al., 1992) but not ongoing states. The constructionist model apparently is compatible with most of the existing empirical evidence, but more research is needed before we can be confident in our claims about inference generation and the construction of situation models.

Comprehending Bona Fide Literature

An adequate model of discourse comprehension would generalize to naturalistic texts rather than being restricted to experimenter-generated 'textoids' (van Oostendorp and Zwaan, 1994). One of the current trends is to explore the process of comprehending actual literary texts, such as short stories and novels (Dixon et al., 1993; Gerrig, 1993; Kreuz and MacNealy, 1995; Miall and Kuiken, 1994; Zwaan et al., 1995).

Literary narrative has a number of properties which are different from the narrative, expository, and pseudotexts that cognitive psychologists have traditionally analysed. Literature is written in part to produce emotional responses in the reader, such as surprise, curiosity, or suspense (Brewer and Ohtsuka, 1988). Literature is written to reveal deep truths about life and reality, even when the plot is entirely fictional. Literature has a high density of nonliteral forms, such as irony, metaphor, understatement, and hyperbole. Literary excerpts are sometimes crafted to support multiple interpretations (that is, intentional ambiguity) rather than to converge on a single intended meaning. Literary texts often violate linguistic and social conventions, thereby encouraging the reader to reflect on language and society. Literary texts have points of view either that are unusual (for example, observing events from the point of view of a dog) or that fluctuate (for example, between a character and an omniscient narrator). Investigations of literary comprehension both open the door to new comprehension phenomena and test the limits of the mainstream cognitive theories of discourse.

The excerpt in Table 11.1 is an example of a literary device. The reader starts out rather confused about the temporal sequence of events in the first two sentences. This confusion exists even though the text exhibits local coherence, namely the argument overlap involving the peach. The third sentence resolves the confusion: time flows backward in that world. From the perspective of the third sentence, all of the events make sense when they are reinterpreted. This device builds confusion, followed by revelation; it creates tension and then abrupt release, which is a common arousal pattern in aesthetic works.

Major Applications

The importance of cognitive research on discourse is not restricted to academic circles. There have been several applications of cognitive models to real world problems. For example, some salient areas of application have been in education, in the design of computer displays and dialogue facilities, and in the construction of printed texts, documents, questionnaires, and forms.

The cross-fertilization between education and cognitive research on discourse has been one of the productive arenas during the last 10 years. The cognitive enterprise has offered some promising new theories and some rigorous experimental methodologies, whereas the education enterprise has forced the cognitive researchers to investigate naturalistic texts and learning environments. A host of practical questions in education have been explored as a consequence of this cross-fertilization (Barr et al., 1991). How do children read stories and expository texts? How can reading be improved? How do readers of all ages differ in reading abilities? How do readers learn from text, and how can this be improved? How can texts be designed or revised to enhance learning and memory? How is learning from text facilitated by auxiliary organizers, such as outlines, questions, highlighting, pictures, diagrams, and animation?

In the best of worlds, learning materials are designed to maximize reading speed, comprehensibility, information delivery, memory, and enjoyment. Unfortunately, however, there sometimes are tradeoffs in meeting these design goals. For example, a text that is pitched for enjoyment may be lean in information delivery. A text that is difficult to comprehend may enhance memory if it promotes active learning on the part of the student. As always, there are individual differences among readers. Researchers have documented a number of counterintuitive effects that reflect various tradeoffs and differences among readers (Goldman and Saul, 1990; Mayer and Sims, 1994). For example, an outline that has a poor match to a text may promote active learning at the deep situation model level, but at the same time reduce memory for explicit text (McNamara et al., 1996;

Mannes, 1994). According to these findings, it is critical to specify the level of text representation that is influenced by manipulations of auxiliary organizers.

One of our favorite gems of wisdom is that there is nothing more practical than a good theory. In this spirit, cognitive models of discourse can be used as a fine-tuned guide to revise text. For example, Britton and Gulgoz (1991) used Kintsch and van Dijk's (1978) model to revise expository texts. The Kintsch and van Dijk model identifies points in the text where there are coherence gaps. Readers are expected to generate inferences to fill these gaps but sometimes they fail and comprehension suffers. Britton and Gulgoz (1991) prepared revised versions of the texts that made these critical coherence-based inferences explicit. Memory for the revised texts was substantially superior to memory for the original texts with coherence gaps. Moreover, the model-based revisions were more memorable than revisions prepared by text linguists and by professional writers for major magazines (such as *Time* and *Life*).

Summary and Conclusions

Studies of cognition and discourse have dramatically increased during the short 25-year history of the field. Early research tested theories of discourse in sister fields, such as text linguistics, computational linguistics, and artificial intelligence. The early work focused on the structures and processes associated with the explicit text and on coherence at various levels. Contemporary research continues to test theories of discourse representation in other fields, but there is a more accurate sense of the plausible representations and processes in humans. There has been a shift toward understanding how these representations are shaped by world knowledge and comprehension strategies. Researchers hardly deny the importance of explicit text, but explicit text is only one piece of the puzzle.

Cognitive researchers have developed sophisticated models of discourse comprehension and production that attempt to explain complex patterns of experimental data. These models of discourse are integrated with general theories of cognition, not just discourse *per se*. Symbolic theories assume that knowledge is represented in the form of propositions, conceptual structures, schemata, and production rules. This content is dynamically activated and created in a limited-capacity working memory as comprehension proceeds. Connectionist theories assume that knowledge is represented in a more distributed mass of neural units, connected by excitatory or inhibitory weights. The activation values of the neural units dynamically change in working memory as comprehension proceeds. The two major models of discourse comprehension, the construction-integration model and the CAPS/reader models, are hybrids of the symbolic and connectionist traditions. These models attempt to account for complex interactions among multiple levels of representation. Future research needs to expand these models by tackling longer texts, global patterns of coherence, a broader array of inferences, richer situation models, diverse reader goals, and pragmatic constraints between communication participants.

An adequate cognitive model accounts for the final meaning representations that get constructed and the process of constructing these representations on-line. According to the structure building framework, for example, the comprehender first builds a framework for a particular structure, then adds new relevant information to the structure, and shifts to a different structure when incoming information is irrelevant. Tests of the final meaning representations involve the collection of memory and judgment data after comprehension is finished. Tests of on-line comprehension mechanisms involve the collection of processing time data, such as reading times, gaze durations, and word naming latencies for test words that are interspersed in the text during comprehension.

Inferences are generated during the course of building the meaning representations on-line. Researchers have proposed several models that predict which classes of knowledge-based inferences are generated during comprehension. Available data appear to best fit a constructionist theory. This theory states that readers construct those inferences that are relevant to the readers' comprehension goals, that establish local and global coherence, and that explain why propositions are mentioned in the text. Future research on inference generation needs to identify the precise conditions under which particular classes of inference are generated, as well as the time-course of their generation. There are almost no data on global thematic inferences and on inferences about the pragmatic communication between writer and reader. Future research needs to continue contrasting different discourse genres. A crude classification distinguishes narrative, expository, persuasive, and descriptive texts. A more mature classification scheme would include numerous subcategories, as well as hybrids. The representations, comprehension strategies, and pragmatic assumptions differ substantially among the various genres. One of the refreshing recent trends has been to focus on naturalistic literary works, such as novels and short stories. Studies of literary comprehension should help us understand the complex relationships among discourse, cognition and emotion.

Cognitive models of discourse have periodically been applied to real world problems. The models provide some guidance in revising text to make it more memorable or easy to comprehend. These efforts have proven useful in several practical arenas, such as education, the design of texts, surveys, and questionnaires, and the design of computer systems. We anticipate that cognitive research will have an important role in the future development of the 'information highway'.

Recommended Further Reading

Gernsbacher's *Handbook of Psycholinguistics* (1994) provides an excellent survey of contemporary research in the psychology of language and discourse. Introductory books by Just and Carpenter (1987) and Singer (1990) introduce the newcomer to cognitive research on language and discourse.

Cognitive psychologists have devoted considerable effort to building computational and mathematical models of discourse. Recent edited books provide a comprehensive survey of these sophisticated models (Britton and Graesser, 1995; Weaver et al., 1995). Original journal articles are available for those who wish to pursue the construction-integration model (Kintsch, 1988) and the CAPS/reader model (Just and Carpenter, 1992).

We have recommendations for those who wish to pursue particular problems in discourse and cognition. Gernsbacher (1990) discusses the structure building framework and supporting research. An edited book by Lorch and O'Brien (1995) presents psychological research on text coherence. The problem of inference generation is covered in an edited book by Graesser and Bower (1990) and in two journal articles (Graesser et al., 1994; McKoon and Ratcliff, 1992). A book of readings edited by Clark (1993) discusses psychological research on the use of language in conversation. For those interested in the comprehension of literature and figurative language, we recommend an edited book by Kreuz and MacNealy (1995). The *Handbook of Reading Research* (Barr et al., 1991) covers educational research on different discourse genres.

References

Albrecht, J.E. and O'Brien, E.J. (1993) 'Updating a mental model: maintaining both local and global coherence', *Journal of Experimental Psychology: Learning, Memory, and Cognition*, 19: 1061–70.

Anderson, J.R. (1983) *The Architecture of Cognition*. Cambridge, MA: Harvard University Press.

Barr, R., Kamil, M.L., Mosenthall, P. and Pearson, P.D. (eds) (1991) *Handbook of Reading Research*. London: Longman.

Bates, E. (1976) *Language and Context: the Acquisition of Pragmatics*. New York: Academic Press.

Bower, G.H., Black, J.B. and Turner, T.J. (1979) 'Scripts in memory for text', *Cognitive Psychology*, 11: 177–220.

Brewer, W.F. and Ohtsuka, K. (1988) 'Story structure, characterization, just world organization, and reader affect in American and Hungarian short stories', *Poetics*, 17: 395–415.

Britton, B.K. and Graesser, A.C. (eds) (1995) *Models of Understanding Text*. Hillsdale, NJ: Erlbaum.

Britton, B.K. and Gulgoz, S. (1991) 'Using Kintsch's computational model to improve instructional text: effects of repairing inference calls on recall and cognitive structures', *Journal of Educational Psychology*, 83: 329–45.

Clark, H.H. (1993) *Arenas of Language Use*. Chicago: University of Chicago Press.

Clark, H.H. and Clark, E.V. (1977) *Psychology and Language*. New York: Harcourt Brace Jovanovich.

Clark, H.H. and Lucy, P. (1975) 'Understanding what is meant from what is said: a study in conversationally conveyed requests', *Journal of Verbal Learning and Verbal Behavior*, 14: 56–72.

Clark, H.H. and Schaefer, E.F. (1989) 'Contributing to discourse', *Cognitive Science*, 13: 259–94.

D'Andrade, R.G. and Wish, M. (1985) 'Speech act theory in quantitative research on interpersonal behavior', *Discourse Processes*, 8: 229–59.

Daneman, M. and Carpenter, P.A. (1980) 'Individual differences in working memory and reading', *Journal of Verbal Learning and Verbal Behavior*, 19: 450–66.

Dixon, P., Bortolussi, M., Twilley, L.C. and Leung, A. (1993) 'Literary processing and interpretation: towards empirical foundations', *Poetics*, 22: 5–34.

Dopkins, S., Klin, C. and Myers, J.L. (1993) 'Accessibility of information about goals during the processing of narrative texts', *Journal of Memory and Language*, 19: 70–80.

Fletcher, C.R. and Bloom, C.P. (1988) 'Causal reasoning in the comprehension of simple narrative texts', *Journal of Memory and Language*, 27: 236–44.

Fodor, J.D. (1983) *Modularity of Mind*. Cambridge, MA: MIT Press.

Frazier, L. and Fodor, J.D. (1978) 'The sausage machine: a new two-stage parsing model', *Cognition*, 6: 291–325.

Gernsbacher, M.A. (1990) *Language Comprehension as Structure Building*. Hillsdale, NJ: Lawrence Erlbaum.

Gernsbacher, M.A. (1993) 'Less skilled readers have less efficient supression mechanisms', *Psychological Science*, 4: 294–8.

Gernsbacher, M.A. (ed.) (1994) *Handbook of Psycholinguistics*. New York: Academic Press.

Gernsbacher, M.A., Goldsmith, H.H. and Robertson, R.R. (1992) 'Do readers mentally represent character's emotional states?', *Cognition and Emotion*, 6: 89–112.

Gerrig, R.J. (1993) *Experiencing Narrative Worlds*. New Haven, CT: Yale University Press.

Gibbs, R. (1994) *The Poetics of Mind: Figurative Thought, Language, and Understanding*. New York: Cambridge University Press.

Givón, T. (1993) 'Coherence in text, coherence in mind', *Pragmatics and Cognition*, 1: 171–227.

Glucksberg, S., Gildea, P. and Bookin, H.B. (1982) 'On understanding nonliteral speech: can people ignore metaphor?', *Journal of Verbal Learning and Verbal Behavior*, 21: 85–98.

Golden, R.M. and Rumelhart, D.E. (1993) 'A parallel distributed processing model of story comprehension and recall', *Discourse Processes*, 16: 203–37.

Goldman, S.R. and Saul, E.U. (1990) 'Flexibility in text processing: a strategy competition model', *Learning and Individual Differences*, 2: 181–219.

Goldman, S.R. and Varma, S. (1995) 'CAPing the construction-integration model of discourse comprehension, in C. Weaver, S. Mannes and C. Fletcher (eds), *Discourse Comprehension: Models of Processing Revisited*. Hillsdale, NJ: Erlbaum.

Graesser, A.C. (1981) *Prose Comprehension beyond the Word*. New York: Springer Verlag.

Graesser, A.C. and Bower, G.H. (eds) (1990) *The Psychology of Learning and Motivation: Inferences and Text Comprehension*. San Diego: Academic Press.

Graesser, A.C., Gordon, S.E. and Sawyer, J.D. (1979) 'Memory for typical and atypical actions in scripted activities: test of a script + tag hypothesis', *Journal of Verbal Learning and Verbal Behavior*, 18: 319–32.

Graesser, A.C., Singer, M. and Trabasso, T. (1994) 'Constructing inferences during narrative text comprehension', *Psychological Review*, 101: 371–95.

Grice, H.P. (1975) 'Logic and conversation', in P. Cole and J. L. Morgan (eds), *Syntax and Semantics. Vol. 3: Speech Acts*. New York: Academic Press. pp. 41–58.

Haberlandt, K. and Graesser, A.C. (1985) 'Component processes in text comprehension and some of their introductions', *Journal of Experimental Psychology: General*, 114: 357–74.

Haenggi, D., Kintsch, W. and Gernsbacher, M.A. (1995) 'Spatial models and text comprehension', *Discourse Processes*, 19: 173–99.

Halliday, M.A.K. and Hasan, R. (1976) *Cohesion in English*. London: Longman.

Haviland, S.E. and Clark, H.H. (1974) 'What's new? Acquiring new information as a process in comprehension', *Journal of Verbal Learning and Verbal Behavior*, 13: 512–21.

Hess, D.J., Foss, D.J. and Carroll, P. (1995) 'Effects of global and local context on lexical processes during language comprehension', *Journal of Experimental Psychology: General*, 124: 62–82.

Just, M.A. and Carpenter, P.A. (1987) *The Psychology of Reading and Language Comprehension*. Boston, MA: Allyn and Bacon.

Just, M.A. and Carpenter, P.A. (1992) 'A capacity theory of comprehension: individual differences in working memory', *Psychological Review*, 99: 122–49.

Kintsch, W. (1974) *The Representation of Meaning in Memory*. Hillsdale, NJ: Erlbaum.

Kintsch, W. (1988) 'The role of knowledge in discourse comprehension: a constructive-integration model', *Psychological Review*, 95: 163–82.

Kintsch, W. and van Dijk, T.A. (1978) 'Toward a model of text comprehension and production', *Psychological Review*, 85: 363–94.

Kreuz, R.J. and MacNealy, M.S. (eds) (1995) *Empirical Approaches to Literature and Aesthetics*. Norwood, NJ: Ablex.

Lightman, A. (1993) *Einstein's Dreams*. New York: Warner.

Long, D.L., Golding, J.M. and Graesser, A.C. (1992) 'The generation of goal related inferences during narrative comprehension', *Journal of Memory and Language*, 5: 634–47.

Lorch, R. and O'Brien, E. (eds) (1995) *Sources of Coherence in Reading*. Hillsdale, NJ: Erlbaum.

Magliano, J.P., Baggett, W.B., Johnson, B.K. and Graesser, A.C. (1993) 'The time course of generating causal antecedent and causal consequence inferences', *Discourse Processes*, 16: 35–53.

Mandler, J.M. and Johnson, N.S. (1977) 'Remembrance of things parsed: story structure and recall', *Cognitive Psychology*, 9: 111–51.

Mannes, S.M. (1994) 'Strategic processing of text', *Journal of Educational Psychology*, 86: 577–88.

Mayer, R.E. and Sims, V.K. (1994) 'For whome is a picture worth a thousand words? Extensions of a dual-coding theory of multimedia learning', *Journal of Educational Psychology*, 86: 389–401.

McClelland, J.L. and Rumelhart, D.E. (eds) (1986) *Parallel Distributed Processing: Explorations in the Microstructure of Cognition*, vol. 2. Cambridge, MA: MIT Press.

McKoon, G. and Ratcliff, R. (1992) 'Inference during reading', *Psychological Review*, 99: 440–66.

McNamara, D.S., Kintsch, E., Songer, N.S. and Kintsch, W. (1996) 'Are good texts always better? Interactions of text coherence, background knowledge, and levels of understanding in learning from text', *Cognition and Instruction*, 14 (1): 1–43.

Meyer, B.F.J. (1975) *The Organization of Prose and its Effect on Memory*. New York: Elsevier.

Miall, D.S. and Kuiken, D. (1994) 'Beyond text theory: understanding literary response', *Discourse Processes*, 17: 137–52.

Millis, K. and Just, M.A. (1994) 'The influence of connectives on sentence comprehension', *Journal of Memory and Language*, 33: 128–47.

Morrow, D.G., Greenspan S.L. and Bower, G.H. (1987) 'Accessibility and situation models in narrative comprehension', *Journal of Memory and Language*, 26: 165–87.

Myers, J.L., Shinjo, M. and Duffy, S.A. (1987) 'Degree of causal relatedness and memory', *Journal of Memory and Language*, 26: 453–65.

Perfetti, C.A. (1990) 'The cooperative language processors: semantic influences in an autonomous syntax', in D.A. Balota, G.B. Flores d'Arcais and K. Rayner (eds), *Comprehension Processes in Reading*. Hillsdale, NJ: Erlbaum.

Potts, G.R., Keenan, J.M. and Golding, J.M. (1988) 'Assessing the occurrence of elaborative inferences: lexical decision versus naming', *Journal of Memory and Language*, 27: 399–415.

Rinck, M. and Bower, G.H. (1995) 'Anaphora resolution and the focus of attention in situation models', *Journal of Memory and Language*, 34: 110–31.

Schank, R.C. and Abelson, R.P. (1977) *Scripts, Plans, Goals, and Understanding: an Inquiry into Human Knowledge Structures*. Hillsdale, NJ: Erlbaum.

Searle, J.R. (1969) *Speech Acts*. London: Cambridge University Press.

Singer, M. (1990) *Psychology of Language*. Hillsdale, NJ: Erlbaum.

Spilich, G.J., Vesonder, G.J., Chiesi, H.L. and Voss, J.F. (1979) 'Test processing of domain-related information for individuals with high and low domain knowledge', *Journal of Verbal Learning and Verbal Behavior*, 18: 275–90.

St John, M.F. (1992) 'The story Gestalt: a model of knowledge intensive processes in text comprehension', *Cognitive Science*, 16: 271–306.

Stein, N.L. and Glenn, C.G. (1979) 'An analysis of story comprehension in elementary school children', in R.O. Freedle (ed.), *New Directions in Discourse Processing*, vol. 2. Norwood, NJ: Ablex.

Trabasso, T. and Suh, S.Y. (1993) 'Using talk-aloud protocols to reveal inferences during comprehension of text', *Discourse Processes*, 16: 3–34.

van den Broek, S. and Lorch, R.F. (1993) 'Network representations of causal relations of causal relations in memory for narrative texts: evidence from primed recognition', *Discourse Processes*, 75–98.

van Dijk, T.A. (1972) *Some Aspects of Text Grammars*. The Hague: Mouton.

van Dijk, T.A. and Kintsch, W. (1983) *Strategies of Discourse Comprehension*. New York: Academic Press.

van Oostendorp, H. and Zwaan, R.A. (eds) (1994) *Naturalistic Text Comprehension*. Norwood, NJ: Ablex.

Weaver, C.A., Mannes, S. and Fletcher, C.R. (eds) (1995) *Discourse Comprehension: Strategies and Processing Revisited*. Hillsdale, NJ: Erlbaum.

Whitney, P., Ritchie, B.G. and Clark, M.B. (1991) 'Working memory capacity and the use of elaborative inferences in text comprehension', *Discourse Processes*, 14: 133–45.

Zwaan, R.A., Magliano, J.P. and Graesser, A.C. (1995) 'Dimensions of situation model construction in narrative comprehension', *Journal of Experimental Psychology: Learning, Memory, and Cognition*, 21: 386–97.

12

Social Cognition and Discourse

Susan Condor and Charles Antaki

What Is Meant by 'Social Cognition'?

Social psychologists have long had an interest in language, and any watcher of the current social psychological scene will notice that what dominates is work on what is called social cognition. But, as two highly knowledgeable commentators point out, there is surprisingly little exploration of the relationship between language and social cognition (Semin and Fiedler, 1991). In this chapter we aim to do that exploration. Against the background of the study of discourse that this handbook provides, we want to give the beginning reader a sense of what the study of social cognition can contribute to the understanding of language in use. But we mean to do a bit more than just set out a simple descriptive story. We want also to make a diagnosis and an argument – namely, that there are two understandings of 'social cognition' abroad in the social sciences, and that they offer very different things to discourse analysts.

Many social psychologists use the term 'social cognition' to refer to the mental processing of information about the social world. In this case, the term 'social' refers to the objects of cognition (that is, people rather than animals, inanimate objects or abstract concepts) and the concern is with the psychological mechanisms which enable isolated individual subjects to perceive themselves and other people in particular ways in particular circumstances. On the other hand, some theorists use the term 'social cognition' to imply a concern for the social nature of perceivers, and for the social construction of our knowledge about the world (see Forgas, 1981 for an overview of the differences between these two approaches). In this case, the concern is with the way in which perception and description of the social world are done by people as members of particular cultures or groups, and the way in which the social world is thought about or described in the course of social interaction.

These different usages of the term 'social cognition' have rather different implications for the study of discourse. In the first place, theorists from the two perspectives often differ in the way in which they treat what people say as data. Mentalist approaches to social cognition are often associated with laboratory and questionnaire research which treats subjects' verbal responses to researchers' questions as reports of inner mental processes (whether 'mindful' or more automatic). On the other hand, some (although by no means all) researchers who are concerned with the social construction of cognition treat people's talk (their descriptions of themselves, their stereotypes of social categories, their articulation of attitudinal 'positions') as public actions, which may serve a number of social functions.

Secondly, researchers adopting these two perspectives on social cognition often differ in the way in which they approach 'discourse' as an academic topic. Those interested in social cognition as individual information processing are often concerned to uncover mental biases in our discourse comprehension or production, which, once identified, can be fixed or skirted. (One commentator (Widdicombe, 1992: 488) notes that one introductory textbook in this tradition holds out the prospect of 'debiasing' people.) Researchers concerned to emphasize the inherently social nature of human cognition tend to be more inclined to treat discourse as a cultural resource. They seek to reveal how people deploy discourses to pursue their plans and projects, and the ways in which discourse may be jointly constructed. We shall try in this chapter to deal with both literatures and both sets of applications, examining each in turn. We shall be perhaps briefer in our account of the mentalist approach, given the nature of this book; and, towards the end, we shall offer a redescription of one of its phenomena in more discursive terms. For a more complete account of mentalist social cognition from within, an excellent source is Fiske and Taylor (1991). We shall, along the way, occasionally be using terminology from one domain which might be unfamiliar to readers from others, but we hope that the terms will make sense in the context in which they are introduced.

Private Enterprise: Mentalist Social Cognition

In this section we shall look at social cognition as it is conceived in cognitively oriented contemporary social psychology. Here the term 'social cognition' refers to attempts to apply basic rules of cognitive psychology to the 'cognizing' – the perception and understanding – of human beings. Researchers addressing 'social cognition' in this sense typically ask questions such as: does your memory play tricks on your recall of people's actions? What mental faculties are responsible for the way you arrive at explanations for social behaviour? Does your use of social stereotypes depend on your focus of attention?

Calling this conception of social cognition 'private enterprise' is a caricature, but a useful one. From this perspective, human beings are seen to operate as isolated information-processing machines or (a commonly used metaphor) as disinterested 'scientists' attempting to glean information about the world through the use of rational (although possibly fallible) processes. The processes involved in the perception, evaluation, explanation and memory of human beings are considered to be similar to those involved in the perception of the physical world. These cognitive processes are deemed to be relatively automatic (although in some circumstances room is made for the processes to be 'mindful' in some way), and are often regarded as unintended, and often not fully understood, by the individuals who use them. All this is true of cognition in general (for which see Graesser, Gernsbacher and Goldman, Chapter 11 in this volume), and social cognition applies it to the social realm. It applies it to information about people, to individuals' knowledge and judgement about themselves and others, and to the guidance of their social behaviour.

In fact, it promises still more than that. Consider this claim from what has become a classic of the social cognition literature, the much cited volume by Susan Fiske and Shelley Taylor:

> the causes of social interaction lie predominantly in the perceived world, and the results of social interaction are thoughts, as well as feelings and behaviour. (1991: 17)

This quote shows just how important cognitive social cognition considers the inner mechanisms. They are the stepping stones between outside stimuli and observable responses; or rather, they are dominoes that fall in distinct (but inevitable) procession on being knocked over by a touch from an outside force. And, in turn, these inner dominoes knock the person into thinking, feeling and doing.

The Relation of Mentalist Social Cognition to Discourse

A proponent of the mentalist position would say that since human discourse – the production and understanding of language above the level of the sentence – is a matter of sense-making, then it is mediated by mental processes. Discourse processes may, therefore, be illuminated by a description of those processes which underlie any sense-making: information selection, handling and judgement, and the decision process that guides the action that follows. If it is the case that mental activity is different from, precedes, and produces discourse, then one can study how the constraints of individual cognitive processes constrain the discourse that they channel.

Discourse as 'Language above the Level of the Sentence' This way of thinking is apparent in that branch of 'discourse analysis' which takes as its topic the production and comprehension of language above the level of the sentence, but freed from the context that frames its exchange. That sense of discourse is illuminated by mentalist cognitive processes like span of attention, ability to make inferences, ability to identify anaphora and ability to be sensitive to textual cohesion. A good source of this kind of cognitive work can be found in texts such as those by Garman (1990) and Stevenson (1993), but, as we shall see below, this is not the only, or even the most current, sense of 'discourse analysis'.

One recent avenue of research which, however, does apply this approach in the social scientific research setting is that which asks how the cognitive processes involved in interpreting questions and selecting appropriate answers produce response biases in interview or questionnaire surveys. These sorts of issues may be illustrated with reference to the work of Norbert Schwarz and his colleagues. Strack et al. (1988), for example, examined the way in which answers to a question might be influenced by the accessibility to memory of particular types of information at the time of answering. In this study, they looked at the way in which students responded to a question asking them to rate their happiness with their 'life-as-a-whole'. They found that when this question followed a more specific question, asking students to rate their 'happiness with dating', the respondents tended to use information about their dating life (which was now accessible to memory) in assessing their overall life-happiness.

Another issue which has concerned Schwarz and other researchers is the cognitive processes involved in answering quantitative autobiographical questions ('how often do you eat at a restaurant?', 'how much time do you spend, on average, watching TV?'). According to Schwarz (1990) answers to such questions often depend on the cognitive strategies used in the recall of information. Subjects may, for example, use decomposition strategies (determining the rate of occurrence for a limited period, and using this as a basis from which to estimate rate of occurrence), or they may use various forms of availability heuristic (recalling specific instances of the behaviour, and using these as a basis for estimating frequency of the act). Research such as this is often used to help researchers to formulate 'better' questions. For example, work on memory processes (in particular, work on autobiographical memory) has been used to recommend that researchers break down questions concerning personal experience into 'chunks' corresponding with the way in which this information was encoded, or may be retrieved, from memory (for example, Loftus et al., 1990).

Discourse as Language Linked with the Larger Circumstances of its Production However, the sense of 'discourse' that the cognitive work we have described above speaks to is not, we think, the kind that is the primary interest of this handbook. Here, the interest is in discourse (as a mass noun, a count noun and a verb, as Potter et al., 1990 put it) which takes its meaning through some kind of identifiable link with the social, cultural or political circumstances of its production. Does 'discourse', understood in the way that most of the contributors to this book would endorse, benefit from being linked in any way with automatic, universal mental processes? Van Dijk certainly thinks so, and lists a procession of classic social psychological phenomena which seem to depend on discourse:

> After all, there are few fundamental sociopsychological notions that do not have obvious links with language use in communicative contexts, that is, with different forms of text or talk. Social perception, impression management, attitude change and persuasion, attribution, categorisation, intergroup relations, stereotypes, social representations and interaction are only some of . . . the major areas of current social psychology in which discourse plays a part. (1990: 164)

The question is just what the 'obvious links' are between discourse and the social psychological phenomena of van Dijk's list, and quite what part they are meant to play. The answer to that depends on which side of the linkage one starts. In this section of the chapter we shall consider approaches which give primacy to cognitive psychological phenomena as explanatory variables. So let us see what mentalist social cognition offers in its traditional strengths in two kinds of domain: how we classify the world around us (the study of *categorization* and *schemata and models*) and how we combine and calculate the information that those categories provide (*attribution of cause*, *attitudes* and *social inference*). We have chosen these two domains because, on the one hand, they are central to the mentalist enterprise; and, on the other, we shall revisit them under a more discursive reformulation when we get to the more social orientation in the latter half of the chapter.

Applications of Mentalist Social Cognition

Categorization   Mentalist approaches to social cognition assume categorization to be a basic feature of human (and perhaps non-human) mental processes. The assumption is that the world contains a bewildering and complex array of stimuli to which any individual has to respond. In order to simplify the task of perceiving, and reacting to, the stimuli we encounter, we tend to utilize general categories. Hence, we walk around with some organized catalogue of the kind of things there are in the world (dogs; furniture; people we like; pilots; people from Argentina; and so on), and fit new instances into the existing set. Categories are mental structures, out of conscious handling, and automatically at work providing us with inferences that guide our action. Of course, the argument continues, such categories necessarily over-simplify the information extracted from the perceptual array. Furthermore, the process of identifying individual cases as members of more general categories, and the processes involved in deducing the characteristics of category members, may involve elements of inaccuracy, or, at least, over-generalization (that dogs are savage, that pilots are male, and so on).

This sort of thinking can be traced back to psychology's prehistory, but in recent times has been crystallized most notably by Rosch's empirical demonstrations of the robustness and centrality of 'prototypes' in people's understandings of everyday categories (a programme beginning with Rosch, 1973). Thus 'lamp' is a better prototype of 'an object that illuminates' than is 'sun', and so on, and there is a gradation in each category from central prototype out to marginal or questionable members ('glow-worm', perhaps, in the case of 'an object that illuminates'). Rosch herself has been determinedly cautious about the implications of such findings, but theorists such as Lakoff (1987) push the cognitive story further into the universalist realm. For Lakoff, categories are formed out of a small range of idealized cognitive models. These models are universalist, the 'general cognitive apparatus used by the mind' (1987: 113). Lakoff is, however, a great deal more willing than the typical social cognitivist to specify the tripartite relation between these models, the people who hold them, and the world they live in. For Lakoff, the fit is an evolutionary one: 'Human conceptual categories have properties that are, at least in part, determined by the bodily nature of the people doing the categorizing' (1987: 371). So we cut the world up into chunks which are by preference human-sized: that is why the prototypical 'object that illuminates' is a (graspable, manipulable, 'object-like') lamp and not the (distant, uncontrollable, 'un-object-like') sun.

The relevance of all this to discourse is that it might explain why it is that we carve up the world to give us certain discursive categories (cats, pilots, countries) and not others (animals whose name begins with the letter 'n'; thin people who have been to the dentist recently; and so on), and how this limitation affects our discursive practices thereafter. The ultimate promise of this sense of categorization is to find evolutionary reasons why we think as we do – reasons to do with our human fit with the environment.

There are, however, approaches to categorization which do not treat it as a given of the human mental system. Discursive approaches, especially those which can trace links to rhetoric or sociology, take categorizing to be a positive activity, and take categories to be variable concepts in the service of whatever ensemble of activities categorizing appears in. We shall see more of this when we come to the work of Billig et al. (1988) and Edwards (1991; 1994) later on.

Social Inference   How do we arrive at judgements about people and events on the basis of what we already know? Does the way in which a person is described prejudice the inferences that can be made about them? Mentalist approaches to social cognition proceed on the basis that faculties of inference work on information coming into the cognitive system to draw conclusions about people and events. This is of course rather like work on categorization, but here the interest can be in atoms of description as small and apparently insignificant as individual words, and has a large armoury of reasoning processes to draw on. Two main kinds of work that are important here are theories of errors and biases in judgement on the one hand, and, with greater emphasis on language, theories of the predisposing effects of words and phrases on the other.

In the former camp are those who describe people's errors (or alleged errors) in dealing with any information (including information about people and the social world) which has some statistical basis. These biases include the under-use of base-rate information, the inability to adjust for the tendency of a number of observations to regress to the mean, the failure to take into account prior probabilities of something happening, and the poor use of covariation information. We can pick one case to stand as an example of this type of work. There is a well-known tendency for people to be inappropriately impressed by extreme or vivid examples and to make the wrong inferences on that basis. Hamilton (1981) weaves this into a theory of stereotyping, arguing that certain sorts of stereotypes are formed when people perceive (falsely) an association between two vivid groups of things: one, the 'vivid' outgroup; and the other, any 'vivid' behaviour (or mis-behaviour) they might be seen doing. Suppose that townspeople from X think that villagers from Y are thieves and robbers – even though, in fact, an impartial count reveals that there are proportionally just as many thieves and robbers among the townspeople as the villagers. What is happening, according to Hamilton's theory, is that the townspeople's mental apparatus is victim to two things which conspire to make thieving villagers unfairly memorable. For one thing, the act of theft is, of course, memorable in itself exactly because it is anti-social. For another, there are numerically fewer villagers than townspeople, and what is rare is, we know, more memorable. These two sources of noise amplify each other and the result is that the townsfolk are fooled into misremembering a correlation – an *illusory* correlation – between being a thief and being a villager.

The relevance to discourse of illusory correlation and other demonstrations of mental processing errors and biases is that they might by themselves explain certain things which we might otherwise put down to motivation, personality or whim, or to ideological and political factors outside the individual. Discourses of racism, for example, could be simply the working through of simple mistakes in people's judgements of the covariation between group membership and a given attribute (criminality, as in the above example).

The other main thrust of social inference is the study of automatic linguistic effects on the production and comprehension of messages. Here, for example Semin and Fiedler (1988; 1991) build on previous work on implicit causality (for example, Brown and Fish, 1983) stemming from Fillmore's (1971) semantic analysis. Semin and Fiedler remind us that even such atoms as individual words (verbs and adjectives, in their model) can play important roles in the disposition of discourses. Any event can be described along a continuum from concrete to abstract by the use, at the concrete end, of verbs like 'kick' and 'hit', and, at the abstract end, by more encompassing verbs like 'defend', and adjectives like 'patriotic'. A certain event might be described by the alternatives 'A hit B', 'A hurt B', 'A hates B' or 'A is patriotic'. The more concrete the description, the more responsibility is assigned to the actor who appears in it, the less enduring the event is perceived to be, the easier to verify and disconfirm, and so on (Semin and Fiedler, 1991). The promise is that such cognitive implications of words and phrases might account for quite significant effects in discourse, and to study the cognitive base is to reveal automatic, inner information-processing mechanisms which the study of rhetoric simply leaves unexamined.

Schemata and Models The claim here is that people keep in their heads fairly well-articulated plans of routine situations and their attendant behaviours. These plans not only click into operation to make life run

smoothly but are ever-available (even, perhaps, intrusive) ways of construing the social world, disposing us to image reality as moulded in just
such ways. Thus the familiar 'script' of what happens in a restaurant (that
we will enter, be shown a table, read a menu, be served, eat, pay and leave)
not only guides our actions, but also channels (and limits) our appreciation
of just what can or might happen in a restaurant – and, of course, the same
can be said for other schemata about other situations or activities. All these
schemata are mentally represented in some organized system, perhaps as a
hierarchy of facts working from abstract prototype down to concrete
example (Rumelhart and Ortony, 1977), or perhaps (as in the restaurant
script) as a prototypical linear sequence (Schank and Abelson, 1977), or
perhaps as a 'mental model' (van Dijk and Kintsch, 1983; Johnson-Laird,
1983) which underlies our non-linguistic representation of any real-world
situation. But in any case, they all have a say in what we attend to in the
world, how we take it in, and what we remember about it afterwards.

The relevance to discourse of this is to explain why certain aspects of our
discourse are as they are. A general principle such as 'schema-consistent
good; schema-inconsistent bad' will be used to cover a lot of ground. It will
be invoked to explain why stories are narrated and recalled in certain ways,
why jokes work or misfire, why this or that example of a category is treated
as a good or questionable one (see also the section on categorization,
above) and so on. These marshalling and filtering powers of cognitive
schemata are also claimed to be useful in explaining discursive practices
like stereotyping and discrimination: thus people with a well-developed
cognitive 'sex-role schema' will, it is claimed, be variously receptive to
information about, and be more or less likely to stereotype and discriminate against, men and women (see, for example, McKenzie-Mohr and
Zanna, 1990). But it is also fair to say that even within the cognitive
community there is a certain discomfort at the potential for tautology that
schema-based theorizing is subject to, and we shall see later that the
relation of schemata to discourse may be quite differently conceived
(Edwards, 1994).

Attribution of Cause   According to mentalist social cognition, the mind has
a process which sorts out the explanation of events that confront us in our
lives. We take in information about the event and work out what rationally
is the most likely *cause* – why a friend declined an invitation, why the
politician resigned, why an old acquaintance has sent us a bunch of flowers.
The mechanism may be a matter of sifting the known information to see
what the best candidate is, as a matter of scientific detective work (Does
this friend often decline our invitations? Does she decline invitations from
others? Has everyone else declined this invitation?). Or the mechanism
might be trying to work out what the questioner already knows and offer
the missing bit of the puzzle (to reveal, say, the unusual fact that the friend
has recently had a bereavement in the family). One way or another, such
mental processes, like those of categorization, are always at work to help us

understand our world and to respond appropriately – for example, to be sympathetic towards (rather than offended at) an apparently unfriendly rejection. Like the processes involved in categorization, these mental processes grapple with an inchoate world and channel it into something we can deal with. Occasional faults and failures make them less than fully rational, but they are perfectible, and the promise of social cognition is to chart the errors they lead us into and suggest ways of avoiding them.

The relevance to discourse of this is that it gives a deterministic mechanism that explains why people arrive at certain explanations merely as a matter of the idiosyncrasies of the mental apparatus they are saddled with. Thus (it might be said) there is a general tendency to see the individual agent, rather than society or local surroundings, as the cause of behaviour (the so-called 'fundamental attribution error': Ross, 1977). So (the argument might run), in some ways of talking about people, what might seem like a 'political' choice to attribute causation in a certain way (to attribute someone's poverty to their lack of effort, say, rather than to failings in society's provision of jobs) may reduce to the operation of blind information-processing mechanisms out of the explainer's conscious control.

Attitudes The cognitive attitude to attitude is that it is a knowledgeable, evaluative, but rather unpredictable, mental animal. It knows some facts and feels something about them, but it is not always reliable in actually managing to turn those beliefs and feelings into consistent action. This three-component mentalist image (beliefs and feelings causing action) has been remarkably stable in psychology over the last fifty years; what has changed is the terms used to describe the 'inner' phenomena of belief and feeling and the technology used to measure the visible behaviour that they are meant to produce. The 'inner' terms now unpack into various sub-components. For example, Fishbein and Ajzen's influential theory (see, for example, Fishbein and Ajzen, 1975; Ajzen, 1988) breaks down the 'beliefs' component into beliefs about the attitude object itself (careful driving, say); beliefs about what other people (friends, the police) would think about it; and, how important their opinions might be to the attitude holder. This approach also illustrates the change in the measurement of the behaviour which these 'inner' phenomena cause: where previously researchers might have been satisfied with asking respondents a general question about their behaviour ('are you a careful driver?'), now they would insist on being very specific about what 'careful driving' (in our example) might mean, and, if they could not directly observe it, they would at least present respondents with a comprehensive battery of things they thought counted as specific examples (checking the mirror before setting off and so on).

There is also a long tradition of social psychological interest in the topic of attitude change. This has involved studying the effects of messages on people's internal beliefs and feelings, and seeing whether their outward behaviour subsequently changes. (This includes the effects of messages on the speakers themselves, or 'the ways in which the communicator's verbalizations can affect the communicator him or herself', as McCann and Higgins, 1990 put it.) Famously, this was given a boost in the years of the Second World War when the state had an urgent interest in getting people to accommodate to the war effort, but it still continues now.

The promise of this kind of research, and the mentalist conceptualization of attitude it works from, is that it will reveal the relationship between discourses of belief and evaluation on the one hand – what people say about minority groups and what they feel about them – and what actually happens on the other – what they do or don't do about them or towards them. If researchers can pin down the inner structure of the beliefs and feelings, they will be able to predict the behaviour that these will cause. But, like all the other threads of this kind of social cognition, the very plausibility of the enterprise depends on the coherence of the picture of input–processing–output that is basic to the mentalist project.

Shared Ownership: the Social Basis of Cognition

In this section we shall turn to consider the second kind of work on 'social cognition' – that which treats human knowledge as a social product under shared ownership. The writers we shall be talking about all seek to differentiate themselves from the 'individualism' of mentalist approaches to social cognition, but they do so in different ways (see Hewstone and Jaspars, 1984; Condor, 1990; for reviews). For the sake of simplicity we shall discuss these approaches in terms of three broad (and often overlapping) perspectives.

1   those which treat individuals as bearers of a particular culture, or set of shared ideologies
2   those which treat social cognizers as members of distinct groups, with particular shared interests
3   those which focus on the processes of interpersonal exchange, which may involve a consideration of the way in which social reality may be jointly constructed.

This classification system is only a rough typology, and it cannot capture the complexities of, and contradictions between, the many approaches which treat cognition as socially shared or as a social product. As we shall see, one thing that many of these approaches share is a tendency to use an analogy of the individual as a social 'actor' rather than as a disinterested 'observer'. This often influences the way in which they interpret the behaviour of their research subjects. A number of theorists tend to prefer to interpret people's use of particular stereotypes to describe others, their explanations of human actions, their stated opinions on particular issues, not so much as reports of private cognitive processes, but as public communicative acts: as discursive *rather than* as cognitive phenomena.

The Cognizer as Cultural Conduit

Even strongly mentalist accounts of social perception often admit that our perceptions of, and beliefs about, the social world cannot be explained entirely with reference to individual information processing. They concede that some aspects of social perception (the stereotypes we hold about particular categories, for example) may reflect the 'society' or 'culture' into which the individual has been 'socialized'. However, researchers who adopt what we have termed a mentalist approach to social cognition tend to treat such 'sociological' considerations – left to the descendants of Émile Durkheim or Talcott Parsons, active elsewhere in the social science forest – as deep background to their major concern of attempting to explain social perception as far as possible with recourse to individual, cognitive processes. In contrast, other perspectives prefer to explain social perception *primarily* in terms of the 'culture' or 'society' to which individuals belong. There are currently a number of psychological approaches which allow that individuals are members, or exemplars, of a common culture (and one such perspective can be found in Moscovici's 1984 discussion of 'the thinking society' and, indeed, in his notion of 'social representations', for a discursive account of which see van Dijk, 1990).

Rather than attempt a detailed account of the many approaches which treat perceivers as cultural conduits, we shall focus on just one such perspective with a clear relationship to discourse: Billig's (for example, 1991) concern with thinking, rhetoric and 'ideology'. Billig makes a number of salient connections. First, he treats the beliefs and percepts of individuals as 'ideological' rather than as merely cognitive phenomena. By that, he means that thought and talk reflect the social heritage of the actors involved. This is most clearly illustrated in his and his colleagues' discussion of 'ideological dilemmas' (Billig et al., 1988), in which phenomena which are often treated as 'merely' cognitive (such as prejudice) are treated as issues which arise in modern (that is, post-industrial) society. This is illustrated, for example, by the way in which Billig and his colleagues treat gender categorization and stereotyping. These are issues which 'mentalist' social cognitivists explain in terms of the automatic, unconscious, information-processing mechanisms used by individual perceivers. At the very most, they are regarded as partially determined by the nature of perceived 'social reality'. Billig et al. (1988), in contrast, prefer to discuss gender categorization and stereotyping as rhetorical positions, adopted by individuals in the course of debate, and meaningful in terms of their relation to wider ideological notions of justice (including notions of human 'rights' and citizenship) in advanced liberal democracies.

Billig distinguishes between the *contents* of social thought (which he regards as historically and culturally specific) and the *mechanisms* of thought, which he prefers to regard as universal. However, Billig's ideas about cognitive mechanisms differ from those who adopt mentalist approaches to social cognition. Billig's focus is not so much on automatic, and possibly unconscious, cognitive processes, as on 'thinking': conscious, purposeful puzzle solving (but puzzle solving in the sense of the setting up, and possible resolution, of arguments). Like Turnbull and Slugoski, Billig sees the social perceiver as engaged in an internal dialogue, in which she or he struggles to make sense of the world, using the contradictory assumptions and 'common senses' provided by his or her culture. This model of the social perceiver as a conscious actor is rather different from the model often used by 'mentalist' perspectives in which aspects of social cognition (such as stereotypes) are seen to stem from unconscious, automatic processes which are brought into play when the individual does not have the available cognitive capacity to 'think' (for example, Gilbert and Hixon, 1991).

An interesting aspect of Billig's approach is the way in which he treats the relationship between 'cognition' and 'discourse'. Whereas, as we have already seen, many social psychologists take the view that a knowledge of human cognition can inform us about discourse processes, Billig adopts the opposite tack. He suggests that a knowledge of human discourse and, in particular, the skills of rhetoric, can inform us about the nature of human thought:

> Human thinking is not merely a matter of processing information or following cognitive rules. Thinking is to be observed in action in discussions, in the rhetorical cut-and-thrust of argumentation. To deliberate upon an issue is to argue with oneself, even to persuade oneself. (1991: 17)

In his research, Billig uses examples of language use, and transcripts of conversations, to reveal the complexity of thought which is often obscured in experimental or questionnaire studies. In particular, he emphasizes how an appreciation of the 'rules' of rhetoric would lead us to appreciate the 'two-sided' nature of human thought often overlooked by 'mentalist' approaches to human cognition. One particular area in which Billig has applied this approach is with respect to the process of social categorization. As we have already seen, mentalist social cognitive approaches treat social categorization as a universal, automatic, and thoughtless device used to simplify the perceived environment. A consequence of this sort of reasoning, Billig argues, is that social categorization and prejudice are often presented as inevitable outcomes of adaptive human cognitive mechanisms. Billig, in contrast, stresses that although human beings certainly use social categories, they are also capable of the obverse – of 'particularization'. Similarly, in contrast to mainstream attribution theorists, Billig argues that people do not 'hold' one explanation of a given phenomenon. Rather, they may be aware of, and juggle with, competing explanations. To use the example cited above, people are likely to believe both the prevailing common senses that poverty is explicable in terms of an individual's lack of effort, and that it is caused by society's failure to provide jobs.

The Cognizer as Group Member

We have seen that Billig's work (like that of many other social theorists) takes both discourse and the contents of our social knowledge to be matters of shared cultural ('ideological') background. Other perspectives, whilst accepting the notion of a 'common culture', also emphasize the significance of the specific group memberships to individual cognition and to action, including discursive acts. We might pull back now and see how a wider European lens draws the individual's community into the picture. (But remember that it does this without ever giving up the notion that the individual is still driven by the mental processing which is churning away inside.) Fiske and Taylor's definition that we saw earlier was rather individualistic. Compare this version, from a pair of authors associated with the European perspective:

> The least one could say is that the study of social cognition concerns the perception of people and ourselves as well as the 'naive' theories we entertain to study those perceptions. (Leyens and Codol, 1988: 94)

Leyens and Codol immediately go on to insist that social cognition

> has a social origin . . . a social object . . . [and] it is socially shared. (1988: 94)

These sentiments come as close as psychology ever does to the 'cultural' sense of social cognition in the sociology of theorists like Talcott Parsons or Durkheim. Leyens and Codol locate individuals out in the groups and institutions that they find themselves having to deal with – but they still maintain the individual base of social cognition. Even if they are willing not to look too closely under the bonnet, psychologists working in this tradition care very much about the driving forces of memory, categorization and the like.

Chief amongst these approaches in social psychology has been Tajfel's (for example, 1978) social identity approach to group membership and intergroup relations. This approach, which has in recent years been modified and supplemented by Turner's self-categorization approach to group membership (for example, Turner et al., 1987), emphasizes the centrality of social categorization to human action. However, the emphasis of this approach is the mechanisms behind, and the consequences of, positioning one*self* as a member of a social category.

The notion of the human subject in this approach is rather different to that used either in mentalist social cognition work, or in work (such as Billig's) which considers individuals as bearers and manipulators of common ideologies. Rather, the concern is for the way in which the social actor speaks and thinks as a part of, and on behalf of, a collective identity. Human social perception and action are, on occasions, shaped by the tendency of individuals to internalize the needs and interests of the specific groups with which they identify. Often this is discussed in terms of a need to perceive and to present the groups to which one belongs in a positive light in comparison to relevant outgroups (see Abrams, 1990), a process which is seen to lead to a systematic bias in social cognition, whereby individuals tend to perceive the characteristics and behaviour of their group more favourably than the characteristics and behaviours of other groups. However, as Tajfel (1981) discussed in some detail, social identity theorists may also regard descriptions of the social world in more sophisticated ways. In particular, they may regard descriptions of social categories as aspects of strategic rhetoric, formulated with the aim of justifying the actions of group members in the context of wider ideologies concerning social justice and legitimacy.

This sort of perspective is well illustrated in van Knippenberg's (for example, 1984) work on social stereotyping. Van Knippenberg emphasizes that, in so far as individuals act as members of definable social groups, they may hold group-specific images of the social world. These images do not merely serve to make their own group appear 'better than' other groups. Rather, they are better regarded as 'political' strategies, meaningful in the context of a wider (shared) ideological system:

> Often, complex presentational strategies are used in group representations. One strategy . . . is to describe groups in such a way that one implicitly advocates the legitimacy or illegitimacy of the existing status relationship. Another strategy is to include in one's group representations a definitely positive, though non-threatening, social identity for the outgroup in order to secure the own group's position. (1984: 560)

A similar concern with the production of strategic imagery is apparent in social identity approaches to attribution. In one much quoted study, for example, Hewstone et al. (1982) examined the achievement attributions made by British schoolboys at state ('comprehensive') and private ('public') schools. The public schoolboys attributed the failure of public schoolboys to lack of effort, and the failure of comprehensive schoolboys to lack of ability. The comprehensive schoolboys, in contrast, tended to attribute the success of public schoolboys to luck. The researchers interpret these results as illustrating that attempts on the part of the public schoolboys to deny 'illegitimate' privilege might account for their academic success.

At present there is little in the way of direct analysis of the possible points of intersection between social identity approaches to cognition and social action and discourse analytic perspectives. Notwithstanding the concern on the part of social identity theorists with strategic (collective) self-presentation, and the function of social stereotypes and attribution in the contexts of arguments concerning social justice and legitimacy, until recently social identity theorists conducted research solely in laboratory contexts. In the last few years, some social identity theorists have attempted to explore their theoretical concerns using natural language as data. For example, Reicher (1991) analysed the way in which the British press constructed social categories during the Gulf War. Amongst other things, Reicher analyses the way in which Saddam Hussein was used to stand metonymically for Iraq, and the ways in which Iraq was referred to metaphorically as a person, with individual motives and attributes.

Cognition in Interpersonal Exchange

In spite of the insistence on social cognition as shared, neither of the two approaches we have considered so far grants a central role to the process of human interaction *per se*. Social identity perspectives generally focus on the individual social actor as relatively (sometimes entirely) isolated from other real human beings (although see Abrams, 1990). Billig's rhetorical approach to social psychology, on the other hand, might appear to grant interaction a central role. However, often his concern is as much with 'conversation' taking place within an individual as with the process of interaction between individuals.

The third sort of perspective that we shall consider here grants a central role to the processes of interaction between two or more individuals (and, indeed, isn't very keen on the analytic notion of 'individual' in the first place). These approaches often grant theoretical priority to 'discourse', and are less concerned with – and sometimes even opposed to – attempts to theorize 'cognition' as a private individual state. There is a long and respectable history, of course, in applying dialectical ideas to psychology (though perhaps some radical attempts are better described as deliberately 'non-respectable', for example Armistead, 1974; Brown, 1973; Parker 1989), but we will focus our attention on more recent, and more language-oriented, discursive work, since it is this that comes closest to the aims and purposes of this volume. The kind of work we have in mind here prefers to see cognition as part and parcel of *action*, and *joint action* at that – as part of the business that people get up to with their neighbours. On this reading, what happens 'inside' is inseparable from its outward manifestation, and the individual's steps only make sense with reference to the other partners in the dance. 'Cognition' joins with *language*, and that is why this sense of social cognition has so much to offer discourse.

Language has always been a thread in social psychology's understanding of social relations (indeed language, as Farr, 1990 reminds us, was one of the major topics of Wundt's ten-volume *Folk Psychology*), but, in the cognitive traditions of the latter half of this century, that thread was hidden among the more dominant patterns of information processing and mental judgement. Nevertheless, traditions as diverse as G.H. Mead's (1934) symbolic interactionism and anglophone linguistic philosophy (from the later Wittgenstein onwards) have always insisted on the primacy of language and its central role in constructing the social (indeed, the physical) world and action within it. This, of course, can be construed in a 'cognitive' way, where the theorists claims that what is important about language is that it furnishes the mind with categories which then in turn furnish the world of objects: this would be the inheritance of the Sapir-Whorf hypothesis in its variously weak or strong forms, and would sit easily with the schema modellers and the others we saw earlier. But the difference here is that there is no need to dig for internal representations; language also (or more importantly) has a public face and is, variously, a device by which social identity is played out, or more generally the prime means of constituting social reality. In each case 'cognition' – if it makes sense still to use the term – is bound up in action: playing out identity, constituting social reality.

The relation between this kind of social cognition and discourse (unlike the case with mentalist social cognition, and perhaps more clearly than the two variants of 'shared ownership' social cognition we have seen so far) can't be the relation of assembly line to finished product, because it doesn't make that separation. On the contrary, it takes discourse to be something inevitably a public enterprise built by many hands, whose 'cause' is not a matter of individuals' mental processing and whose effects go beyond the individuals involved.

'Social cognition' with this orientation promises to identify how discourse is jointly formulated, and to uncover what local and institutional ends it serves. In the next sections we shall see its strengths in identifying the co-operative construction of utterances, and how that helps us understand such things as the formulation of social business in talk, the maintenance of social identity through its public negotiation, and even such apparently psychological questions as 'attitudes', 'thinking' and 'memory'.

Attitudes as Discursive Constructions   The central notion of 'attitude' was the first to attract an anti-mentalist discourse analysis reading. Potter and Wetherell's *Discourse and Social Psychology* (1987) was a landmark in the application of anglophone discursive thinking to social phenomena and has recently been extended by Edwards and Potter's *Discursive Psychology* (1992) with a remit ranging over the wider spectrum of cognitive processes. What both share is the foundational belief in the primacy of language as a constitutional part of social life; in the emergence of social reality through the interchange between speakers in a society. For these authors, interpersonal interaction via the medium of language is what is crucial to social processes.

Potter and Wetherell's focus is not on individuals in that interchange, but on what is distributed between them. Following Gilbert and Mulkay (1984), they identify themes in the talk ('linguistic repertories') which mesh together to promote or sustain certain visions of reality. In Wetherell and Potter's (1988; 1992) analysis of racist talk, for example, such repertoires are explicitly identified and their variation plotted. In the following extracts, the speakers (white New Zealanders) seem to be expressing rather warm attitudes towards Maoris:

I think the sort of Maori renaissance, the Maoritanga, is important like I was explaining about being at that party on Saturday night, I suddenly didn't know where I was, I had lost my identity . . . I think it's necessary for people to get it [Maori identity] back because it's something deep rooted inside you. (Reed)

I'm certainly in favour of a bit of Maoritanga it is something uniquely New Zealand. I guess I'm very conservation minded and in the same way that I don't

like seeing a species going out of existence I don't like seeing a culture and a
language and everything else fade out. (Shell) (Wetherell and Potter, 1988: 179)

Wetherell and Potter cast these two as being in some senses contradictions,
or at least inconsistencies. On the one hand, new emphasis on Maori
culture is valued because everyone should have one's roots for the sake of
securing their identity: the implication is that the current generation of
Maoris have 'lost' it, possibly through their own negligence. On the other
hand, the second extract promotes Maori culture as being positively
unmistakeable: it is as vivid and unique as a rare species. This contradiction
(or inconsistency) suggests to the watching analyst, as scientists' variable
use of error suggested to Gilbert and Mulkay (1984), that there is some
important work going on.

Wetherell and Potter interpret it as being the manifestation of what they
call the repertoire of 'cultural fostering' – the idea that Maori culture is a
rare bloom that can only survive by the sympathetic attention that any
exotic specimen would demand. In other words, the Maoris need the
patronage and sympathetic husbandry of the whites to survive; otherwise,
unable to meet the demands their own exoticism makes on them, they will
'lose their identity' and die out. This sentiment is much more clearly racist
than either of its two constituent parts which, on their own and without
being set against each other, might pass muster. Unlike the singleton notion
of the 'attitude statement', it is the meshing together of multiple utterances
that does the work.

Wetherell and Potter's analysis makes a linguistic exercise do discursive
work by fuelling it with an appreciation of cultural meaning. But they are
clear in their insistence on engaging the reader's cultural, or perhaps it
would be better to say *political*, understanding of the issue at hand; it is
perhaps inevitable that, once analysts move beyond the notion of independently meaningful atoms like 'attitude statements', they are bound to
acknowledge their own interpretational work in their discursive readings.

Thinking and Memory   To push the notion of shared ownership of cognition still further into the realms of 'hard-wired' cognition, it is instructive
to follow Edwards and Middleton's (1987) refreshing look at one of the
founders of modern cognitive psychology, the English psychologist
Frederick Bartlett. Edwards and Middleton make the point that, in his
classic work *Remembering* (1932), Bartlett was more interested in how
symbols became a matter of public property than in how they were
individually processed. Indeed, Edwards and Middleton show that (unlike
virtually all his followers) Bartlett had a keen interest in how remembering
was a function of conversational discourse.

We might press the case further and have a look at one of Bartlett's later
works, *Thinking* (1958). Certainly there is nothing in this quote that would
cause any discomfort to his modern successors in mentalist social cognition:

The broad objectives of thinking remain very nearly the same, in whatever field the thinker operates, and with whatever kind of evidence he is concerned. Always he must try to use the information that is available to him so as to reach a terminus, based upon that information, but not identical with it. (1958: 97)

So far, so cognitive. But it is instructive to carry the quote on a little further, and see that Bartlett meant to put this thinking into a social, and socially accountable, context:

and he must so set out, or be prepared to set out, the stages through which he passes, that he can reasonably hope that where, for the time being, he comes to rest, everybody who is not mentally defective, or mentally ill, or abnormally prejudiced, must come to rest also. (1958: 97)

This could have been written by any rhetorician, and introduces a note of intellectual relativity which will make rationalist cognitive psychologists' hair stand on end: Bartlett is willing to let the validity of his subjects' thoughts be judged against *social*, not abstract, information-processing criteria. This gently opens the door to a thoroughly contextualized account of thinking which

seeks to discover the 'methods' that persons use in their everyday life in society in constructing social reality and also to discover the nature of the realities they have constructed . . . Only by examining their procedures and discovering what they consist of, can one fully understand what they mean by correctness, as correctness is decided by those who construct it. (Psathas, 1972: 132)

This quote comes not from Bartlett but from an early account of ethnomethodology. We are not, of course, claiming that Bartlett was a founder of ethnomethodology; but it does show what he put into the social scientific air, ready for crystallization by a later generation.

We used the example of Bartlett because we wanted to follow Edwards and Middleton's pioneering project of rehabilitating the work of someone who had been unfairly recruited into the mentalist school, and to show that even such an eminent cognitivist had an account of language and rationality difficult to square with a purely individualist idealism. If there is a case that language and rationality have to be set into a context, then there is a strong argument that the better we can specify that context, the more successful we shall be in understating the language it supports. If that is the case, then we have to attend to 'language' in more than just the sense of words and phrases that can be tidied up and paraphrased by the analyst looking to reduce the messiness and clarify the obscurity of the printed argument. Rather, we shall have to attend to the words used as exactly as possible to see what might be going on: all the literary, stylistic and persuasive devices which speakers use to win over their listeners, with or without recourse to the hard coupling of formalizable premise and conclusion.

Joint Construction of Knowledge   One objection that some have to the kind of discourse analysis we saw above is that, although it is founded on the belief that the interchange of language constitutes reality, its followers tend not to dwell on the very local context of the talk in their reports. There are other kinds of analysis which do that, adding to the foundational constructionist belief the extra ingredient that the exact sequencing and ordering of the talk is as crucial as its apparently surface content. This builds on the notion of the philosopher G.H. Mead and the philologist Bakhtin that parcels of language were not simply posted from one speaker to another but somehow packed together jointly. For Mead, it was a matter of collusion between speaker and audience; and for Bakhtin, a matter of the infiltration into one speaker's utterances of the interests and perspectives of the other. In both cases, the utterance – and the 'cognition' from whence it came – was meaningless without an appreciation of its joint, or multiple, authorship.

The most dynamic inheritor of this tradition in the social sciences is ethnomethodology and, in particular, conversation analysis which insists on close observation of the sequential organization of utterances as the proper basis for their understanding. Conversation analysis will be properly explained by Pomerantz and Fehr in Chapter 3, Volume 2 of this handbook, but here we can just note a few outlines. Garfinkel (1967) launched ethnomethodology with a series of observations about the irredeemably *local* determination of meaning. Conversation analysis, especially in the hands of Harvey Sacks (1992), developed the spirit of ethnomethodology's concerns with the local to show in close detail how people's words will propose, and dispose of, actions differently at different points in an interaction. To take a banal but pervasive case, the word 'hello' has a different force when it comes at the beginning of a conversation (say a telephone conversation), when it will be a greeting and a means of identifying the speaker, than when it comes somewhere in the middle, when it might be a check that the caller is still there. What one speaker proposes will be disposed of by the next speaker, and both speakers exploit the complex regularities of interaction to get across their meaning subtly and economically. There is, of course, a great deal more to ethnomethodology and conversation analysis than this poor sketch (see Chapter 3, Volume 2); but it gives the background for two examples of the sort of contribution it makes to the debate about social cognition and discourse.

One very telling set of examples is from the work of Derek Edwards, who has long been at the forefront of offering a more grounded, non-mentalistic alternative to 'cognitive' phenomena. He follows the ethno-methodological injunction to treat (what cognitivists take to be) mental objects as things whose 'reality' is their *invocation* in whatever human activities they appear in – in work talk', 'intimate talk' and 'casual talk' as much as in 'scientific talk'. Edwards shows how a number of phenomena of social cognition are matters of situated accounts. In Edwards (1991) he shows how the apparently universal mechanisms of 'categorization' which humans are supposed to share can be successfully replaced with an understanding of categories as contingent, situated descriptions which play their part in the promoting of certain projects at the expense of others, and whose alleged universalities are to be taken not as 'true' but as part of their rhetorical payload. Another example of Edwards's discursive approach to 'cognitive' phenomena is the argument (Edwards, 1994) that the notion of mental 'scripts' (which we described earlier), taken by cognitivists to reside in people's mental representations, can be profitably reconceived as cultural rules ready to be invoked by people at appropriate times and places. Thus, rather than think of a script for eating in a restaurant as being something you 'have', we can see it as something that you can hearably invoke or exploit in appropriate situations. As Edwards puts it, 'The aim is not to do away with the powerful explanatory notions of goals, plans, and scriptedness; rather, the intent is to investigate exactly how these kinds of notions may feature as *participants' own* explanatory resources, if and when they do' (1994: 216, emphasis in original).

For our second example, we choose another account that directly rivals the mentalistic trend of psychological social cognition. An attractive candidate here is the explanation of people's causal attributions. In mentalistic social cognition, these are supposed to issue from one individual's inner mechanisms of judgement, and the study of those mechanisms promises to eliminate poor reasoning. In actual discourse, one can instead read causal attributions as being jointly constructed by two or more participants acting in unison. That programme then has the less pedagogic promise of identifying how business is done. Since we shall go through this example in rather more detail than Edwards's work on scripts, we have put it into its own section, immediately below.

Example of an Analysis of Social Cognition as Being in 'Shared Ownership' It might help if we finish off this chapter by extending the previous section to see an example of the kind of analysis that tries to make the case that the phenomena of 'social cognition' can usefully and productively be considered as being shared between people, rather than located in the mental representations of one individual.

But note: by placing this extended example here at the end of the chapter, we might be taken to be suggesting that the analysis we offer solves all the problems we mentioned along the way. We do not mean it to be read like that. We mean it to be a closely worked illustration of just one way of treating social cognition as being public. There are other ways of doing it, and there are, of course, rebuttals of this way of doing it. But it is here as, at least, an example of what can be done.

We will keep to the domain introduced earlier and reprised in the material just above: the battle in the literature over ordinary reasoning. A social cognitive approach, as we have seen, would start from the notion that reasoning is a private mental activity, and seek to find the information-processing machinery which is responsible for the selection, retrieval and production of social judgements, and then to chart the variables that affect its working, and those that are in turn affected by its outcome. A good example of that would be the social cognitive approach to causal attribution, which, again as we have seen, describes the mental processes by which the individual combines current, or remembered, information about an event's history to arrive at its probable cause.

A sophisticated version of this cognitive approach to causal attribution is taken by Hilton (1990; 1991), who proposes that an explainer works out what the questioner assumes to be the difficulty at issue, then works out what it is in the history of the problem that is the 'abnormal condition' – what distinguishes between the case as it is now, and as it might have been. For example, suppose we were both members of a culture which was exposed to Western news media, and, perhaps prompted by some casual mention of space disasters, you asked 'why did the *Challenger* space shuttle blow up?' (to use an example from Hilton, 1991), I would assume that you were interested in one thing; but if you asked 'why did the *Challenger* space shuttle blow up, and not simply crash to the ground?', I would assume you wanted to know something slightly different; and if you asked 'why did the *Challenger* space shuttle blow up on that launch and not on the previous one?', I would assume a still different question; and so on.

Once I had that mental representation of the question (and let us take it to be the first version of the question), the cognitive argument is that I would then consider the conditions that were present in the case of the craft exploding as opposed to occasions on which it (or its equivalents) did not explode. So I would advance (say), as an answer, the unusual coldness of the night preceding the launch. However, I would not suggest (say) the fact that a certain sort of seal in one of its sections was made of thin rubber: that is not in itself an explanation, given that it was the case in both the explosion and the non-explosion conditions.

At first sight, this is a very plausible account of explanation. After all, it is recognizable as the kind of thing people do, at least sometimes. But they do not do it all the time, or perhaps even much of the time. Or rather: they have it available as one among many ways of 'explaining' and they will use it in certain circumstances. We have put the word 'explaining' in quotes to signal that the business of explaining is what Wittgenstein calls a language game, and what discourse analysts of a certain kind might call a discourse. To the extent that people in any given interaction actually are engaged in the particular language game of 'information sorting', then the attribution model is a good description of the rules they play to. But there is a good deal more to social interaction than this particular language game.

We shall have to move away from idealizations and into real encounters to illustrate what we mean. Suppose you asked me this blank and, on its own, incomprehensible question: 'why was it a mistake from their point of view?' We have chosen this example because it is – out of context – very obviously queer, and that is an immediate contrast to the misleading clarity of the question we saw above: 'why did the *Challenger* space shuttle blow up?' We say misleading clarity because we went out of our way to make that question understandable when we introduced it, as you will see if you refer back. The uninterpretability of 'why was it a mistake from their point of view?' immediately demonstrates that language is thoroughly indexical, as linguists and others have pointed out since the late nineteenth century. It is impossible to understand some utterance like *why was it a mistake from their point of view?* without knowing the deictic referents of *it* and *they*, and without the context in which such deixis makes sense. And, of course, that is equally true of the (apparently) 'clear' question about the *Challenger*; there too, we have to mobilize a context in which such a question makes sense (why should it be assumed that the hearer or reader has heard of the *Challenger*, or the '*Challenger* disaster', and so on?).

Let us have a look, then, at the real interaction which gives the local context in the 'mistake' case:

A: the first Belfast blitz had *sha*ken Catholic Ireland *sil*ly because ((in)) nothing had ever happened including the troubles ((that)) had killed so many holy Roman Catholics in one moment and the *se*cond Belfast blitz was the [tu th] the the mistake the Germans made – – –

B   why was it a mistake from their ((point of view))

A   because they should *nev*er have put they should never have blitzed Belfast again they should've [ko] left it com*plet*ely alone and they'd have got Southern Ireland perhaps back into the [t] *fold*

(This transcript comes from a collection of naturally occurring conversations between native speakers of English, recorded in Britain in the 1970s, and published as the London-Lund corpus (Svartvik and Quirk, 1980). This is an extract from conversation 1.14, with the notation much simplified. Here, italics denote emphasis, words in double parentheses are guesses at unclear speech, dashes indicate pausing, and material in square brackets is phonetic renditions of incomplete words.)

Even this is not really enough contextualization, as we shall show in a moment; and of course it mobilizes very particular sorts of cultural knowledge which would be encompassed only by a 'context' very much larger than a few paltry lines of text. But what we have now is enough to show – whether the reader is familar with the politics referred to in the words or not – that what is at stake here is not a matter of information sorting, neither in the classical attribution theory sense of searching for covariates of an effect, nor even on the linguistically more sophisticated abnormal conditions model. The way the participants set the explanation up, and dispose of it, shows us that the language game is of a very different kind.

For one thing, as Edwards and Potter's (1992) discourse action model persuasively argues, the solicitation of the account is not disinterested. The call for an explanation here comes from someone who is breaking into what is hearable as a story, a recounted episode told from the point of view of, and in promotion of the interests of, a certain speaker. In that context, the request for an explanation cannot be neutral, nor can the answer be immune from the expectation that it orient to the accountability that the explainer is under. Neither party tailors their talk to be consistent with the (rather unusual) 'information-sorting' language game that cognitive social psychology assumes to be the general case. They could have done: we could have been eavesdropping on two people talking as scientists or accident investigators and mobilizing the rules of an information-sorting language game; but the participants in this encounter seem not to be doing so.

What grounds are there for this kind of assertion? They are there in the actual words of the speakers themselves or, more accurately, in the speakers' exploitation of the regularities of conversational structures – what conversation analysts call the preference order of conversation (see Chapter 3, Volume 2). For example, the fact that the solicitation of the explanation is moderated by the phrase *from their point of view* suggests that the speaker is shying away from the direct challenge of questioning the story-teller himself. To pose such a question on one's own footing is to break into the space normally allowed to someone who has started a story and is in its midstream (Sacks, 1972). What the speaker does to disarm the non-normativeness of his intervention is to pose the question in something hearable as being in the story-teller's *own* voice – that is to say, to pose the question as being about something consistent with claims that the story-maker was making. The questioner's formulation does not dispute that 'it' (the bombing) was a mistake, but asks why it was a mistake from the point of view of the Germans – and, in contrast, not from the point of view of the story-teller. In other words, the question is hearable not as a challenge (let alone a prompt for information sorting) but rather as a spur for the story to continue in the terms that the story-teller has already set – in fact, very like the (very frequent) back-channel responses which pepper the telling of a story and signal that the audience is appreciating what is being said (Sacks, 1972).

All this has taken us three paragraphs, and we haven't got to the putative 'explanation' itself; nor have we said anything explicitly about the sort of political and historical discourses that could be wrung out of the extract by analysts who were or were not privy to the speakers' particular culture. At the very least, even if we went no further, we have shown that questions soliciting an explanation are not necessarily like the standard social-cognitive ones which presume a concern solely for the sorting of information and the arrival at a causal candidate. What we also hope to have done is to show that the 'meaning' of the explanation that will now fall into the slot opened up for it is not going to be wholly determinable from its semantic content, in other words, that it cannot be understood as being representative of something in the speaker's mind, and the outcome of some calculating process. Whatever it is, it is informed by its position in a jointly constructed dialogue as much as (or perhaps, some conversation analysts would say, more than) by its lexical content.

Some analysts would want to go further and, supported still by the way the participants interact, say something about the discourse of which the explanation forms a part. Recall that speaker A is telling a story involving (at this point) 'Northern Ireland' and 'the Second World War'. It is a legitimate question to ask what kinds of discourses (in the sense common to many chapters of this handbook) might be at play here, and how they would appear to analysts of different persuasions and with different degrees of familiarity with the matters apparently at hand. We can hardly hope to answer that question here. In principle, however, it is sensible to see explanations as being available, as are accounts (Gilbert and Mulkay, 1984), descriptions of fact (Edwards and Potter, 1992) and other rhetorical devices (Billig et al., 1988) for the promotion of speakers' or groups' interests and ideologies. For these writers, as for those who would look to participants' orientation to explanations in the run of conversational interaction, it is misleading and inappropriate to consider social reasoning to be a private, individual matter of sorting through rational information. It is, rather, a matter in the social domain, and whose force is in its public expression.

The above abbreviated analysis was, we hope, an illustration of the kinds of ways a shared ownership perspective might interpret something (here, explanation) which would also attract interest from the private ownership camp. We are aware, though, as we mentioned earlier, that putting an example sympathetic to conversation analysis and anglophone discourse analysis here at the end of the chapter is tendentious, and we would draw back from any claim that this kind of analysis is preferable to others.

Summary and Conclusions

'Social cognition' as an intellectual domain – the study of people's knowledge of the social world in which they live, speak and act – can lean in one of two directions. The tendency that has most currency among cognitively oriented psychologists is towards studying the psychological mechanisms by which individuals mentally represent social objects – themselves and other people. On the other hand, social cognition can orient to the social *nature* of perceivers and the social world they construct. Here, the concern is with how people function as members of particular cultures or groups, and with studying the way in which the social world emerges in the course of social interaction.

The two senses of social cognition have different applications to discourse. Mentalist social cognition promises to tell us about the operation of universal, automatic and unconscious information processing on the production and comprehension of text and talk. It promises to identify mental errors in discourse production and understanding, and help us overcome them. For example, it shows the operation of pre-formed schemata on the reception of new information, the organizing effect that cognitive structure imposes on narrative, and so on. It is, in that sense, a rational (or perhaps, rationalistic), rather didactic pursuit, and one committed to the notion that the mental events involved in discourse are to a large degree automatic, causal and indeed deterministic.

The alternative tendency of social cognition leans towards the study of things outside the individual, and, in at least some of its versions, refuses to acknowledge a split between internal and external processes. Social cognition is conceived of as *distributed* among people, and its study is uninterested in individual processing as such. On this reading, social cognition is part of the public domain and is bound up in actions into which people enter jointly. This means that a broad range of questions which mentalist social cognitivists ask about discourse simply fall away as not being properly askable questions at all – and the deterministic solutions they come up with as being unnecessary and misleading. On this alternative reading of social cognition, discourse is conceived not as a matter of the comprehension and production of unsituated propositions, but rather as a social event which is in some sense *action* in its own right, and in either talk or text: for example, the co-operative joint construction of utterances in adjacent turns, the formulation of decisions in group talk, the maintenance of belief structures through their public negotiation, and so on. Social cognition of that kind promises to identify how discourse is jointly occasioned and jointly formulated, and promises to uncover what local and institutional ends that discourse serves.

Recommended Reading

The interested reader may like to explore further the two traditions of social cognition, and their crossover and modern development. The references below (some of which have already been cited in the body of the chapter) should, we hope, provide good starting points.

Bartlett (1932): elegantly and subtly written, this has been used as stimulus and warrant for very different interpretations of what 'memory' is.

Edwards and Potter (1992): a strongly discursive reading of a wide range of 'psychological' phenomena usually the preserve of the mentalist tradition.

Fiske and Taylor (1991): the second edition of a textbook that has, in its two editions, served as an emblem of, and a touchstone for, the mentalist project.

Greenwood (1992): to be read along with the commentaries that follow it in that volume of the journal *Theory and Psychology*; a stimulating debate on the epistemology and ontological issues in social cognition.

Heider (1958): a prototypical example of the promise that was held out by the description of social action according to mental faculties.

Mead (1934): a philosophically knowing statement of the place of cognition in the social world.

Sacks (1992): edited transcripts of Sacks's lectures from the 1960s and 1970s; a fascinating and stimulating store of insights into human action, putting the argument that it is to be understood without risking the epistemological dubiousness of mental entities.

Schegloff (1993): a recent statement of the conversation analytic sense of (socially shared) cognition, explicitly directed at a psychological audience.

Widdicombe and Wooffitt (1994): an engaging example of a discursive account of traditionally 'psychological' phenomena; here, identity and behaviour.

Notes

The authors are grateful to Nikos Bozatzis, Derek Edwards, Steve Reicher and Teun van Dijk for comments on an earlier draft of this chapter.

References

Abrams, D. (1990) 'How do group members regulate their behaviour? An integration of social identity and self-awareness theories', in D. Abrams and M. Hogg (eds), *Social Identity Theory*. Brighton: Harvester Wheatsheaf.

Ajzen, I. (1988) *Attitudes, Personality and Behaviour*. Milton Keynes: Open University Press.

Armistead, N. (1974) *Reconstructing Social Psychology*. Harmondsworth: Penguin.

Bartlett, F. (1932) *Remembering*. London: Unwin.

Bartlett, F. (1958) *Thinking*. London: Unwin.

Billig, M. (1987) *Arguing and Thinking: a Rhetorical Approach to Social Psychology*. Cambridge: Cambridge University Press.

Billig, M. (1991) *Ideology and Opinions: Studies in Rhetorical Psychology*. London: Sage.

Billig, M., Condor, S., Edwards, D., Gane, M., Middleton, D. and Radley, A. (1988) *Ideological Dilemmas: a Social Psychology of Everyday Thinking*. London: Sage.

Brown, P. (ed.) (1973) *Radical Psychology*. London: Tavistock.

Brown, R. and Fish, D. (1983) 'The psychological causality implicit in language', *Cognition*, 14: 237–73.

Condor, S. (1990) 'Social identity and social stereotypes', in D. Abrams and M. Hogg (eds), *Social Identity Theory*. Brighton: Harvester Wheatsheaf.

Edwards, D. (1991) 'Categories are for talking: on the cognitive and discursive bases of categorization', *Theory and Psychology*, 1: 515–42.

Edwards, D. (1994) 'Script formulations: an analysis of event descriptions in conversation', *Journal of Language and Social Psychology*, 13: 211–47.

Edwards, D. and Middleton, D. (1987) 'Conversation and remembering: Bartlett revisited', *Applied Cognitive Psychology*, 1: 77–92.

Edwards, D. and Potter, J. (1992) *Discursive Psychology*. London: Sage.

Farr, R.M. (1990) 'Waxing and waning of interest in societal psychology: a historical perspective', in H.T. Himmelweit and G. Gaskell (eds), *Societal Psychology*. London: Sage.

Fillmore, C. (1971) 'Verbs of judging: an exercise in semantic description', in C. Fillmore and D.T. Langendoen (eds), *Studies in Linguistic Semantics*. New York: Holt, Rhinehart and Winston.

Fishbein, M. and Ajzen, I. (1975) *Belief, Attitude, Intention and Behaviour: an Introduction to Theory and Research*. Reading, MA: Addison-Wesley.

Fiske, S.T. and Taylor, S.E. (1991) *Social Cognition*, 2nd edn. New York: McGraw-Hill (1st edn Random House, 1984).

Forgas, J. (ed.) (1981) *Social Cognition: Perspectives on Everyday Understanding*. London: Academic Press.

Garfinkel, H. (1967) *Studies in Ethnomethodology*. Englewood Cliffs, NJ: Prentice-Hall.

Garman, M. (1990) *Psycholinguistics*. Cambridge: Cambridge University Press.

Gilbert, D. and Hixon, J. (1991) 'The trouble of thinking: activation and application of stereotypic beliefs', *Journal of Personality and Social Psychology*, 60: 509–17.

Gilbert, G.N. and Mulkay, M. (1984) *Opening Pandora's Box: a Sociological Analysis of Scientists' Discourse*. Cambridge: Cambridge University Press.

Greenwood, J. (1992) 'Realism, empiricism and social constructionism: psychological theory and the social dimensions of mind and action', *Theory and Psychology*, 2: 131–52.

Hamilton, D.L. (1981) 'Illusory correlation and stereotyping', in D.L. Hamilton (ed.), *Cognitive Processes in Stereotyping and Intergroup Behaviour*. Hillsdale, NJ: Erlbaum.

Heider, F. (1958) *The Psychology of Interpersonal Relations*. New York: Wiley.

Hewstone, M. and Jaspars, J. (1984) 'Social dimensions of attribution', in H. Tajfel (ed.), *The Social Dimension*, vol. 2. Cambridge: Cambridge University Press.

Hewstone, M., Jaspars, J. and Lalljee, M. (1982) 'Social representations, social attribution and social identity', *European Journal of Social Psychology*, 12: 241–70.

Johnson-Laird, P.N. (1983) *Mental Models*. Cambridge: Cambridge University Press.

Hilton, D. (1990) 'Conversational processes and causal explanation', *Psychological Bulletin*, 107: 65–81.

Hilton, D. (1991) 'A conversational model of causal attribution', in W. Stroebe and M. Hewstone (eds), *European Review of Social Psychology*, vol. 2. Chichester: Wiley.

Lakoff, G. (1987) *Women, Fire and Dangerous Things*. Chicago: University of Chicago Press.

Leyens, J.-P. and Codol, J.-P. (1988) 'Social cognition', in M. Hewstone, W. Stroebe, J.-P. Codol and G.M. Stephenson (eds), *Introduction to Social Psychology*. Oxford: Blackwell.

Loftus, E., Klinger, M., Smith, K. and Fiedler, J. (1990) 'A tale of two questions: the benefits of asking more than one question', *Public Opinion Quarterly*, 54: 330–45.

McKenzie-Mohr, D. and Zanna, M.P. (1990) 'Treating women as sexual objects: look to the (gender-schematic) male who has viewed pornography', *Personality and Social Psychology Bulletin*, 16: 296–308.

McCann, C.D. and Higgins, E.T. (1990) 'Social cognition and communication', in H. Giles and W.P. Robinson (eds), *Handbook of Language and Social Psychology*. Chichester: Wiley.

Mead, G.H. (1934) *Mind, Self and Society*. Chicago: Chicago University Press.

Moscovici, S. (1984) 'The phenomenon of social representations', in R. Farr and S. Moscovici (eds), *Social Representations*. Cambridge: Cambridge University Press.

Parker, I. (1989) *The Crisis in Social Psychology – and How To End It*. London: Routledge.

Potter, J., Wetherell, M., Gill, R. and Edwards, D. (1990) 'Discourse: noun, verb or social practice?', *Philosophical Psychology*, 3: 205–17.

Psathas, G. (1972) 'Ethnomethods and phenomenology', in J.G. Manis and B.N. Meltzer (eds), *Symbolic Interaction: a Reader in Social Psychology*. Boston: Alleyn and Bacon.

Reicher, S. (1991) 'Mad dogs and Englishmen: telling tales from the Gulf'. Paper presented to the British Association 'Science 91' meeting, Plymouth.

Rosch, E. (1973) 'Natural categories', *Cognitive Psychology*, 4: 328–50.

Ross, L.D. (1977) 'The intuitive psychologist and his shortcomings', in L. Berkowitz (ed.), *Advances in Experimental Social Psychology 10*. New York: Academic Press.

Rumelhart, D.E. and Ortony, A. (1977) 'The representation of knowledge in memory', in R.C. Anderson, R.J. Spiro and W.E. Montague (eds), *Schooling and the Acquisition of Knowledge*. Hillsdale, NJ: Erlbaum.

Sacks, H. (1972) 'On the analyzability of stories by children', in J.J. Gumperz and D. Hymes (eds), *Directions in Sociolinguistics: the Ethnography of Communication*. Holt, Rinehart and Winston. Reproduced in R. Turner (ed.), *Ethnomethodology*. Harmondsworth: Penguin, 1974.

Sacks, H. (1992) *Lectures on Conversation* (ed. Gail Jefferson). Oxford: Blackwell.

Schank, R.C. and Abelson, R.P. (1977) *Scripts, Plans, Goals and Understanding*. Hillsdale, NJ: Erlbaum.

Schegloff, E.A. (1993) 'Conversation analysis and socially shared cognition', in L.B. Resnick, J.M. Levine and S.D. Teasley (eds), *Perspectives on Socially Shared Cognition*. Washington, DC: APA.

Schwarz, N. (1990) 'Assessing frequency reports of mundane behaviors', in C. Hendrick and M. Clark (eds), *Research Methods in Personality and Social Psychology*. Newbury Park, CA: Sage.

Semin, G.R. and Fiedler, K. (1988) 'The cognitive functions of linguistic categories in describing persons: social cognition and language', *Journal of Personality and Social Psychology*, 54: 558–68.

Semin, G.R. and Fiedler, K. (1991) 'The linguistic category model, its bases, applications and range', in W. Stroebe and M. Hewstone (eds), *European Review of Social Psychology*, vol. 2. Chichester: Wiley.

Stevenson, R.J. (1993) *Language, Thought and Representation*. Chichester: Wiley.

Strack, F., Martin, L. and Schwarz, N. (1988) 'Priming and communication: the social determinants of information use in judgements of life satisfaction', *European Journal of Social Psychology*, 18: 429–42.

Svartvik, J. and Quirk, R. (1980 *A Corpus of Conversational English*. Lund, Sweden: Gleerup.

Tajfel, H. (1978) 'The structure of our views about society', in H. Tajfel and C. Fraser (eds), *Introducing Social Psychology*. Harmondsworth: Penguin.

Tajfel, H. (1981) *Human Groups and Social Categories: Studies in Social Psychology*. Cambridge: Cambridge University Press.

Turner, J.C., Hogg, M.A., Oakes, P.J., Reicher, S.D. and Wetherell, M.S. (1987) *Rediscovering the Social Group: a Self-Categorisation Theory*. Oxford: Basil Blackwell.

van Dijk, T.A. (1990) 'Social cognition and discourse', in H. Giles and W.P. Robinson (eds), *Handbook of Language and Social Psychology*. Chichester: Wiley.

van Dijk, T.A. and Kintsch, W. (1983) *Strategies of Discourse Comprehension*. New York: Academic Press.

van Knippenberg, A. (1984) 'Intergroup differences in group perceptions', in H. Tajfel (ed.), *The Social Dimension: European Developments in Social Psychology*, vol. 2. Cambridge: Cambridge University Press.

Wetherell, M. and Potter, J. (1988) 'Discourse analysis and the social psychology of racism', in C. Antaki (ed.), *Analysing Everyday Explanation: a Casebook of Methods*. London: Sage.

Wetherell, M. and Potter, J. (1992) *Mapping the Language of Racism: Discourse and the Legitimation of Exploitation*. Hemel Hempstead: Harvester Wheatsheaf.

Widdicombe, S. (1992) 'Subjectivity, power and the practice of psychology', *Theory and Psychology*, 2: 487–99.

Widdicombe, S. and Wooffitt, R. (1994) *The Language of Youth Subculture*. Brighton: Harvester.

Name Index

Subject Index